Mahkot

THE LANDMARK HISTORY OF THE
AMERICAN PEOPLE

THE LANDMARK HISTORY OF THE
AMERICAN PEOPLE

VOLUME 1
From Plymouth to Appomattox
NEWLY REVISED AND UPDATED

BY DANIEL J. BOORSTIN
With Ruth F. Boorstin

Illustrated with prints and photographs

Author's Acknowledgments

This book has benefited from the suggestions of many friends and fellow historians, especially those at the University of Chicago and the Smithsonian Institution. At Random House, Janet Finnie proposed the book to me and helped shape it; Karen Tobias helped find and select the illustrations. Janet Schulman of Random House suggested the new edition and with the assistance of Kate Banks helped guide the updating and revisions.

PICTURE CREDITS: American Antiquarian Society, 115, 122; William T. Anton, 74; Boatmans National Bank of St. Louis, 143; British Museum, 66; Brown Brothers, 77; Chase Manhattan Money Museum, 74; City Art Museum of St. Louis, 52; Colonial Williamsburg, 38, 125 bottom; in the collection of the Corcoran Gallery of Art, 93, 163; Culver Pictures, 118, 138 bottom, 181; Friends Library, Swarthmore, Pa., 16; Thomas Gilcrease Institute, 17; Reprinted from Heritage Magazine, a division of Forbes, Inc., ix; Henry E. Huntington Library, 135; Thomas Jefferson Memorial Foundation, 40, 41; Library of Congress, 63, 109, 144, 169, 172, 184; Nina Leen, *Life* magazine © Time Inc., 61; Mansell Collection, 90, 95; Maryland Historical Society, 98; Metropolitan Museum of Art, 67, 68, 71; Metropolitan Museum of Art, on loan from Edward W. C. Arnold Collection (photograph courtesy of the Museum of the City of New York), 112; Metropolitan Museum of Art, Harris Brisbane Dick Fund, 21, 113, 149, 171, 174, 180, 183; Metropolitan Museum of Art, gift of Edgar William and Bernice Chrysler Garbisch, 47; Metropolitan Museum of Art and the Huntington Library, 164; Metropolitan Museum of Art and the New York Public Library, 5; Missouri Historical Society, 128; Museum of the City of New York (J. Clarence Davies Collection), iv–v; National Gallery of Art, gift of Edgar William and Bernice Chrysler Garbisch, 36; courtesy of the New-York Historical Society, New York City, cover, 30, 55, 81, 97, 100 both, 101, 121, 140, 147, 152, 154, 158, 166, 177; New York Public Library, 73; New York Public Library, Picture Collection, 19; New York Public Library, Print Room, 1, 24, 26, 28, 43, 54, 56, 59 top, 79, 104 both, back endpaper; New York Public Library, Rare Book Room, vi, 4, 7, 10, 13, 14, 31, 35, 48, 50, 125 top, front endpaper; Otis Elevator Company, 107; Otis Historical Society, 146; Oxford University Press (from *English Men and Manners in the Eighteenth Century*), 22; Plymouth Plantation, 8; Princeton University Library, 103, 132, 137, 138 top, 178; Abby Aldrich Rockefeller Folk Art Collection, Williamsburg, Va., 87, 159; State Historical Society of Wisconsin, 130, 131; University of Chicago Library, 106; University of Michigan, Clements Library, 84; University of Michigan Museum of Art, bequest of Henry C. Lewis (1895), 129; Yale University Art Gallery, 59 bottom, 168; Yale University Library, 110 both; courtesy of Washington and Lee University, 39.

Current edition published by Sonlight Curriculum, Ltd. 2000, by arrangement with the author.

Library of Congress Cataloging-in-Publication Data:
Boorstin, Daniel J. (Daniel Joseph), 1914— .
    The landmark history of the American people.
    Includes bibliographies and indexes.
    Contents: v. 1. From Plymouth to Appomattox—
v. 2. From Appomattox to the moon.
    1. United States—History—Juvenile literature.
[1. United States—History] I. Boorstin, Ruth Frankel.
II. Title.
E178.1.B717 1987   973   87-9603
ISBN 1-887840-02-8

Manufactured in the United States of America   3 4 5 6 7 8 9 0

For a catalog of Sonlight Curriculum materials for the home school, write:
Sonlight Curriculum, Ltd.
8042 South Grant Way
Littleton, CO 80122-2705
USA
Or e-mail: catalog@sonlight.com

Photo, facing page: *Dutch Traders, circa 1670*

*Dedicated with love
to our grandchildren,
Julia, Eric, Adam, and Ariel*

CONTENTS

Part Three: American Ways of Growing

Part Four: Thinking Like Americans

Part Five: The Rocky Road to Union

Appendixes

PROLOGUE
The Best-Kept Secret

America was the best-kept secret in history. Before Columbus the peoples of Europe did not even imagine that this continent was here. Their maps and globes of the earth showed only Europe, Asia, and Africa and left no room for another continent. The greatest surprise was that there really *was* an America. Columbus himself believed that he had reached the shores of Asia. It was another Italian, Amerigo Vespucci, who suggested that this was a whole new world. And mapmakers wrote the word *America* on their maps in honor of him. But at first America seemed only an unlucky obstacle between Europe and the riches of India and China. America was discovered by accident.

And what a surprise it was! Europeans could not believe that such vast lands could have been here all the time without their even knowing it. Was it really possible that there was an "extra" continent? The Romans had sailed thousands of miles, even to India. The Spanish and Portuguese explored all the way to Iceland and down and around Africa. How could so much of the earth have been kept a secret? If there could be continents that the peoples of Europe never even imagined, how much more might there be in the world that they had not imagined? It was just a few years before the Puritans landed in New England that Shakespeare warned, "There are more things in heaven and earth, Horatio, than are dreamt of in your philosophy." The American surprise promised a world of endless surprises.

The ocean was the great protector of the American secret. European sailors were afraid to sail straight westward into this vast unknown. That way to Asia seemed too many miles. For you had to be able to go there *and back*. Finally the bold and enterprising sailor Columbus was willing to take his chance and persuaded a doubting crew to go along. He knew the winds and the current from sailing far north and south along Europe's Atlantic coast. And he knew how to bring his ships back.

At first only a vast ocean could have kept America from the greedy adventuring peoples of Europe. And later only the ocean could have carried so many so far seeking homes. They could hardly have come in such large numbers over three thousand miles by land. In those days land travel was a bumpy and muddy misery—on horseback, in wagons, or even in lordly carriages. There were few highways but many highway robbers who skulked behind high rocks and around bends in the road or hid in ravines, ready to relieve passengers of their baggage or even of their lives. Unless you walked, you needed teams of horses, which tired, got stuck in the mud, and had to be fed and watered along the way.

But the ocean was convenient and pleasant and usually friendly. Though, of course, the sea was sometimes rough, still often enough it was calm. If you knew the winds and the currents, had a compass, and could follow the stars at night, you would make your way faster and safer than on land. There was always the off chance that you might be becalmed and have to wait days for the winds to come again. But the winds never had to be fed, and they worked around the clock. On the sea, robbers found no place to hide, and pirates themselves had to take great risks in the wide ocean.

The ocean was lucky in still other ways, for it made people travel in large groups. You could not cross the ocean in a rowboat with a few friends. Only a large vessel could survive the stormy seas and carry provisions for the seven weeks' passage. In the *Mayflower* you were traveling with a hundred other passengers, besides captain and crew. You could walk about the deck, dance and sing and play games on the way. You sailed in a little traveling town. You heard sermons, made laws, and exchanged stories as you went.

You did not have to trust to innkeepers on the way. The ship carried food and water and could even bring along treasured pieces of furniture, musical instruments, and favorite books. Cows on board, when they were not seasick, could provide fresh milk. By the time you landed you had come to know your neighbors, had found out who were troublemakers and who were leaders. Then when you first stepped on the unmapped coast, you were already surrounded by friends, prepared to work together building houses and churches and schools, hunting turkey, deer, and wild pigeons, and facing the perils of unfriendly residents. The ship landed in a ready-made community.

As the colonists settled on the Atlantic coast, they did not have to wait for roads to be built to receive passengers and produce from the world or to send out their produce in exchange. Safe harbors —Boston, New York, Savannah— opened on ready-made highways to the whole world. The spacious holds of ships that brought settlers could send out furs and corn and rice and tobacco. An elegant London-made coach could be delivered directly to George Washington's dock at Mount Vernon on the Potomac River.

The English who settled the thirteen American colonies were not the first Europeans to start colonies in America. Adventurers from Spain and Portugal, France and the Netherlands, along with others, had long been competing for the treasures of faraway places. A century before the Puritans came to New England, the bold Hernando Cortés, with only two hundred men, conquered the armed hordes of the Aztec empire. In two years (1519–21) he had made Mexico a colony of Spain. Ten years later the swashbuckling Francisco Pizarro, who could not even write his name, overcame the grand Inca empire and added Peru to the realm of the Spanish king. These *conquistadores* were as ruthless and as courageous as any who would ever set foot on the Americas. They aimed to convert the Indians to Christianity and brought friars to help them. But they were better at robbing than converting. They lived and died for gold and glory. They had no desire to settle down with their families as hardworking farmers.

In 1620, when the sober William Bradford and the prudent John Winthrop came to "New" England, they had another idea. They came not for gold and glory but to build homes for themselves, their children, and their grandchildren. They aimed to make a "city upon a hill" for all the world to admire. Theirs was not a violent adventure of conquest but a long-lasting tale of building. They were a bit kinder to the Indians than the *conquistadores* had been. One of them, John Eliot, set a friendly example and even translated the Bible into the Algonquian Indian language. The Indians in New England were few in number and had no riches of gold or silver to tempt the newcomers. But they had much to teach the colonists —how to survive in the wilderness, how to hunt, and what would grow. The English colonists planted themselves and put down roots in the New World.

When the thirteen English colonies began, the English people were already centuries ahead of most of the rest of Europe in their struggle for self-government. Their Parliament was already five hundred years old. Only a few years after the Pilgrims arrived here, the English back home were fighting a bloody civil war for the rule of law and their right to govern themselves with a parliament. They did the unthinkable when they beheaded an anointed king (1649) because they would not tolerate a tyrant. When the English colonists arrived here, they were already familiar with the ways of self-government. And they expected each colony to have its own way of self-governing. Their English inheritance would help make them willing to risk their "Lives . . . Fortunes and . . . sacred Honor" to make a new self-governing nation.

The very shape of North America lent itself to bringing people together in a new nation on a vast continent. For North America was blessed by broad rivers running inland from the coast— the Kennebec, the Charles, the Hudson, the Potomac, the Ogeechee, and countless others. These highways into the country would unite inlanders with their fellow Americans on the coast. The St. Lawrence River and the chain of Great Lakes led deep into unknown territory. The Colorado River reached fifteen hundred miles down from the snow-covered Rockies out to the Gulf of California. The wide-rushing Columbia and the Snake River opened a westward way into the Pacific Ocean.

The river monarch of the continent, which the Indians called the Father of Waters, was the magnificent Mississippi. It drew together the outreaching waters of the Ohio, the Missouri, and countless rivulets, carrying them four thousand miles into the Gulf of Mexico. This river-rich continent was made to order for explorers, for people and produce on the move. Long before the age of the automobile, these lucky river arteries were bringing people together, nourishing a continental nation.

The wondrous variety of the lands of North America took some time to discover. When the first New England settlers walked westward to the top of the nearest hill, they really expected to see the other ocean. Who could imagine that they were standing only on the remote edge of a three-thousand-mile living museum of the whole world's geography? Deserts and mountains and prairies, snowcapped peaks and tundras and arid, sandy stretches. English settlers in New England found the climate harsher and snowier than back home but mostly familiar. The varied continent would eventually provide cold northern plains to make people from Norway or Sweden or Russia feel at home—and warm, sunny seacoasts to attract growers of grapes and oranges from Greece or Spain or Italy. North America seemed designed to be a world in itself, offering a familiar landscape to people from almost anywhere.

How the world looked to Europeans before Columbus. This map, drawn by the famous Italian geographer Andrea Bianco in 1436, showed the three continents (Europe, Asia, and Africa) joined together in an "Island of the Earth" surrounded by the Ocean Sea. Jerusalem was in the center. There was no place for another continent.

PART ONE

AN ASSORTMENT OF PLANTATIONS

The American colonies were an assortment of dreams and hopes and fears. They offered samples of nearly every kind of feeling. The first settlers, who thought anything was possible here, were not far wrong. Some came with definite plans, others with troubled consciences. Some came as charity cases, owing everything to a few rich men in London. Some came simply for profit. Others came desperately seeking refuge. All would become Americans.

From the beginning America was a place of testing and trying. "Plantations" is what they called the settlements along the Atlantic fringe in the earliest days.

It was a good word. A "plant" first meant a cutting from a growing thing set out to grow in another place. These plantations (we later called them colonies) were European cuttings set out to grow three thousand miles across the Atlantic.

The English were experts at planting people in faraway places. They were never more successful than when they planted in America. For the people here were really *planted*. They did not come only as explorers or as gold diggers. Instead, they took root, found new nourishment in American soil, grew in new ways in the varied American climates, and in a few centuries would outgrow Mother England.

But they were not always successful. Whether a plantation died or lived and how it grew depended on many things. Much depended on the climate and the soil and the animals and the Indians. Much depended on whether the settlers had planned, and what they had planned, and how quickly they could learn what the continent had to teach. And much depended on luck.

CHAPTER 1

The Puritans: Love God and Fight the Devil

America was a land of mystery. Englishmen in the age of King James I knew even less than they thought they knew, because most of their "facts" were wrong. Their misinformation about the New World came in all kinds of packages. Some came in fantastic advertising brochures written by men who wanted to sell land in America.

Men who had put their money and their hopes into new American settlements knew that success depended on attracting people to a strange and remote land. If nobody came, the land would remain a wilderness. But if people did come there would be cities and roads, farms and mines. The wilderness would become valuable real estate. Still more people—more carpenters, shoemakers, tailors, and merchants—would come because they would know they could make a living from the people already here.

The promoters had to offer "facts," but

Virginia, in this seventeenth-century view, was an earthly paradise. Finding fish and game for your table was not hard work, but simply good sport.

they did not know the facts. So they drew imaginary pictures, using ancient legends mixed with their wildest hopes and fondest dreams. The weather in America, they said, was always sunny. The oranges, lemons, apples, pears, peaches, and apricots were "so delicious that whoever tastes them will despise the insipid watery taste of those we have in England." The American venison was so juicy that Englishmen would barely recognize it. The fish were large and easy to catch. In America there were no diseases, and no crowds. Everybody stayed young and everybody could live like a king. Come to this American paradise!

If Englishmen turned to their scientists to check up on all this, they did not get much help. The geography of the New World was quite befuddled. Maps were about as detailed as those we have of Mars—and a good deal less accurate. They had no idea how wide the continent was. When they found a lake or a river near the Atlantic seacoast, they often believed that it would take them to India. When they heard of peculiar animals in America like the raccoon, the opossum, and the bison, which were unknown in Europe, they imagined they must be like unicorns and dragons and other mythical beasts.

When they heard that there were already "red-skinned" men and women in America their religion gave them a ready-made explanation in advance. According to the Bible, all men and women everywhere were descended from Adam and Eve, who once lived in the Garden of Eden. If men in America had red skins, it was simply because of sunburn or dyes. Englishmen took it for granted that the red men in America were one of the ten "lost tribes" of Israel mentioned in the Bible. Because people were so confused about their geography and at first believed that the New World was really a part of India, they had quite naturally called these red people "Indians."

When Englishmen thought about coming to America, one of the questions that interested them most was what sort of

The great "Sea of China and the Indies," this 1651 map showed, was just over the first range of mountains from the Atlantic coast. (The west is at the top.)

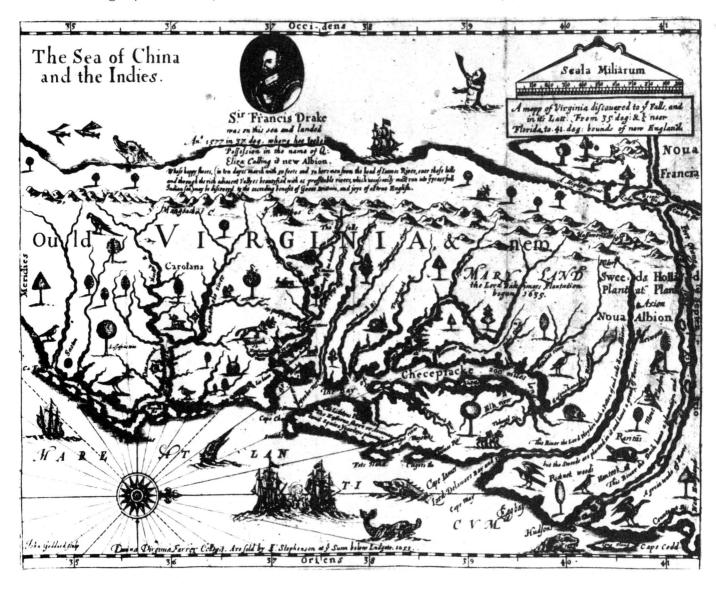

people were these American descendants of Adam and Eve who would greet them over here. Would they be friendly and helpful? The rumors were not encouraging. It was said that the "savages" of America were not content merely to kill but delighted in tormenting their victims. There were tall tales of how they used sharp sea shells to skin their enemies alive, cut off limbs and joints one by one, and broil slices of human flesh on hot coals. Then they smacked their lips over the sizzling meat before the very eyes of their victims, whom they somehow managed to keep alive. Other Indian cruelties were supposed to be too horrible to tell.

It is surprising that Englishmen dared come to America at all. For in addition to all the real threats of a "hideous and desolate wilderness," they were haunted by these horror stories and nightmares. Against these, all the cheery advertising boasts were not much help. And it is still more surprising that despite all of this vivid misinformation, they not only survived but managed to build durable cities.

In the mysterious New World, you would surely be lost unless you had some plans of your own. If you had goals, they could encourage you while you were discovering what America was really like. Your plans had to be definite, but not too definite. You had to be willing to change your plans when you ran into trouble, or when the New World did not offer what you expected. You had to be prepared for disappointment. Yet you had to have unending self-confidence, faith in your mission and in yourself.

In England about the year 1620, some people happened to be equipped with precisely this odd combination of hopes and fears, optimism and pessimism, self-confidence and humility. They were called "Puritans." And when they were persecuted for their religion, they showed just the courage needed for the American adventure.

Among the Puritans were the Pilgrim Fathers. When they left England in the *Mayflower* on September 16, 1620, they aimed for Virginia. Even before they landed they showed how well they could face the unexpected. At the end of over seven weeks on the ocean they found themselves far north, outside the boundaries where they had permission to settle. Some unruly passengers noticed this, and threatened "that when they came ashore they would use their own liberty, for none had power to command them, the patent they had being for Virginia." But the *Mayflower* leaders, anxious to land, could not tolerate a community without government. Why should their plans be spoiled by a few roughnecks?

So they decided on shipboard, then and there, to create a new government to serve their very special purposes. The leaders, including the steady William Bradford (who would be governor of Plymouth Colony for thirty-one years) and Captain Miles Standish (whom they had hired to head their militia), came together. Like people making up rules for a club that already existed, they wrote out and signed an agreement (or "compact"). This was the famous Mayflower Compact:

In the name of God, Amen. We, whose names are underwritten, the loyal subjects of our dread sovereign Lord, King James . . . having undertaken, for the glory of God,

A European view of the kind of welcome the Indians were apt to give the first settlers.

and advancement of the Christian faith and honor of our king and country, a voyage to plant the first colony in the northern parts of Virginia, do . . . solemnly and mutually in the presence of God, and one of another, covenant and combine ourselves together into a civil body politic; for our better ordering and preservation . . . to enact . . . such just and equal laws, ordinances, acts, constitutions, and offices, from time to time, as shall be thought most meet and convenient for the general good of the colony: unto which we promise all due submission and obedience.

They created an instant government. It worked surprisingly well for the infant colony, and later became the foundation for the great State of Massachusetts.

The Puritans had a grand purpose. In old England they had been called "Puritans" because they wanted to cleanse and purify their church from fancy ceremonies, from rituals which had lost meaning. In New England they wanted to build a Zion in the wilderness. "Zion" was a Hebrew word for "hill," and to the

Puritans it meant the hill where Jerusalem, the first Holy City, was built. Just before the Pilgrims came here, some of them had tried, and failed, to build a purified city in Holland. Now they wanted to try again, far from crowded, decaying old Europe. Perhaps in America they could actually go back to the simpler life of the early days when the first Holy City had been built.

But how would you lay out your city?

What did it all have to do with America—a land that the men of Bible times had never heard of? Some Bible stories are cryptic or complicated, others are bewilderingly simple. Daily life, too, seems complicated, aimless, or confusing. Puritan ministers and teachers tried to find some meaning and make it all less confusing.

To discover this meaning, and the details of God's plan for Zion, the Puri-

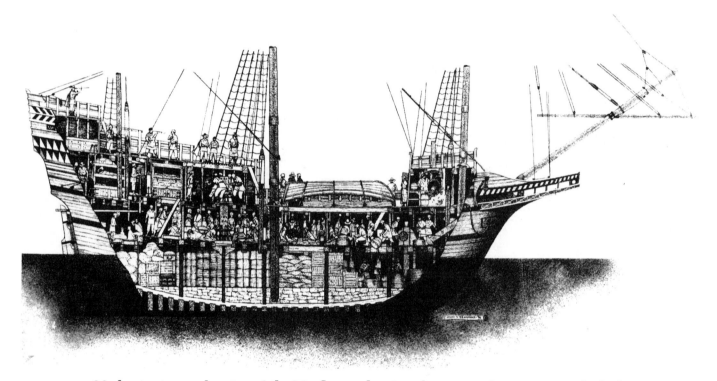

Modern cutaway drawing of the Mayflower *showing the cramped quarters in which the Pilgrims made their seven-week voyage.*

What would you write into your laws? The Puritans, luckily, had a guide. The plan for their community had already been written out, by God himself, in the Bible.

Still, it was no easy matter to find it there. The Bible was a long book, full of stories and poems and prophecies.

tans had a very special way of reading the Bible. For them it was not just a book of quaint tales about people far away and long ago. Instead it was a kind of catalog prepared by God himself, listing all the things that could happen to man. The Puritans believed that everything had, somehow or other, already happened in the stories of the Bible. If you knew how to read the Bible, then, you could find the meaning of what was happening to you today— wherever you were, even in newly discovered America. And from the Bible you could actually predict the future.

The Bible, then, was the key to everything. The Puritans in New England said they themselves were just like the ancient Hebrews, a Chosen People in the Wilderness. The small band of Puritans fighting against scores of Indians were just like little David fighting giant Goliath. And remember that David won!

Everyday events were filled with wonderful meanings. Ministers and teachers helped, but everyone became his own preacher, solving his own Bible puzzles. Some New England leaders kept diaries where they explained these meanings to themselves. Judge Samuel Sewall left one of the best. In his diary for November 6, 1692, he wrote that his little son Joseph threw a brass knob and hit his sister Betty on the forehead, making it bleed and swell. To make matters worse, Joseph did not even repent, but insisted on playing during prayers and actually started eating before grace was finished. Judge Sewall "whipped him pretty smartly" and sent him to bed.

Joseph's grandmother intervened, asking the father to come into the bedroom to forgive his naughty son. "When I first went in (called by his grandmother), he sought to shadow and hide himself from me behind the head of the cradle: which gave me the sorrowful remembrance of Adam's carriage [behavior]."

Judge Sewall at once had found a Bible story to fit his son's misbehavior.

His little son was acting just like Adam in the Garden of Eden. After Adam ate the forbidden apple, he tried to hide from God. Adam knew he had done evil, and that he had something to hide. Puritans called this the "fall" of Adam. Were not all men, and all children too, like Adam? And did this not make it easier to see the dangers of sin, and yet forgive all sinners?

For the Puritans, then, every little fact had a big meaning. And they could be sure, too, that all their little troubles served some large purpose.

There were many advantages to this way of looking at things. You might make mistakes in your own particular explanations and yet believe some purpose was hidden there for you or somebody else to discover. You had just chosen the wrong Bible story to explain your experience. If you ran away from an enemy, you might be escaping from the tyrant Pharaoh. Or then again, maybe you were the sinner Cain, hopelessly wandering after you had killed your brother Abel. Which were you?

Every Bible story was itself a kind of puzzle. You had answered one puzzle with another. But the Puritans were not discouraged. Sometimes, of course, they wondered whether they themselves had actually figured out the meaning of life. But they seldom doubted that there was a meaning to be figured out.

They never doubted that God had assigned them some large purpose—"an errand into the wilderness." If they could not understand the errand, this was only one more proof of how great was God. He alone knew all the answers. The Puritans spent hours listening to

The Burning of Mr. John Rogers

A picture like this enlivened The New England Primer, *from which Puritan school-children learned to read and to love God.*

sermons, giving sermons, hearing lectures, and keeping diaries. All these showed both their wonderment over the answers to the daily puzzles and their firm belief that somehow there *was* an answer.

Going to school in New England meant learning God's plan for the Puritans. Children were taught to read from a book called *The New England Primer*. In those days "primer" meant not only a first reader but also a "catechism," or first book of religion. While the young Puritan was learning how to read he was also learning what to believe. Even when he memorized the alphabet it was in little ditties about the Bible. The first item read: "In Adam's fall we sinned all." The last item told about Zaccheus. "Zaccheus, he did climb the tree, his Lord to see." The pictures did not show boys and girls playing with their friends. Instead they showed the martyr Rogers being burned at the stake while his wife, with nine small children and a baby, saw her husband give up his life for the true religion.

Harvard College, the first in the English colonies, was founded by the Puritans in 1636 "to advance learning and perpetuate it to posterity; dreading to leave an illiterate ministry to the churches, when our present ministers shall lie in the dust." Many Harvard students did not intend to be ministers. But even for them there was no choice about the subjects they studied. Students spent their time on Biblical topics, on difficult Biblical languages (Hebrew, Aramaic, Syriac, and Greek), and on learning how to preach. They discussed God's blueprint for Zion.

Of course it was important to have a plan for building your community. But it was just as important not to expect too much success, and not to expect success too fast. You must expect to succeed, yet you must be more surprised by your successes than by your failures. You would never be disappointed if you were always prepared for the worst.

To explain the Puritans' success in their "hideous and desolate wilderness" we must understand that they were pessimists. Odd though it may sound, they were actually enthusiastic pessimists. For no people has ever believed more strongly in the power of evil. To them the Devil was as real as God. The more powerful the Devil was, the more powerful it proved that God was, because in the long run God always won.

The Indians, according to the Puritans, were armies of the Devil especially equipped to fight against God's Chosen People. No one should be surprised if they were strong or cunning. When Puritans first visited nearby Indian villages they found piles of bones and skulls, reminders of the plague that had hit only a few years before, killing about a third of the Indians in the neighborhood. That plague, the Puritans said, had been specially arranged by God to reduce the Devil's armies and so "make way for the quiet and peaceable settlement of the English in those nations."

Yet the Puritans did not really hate the Indians or believe they were an inferior race. On the contrary, it was a Puritan duty to give "some light to those poor Indians, who have ever sat in hellish darkness." If the Puritans did not convert the Indians to Christianity, the Indians would "go down to hell by swarms without remedy."

John Eliot decided that the best way to convert the Algonquian Indians who lived in the neighborhood was to translate the Bible into the Algonquian language. But the Algonquians had no written language, and Eliot scarcely knew their spoken language at all. By ingeniously using the English alphabet to make the Indian sounds he finally managed to translate the Bible into Algonquian in 1661. That was the first Bible printed in the New World. At Harvard they even built a building called the Indian College to train Indians to be missionaries.

Some Indians took up the Puritans' religion, but still they did not want to change their own way of life. The Indians had the habit of greasing their bodies with fish oil, with the fat of the eagle or the raccoon, or the grease of the bear or the pig. This was useful because the grease protected against heat and cold, and kept off mosquitoes. Also it took the place of clothing. The Puritans noticed only that it was smelly. But they found it easier to persuade Indians to stop following Satan than to stop covering their bodies with grease.

The Puritans believed that the Indian medicine men, who were called "powwows," could actually practice witchcraft. Cautious Puritans like Roger Williams refused to watch the powwows at work because it was dangerous to get so close to the Devil.

When the Indians attacked the Puritan settlements, the Puritans fought back and fought hard. In 1637, because the Pequots (a tribe of Algonquians) were killing settlers and traders, the Puritans made war on them. The war came to an end when Puritans massacred a village of about five hundred Pequot men, women, and children in about half an hour. "Thus did the Lord judge among the heathen," they boasted, "filling the place with dead bodies." They compared this to David's war in the Bible, and proclaimed a day of thanksgiving to God for their victory.

By the time of King Philip's War in 1675, the Indians were more troublesome. The Wampanoag Indians (another Algonquian tribe) had secured firearms from the English and now actually hoped to conquer back the lands taken by the Puritans. This, their bloodiest war with the Indians, was a long fight. Young Puritans had the arrogant notion that one of them could beat ten Indians. They soon learned better. For to win the war against King Philip's tribe, the Puritans had to have the help of some of the Indians themselves. King

Philip (son of Massasoit, an old friend of the Puritans) was finally betrayed by one of his own men.

In many ways the Indians actually helped the Puritans. During their very first bitter winter of 1620–21, the Pilgrims at Plymouth would have died without some reliable advice about how to survive in the American woods.

Squanto was an Indian kidnaped a few years before by an English sea captain, who had sold him into slavery in Spain. He escaped to England, where he learned some English, and then returned to New England in 1619. There he found that his whole village had died of the plague. Now, in March 1621, it was Squanto of all the thousands of Indians in America who happened to turn up in Plymouth! He knew enough English to act as an interpreter. And he showed the Pilgrims how to plant corn (which was not known in England), how to fertilize the soil, where to catch the fish, and how to trap beaver for their fur. No wonder the Pilgrims called him a "special instrument sent of God for their good beyond their expectation."

The Indians helped in still other unexpected ways. When the Puritans needed money to use among themselves and with the Indians, the Indians taught them about "wampum." Wampum was small white or blue-black beads, which had been carved from sea shells. The wampum beads were strung together, and the amount of money they counted for was measured by the length of the string. Using six-foot lengths of wampum, Puritan traders could buy beaver and otter skins from the Indians. During the many years when gold and silver were scarce and they had no paper money, the Puritans traded among themselves by using these odd coins. Even the Devil's own agents could not avoid helping God's Chosen People!

In this mysterious New World, it was easier than in England to give credit for everything to God. Newcomers from Europe did not know what animals or plants or weather to expect here. When New England Puritans found lobsters in the ocean they knew it was God providing for them in their need. When Squanto showed them how to raise corn, he was really God's helping hand. The wild turkey was God's special gift to the Puritans. Was not the turkey unknown in England?

These and all the other provisions of God, the Puritans called "providences." They were God's way of *providing* for his own Chosen People. Over there in England everything had a familiar explanation. In unknown America—still a dark continent—there seemed to be remarkable providences every day.

The Puritans knew it would be a great victory for the Devil if he could discredit God by defeating his Chosen People in the Wilderness. In 1642, when Plymouth Colony suffered a crime wave, Governor Bradford was not surprised or downhearted. "The Devil," he explained, "may carry a greater spite against the churches of Christ and the Gospel here, by how much the more they [the Puritans] endeavor to preserve holiness and purity

---

Tobacco (at top) and corn (at right) were strange crops that the Europeans learned about from the Indians.

The Indians had much to teach the settlers about hunting.

amongst them." What the Devil most wanted was to "cast a blemish and a stain upon them in the eyes of the world."

In all these ways America gave the Puritans a lively feeling for God—and also sharpened their sense of the Devil. But even the Devil could not drive them to despair. Sooner or later, God would always win. He would see that his own people were not destroyed. The troubles of this world—New England blizzards, Indians' arrows, the plottings of enemies in England, or the crimes of their own sinful New Englanders— never overwhelmed them. They knew too well that *all* men were the children of sinful Adam and had inherited Adam's sin. Man was weak and confused, always giving in to temptations.

The Puritans were not disappointed, then, that they did not build New England quickly. Instead they were surprised and pleased that in a howling wilderness, with the Devil constantly plotting against them, sinful men like themselves actually managed to build anything at all.

So, the saying went, there could never be a disillusioned Puritan—simply because Puritans did not have illusions.

CHAPTER 2
The Quakers Refuse to Fight

In the front and center of a Massachusetts Puritan church was the pulpit. There the learned minister expounded God's plan in the Bible. He gave long and carefully prepared sermons, while the listening congregation took notes. Only those few who had had a very special experience had a voice in running the church. The Puritans called it a "converting" experience, because it converted a sinful soul into one that would be saved in heaven. The converted few were called "Visible Saints." In the early years in Massachusetts, in order to vote you had to be one of these Saints, in addition to having some property. Puritan government was a Dictatorship of the Saints.

In a Quaker meeting house in Pennsylvania, the feeling was entirely different. The whole hall was full of benches. There was no pulpit because there was no minister. In the front a few benches faced the others. Here sat older and more prominent Quakers, called "the weightier members." Their opinions actually carried more weight with their neighbors—but not because they had any high-sounding title or had been anointed as priests. Anyone could sit on the front benches if he felt himself worthy. There was no program, and no regular order of services.

A Quaker Meeting had no chairman, yet it was not noisy or disorderly. Members sat quietly. They waited and waited and waited until someone—anyone—was moved by God's spirit within him. That person would stand up and say whatever God had told him to say, on any subject at all. No one was supposed to prepare anything in advance. And, of course, there was no sermon. If no one felt God's spirit within him, then no one said anything. After sitting awhile, the members would get up and return to their homes.

If there was a practical question, like whether to repair the meeting house roof or where to build a road, the Quakers would not take a vote. Instead, after everybody had had his say, then somehow (without any counting of hands or hearing of voices) members seemed to agree on what was the "sense of the meeting." It is amazing that an organization run this way could run at all. Yet the Quaker Meetings prospered. They gained new members, and for a long time they were the backbone of the new plantation of Pennsylvania.

There was much to be said for this way of running a church. Within the Society of Friends (as the Quakers called their church) it worked surprisingly well. We must remember that each Quaker Meeting was a small number of God-fearing people who knew one another and who shared beliefs. But Pennsylvania was a big place. Within a few years the Quakers' numbers were overwhelmed by others. Many of these disliked or even hated the Quakers. The fringes of settlement were besieged by tribes of Indians and by small armies of French and Spanish. In dealing with this larger world outside, the Quakers did not do so well.

The Quakers who founded Pennsylvania in 1682 were a kind of Puritan. Their leader, William Penn, was the son of a rich British admiral. When he published a pamphlet against the established religion he was imprisoned in the Tower of London, but this simply confirmed him in his Quaker beliefs. He determined to found a colony for refugees in far-off America. A shrewd and persuasive man, he secured a vast grant from King Charles II, which he named Pennsylvania in honor of his father.

Penn's eloquent advertising brochures brought thousands of settlers to Pennsylvania. And much of the prosperity of the colony depended on the sensible constitution that he wrote. He was afraid of neat schemes which could not be changed. "Let men be good," he said, "and the government cannot be bad; if it be ill, they will cure it." He distrusted men who were too bookish, "for much reading is an oppression of

A Quaker meeting house, in America as in England, had no pulpit or altar at the front. An eighteenth-century print by the English illustrator, Thomas Rowlandson.

William Penn is shown here making a treaty with the Indians. The painter, Edward Hicks, was an amateur whose works have a special strength and charm.

the mind, and extinguishes the natural candle; which is the reason of so many senseless scholars in the world."

The Quakers, like other Puritans, wanted to "purify." But they went much further than the Puritans of New England. They were afraid of *any* rules. Even those rules copied from the Bible, they said, would destroy the true religious spirit. Then people would take their religion for granted. God, they said, did not limit his Chosen People only to those who knew the Bible or to those who could read and write. That

was why Quakers had no ministers. They believed in the "universal priesthood of all believers." They believed God had put his spirit into every man, woman, and child. They overflowed with God's spirit. But they were suspicious of anyone who said he knew God's plan.

Just as the Puritans were enthusiastic pessimists, so the Quakers were fanatics about their consciences. Keep looking inward, they said. Let your conscience be your guide. They were afraid of any scheme that was cut and dried, even if some people thought it came from

God himself. God, they said, did not really communicate with man from any printed page. He spoke to each man from within, brightening each man with an Inner Light.

Back in England, the Quakers had been strict pacifists. They opposed war, and refused to fight in any war for any reason, even self-defense. "We are heirs of the gospel of peace," said George Fox, an early Quaker who had gone to jail rather than fight. Fox reminded people that Christ had said, "My kingdom is not of this world." Therefore Christ had told Peter to put away his sword, "for all they that take the sword shall perish with the sword."

It was one thing for Quakers to be pacifists back in England. There they were nothing but a small group of peculiar people. Even if all the Quakers in England refused to fight and went to jail, the country would still be defended. It was quite another matter in Pennsylvania. For there at first the Quakers were a majority. And they ran the Pennsylvania government till the middle of the eighteenth century, long after they ceased to be a majority.

In Pennsylvania, if the Quakers refused to raise an army, the countryside was left defenseless. This is precisely what happened.

The Indians were surely not pacifists. Nor were the French or the Spanish, who were the leading rivals of the British for possession of the New World. The British Empire was continually entangled in wars for America. The English government naturally expected the Quaker colony to bear its share of the war burden. But the Quakers stuck to their pacifism. They would have nothing to do with these colonial wars, even when Spanish privateers sailed up the Delaware River, in sight of Philadelphia.

The most the English government could do was persuade the Quaker legislature in Pennsylvania to use certain dodges, so the Quakers could help defend the colony without violating their pacifism. Once the Quakers pretended they were giving money "to feed the hungry and clothe the naked" Indians, but it was silently agreed the money would be used for defense. In 1745, non-Quakers maneuvered the Pennsylvania legislature into giving £4,000 to supply a military garrison with "bread, beef, pork, flour, wheat, or other grain." It was quietly understood that "other grain" meant a not-very-nourishing grain called gunpowder.

We can understand why American Quakers did not want to join in far-flung wars for empire. What did they care whether the British or the French or the Spanish owned this or that piece of remote wilderness?

It is harder to understand how Pennsylvania Quakers could remain indifferent to the murder of their fellow Pennsylvanians. From the beginning, raiding Indians made life miserable for the backwoodsmen. In 1755 came a terrible climax. During that summer the British General Edward Braddock set out with 1,400 British regulars and 450 colonial troops to take Fort Duquesne from the French. It was strategically located at the river junction where Pittsburgh is now.

Benjamin Franklin, who was shrewd even in military matters, had warned

Braddock against the surprise tactics of the Indians. Braddock, however, was a stiff British general. He believed everybody would follow the genteel rules of European warfare. He thought the Indians would wait till the opposing armies were neatly arrayed in an open field.

But the Indians knew nothing of such rules. Using the surprise tactics which Franklin had predicted, a mixed force of nine hundred French and Indians overwhelmed the British in the Battle of the Wilderness. Braddock was mortally wounded. His chief of staff, the ambitious young Colonel George Washington, after burying Braddock in the forest, took command of the retreating remnant. The French were now in firm control of all western Pennsylvania. They were better situated than ever for inciting the Delaware tribes of Indians to sudden and bloody attacks.

Backwoodsmen now suffered the ravages of total war. Nothing could have been more different from the polite exchanges of musket fire—on prearranged battlefields (in good weather) between professional soldiers—which were called warfare in Europe in those days. American colonists' homes went up in flames, crops were ruined, women and children were scalped or captured. Massacres mounted. Panic gripped western Pennsylvania. Should they stand or run? "Most are willing to stand," reported a citizen in the western town of York

---

General Braddock, with his British colonial troops in their conspicuous uniforms. At left, hiding behind a rock, is an Indian enemy scout preparing for the surprise attack. Young George Washington was Braddock's chief aide.

in November 1755, "but have no arms or ammunition." Towns farther east were flooded by refugees, while innocent backwoodsmen paid the price for Quaker pacifism.

But the Pennsylvania Quakers still remained pacifists. In their meetings that winter they still refused to give money for defense. They still wanted, as they said, "to walk in white"—to be purer than the pure—even while western Pennsylvania ran red with innocent blood.

In that bloody year of 1755, the Quakers were still very much in control of the government of Pennsylvania. At the beginning of 1756, although Quakers now numbered only one-fourth of the colony's population, they still held 28 of the 36 seats in the legislature. An enraged and exasperated citizenry, led by non-Quakers (and including a number of moderates like Benjamin Franklin), forced the Quakers to resign the government. They never ruled the colony again.

When the American Revolution came, many Quakers stuck to their pacifism. They became gadflies and prophets. They warned against the evils of slavery. Quakers refused to hold slaves themselves, or to buy anything made by slave labor. They opposed alcoholic drinks— and developed the chocolate business in which they prospered.

They were the voice of everybody's conscience. But they were not made for politics.

CHAPTER 3

The Woes of a Charity Colony

The twenty-one men in Great Britain who secured a charter for Georgia in 1732 thought they were very practical. The best known of them was James Oglethorpe, a tough-minded military man who combined a passion for building the British Empire with a passion for reform. He was against strong alcoholic drinks, he wanted to make British prisons more humane, and he opposed slavery. Oglethorpe and his friends had their eyes not so much on the Bible or on their own consciences but rather— so they thought—on the facts and problems of their day.

Their practical worries started right at home in London and reached out to the empire. They were bothered by the "numbers of poor children and other poor that pester the streets of London." They were bothered, too, by the idleness and crime, and especially by the drunkenness. Signs outside some London pubs read: "Drunk for a penny. Dead drunk for two pence." Could not something be done to rid London of its criminal element, its drunken, idle poor?

When they cast their eyes overseas to North America, they saw a vast empty continent where their country was trying to build an empire. On the southern boundaries of the empire, just below the

*These were some of the "poor children and other poor that pester the streets of London,"
as drawn by the bitter English caricaturist William Hogarth. Conditions like these led
the London philanthropists to dream of a Georgia haven.*

General James Oglethorpe, rugged leader of the Georgia scheme, as sketched in London in his old age.

Carolinas, between the Altamaha and the Savannah Rivers, was a land rumored to be ideally suited for a new paradise. By a happy coincidence, that was precisely where it was most important to have strong armed settlements. For the Spanish had established themselves in Florida farther south, and were always pushing northward.

Of course, the thing to do was to plan a settlement in that area (which they proposed to call "Georgia" after King George II). What could be more obvious? If they planned right they could kill two birds with one stone. They could drain off some of the London poor, while using them in far-off America for a human barricade against the Spaniards who threatened the empire. They could accomplish still another good purpose by setting the poor people to work producing what the empire most needed. A strong empire, they figured, should grow and make everything for itself. When the British bought anything from another country, British gold drained away and made the other country richer. They measured wealth mainly in gold. All the countries in the world were competing for the world's limited gold supply. Therefore anything that kept British gold at home made Britain stronger.

One problem for a country like Britain —a small island-nation in a cool climate—was that many crops could not be raised at home. Britain had to buy these products from other countries. This weakened the empire by sending British gold abroad. One important product that the British bought from other countries was silk. Every year, as the founders of Georgia pointed out, in order to buy silk the British people were sending out of their country—to the Italians, the French, the Chinese, and others—a fortune in precious metals.

If the British could only produce silk inside their own empire, they would keep all this gold at home. Why not use Georgia? Why not make Georgia into a vast silk plantation?

In London the founders of Georgia embraced this idea with quick enthusiasm. Even before a single silkworm had been taken out to the colony, they announced that silk raising in Georgia would surely give work to at least twenty thousand people there during the four months of the silk season. During the whole year round, they said an additional twenty thousand people in England would be employed making the silk thread into cloth. They predicted that before long all silk worn by Englishmen would be raised in their own empire. The British would soon be exporting silk. They might eventually capture the whole European market.

The longer they dreamed these dreams, the more they discussed them, the more plausible and beautiful the dreams seemed. One special advantage of raising silkworms was that it was not heavy work. It required only a delicate touch and nimble fingers. Did this not make it a perfect employment for the poverty-stricken, undernourished Londoners? Their women and children especially needed work. The Georgia founders happily concluded: "Most of the poor in Great Britain, who are maintained by charity, are capable of this [silk raising], though not of harder labor."

Of what "facts" had the charitable men of London woven this fabric of beautiful illusions? Much of their information had come from earlier advertising brochures. In 1609 some of the adventurers to Virginia (only a few hundred miles north of Georgia) reported finding "silk worms, and plenty of mulberry trees, whereby ladies, gentlewomen and little children (being set in the way to do it) may be all employed with pleasure, making silk comparable to that of Persia, Turkey, or any other." Some of the promoters of Virginia, seeking publicity, had actually presented to King Charles II a coronation robe that they said was woven of Virginia silk.

If the silkworm flourished in Virginia, declared the Georgia promoters in London, surely the silkworm would grow still better in Georgia, because Georgia was farther south. "The air, as it is healthy for men (the latitude about thirty-two)," they advertised, "is also proper for the silk worms." They hired Sir Thomas Lombe, who had become the national expert on silk, to advise them. Lombe had smuggled himself into an Italian silk mill in 1718 in order to steal the secret of silk-making. He had never been to Georgia, but he testified anyway to the sure-fire wonders of silk-raising out there. The promoters of Georgia began to believe their own advertising.

Now the silkworm is a delicate and peculiar animal. It has its own ways, and would not change its diet for anybody—not even to help the suffering poor of London or to protect the great British Empire. It feeds mainly on the leaves of the mulberry tree. But not just any mulberry tree will do. The silkworm feeds only on the *white* mulberry. Unfortunately the Georgia mulberry trees were not of this type. Instead they were *black* mulberry trees, whose leaves do not satisfy the silkworm's choosy appetite. The white mulberry trees would not grow well in Georgia.

This was a little fact which the London promoters had not bothered to notice. It would soon wreck their whole plan for silk-raising. Along with other miscalculations, it would make Georgia's early years a failure.

Plans breed more plans. The ill-informed trustees of Georgia, sitting in their easy chairs in London, went on drawing their plans in ever more minute detail. They required people who received Georgia land to plant mulberry trees in certain quantities. To insure a strong border defense with a well-armed population, each settler had to live near

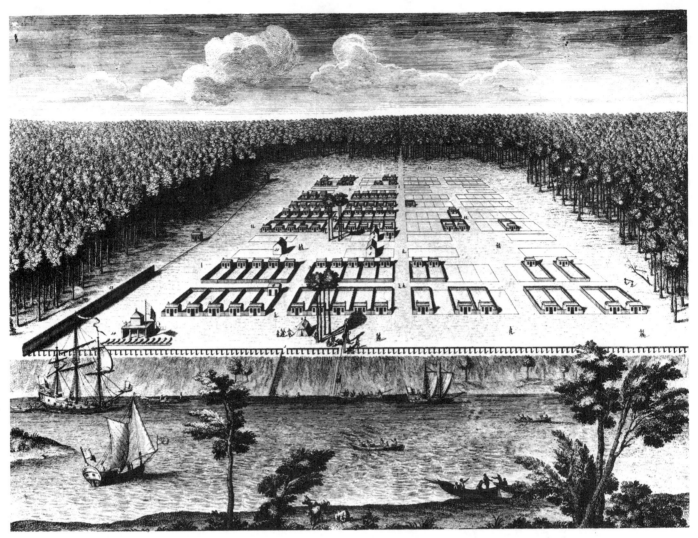

The neat checkerboard scheme which the London planners imagined for the city of Savannah in Georgia (1734).

the others. To keep the settlers sober and industrious the trustees prohibited "Rum, Brandies, Spirits, or Strong Waters." All kegs of liquor in the colony were to be publicly destroyed, and sale of liquor was punished as a crime. No settler was allowed to own or sell the land he worked on. He could use it only according to company rules. No Negro slaves were to be allowed.

This was a charity colony. It was the only colony whose founders did not expect to make money for themselves. To find settlers, they actually advertised for the most worthy charity cases—"such as were most distressed, virtuous, and industrious." Charity cases were in no position to make demands, nor were they allowed to govern themselves or decide what to do with other people's money. Where the people would live, what tools and weapons they would have, what their food rations would be, what clothing they would wear—all these items were settled in England. Georgia became a vast poorhouse. The official storekeeper of the colony (who gave out everything to the settlers) declared that the colonists themselves "had neither lands, rights or possessions; that the trustees gave and that the trustees could freely take away."

A first group of charity settlers arrived in Georgia in 1732. While the high-minded trustees in London made neat rules, the settlers in far-off America had to face the rough facts. They had to live in torrid heat while they tried to farm the pine barrens. They were tempted by slave traders and rum salesmen. They were attacked by Indians and Spaniards. They had to suffer everything. But they could decide nothing.

Since the colony was not operated for profit, when the silk crops failed, the London trustees did not quickly try to find a more profitable crop. Instead they blamed the good-for-nothing settlers, and tried to raise more money to pay for more failures. When the trustees proudly presented to Queen Caroline a gown of "Georgia Silk," it actually had

in it only a few, if any, threads from Georgia. The leader of the trustees, Lord Egmont, modestly boasted to the Queen: " 'Tis for persons in high station, who have the means in their hands, to do good."

We cannot be surprised that Georgia did not flourish. An empire-builder's dream turned out to be a nightmare. The settlers rebelled, the trustees gave up. By the time of the American Revolution, Georgia—the spoiled child of charitable London—was the least prosperous and least populous of all the colonies. "The poor inhabitants of Georgia," a settler lamented, "are scattered over the face of the earth; her plantations a wild; her towns a desert; her villages in rubbish, her improvements a by-word, and her liberties a jest; an object of pity to friends, and of insult, contempt and ridicule to enemies."

CHAPTER 4
How British Laws Made Smugglers and Pirates

The settlers who came to New York in mid-May 1623 did not have a grand purpose. They were brought over here by the Dutch West India Company, whose goal was to make money. They called their colony New Netherland, but they did not really want it to be a renewed little Netherland—a new Holland overseas. When the English called *their* settlements New England, they really meant what they said. They expected to build a purified, renewed little England. But not the Dutch. They aimed to set

up a trading post and a marketplace.

For Holland was the great merchant of the world. The Dutch were not too particular about what they bought and sold (or sometimes even stole) provided there was a profit in it. And they were not too particular about who came, or what the settlers believed, provided they were willing to trade or to help the Dutch to trade.

The company started dealing in furs, which they gladly bought from Indians or anybody else. Within a year of the

first settlements they sent back to Holland over four thousand beaver skins and seven hundred otter skins. They traded in the tobacco which grew on Manhattan Island. A tobacco plantation stood where we now see the United Nations Building, and Manhattan Island tobacco was as good as the best from Virginia.

The most valuable commodity on Manhattan was, of course, land. Very early the Dutch began "buying" land from the Indians. Fearing they could not establish their right by discovery, the Dutch wanted to be able to say they had actually bought the land from its "owners." The Indians had not settled on Manhattan, but used it only for fishing and for hunting beaver, deer, fox, wild turkey, and the other plentiful game. Not having an idea of landownership anything like that of the Europeans, these Indians probably did not understand what "selling" land to the Dutch meant. The Indians did not know that once the land was sold, the Dutch would have the right to keep them off.

For some trinkets worth 60 Dutch guilders (about $24) several Indian chiefs "sold" Manhattan Island in 1626. Of course, in those days when money was so scarce, $24 was probably worth what several thousand dollars would be worth now. The Dutch were really paying "protection money." They wanted to be allowed to go about their business,

New Amsterdam in 1660 (a modern copy of an old map). The fortified wall near the top gave its name to New York's Wall Street. A gate guarded the entrance to the wide thoroughfare known as Broadway.

and one kind of insurance was to try to keep the Indians happy.

The cluster of islands (Long Island, Staten Island, and Manhattan Island) around the mouth of the wide Hudson River provided a safe natural harbor that was less troubled by ice or fog than were other ports in the temperate regions of the world. The broad Hudson River was a superhighway for bringing furs and farm goods from the interior. The city (which the Dutch called New Amsterdam but which became known to history as New York) was conveniently located also for trade to the West Indies and to Africa.

New Yorkers very early began building ships. They built canoes, small sloops (with one mast) and shallops for shallow water, ketches (with two masts), and large yachts. "Yacht" (like "sloop") was originally a Dutch word, meaning a large hunting ship or pirate ship. The beautiful harbor surrounded by virgin timber tempted Peter Minuit in 1630 to finance Belgian shipbuilders in the construction of the *New Netherland*. A ship carrying thirty cannon and displacing some seven hundred tons, it is said to be the largest ship built in America during the next two centuries.

Of the varied enterprises which made New York a great city, none was more profitable than piracy. This began to flourish after the English had conquered New Netherland in 1664 and renamed it New York.

The pirate's trade was a byproduct of certain laws called the Navigation Acts, which the British had passed to make their empire strong. Colonies were supposed to exist not for their own sake, but for the sake of the mother country. The farmers and manufacturers back home in England were the important people. Colonists, therefore, would not be allowed to produce anything to compete. They must not buy from anybody but the English; they must not ship their products to any country but England. Since the English shipbuilding industry had to grow, the colonists must be forced to use English ships.

This was the purpose of the Navigation Acts. Laws beginning in 1650 and coming right down to the era of the American Revolution told the colonists what they could make or raise, what ships they could use, and where they were allowed to sell their products.

Early laws listed only a few items which had to be brought direct from England, but the list gradually became longer and longer. At first goods could be carried in any ships provided these were *owned* by Englishmen, but by 1696, *all* trade between the colonies and England had to be carried in English-*built*

Background: New Amsterdam (New York) twenty years after the arrival of the first Dutch settlers. Foreground: The miscellaneous population of New York included people of many faiths and several races. Here are Quaker tobacco growers from the West Indies.

ships. *All* European goods for the colonies had to come from or through England. The principal colonial products could be exported only to England or to another British colony. Trade with the English or do not trade at all!

It is not surprising that energetic people, who had crossed the ocean and were just beginning to explore the resources of a vast new world, would not let themselves be fenced in. They wanted to ship everywhere and to buy everywhere.

But the Navigation Laws were not regularly enforced. In fact they were largely unenforceable. The British Empire, from the time of the first Navigation Act till the age of the American Revolution, was continually engaged in wars. Sea battles with other European nations—the Dutch, the French, and the Spanish—kept the British navy busy with work more exciting and more urgent than catching a few smugglers. The British navy could not be bothered with the chores of colonial policemen.

Smuggling then became one of the most profitable occupations of the colonial period. It was the foundation of the fortunes of famous American families. Many a nineteenth-century aristocrat looked down his nose at the new immigrants. He said they were enemies of law and order. Yet he perhaps owed his own fortune to smuggling done by his father or his grandfather.

"Privateer" was the name for a legally licensed pirate. The word came into use about 1664, after the first Navigation Acts. It described someone who had a "private" ship which he used for government purposes. The owner of a private vessel in time of war could get a license from a government official (called a "letter of marque" after the Old French word meaning to seize) allowing him to seize enemy ships. Since he helped the war effort by crippling the enemy, he was allowed by his own king to keep a share of the loot. But when a privateer with letters of marque happened to find a ship with a rich cargo, he was tempted not to take too much trouble to find out its exact nationality.

Once a privateer (or "pirate," to use the less respectable name) had loaded his ship with treasure he would hurry into New York port. In port, he simply showed his letter of marque and explained that he had seized his rich cargo as a patriotic duty to help the war effort. New Yorkers themselves did not want to know whether the goods were really from enemy ships or whether they were simply stolen goods. They were only too glad to have merchandise they could not buy from England, and which they were forbidden to buy elsewhere.

The pirates naturally found New York harbor much to their taste. His Majesty's governor and officers were pleased to have them around. The pirates paid handsome "protection money" to the governor who issued their letters of marque, and who also protected them while they sold their booty.

There were few other places in the world where the market for pirates' booty was so good. Prosperous New Yorkers were ready to pay high prices for all the glittering items—heavily carved and inlaid tables and chairs, filigreed daggers, feathered fans, ornate porcelain, and gold-embroidered cloth—which the pirates had captured from

Busy New York Harbor in 1716.

"enemy" ships trading to the Orient. In this way the unenforceable laws and the unwinnable wars of the British Empire transformed reckless pirates into respectable merchants!

These were not the last pirates or the only kind of pirates who frequented New York City. But no others were more flamboyant. Captains and officers of privateers wore the flashy costume of the new rich. They were hearty and hot-tempered. And they spent money freely—on drink, on women, and on luxuries sold by other pirates. They helped make New York a great, rich, and colorful metropolis.

In colonial New York appeared the most celebrated pirate of modern times: Captain William Kidd. For a while he was one of New York's most respected citizens and a sought-after dinner guest. His success was an example of the wide assortment of new opportunities for enterprise in the New World. His real career was so legendary that it is hard to separate fact from fiction.

When Captain William Kidd arrived in New York City about 1690 at the age of forty-five, he was already a substantial citizen. Son of a Scottish minister, he had risen through the ranks. The fact that he was a privateer did not prevent his being respectable. On the contrary, it proved he was risking his own private ships to punish the King's enemies. The New York colonial legislature voted him £150 for his services!

About the same time that Captain Kidd had established a reputation in New York as a patriotic privateer, King William himself, who was trying to hold together a British Empire that stretched around the world, heard disturbing reports from the Far East. Tales were coming back that out there ships under all flags (some belonging to Englishmen and others to East Indians themselves) were being seized by pirates. One of the headquarters of those pirates, the King learned, was New York. So the King removed the old governor, who had taken bribes to leave the pirates alone, and he sent out a new governor, the Earl of Bellomont.

Bellomont was determined—if possible, at some profit to himself—to exterminate pirates in those far-off Asian waters. He personally organized a company to send ships out to the Indian Ocean to capture the pirates with all their booty. Captain Kidd, whom Bellomont called "a bold and honest man," and who had already proven his ability to chase and capture treasure-laden ships, was Bellomont's choice for the top command. The profits would be spread around—10 percent to the King, the rest shared among Governor Bellomont and the other investors, including, of course, Kidd himself. To divide the booty according to company rules, Kidd had to keep careful records of everything taken in.

We cannot be surprised that a man of Captain Kidd's active temperament did not relish this work of a bookkeeper. Once in the Indian Ocean he found it both more interesting and more profitable to be a pirate making his own rules (and keeping all the booty) instead of working under company rules to chase pirates for a small commission.

Seizing every ship in sight, Captain Kidd was not careful about whether or not a particular ship was owned by the

A pirate about to be hanged. In those days hangings were a form of public entertainment. (From an English book on piracy, 1724.)

King's enemies. Within two years he became a name to frighten children with. Rumors arriving in England and New York told how the pirate-chaser had become a pirate, how he had plundered innocent villages all over the Indian Ocean. He was said to be ingenious in devising tortures which would persuade the most courageous seaman to reveal the whereabouts of his treasure.

One of Kidd's boldest enterprises, oddly enough, was his final return to New York. There he made a last desperate effort to prove he was not a pirate at all. He actually argued, with elegant technicality, that the ships he captured were all lawful "prizes." Somehow or other, he said, those ships had been under the protection of the enemy French. Bellomont sent Kidd to London, where he was tried for the murder of a sailor and for five instances of piracy. He was hanged on May 23, 1701, still calling himself "the innocentest person of them all." The King confiscated Kidd's property. But rumor has it that the most valuable of all Kidd's treasure still remains to be found—buried in some secret place on an island in New York harbor.

CHAPTER 5

A Scrambling Place— for Refuge and for Profit

There on Manhattan Island began the great American democracy of cash. Nothing is quite so democratic as money (if you have it). It was lucky for us that the city was founded by the Dutch. They were shrewd and ruthless merchants. If you really want to sell something or buy something, you are not apt to bother people with questions about their religion—or about anything else they believe. You are interested only in their money or their goods. The Dutch, therefore, kept their doors open. They let everybody in, and were slow to persecute—not so much because they believed in toleration, but simply because it was good business. New York City became a place of refuge precisely because it was a place of profit.

This also made it a scrambling place. All sorts of people came from all over. The very first settlers whom the Dutch West India Company sent out in 1623 were not Dutchmen at all. They were Walloons—Protestants who came from southern Belgium, where Spanish Catholics were persecuting them—and they spoke French. From New England soon came refugees from the dictatorship of the Puritan Saints. From Virginia came indentured servants, who wanted to exchange the heavy labor of the plantation for the anonymous freedom of the city. And from time to time there came groups of Huguenots, French Protestants who were persecuted in their own country for their religion.

From Brazil came Jews. They were descendants of those who had been expelled from Spain and Portugal by Ferdinand and Isabella in 1492, and they had first sought asylum in the Netherlands before coming to South America. But they needed a new American haven when the Portuguese, who took over Brazil in 1654, threatened them with the tortures of another Inquisition. The stern and narrow-minded Dutch Governor Peter Stuyvesant hesitated to receive them. But the directors of the Dutch West India Company reminded him that the Jews actually held shares in the company. The Jews must be welcomed, provided they looked after their own poor. Then began the privately supported Jewish charities which have flourished ever since in New York.

Religious freedom in New York City was still, by twentieth-century standards, far from complete. With only a few exceptions, Catholics were kept out during most of the colonial period. They were sometimes persecuted on the fancied grounds that they were threatening to take over the government or that they were the natural allies of the French. The Quakers, who came to preach and to convert only twenty years after the colony was founded, were suspected of being anarchists. They were imprisoned and tortured, but they kept coming back. Still, in an age which in Europe was a time of bloody persecution, of religious wars, and of bigotry, New York City was a surprisingly open marketplace of ideas. Anything else was bad business.

Merchants brought with them their Negro slaves, whose number increased until about the time of the Revolution. As early as 1658, a law controlled the treatment of slaves. Some were freed and even owned land. But the city was an excitable place. In 1741, hysteria over the supposed efforts of Spanish Catholics to conquer America was focused on the innocent Negroes. During that summer, fourteen Negroes were burned alive and eighteen were hanged for imaginary crimes. But within another decade that hysteria had passed and Negroes were actually allowed to vote. In 1817 the State of New York voted to abolish slavery.

Big-city politics was turbulent. New York's simmering conglomeration of peoples, languages, and ideas boiled up from time to time. The English, who began fighting to conquer New Netherland as early as 1661, finally occupied the city in 1664. The Dutch managed to reconquer it ten years later, but shortly lost it again to the English. Jacob Leisler, a German merchant adventurer, profiting from the political confusion in England in 1688, seized and held the government of the colony until he was tried and executed for treason in 1691. In 1733, a bold printer, John Peter Zenger, fought for the right to print unpleasant political facts in his newspaper. His trial aroused public enthusiasm and riots. A few years later came the anti-Spanish Catholic hysteria. Then came the Stamp Act riots and the troubled days of the Revolution.

All this helped explain why New York was a place of vitality and of excitement. By 1771 the city had a population of 22,000. People prospered together even while they fought one another.

CHAPTER 6

How a Few Gentlemen Ruled Virginia

In the years before the Declaration of Independence almost nobody, even in America, believed that anyone who owned very little property could be trusted with governing himself, much less governing others. Democracy—government by and for all the people—seemed a dangerous word.

Nearly everybody believed that a man ought to have a good deal of property to vote at all and that he ought to be rich to be qualified for high office. Poor people, it was said, could not be trusted to run a government, because they needed money so badly that they could be too easily bribed. But rich people, the argument went, because they did not need money so badly, were more likely to be honest. It seemed pretty generally agreed that an "honest" government was a government by and for the rich.

Many of the rich and educated who feared the instincts and the power of the common people did believe that a good government somehow had to be a representative (or "republican") government. Of course, they thought, a decent representative government would have to be run by the "better element"—that is, by people with some property.

Most Americans in the era of the American Revolution probably believed in some form of representative government. There were, on the one hand, those who more than anything else *feared* the people. Their first worry was to preserve the lives and property and liberties of everybody from the violent whims of the dirty, uneducated masses. On the other hand, there were those who *trusted* the people. They did not yet trust them enough to believe they all ought to be allowed to vote. But they thought the natural instincts of most ordinary people were good. The men they feared most were the men in power.

Much of American history during its early years was a struggle between these two kinds of people: those who most feared the people and those who most feared kings and governors and dictators. The different experiences of the colonial years prepared men to take one side or the other.

Four of the first five Presidents of the United States were Virginia men. These were Washington, Jefferson, Madison, and Monroe. We usually call them the "Virginia Dynasty." They included some of the most powerful leaders who put their faith in the people. How did it happen that in the fifty years just after the Declaration of Independence—when there were thirteen and then more States—so large a proportion of our leaders came from a single State?

One answer lies in some special features of life in colonial Virginia. When these men first learned about government, Virginia was still a colony. James Monroe, the last of the Virginia Dynasty, was seventeen years old at the start of the American Revolution. In colonial

Hogsheads of tobacco being prepared for shipment. This is an illustration for a map made in part by Thomas Jefferson's father, Peter, who was a surveyor. He encouraged his son's interest in map-making.

Virginia, where they had formed their political ideas and habits, these future Presidents had learned to trust the people.

Life in mid-eighteenth century Virginia, when Washington and Jefferson and Madison and Monroe were young men, was extremely cozy—at least for young aristocrats like them. A few families ran nearly everything. They owned the largest tobacco plantations, and tobacco was the foundation of everything else. These same people owned the largest number of slaves. If you wanted to be invited to the most elegant parties, you had to come from one of these families. Sons and daugh-

ters of these families usually married daughters and sons of the same small tobacco aristocracy. It was a good time and place to be alive—at least if your father's name was Burwell, Byrd, Carter, Custis, Harrison, Lee, Ludwell, Page, or Wormley.

We know a good deal about the pleasurable life of the young Virginia blue bloods. They were a well-educated lot, and they kept diaries. Since there was no telephone, they were constantly writing one another letters. When we read the letters which Jefferson wrote in his teens (he was born in 1743, and left us letters written as early as 1760), we can see how different was his life from that of the earlier builders of New Zion in New England, or of the crude backwoodsmen farther west. Almost every name Jefferson mentions was from one of the "best" Virginia families. His first sweetheart, Rebecca Burwell, came from the same Burwell family that had already been running the Governor's Council in Virginia a half-century before.

"Dear Will," young Jefferson wrote to his friend Fleming, "I have thought of the cleverest plan of life that can be imagined. You exchange your land for Edgehill, or mine for Fairfields, you marry Suckey Potter, I marry Rebecca Burwell, and get a pole chair and a pair of keen horses, practice the law in the same courts, and drive about to all the dances in the country together. How do you like it?"

The same Virginians who had played together as children, and partied together when they were young men, ran the government together when they grew up. Whenever the Governor of Virginia tried to fill his Council, he had trouble finding candidates from "suitable" families who were not already overburdened with public offices and government honors. On the list of 91 men who served on the Virginia Governor's Council from 1680 to the American Revolution, there were only 57 different family names. Nearly a third of the councillors were from only nine

Riding to hounds was a favorite sport of the Virginia aristocrats.

different Virginia families.

Many members of these lucky families held more than one office. Sometimes they found themselves actually sitting as judges in cases where they were supposed to hear their own arguments as government lawyers. And besides the colony-wide offices there were many local offices that went to these same families. The young George Washington, for example, was at the same time a church vestryman, a justice of the peace, a commander of the militia, and a delegate to the House of Burgesses. This was an American-style aristocracy, but still an aristocracy.

Since Virginia was a representative government, there had to be elections. These elections of members of the House of Burgesses—the Virginia legislature—were very different from the rough-and-tumble contests we know in modern cities. Nowadays, anybody can run for some office, and nearly everybody can vote. In colonial Virginia, however, everything was organized so that few of the "wrong kind" of people voted and none of them were elected.

Election day was a friendly occasion when George Washington ran for Burgess. To be a voter you had to be a "freeholder"—that is, own land of a certain value. Technically any Virginian qualified to vote could run for the House of Burgesses, but actually no one dared who was not a member of the tobacco aristocracy. There was hardly any campaigning. It was considered rather silly to make a campaign speech since you were appealing entirely to a small number of old friends and neighbors. They had known you since childhood.

It was considered ungentlemanly to solicit votes or to vote for yourself, and there were no organized political parties.

The usual means of persuasion were not complicated arguments or dull statistics about trade and commerce, but large quantities of barbecued beef and pork, served with rum punch and ginger cakes. To persuade people in this way was expensive. Each time he ran for Burgess, Washington spent at least £25, and once his bill came to £50. This was several times what it cost a man in those days to buy the house and land required to qualify him as a voter.

A Virginia law forbade a candidate to offer voters any "money, meat, drink . . . present, gift, reward, or entertainment," but it was seldom enforced. A candidate who entertained his voters lavishly actually proved he was a generous and substantial gentleman. And wasn't that exactly the sort of person you wanted to represent you? Anyway, rich gentlemen were always giving parties. Wouldn't it be ungrateful to accuse them of bribery at election time?

The election itself was a kind of spectator sport. In good weather it was held in the open air on the courthouse lawn. There were no paper ballots. Voting was anything but secret. At the table sat the sheriff, with the candidates, who were expected to be present, and the clerks to count the votes. Each voter came up and announced his choice aloud. Then his vote was recorded on a scoreboard for all to see. As each voter declared his preference, shouts of approval went up from one side and good-natured hoots from the others. The betting odds changed, and new wagers were laid.

In the Governor's Palace, the colonial Governor of Virginia lived in royal style, providing the local aristocracy with a court and social center. Here also lived Patrick Henry and Thomas Jefferson, the first two Governors of the new State of Virginia. Reconstructed on the original foundations at Colonial Williamsburg.

When a candidate received a vote he would rise, bow, and personally thank the voter: "Mr. Buchanan, I shall treasure that vote in my memory. It will be regarded as a feather in my cap forever." When George Washington was running for Burgess in 1758, but had to be away commanding the militia at election time, he sent his friend, the most influential man in the county, to sit at the polls and thank each voter for him.

There was very little danger of voters electing the "wrong kind" of person because the sheriff himself was chosen by the wealthy gentlemen, and the sheriff managed the elections. The sheriff decided who was qualified to vote. He set the date of the election. He decided when voting should begin and (most important) when the voting was closed. If the sheriff's favorite candidate was ahead he might declare the voting closed at two o'clock in the afternoon. But if his candidate was still behind at nightfall he could continue the voting into the next day, while the needed votes were rounded up.

According to Virginia law, a gentleman could vote in every county where he owned enough land. If he owned land in three counties, he could vote three times—once for each of three sets of Burgesses. And he could run for Burgess from any one of the counties where he could vote. A large planter would, of course, choose to run in the most promising constituency. It was normal for Virginians—including George Washington, Patrick Henry, John Marshall, and Benjamin Harrison—to use their large landholdings to help their political careers.

The choice of a Burgess was usually between two equally well-qualified gentlemen from two equally well-to-do families. Virginia, therefore, remained for the whole colonial period in the hands of its "best" people. Slaves or working people could not make trouble at elections. They had no vote. And Virginia had no cities where newly arrived immigrants might vote unpredictably or where vagrant or discontented working people might vote for one of themselves. The largest town in all Virginia during the colonial period was tiny Williamsburg. Although it was the capital, it had a year-round population of less than two thousand people.

Virginia, then, actually was a kind of republic. It did have a representative government elected by "the people." But what a safe and snug republic it was!

Is it any wonder that Virginians like Washington and Jefferson and Madison and Monroe had great faith in what *they*

called representative government? The only kind of representative government they knew was safe and sane—especially for people like themselves who were lords of the tobacco aristocracy. They had a great deal less fear of "the people" and a great deal more confidence that "the people" would select good representatives than did other thoughtful Americans of that age. John Adams of Massachusetts, Alexander Hamilton of New York, and Gouverneur Morris of Pennsylvania—who all lived in or near big cities—knew the fickle, frightening mobs. They put their faith elsewhere.

George Washington wearing his French and Indian War uniform, with the "gorget" of an officer hanging from his neck. By the American artist, Charles Willson Peale, who painted many Revolutionary leaders from life.

Monticello, the house which Thomas Jefferson designed for himself and was continually remodeling. This is the shape he finally gave it, adding the central dome to make it resemble buildings he admired in France and Italy.

Considering how small and cozy was the ruling group, how large was the colony of Virginia (it was the largest colony in square miles, and for most of the eighteenth century had the largest population), and how tightly the aristocracy limited their membership, we must be amazed at how well they ran things. They succeeded partly because they had the same interests. Members of the House of Burgesses, where laws were debated, knew one another intimately. Since newspapers were few and communications were slow, it was hard for Burgesses to be demagogues. In the House of Burgesses the members really debated with one another. They were seldom tempted to speak simply to get votes back home. They discussed what was good for Virginia.

The most valuable power of the House of Burgesses was to give out land. There were vast, unsettled, fertile tracts within the colony which the Burgesses had power to give away—or to sell at a price which amounted to a giveaway. In 1769, for example, George Washington used his influence to extract from the Burgesses a grant of about 200,000 acres (an area about one-third the size of Rhode Island) to his veterans and himself for their service in fighting against the French and the Indians in western Pennsylvania. He even boasted that his men owed all the land they received to his own successful lobbying. Since he had been their commanding officer, he naturally got the largest share.

For the most part, Burgesses were honest men. They believed it was every gentleman's duty to serve in public office. Any man elected Burgess was expected to attend to the public business, and regularly. As early as 1659, a Virginia law fined every Burgess three hundred pounds of tobacco for every day he was absent from the House without a good excuse. Sometimes a man was elected Burgess even when he did not want to run. He was not allowed to refuse the job. In May 1782, the war-weary Jefferson was unhappy because he had been censured for his conduct as Governor during the British invasion. The people of his county elected him a Burgess without his permission. He tried to refuse, but when the Speaker hinted that he might be seized and taken forcibly to Williamsburg, he gave in reluctantly.

The tobacco aristocrats who governed Virginia were, of course, practical men. But to be practical they had to have broad interests. They had to know all sorts of things which a city merchant did not need to know. They had to know about the weather, for the delicate tobacco plant was killed by frost or too much rain. They had to know about the care and breeding of livestock in order to feed their plantation community. Since they were a great distance from big-city doctors or hospitals, they (and their wives, too) had to be amateur doctors in order to give emergency treatment for dysentery or smallpox, or to help deliver a baby. They had to know something about the law (at least as much as an English justice of the peace) in order to decide disputes and punish crimes of the neighborhood. And of course they had to know about politics and the constitution in order to do their job in the House of Burgesses.

If they were going to hear music, they had to know about music, or at least know how to judge musicians. Jefferson imported some Italian grape-raising and wine-making experts who could also entertain his plantation with chamber music. Since their tobacco went from the plantation docks across the ocean to England, Virginia planters also had to know something about world trade and how prices changed with the fortunes of peace and war.

Life in the midst of the remote acres could be lonely and monotonous. When George Washington became bored with seeing the same people day after day, he would send a slave to the nearest crossroad to waylay a passing traveler, to bring him to Mount Vernon for dinner and the night. The proverbial Southern

---

This "polygraph," one of many ingenious machines devised by Jefferson, made a copy of a letter while the original was being written. In the days before carbon paper and before photocopying, this saved the trouble of making a copy by hand. It was especially useful for Jefferson, who was a prolific letter writer.

hospitality grew in the lonely, isolated plantation whose owner was anxious for fresh company with news from the outside world.

When there were no big-city amusements, and neighbors might be several hours' horseback ride away, men of lively minds turned to books. In 1744, for example, William Byrd's collection of more than 3,600 titles was one of the two or three largest private libraries in North America. Jefferson early in his life began bringing together at Monticello a remarkable library. The whole nation later profited when it became the basis of the Library of Congress. Great libraries like these were, of course, rare. But every plantation had its small collection of books—manuals of farming, religion, law, medicine, and politics for men who had to run their own small world.

Though the men who ran Virginia often turned to books, they were not bookish. They did not read books in order to make learned or witty conversation in somebody's living room after dinner. They were not men of theory. They looked for what was best that could be transplanted from England. Their first goal was to keep Virginia going—to keep the tobacco plantations profitable and at the same time, if possible, to keep workers healthy and happy. Incidentally they learned many things which drew them out to the other colonies, and even to the world. The great Virginians became leading citizens of what was (in Jefferson's own phrase) a world-wide "Republic of Letters."

PART TWO

THIRTEEN STATES ARE BORN

Winning the American Revolution, John Adams once said, was like trying to make thirteen clocks strike at once. The colonies were so different that it would have been an astonishing coincidence if they had come to the same idea at the same time. Starting as colonies at different times and with different goals, they moved to independence in thirteen different ways. To bring the people of any one colony—of Massachusetts or Pennsylvania or New York—to agree was difficult enough. To lead thirteen different plantations to take common action seemed next to impossible. This was the main American problem in the War for Independence.

But this same variety turned out to be a secret weapon in the war. If the Americans were dispersed, if they lacked any single headquarters, this made trouble for the enemy. The colonies were like a monster with many heads. They could survive the loss of several of them. Nothing was more baffling to the British generals. Nothing did more to make it impossible for the British to win the war.

In peacetime, when the new nation was being born, this American peculiarity again became a secret strength.

For here in America it was possible to try many different ways of life within the same country. Not until after the Civil War—a century after the outbreak of the American Revolution—did the States finally decide that they really were a single nation. And that was to be the bloodiest and most painful decision ever made by the American people.

Meanwhile, America was discovering that it was a nation of nations, a people of many peoples. The chance for men and women with two thousand years of Old World civilization behind them to experiment on an unspoiled continent—this was something new under the sun.

To weld these varied communities into a single nation was a chance for a new and unpredictable kind of greatness. The precise character of the nation, like the continent itself, would long remain a mystery. In these next chapters we will see a nation being born. It was born in a puzzling twilight—in the dusk of an old Europe which was the dawn of a new America. Many decades would pass before Americans themselves began to feel sure of the grand outlines of their civilization which was filling a continent.

CHAPTER 7

How the Ocean Tied Some to England ❧

Great Britain—the motherland—was of course an island. Water separated the British from all the world, and water was their only highway to the world. The thirteen American colonies were also a kind of island. They stretched like a string of beads down the Atlantic seacoast. Every one touched the sea. During the colonial years every important American city was on the Atlantic seacoast, where it could look eastward and oceanward.

What separated every colony from the mother country—and what tied every colony to the mother country—was the ocean. It was the ocean (as Governor Bradford had said) that separated them "from all the civil parts of the world." Westward of the colonies stretched the vast, unfathomed, trackless continent. That was (in a new American phrase) the "back country"—so called because it was away from the ocean. The continent was even more unknown than the ocean and there was no known civilization on the other side.

American independence was, of course, independence from Europe. To become independent meant to turn inland. Future Americans more and more would look and think *westward*. When the inner American continent ceased to be a threat, and became a promise, when the unknown land ceased to be a wall holding them to the sea, and instead became their hope, then (and not until then) did the New World bring forth a new nation. But that was many years coming.

The different feelings of the different American colonies about the mother country and about themselves depended very much on how they used the ocean. Was the ocean mainly a highway connecting them to a modern, civilized homeland? Or was it mainly a gulf separating them from a dying Old World?

The feelings of the different colonies about the ocean depended, of course, on what they hoped to make of themselves. It also depended on what the ocean had to offer them—on how the water came up to their land.

Virginia was a land of riverways. Looked at from the ocean, Virginia had no solid seacoast, but was a half-dozen outreaching fingers of land separated by inreaching fingers of water. In these rich lowlands of "tidewater" Virginia (so called because the ocean tides reach there), the land and the sea seemed perfectly married. Deep navigable rivers—the Potomac, the Rappahannock, the York, and the James—divided Virginia into strips stretching southeastward. Each of these strips was nearly an island. Each in turn was veined by smaller rivers, many large enough to carry traffic to the ocean.

These riverways brought the whole world to the door of every great plantation. From the ocean came ships carrying Negro slaves from Africa and the West Indies, carrying muskets, hoes, clothing, furniture, and books from London. Down to the ocean went ships carrying large barrels (called hogsheads) of tobacco from the broad plantations of the Lees, the Carters, and the Byrds.

Every large plantation had its own dock. Goods arrived there direct from London. Virginians felt little need to have their own cities. For London was their shopping center.

In 1688 an English traveler to Virginia wrote:

No country in the world can be more curiously watered. But this convenience, that in future times may make her like the Netherlands, the richest place in all America, at the present I look on [as] the greatest impediment to the advance of the country, as it is the greatest obstacle to trade and commerce. For the great number of rivers, and the thinness of the inhabitants, distract and disperse a trade. So that all ships in general gather each their loading up and down a hundred miles distant; and the best of trade that can be driven is a sort of Scotch Peddling, for they must carry all sorts of truck that trade thither, having one commodity to pass off [for] another. . . . The number of rivers, is one of the chief reasons why they have no towns.

Planters with riverways running direct to London from their door felt very close to Old England. In those days before railroads, it was slow and expensive to carry anything across the land. "Most houses are built near some landing place," the Rev. Hugh Jones wrote from Virginia in 1724. "Anything may be delivered to a gentleman there [in Virginia] from London, Bristol, etc. with less trouble and cost, than to one living five miles in the country in England; for you pay no freight for goods from London, and but little from Bristol; only the party to whom the goods belong, is in gratitude engaged to freight tobacco upon the ship consigned to her owners in England."

Tobacco was a bulky crop, packed in huge barrels weighing hundreds of

A tobacco plantation was a little village. This painting (about 1825) shows the planter's house on the hill at the center, for it was the center of power and government. Below the slave quarters, barns, and stables is the plantation's own wharf.

pounds. These filled the holds of ships going back to England. What could these ships bring from England? Anything and everything needed by the tobacco planters of Virginia. In the empty holds of ships returning from England, bulky objects could be carried at very little cost. Some wealthy Virginians therefore pleased their families by importing from London heavy furniture and grand coaches elegantly carved and covered with gold leaf.

To make his purchases the Virginia planter naturally had to rely on his agent in London, who was usually the same person who helped him sell his tobacco there. The London agent ran a kind of mail-order shopping service. He supplied all sorts of things—a set of lawbooks, a fancy bonnet for a wife's or daughter's birthday, a case of wine, a dozen pairs of shoes for slaves.

This man in London (called a "factor," from the Latin word *facere,* to make or do) did almost anything the Virginia planter required. He arranged the English education of the planter's son or daughter, he reported this season's London styles, he sent the latest market news, he advised which recent books were worth reading, and he recounted court scandal or the latest trends in English politics. Sometimes he even helped a lonely bachelor-planter who offered to marry "on fifteen days sight" if the factor would ship with his other supplies a young woman "of an honest family between twenty and twenty-five years of age; of a middle stature and well-proportioned, her face agreeable, her temper mild, her character blameless, her health good, and her constitution strong enough to bear the change of climate."

Virginia planters thought of themselves not so much as Americans, but as English country gentlemen who happened to be living in America. They still relied on England for books, clothing, furniture, carriages—even for religion and political ideas. During most of the colonial period, the normal way to ship something from a Virginia plantation to Boston was first to send it all the way back to London, from where it would be shipped out to Boston on an English vessel. Virginia Englishmen—including leaders of the American Revolution like George Washington and Thomas Jefferson—owed most of their civilization to England. Many, like Washington, had fought for the King and the British Empire against the French and the Indians.

The ocean which tied them to the English homeland helped them keep the habits and ideas of English gentlemen. With few exceptions they were moderate, sensible men. They would make no trouble so long as they could prosper as loyal Englishmen.

CHAPTER 8
How the Ocean Led Others Out to the World

The same ocean highway that tied Virginia tobacco planters to Mother England led men of Massachusetts Bay elsewhere. The rough and rocky coast of New England offered few gateways to the interior. There were sheltered bays and deep harbors—Salem, Boston, Plymouth, and many others. But New England rivers, with few exceptions, ran steeply downhill. Although they were good for turning a millwheel, they were, for the most part, one-way streets tumbling to the ocean. You could not take an ocean vessel very far inland.

New England bays became havens for big ships that traveled the oceans of the world. On the rocky New England soil, covered by snowy winters far colder than those of Old England, there grew no single staple crop. There was little tobacco, no sugar or silk or rice. New Englanders found their wealth in the sea.

"The abundance of sea-fish are almost beyond believing," Francis Higginson, one of the earliest New Englanders, wrote in 1630, "and sure I would scarce have believed it except I had seen it with mine own eyes." There was fish for every taste: mackerel, bass, lobster, herring, turbot, sturgeon, haddock, mullets, eels, crabs, mussels, and oysters. A small quantity the New Englanders themselves ate. Most they dried, salted, and carried to far parts of the world. Some they sold to the Catholics of Europe, who ate much fish on Fridays. The scraps and leavings went to the slave owners of the Caribbean as cheap food for their Negroes.

Before the end of the seventeenth century, fishing was the main industry of Massachusetts Bay. In 1784, the Massachusetts House of Representatives voted "to hang up a representation of a codfish in the room where the House sit, as a memorial of the importance of the codfishery to the welfare of the Commonwealth." The codfish became the totem of the State. It hung over the Speaker's desk until the middle of the twentieth century.

The New England fisheries actually helped bring on the Revolution. Deep-sea fishermen need ships, and New Englanders began building their own fishing ships in large numbers. This especially worried the English. They feared the colonists would build their own merchant marine and eventually do all their own shipping. And this was one of the reasons why the English clamped the Navigation Acts on the colonies, and went on to tighten their senseless and unenforceable restrictions against colonial trading. Faneuil Hall (which still stands in Boston), the meeting place of the Massachusetts rebels, was given to the city by Peter Faneuil, one of the many merchants who had become rich by shipping New England codfish to forbidden distant markets.

Why should bold and adventurous New England sailors keep inside the boundaries marked off by a few English politicians? Even before the new United States was launched as a nation, New England sailors showed their independence by shipping whatever they could find or make—and to wherever they were carried by whim or profit.

New England ships roamed the world. Their sailors were the first Americans to reach China, where they peddled large quantities of ginseng, a rare herb sup-posed to prolong life. They were the first to reach St. Petersburg in Russia. New England vessels traded with the west coast of Africa, and they went to Zanzibar on the east coast, where they found copal (a substance from tropical trees) to make varnish. They brought the elegant sandalwood (for carved cabinets or for burning as incense) from Hawaii. They picked up otter skins in British Columbia on the Pacific, which

Codfish, the mainstay of New England fisheries, were brought to shore in small boats, then dried and salted for shipment. The cannon were intended for protection against Indians or against the French or other imperial rivals.

they carried to China in exchange for the tea which they brought back home for great profits.

Nothing was too small or too big for their commerce or their imaginations. Salem became the world headquarters for trade in the tiny peppercorn, the seed we put in our pepper grinders. Pepper and spices were especially important in the days before refrigeration—both as preservatives and as a cover-up for the foul smell of aging meat. To get oil for lamps, whaling expeditions—which might last three years at a time—went out from New Bedford and Nantucket.

In the days before independence, when English laws still hemmed them in, enterprising New Englanders had to be smugglers. For them, American independence would be a great relief. It would make them into honest, law-abiding men. But long before the American Revolution, the minds and hearts and pocketbooks of bold New Englanders were attached to the whole world.

New Yorkers, too, had their own special reasons for making the ocean a highway away from England. Families of many of the Dutch settlers were still in the Netherlands. New Jersey had been settled by Swedes from the remote Scandinavian north. Pennsylvania had already attracted large numbers of Germans—wagon makers and tailors and cabinetmakers—who still spoke the German language. They naturally wanted German books which could not be found in England. All over the colonies were sprinkled immigrants who had come in groups. Austrians from Salzburg were in Georgia to make silk, Italians in Virginia to teach plantation owners how to raise grapes. Huguenots in Massachusetts and New York and South Carolina were fleeing from persecution in their French homeland. All these learned English only slowly. Their mother country was not England.

Even if colonists had not been independent-minded and determined to run their own lives, the vast ocean barrier would have made them so. The ocean was the father of self-government. The English colonial office, which was supposed to control the governments in the American colonies, had to run its affairs by mail.

Each colony had its own representative assembly. But in each colony the natural leader and the greatest single power was the Governor. He came from England and received his orders from London. The English government in turn depended on him for information about the colony. Getting a message from England to a colony was complicated. Ships were slow and far between. If no ship was sailing, no message could go. The Governor of North Carolina, for example, normally received his communications by way of Virginia. In June 1745 the Board of Trade in London wrote Governor Johnson of North Carolina complaining that it had had no letter from him in the past three years. A full year later he replied from North Carolina that their letter had only just reached him.

During the long New England winter when Boston harbor was frozen or impassable, the whole colony received no word from the outside world. A letter which the Governor of Massachusetts Bay wrote in late November was not

New England sea captains, away on long business trips, caroused in the taverns of the Caribbean—much like modern conventioneers.

likely to reach London before the following April or May. By that time the information it carried would be ancient history. Even if the mail actually reached an English port, there were more delays. It might take weeks or months for mail arriving at Bristol or Falmouth to be carried overland to London. Papers addressed to the Board of Trade were sometimes lost in the customs house, or they might lie for a year before anyone troubled to deliver them.

To avoid these delays of official mail, messages were sometimes sent through friends. Then even the most confidential information might be leaked to people who read the messages on the way.

Parliament was frequently passing laws for the colonies. With nothing but out-of-date information, how could Parliament really know what it was doing?

The continual wars for empire added to all the other difficulties. Britain's enemies aimed to sink all British ships. French and Spanish men-of-war saw that many an urgent government message was delivered to the bottom of the ocean. Not until 1755 was a regular monthly packet boat going back and forth between Falmouth, on the southwestern tip of England (about four hundred miles overland from London), and New York.

By then it was too late. In the American colonies there had already grown up thirteen separate centers of government. Self-government had come to stay, simply from force of circumstance—from the force of three thousand miles of ocean. If Americans wanted to be well governed, they had to govern themselves.

CHAPTER 9

The British Take a Collision Course

The British finally won their colonial war against the French and the Indians in 1763. According to the custom of empires, the loser handed over vast lands and the people in them to the winner. The British Empire was now bigger than ever, which made the thirteen American colonies a smaller part of the empire than ever before. To the north of the thirteen colonies the British had now added all of Canada, and to the south all the regions east of the Mississippi River, including Florida. The people living in these vast lands became new members of the British Empire.

Trouble really began when the well-meaning men running the government in London decided in 1763 to set this far-flung empire in order. Their plans were much too orderly to work well on a continent that was nearly all wilderness. To prevent fighting among the colonies, and to avoid war with the Indians, the men in London decided to try to keep the colonists confined where they already were. The British thought that the Appalachian Mountains, which ran roughly parallel to the Atlantic coastline a few hundred miles inland, would be a useful barrier to keep the colonists separated from the Indians on the west. They proclaimed that in the future the colonists should not settle on the western side of those mountains, and that the Indians should not go eastward.

This was a neat enough idea, but hardly designed to please Virginians, who were always looking for new tobacco land and who were hoping also to make money from wilderness real estate. Was not the continent theirs every bit as much as the Indians'?

At the same time George Grenville, who was in charge of the British treasury (his title was "Chancellor of the Exchequer"), was desperately looking for ways to pay the bills left over from a century of wars. Had not the American colonists eventually profited from the British wars against the enemies of the empire? In the backwoods, colonists had seen their homes burned and their families murdered by French and Indians. On the sea, colonial merchants had lost ships and goods to marauding French and Spanish and Dutch privateers. Why should not Americans now at last pay a fair share of the bills for keeping peace and defending the empire?

Grenville therefore persuaded Parliament to pass the Sugar Act in 1764. It raised the old taxes and imposed many new taxes. Its purpose was not so much to control American trade as to extract American money. That was a fatal mistake. It was the first law ever passed by Parliament to get money from the colonies to send back to support the British government.

This was only the first of a series of disastrous experiments. The British government tried one way after another to get money from the colonies. The men in London raised the taxes on sugar and

Bostonians rejoiced at the burning of British tax stamps.

coffee and wines imported into the colonies. Then, in addition to taxing imports into the colonies, in the Stamp Act of March 1765 they tried a new kind of tax. They now put taxes on all sorts of everyday things which the American colonists used, even if they were not imported. To show you had paid the tax, you would buy a stamp, like a postage stamp. A stamp had to be put on nearly every piece of printed matter in daily use—on newspapers, magazines, calendars, receipts, legal papers for buying and selling land, on ships' papers, on insurance policies, and even on playing cards. If your papers did not have stamps on them they would be seized, you would

be tried (without a jury) and be fined or jailed.

It was bad enough for an ignorant Parliament three thousand miles away to control what came into the colonies. But many colonists still thought that might be a reasonable price to pay for preserving the empire and supporting the British navy. It was quite another matter—and far more serious—when the Parliament in London now started meddling inside the colonies. If Parliament taxed newspapers they could tax books, and then what couldn't they tax? If they could tax everything in the colonies, they could control all daily life. Where would it end?

In a new push to organize trade in the enlarged empire, and to improve business in England, Grenville now also decided to control the trade of the colonies more tightly than ever before. The old Navigation Laws controlling imports and exports had not been strictly enforced. Otherwise Americans would not have tolerated them. Under the new, stricter laws, Americans would be tried *outside* the colonies. They could no longer appeal to juries of their friends and neighbors. And still more laws were added to be sure that no colonial trade leaked to any non-British part of the world.

If these new policies continued, Americans thought, they would no longer be American Englishmen, with all the rights of Englishmen. They would simply be slaves of Parliament. Even in England, some people warned against the new policies.

The colonists quickly replied to British tyranny. They organized town meetings to protest. In order to punish British businessmen, colonists decided not to buy British goods. Some of the richest and most respectable Americans formed a secret society, called the Sons of Liberty, to terrorize the British agents who were trying to sell the hated tax stamps. They persuaded many of the British agents to resign. The Americans used all sorts of arguments, including brickbats and tar and feathers.

Hundreds of merchants in New York City, Philadelphia, and Boston agreed not to buy imported goods until the Stamp Act was repealed. Nine of the thirteen colonies sent official representatives from their colonial assemblies to a special Stamp Act Congress in New York City in October 1765, to combat British tyranny.

All this began to empty British pocketbooks. In a single year, 1764–1765, British sales to America fell off by £305,000.

The London merchants began to worry. To save themselves, they demanded that Parliament repeal the Stamp Act. Benjamin Franklin, representing the colonies in London, went to the House of Commons and warned the British that they were on the road to ruin. If they did not change their policies, there would very likely be rebellion. The Americans, he explained, dearly loved their Mother England, but they loved their liberties even more.

The rulers of Britain might still have saved the situation. If they had known the colonists better, they would have realized that Americans would not let their lives be run by others. A shrewder British government might have worked out a cooperative empire. Then there might never have been a War of Inde-

---

The Sons of Liberty published notices like this to announce their meetings. In those days the letter "s" was sometimes written much like the letter "f."

ADVERTISEMENT.

THE Members of the Affociation of the Sons of Liberty, are requefted to meet at the City-Hall, at one o'Clock, To-morrow, (being Friday) on Bufinefs of the utmoft Importance;—And every other Friend to the Liberties, and Trade of America, are hereby moft cordially invited, to meet at the fame Time and Place. *The Committee of the Affociation.*

Thurfday, NEW-YORK, 16th December, 1773.

pendence. But the rulers of Britain were near-sighted and short-sighted. They thought that government by Parliament had to be all-or-nothing. Unlike the Americans, they were not willing to compromise.

The colonists were practical men.

They knew it was possible for Parliament to run their foreign relations, and that Americans could still have their own assemblies—in Massachusetts, in Virginia, and in all the other colonies—to run life inside the colonies.

The men in London did not see it that

This engraving of the "Boston Massacre," as imagined by Paul Revere, became effective propaganda against the British. In the background Revere shows the Old State House (still standing), and in the foreground are the victims.

way. They thought that government by Parliament had to be all-powerful or that it would have no power at all. Even when they repealed the Stamp Act they stupidly declared that Parliament still had power to make laws for the Americans "in all cases whatsoever." They did not realize that a new age had arrived. Two million people were now living in the thirteen colonies. Englishmen in America were beginning to be Americans.

The British government continued its collision course. Needing money at home, they increased the import taxes in America. When colonists resisted, they sent British troops to Boston. All this simply increased colonial resistance.

One of the ablest organizers of colonial rebellion was Sam Adams of Boston. He was a strange man who always had trouble managing his own affairs, but could persuade others how to run theirs. He came from a well-known family and went to Harvard College, where he studied Latin and Greek. His father set him up in business, but he soon lost his father's money. He became tax collector for the Town of Boston, but got into trouble when he failed to hand over all the taxes he collected. He was always in debt, and many Bostonians considered him a shady character.

But Adams made himself a master of propaganda and mob tactics. He was clever at making a sensation out of every incident, and blaming it all on the British. British troops in Boston late one March night in 1770 had been taunted by a few restless unemployed workers. In their confusion, the British troops fired and killed five colonists. Sam Adams advertised this as the "Boston Massacre."

Since it was easier to organize big-city crowds, Boston became a center of agitation. On the night of December 16, 1773, a group of townspeople who had been organized by Sam Adams put on the disguise of Mohawk Indians, boarded the tea ships in Boston Harbor, and made their protest against the tea tax by throwing overboard 342 chests of tea. This "Boston Tea Party" helped Americans prove that it was the principle of taxation without representation and not merely the taxes that worried them. For the British government had just made complicated arrangements with the British East India Company that reduced the actual price of tea for the American colonists. But at the same time the British government had preserved the hated tax.

Still the British rulers of empire refused to retreat or to compromise. Instead they used force. In 1774 they closed the port of Boston. They seized the government of Massachusetts and then filled the legislature with their stooges. They altogether deprived colonists of the right of trial by jury. They gave British troops in America the power to take over taverns, and even to live free of charge in private homes. The worst American fears had come true.

CHAPTER 10

Americans Declare Their Independence ɔⱱ

When Americans began to realize that it was hopeless to argue good sense into the heads of the British rulers, they also realized that they were in for a long, hard fight. If thirteen disunited colonies were to win independence from the world's greatest empire, they would need all the help they could find. Most of all, they needed help from the second-greatest empire of the day—France. The French army, and especially the French navy, might make all the difference.

But to win the all-out help of France, the Americans would have to convince the French that the Americans had really cut the British tie—that they were no longer trying simply to patch up a family quarrel. Then France, by helping the Americans, would really be weakening the British Empire. For this reason, if for no other, Americans would have to declare their independence loud and clear.

Until the unpleasantness with the mother country, the colonies had gone their separate ways. There had not been any Congress or any central government where all thirteen colonies could meet and talk about their problems. Franklin and others had tried to persuade them to come together, but with very little success. Now within only a few years the bungling politicians in London did more to push the colonies together than colonial statesmen had accomplished in over a century.

Twelve of the colonies sent delegates

(fifty-six altogether) to Carpenters Hall in Philadelphia on September 5, 1774. The meeting called itself the First Continental Congress. It was not really the Congress of any government, for there was no *American* government. It could be nothing more than a *continental* Congress—a collection of delegates from colonies that happened to be neighbors on the same continent.

At first each colony believed it had all the powers of a nation. Yet, because each had been part of the great British Empire, many of the usual jobs of a national government—for example, building an army or a navy, or conducting diplomacy—had been left to London. When the First Continental Congress met, then, it had to start from scratch, taking on many of the jobs of a national government.

The dramatic and disastrous events of April 1775 would put an end to the hopes which some Americans still had that they would somehow find their way back into the empire. Massachusetts

---

Two early battles of the Revolution, shown by two Connecticut artists of the time. Top: Amos Doolittle's matter-of-fact engraving of the British troops marching into Concord, while their commanding officer keeps an eye on the Minute Men. Below: John Trumbull's flamboyant European-style painting of the Battle of Bunker Hill. There the Americans, though forced to retreat, taught British troops to fear militiamen.

had been hardest hit by the British acts of force. And, without waiting for others, Massachusetts began to prepare for war by collecting military supplies in the little town of Concord, about twenty miles inland from Boston.

When the British Secretary of State for Colonies heard of this, he decided to act quickly to destroy that first supply base before the Americans were any better organized. Bostonians learned of the British plan and on the night of April 18, 1775, sent Paul Revere and William Dawes on their celebrated ride to Lexington, which was on the road to Concord. They warned Americans to form ranks to stop the King's troops before these could reach and destroy the colony's Concord supply base. Early the next morning when the seven hundred British troops reached Lexington, they found seventy American Minute Men arrayed against them on the town common. The British killed eight and wounded ten Americans before hastening on to Concord. As if by magic, the countryside sprang to arms. From nowhere appeared thousands of American militiamen. They harassed the British troops, who, before returning to their ships in Charlestown harbor, suffered nearly three hundred casualties.

Now talk was at an end. War had begun. There was no turning back.

When delegates from twelve colonies met again in their Second Continental Congress in the Philadelphia State House in May 1775, they were no longer American children pleading for better treatment from their British mother country. Now they were armed colonists demanding their rights. George Washington of Virginia was chosen commander in chief of the "Continental Army." It could not be called the Army of the United States, for there was yet no United States.

The Continental Congress quickly realized that they would need a navy. Following the old British example, the Congress, with their own letters of marque, began creating privateers. But now they were *American* privateers in hot pursuit of all British ships. What the Americans most needed was the aid of France, who had a great navy, and, if possible, also the aid of Spain. To encourage this aid, the Continental Congress on April 6, 1776, at one stroke abolished a whole century's accumulation of Navigation Laws. They opened all American ports to all nations in the world, except Britain.

Meanwhile, fortunately for the Americans, who still had no definite word of what was happening in Europe, the French were already conspiring with the Spanish to use this opportunity to tear apart the British Empire. The French King, Louis XVI, secretly arranged to supply gunpowder to the American rebels. From the French the American armies received nearly all the gunpowder they used during the first two years of war. But this was only a beginning.

American independence was already becoming a fact. The Americans had set up their own Congress, they had organized their own army, they were beginning to organize a navy. They had already plainly declared commercial independence by abolishing all the British laws of navigation. Then, on July 2,

1776, the Continental Congress adopted a short resolution "that these United Colonies are, and of right ought to be, free and independent States, that they are absolved from all allegiance to the British Crown, and that all political connection between them and the State of Great Britain is and ought to be totally dissolved."

In many ways this was a mere formality. But John Adams, who had a good sense of history, wrote to his wife on the very next day that July 2 would be "the most memorable" day in the whole history of America. "It ought to be commemorated as the day of the deliverance, by solemn acts of devotion to God almighty . . . with pomp and parade, with shows, games, sports, guns, bells, bonfires, and illuminations, from one end of this continent to the other, from this time forward, forever more."

With the resolution on July 2, Americans had *announced* their independence. They gave out the news that a new nation was born, but they had not yet given out the reasons. Strictly speaking, American independence was not yet *declared*. ("Declare" comes from the Latin word meaning to make clear.) It was not yet officially explained and made clear. And, despite what John Adams said, it was not the mere announcement but the "declaration"— the explanation—of independence that Americans would always celebrate. For Americans were proud of the reasons for the birth of their nation, which they thought were worth fighting for. These reasons gave the new nation a purpose which it would not forget.

One of the remarkable things about the United States, which made it different from the older nations of Europe, was that it could actually point to the reasons why it had become a separate nation. These reasons were listed in a Declaration of Independence prepared and approved by the very men who made the nation independent.

Three weeks before the Continental Congress adopted its brief resolution an-

Thomas Jefferson became an international hero for his authorship of the Declaration of Independence, for his broad scientific activities, and for his faith in the powers of the New World. This portrait bust was made by a French sculptor, Houdon, while Jefferson was serving as ambassador in Paris.

nouncing independence, it had named a committee to prepare a longer Declaration of Independence. The brilliant Jefferson, then only thirty-three years of age, was appointed chairman. Also on the committee were John Adams of Massachusetts and Benjamin Franklin of Pennsylvania, but Jefferson did the writing and the others only changed a word here and there. Some said it was lucky Franklin had not been given the job, for he might not have resisted the temptation to put in a joke. And John Adams, who was also a learned lawyer, might have made the Declaration hard for the average man to read.

Jefferson was the perfect choice. Not only was he a learned lawyer, but he wrote so everybody could understand. And he used phrases that people could not help remembering. He also knew how a new nation ought to explain itself to the world.

The first sign of Jefferson's good sense was that he did not make the Declaration too original. Some years later, John Adams complained that Jefferson's Declaration did not have a new idea in it. Jefferson replied that Adams was correct. The object, Jefferson said, was not to be original, but to say what everybody already believed. He wanted to write down the "common sense" of the subject. The common sense that Jefferson was talking about was not what only the Americans believed. He was speaking to the whole world. It was no good trying to persuade the world unless you started from what lots of people everywhere already believed. That is precisely what Jefferson did.

The opening part of the Declaration, usually called the "preamble," was cribbed from the various books and declarations that Englishmen had written a hundred years before. The English people in England had had a revolution of their own back in 1688. They called it their Glorious Revolution. At that time they had removed one ruler (King James II) who seemed to believe that the nation was his own private property, and then replaced him with King William and Queen Mary, chosen by Parliament.

The British, then, could not possibly deny Jefferson's words in his declaration —that governments derive "their just powers from the consent of the governed." Nor "that whenever any form of government shall become destructive of these ends"—life, liberty, and the pursuit of happiness—"it is the right of the people to alter or to abolish it, and to institute new government . . . in such form as to them shall seem most likely to effect their safety and happiness." Their own British government, as they were repeatedly saying after 1688, was made by precisely that formula. You could hardly call an idea radical if it was the basis of the very respectable government of England.

After the "common sense" in the preamble there came a long list—"a long train of abuses and usurpations." Every item showed how the British King, George III, had disobeyed his own laws. The King aimed to reduce the colonists to "absolute despotism," to establish "an absolute tyranny over these states." His many crimes included "cutting off our trade with all parts of the world," "imposing taxes on us without our consent," and "quartering large bodies of armed troops among us." They also included the King's crimes against the very special rights of Englishmen—for example, taking away the right of trial by jury, and violating the legal charters given to the colonies.

The colonists, Jefferson explained, had shown great respect for their King, and great love for their "British brethren." "In every stage of these oppressions we have petitioned for redress in the most humble terms: Our repeated petitions have been answered only by repeated injury." The King had proved himself a tyrant, "unfit to be the ruler of a free people." If the King would not respect

duty to hold the empire together and to protect all his subjects. The Americans demanded nothing but their simple rights as Englishmen. The King had denied those traditional rights. The colonists wanted to preserve them. Now it was not the colonists, but the King, who was really revolutionary.

The King had proved himself a criminal. He did not respect his own laws. How could Americans any longer respect him? The law was now on the side of the Americans. If Americans wondered why they were fighting, here was their simple answer.

On July 4, 1776, Jefferson's Declara-

The French were glad to help American colonists dismantle the British Empire. Here we see the French navy (foreground) in 1778 blockading the English ships (background) in New York Harbor.

the colonists' rights as Englishmen, the Americans had no choice. They had to set up their own government.

Till the very end, Jefferson explained, the colonists had tried appealing to the King. Jefferson's declaration simply ignored the British Parliament. It did not mention Parliament even once. For, according to Jefferson, Parliament had no rights over the colonies. It was the King's

tion of Independence was approved by the Second Continental Congress, signed by John Hancock, the president of the Congress, and certified by the secretary. Then copies were sent out to all the States. As new members came to represent colonies in Congress, they too signed the declaration, even though they had not been there when Jefferson first presented it. As late as November some representatives were still signing (there were finally fifty-five signatures altogether). In this way, they showed that they believed in the Revolution.

Congress now sent diplomatic representatives abroad to make treaties and promise commercial benefits in return for help in the war. From all over Europe came officers. Some were really inspired by the American cause, some hated the British Empire, others were simply looking for adventure. From France came the aristocratic young Marquis de Lafayette (commissioned a major general in the American army at the age of twenty!). From Germany came "Baron" de Kalb (also to be a major general) and Baron von Steuben (who became Washington's right-hand man). From Poland came Thaddeus Kosciusko (who built the fortifications at West Point and reached the rank of brigadier general).

In France, Jefferson's Declaration was especially well received. Early in 1778, the French government made a full-fledged treaty of alliance with the Americans—in order to "maintain effectually the liberty, sovereignty, and independence" of the new nation. The French sent thousands of experienced troops. Without the French navy, the final battle could never have been won at Yorktown. In all these ways, the Declaration of Independence proved a decisive weapon in the war.

That was just what the Americans had hoped. But what they had not expected —and could not even have imagined— was that this eloquent birth certificate of the new United States would fire the imaginations of people all over the world. A few years after the American Revolution was won, when the French people decided to defend their own rights against their king, they found inspiration in Jefferson's words. In the 1820's when Spanish colonists in South America separated from their mother country, they turned to the same source. Jefferson's Declaration of Independence, like other documents that live and shape history, has had the magical power to be filled with new ideas. In the twentieth century, when colonists in Asia and Africa try to explain to the world why they fight for their independence, they still look back to the Declaration of Independence of the thirteen American colonies.

CHAPTER 11

Why the British Lost the War ᘓᖆᓂᓂᓅᘓᖆ

America produced a new style of warfare. Here the skirmish, not the battle, was important. Communications did not exist, the land was vast. There was no way of directing operations from a cen-ter. Every man for himself! Colonists had learned to hide behind rocks and tree trunks. "In our first war with the Indians," the Puritan missionary John Eliot noted back in 1677, "God pleased to show us the vanity of our military skill, in managing our arms, after the European mode. Now we are glad to learn the skulking way of war."

Here grew a new and American kind of army. The colonists called it their "militia." The militia was not really an army at all, but only a name for all the citizens who bore arms. As early as 1631, Massachusetts Bay passed a law requiring each town to see that every able-bodied man was armed. Usually each citizen had to buy his own musket. Of course he had plenty of private use for it, hunting game for his table and defending his own house against surprise attack. Regular membership in the militia usually began at about sixteen years of age, and might last till a man was sixty. There was no uniform, and little of the colorful ritual of the European battlefields.

In Europe it was the Age of Limited Warfare. Over there armies fought according to certain definite rules, which made a battle in many ways like a football match. Battles took place on open fields, in good weather. Each side set up its men in neat array. Each side knew what forces the other possessed, and each part of an army was expected to perform only certain maneuvers. To begin a battle before the heralds had sounded their fanfares, to use sneak tactics or unusual weapons, was generally frowned upon.

The only people who fought were the professionals out there on the battlefield. Officers came from the international European aristocracy. They knew the rules and were willing to abide by them. At nightfall, or when the weather was bad, officers from opposing armies would actually entertain one another at dinner parties, concerts, and balls. Then the next day they would take up their places on the battlefield. The privates were human dregs who had been dragged out of jails and bars. The best trained and most reliable soldiers often were mercenaries—like the Swiss or the Hessians—who made a living from hiring themselves out to the highest bidder.

Patriotism had very little to do with those battles. Armies were small. The men were seldom fighting to preserve their country, but more often for some secret purpose known to nobody but the sovereign and his few advisers. By modern standards, the casualties were few. Weapons were crude. The old-fashioned musket had a poor aim, was hard to reload, and would not fire at all in wet weather. Kings could have their battles, and yet interfere very little with the peaceful round of household, farm and fair.

Battles gave nobles a chance to be brave in public while they wore swords, bright costumes, and plumed helmets. Citizens would sometimes stand on the battlements of their town and there at a safe distance watch the colorful clash of arms. War still consisted of a few dramatic battles. It had not yet become a universal misery.

Unfortunately, the American Indian had never heard of these polite traditions of war-by-the-rules. The Indian did not know he was not supposed to use sneak tactics. He especially liked to find a hiding place behind a tree while he surprised his enemy in the dark or in wet weather. For this kind of fighting, the

Indian's simple weapons actually had advantages. Unlike the musket, his bow was silent and accurate, quick and easy to reload. Compared to the European soldier's fifteen-foot pike, his tomahawk was light, easy to maneuver in thick woods, and handy at close range.

The Indian had never heard of the law of war that required him to take prisoners, to treat them kindly according to their rank, and exchange them for prisoners taken by the other side. His custom was to massacre or torture his enemy, sometimes peeling off his skin or bleeding him to death by jabs of pointed sticks.

The Indians conducted a primitive form of total war. And the colonists' only good protection was a primitive form of total defense. When the Indian danger was greatest, whole communities moved into their garrison—a crude fortress-town surrounded by a high stockade. Colonists could not leave their defense to professional soldiers far away on some neat battlefield. Where everybody was a target, every man, woman, and child had to be a soldier. "A grown boy at the age of twelve or thirteen," one back-woodsman noted in the 1760's, "was furnished with a small rifle and shot-pouch. He then became a fort soldier, and had his port-hole assigned him. Hunting squirrels, turkeys, and raccoons, soon made him expert in the use of his gun."

Americans had to defend themselves in their own backyards. They came to believe that every man had a right to carry a gun. In Europe, kings and nobles

American soldiers often did not follow the European rules of war. In Germany, when the British (foreground) fought against the French (background) at the Battle of Dettingen in 1743, both sides were in neat array, giving the British a good view of the enemy.

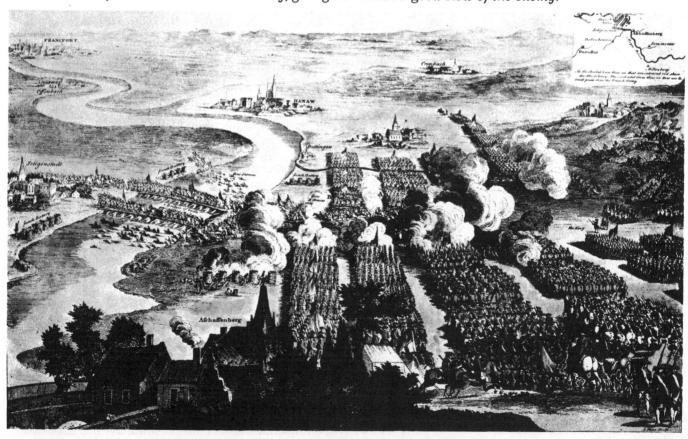

were afraid to let civilians have firearms for an armed people might overthrow the government. When Americans finally wrote their new constitution in 1787, they actually wrote into their bill of rights: "A well regulated militia, being necessary to the security of a free state, the right of the people to keep and bear arms, shall not be infringed." The warfare Americans had learned from the Indians must have seemed very odd to the regular European soldier.

Most remarkable (and most unprofessional by European standards) was the colonial practice of electing officers. This changed the relations between the officers and the men. In the professional armies of the Old World, discipline was not only strict but brutal. Service in the ranks of a European army was a form of punishment for crime. Flogging was the usual means of discipline, food and supplies were meager. But in the American militia, an officer was not likely to be reelected if he treated his men brutally. The relation of officers to men was much more friendly.

Defense of the colonies from south to north depended on these militia groups. They were more like clubs than like what Europeans meant by an army. What a man did in his militia depended on how much he was interested and on what he himself really wanted to do.

Against surprise attacks the militia system could not work unless men came of their own accord, and came on a moment's notice. A visitor to Plymouth in 1627 noticed that men were on the alert day and night. Each man went to

The colonists, who had learned sneak tactics from the Indians (page 19), bewildered and confounded the British by shooting from behind rocks and trees. The British considered such behavior cowardly.

THE AMERICAN RIFLE MEN.

The American militiamen were at first ridiculed, as in this British cartoon, for their lack of discipline and of spit-and-polish.

---

church with his musket in hand, and even during the service he had it beside him. When the Indians attacked in King Philip's War in 1675, an alarm sounded at a town thirty miles outside Boston, and twelve hundred militiamen were there within an hour.

It was the militia that was alerted by Paul Revere and William Dawes in 1775, and that sprang to arms within a few hours in the neighborhood of Lexington and Concord. They had agreed to be ready at a minute's warning. With good reason they called themselves "Minute Men."

All this was possible in America only because men here knew what they were fighting for. They were not fighting to preserve a dubious alliance between some king and his cousin, or to gain another spice island for an empire, but to defend their own homes and families.

But still, against a professional army like that of the British Empire, the militia had some grave disadvantages. When American militiamen did not understand the strategy, or when they no longer agreed with the reasons of battle, or when they simply had other personal business, they would give up the fight. The very idea of enlistment—which kept men in the army even when it was personally inconvenient—did not suit militiamen. George Washington's most vexing problems came from these peculiarities of the militia. Since his forces consisted largely of militiamen, he could never be sure how many he could count on.

A large number of the "losses" of Washington's army were due to desertion rather than to death or capture. Within a few weeks before the Battle of Bennington on August 16, 1777 (which helped prepare for the defeat of Burgoyne at Saratoga two months later), over four hundred men deserted. A year later over five thousand militiamen deserted in a few days, so weakening the American forces at Newport that they had to abandon their plan to attack. On March 15, 1781, when the Americans greatly outnumbered the British at Guilford Courthouse in North Carolina, they might have routed the forces of the British General Cornwallis. But the American militia fled to the woods and left victory to the British.

Forces of American militiamen melted away whenever the men decided to go home to help bring in the harvest, or to be present at the birth of a child, or sometimes simply because they were tired of fighting. "Put the . . . militia in the center," the American General Daniel Morgan ordered on one occasion, "with some picked troops in their rear with orders to shoot down the first man that runs." "Militia won't do," he complained. "Their greatest study is to rub through their tour of duty with whole bones."

When General Washington begged the Continental Congress for a regular army organized in the European way, he complained that he had never seen a single instance of militia "being fit for the real business of fighting. I have found them useful as light parties to skirmish in the woods, but incapable of making or sustaining a serious attack."

Militia were a home guard and not an imperial army. That meant they were accustomed to fighting only close to home. But the American Revolution had to be fought wherever the battle required and against a large regular army. A lot of scattered forces, each consisting of a militia "pick-up team" was not good enough. To fight a full-size war you had to be able to send forces far from home. Strategy often demanded that you collect thousands of men for a decisive battle—to destroy the enemy's forces, to seize a dominating hill or an essential port. If Americans were to have a massed army, they had to bring together militia from all over the colonies. But if you sent your own col-

ony's militia far away to defend *all* the colonies, you might leave your own colony and your own home naked to the Indians.

Americans in one colony were unwilling to send their militia to help defend a neighboring colony. This was an old story and was an American problem long before the Revolution. The local militia of New York City, organized when it was still New Amsterdam in order to fight the Indians in 1644, would not even go outside the city limits. In midsummer 1691, the Governor of New York wrote asking the Governor of Massachusetts to combine their militias to conquer Canada and so capture the source of the Indian and French marauders that menaced them both. The Governor of Massachusetts begged off with a half-dozen inconsistent excuses, but in return he dared ask the Governor of New York to send some New York militia to help defend Massachusetts from the east. Of course, the Governor of New York also refused.

When Virginia was asked to send its militia north for a common plan of defense, Virginia replied that she had always been her own best defense. And so it went.

In the middle of the eighteenth century, when the British tried to unite colonial troops against the growing threats to all the colonies from the French and the Indians, the British found the task hopeless. Militia of all the colonies together numbered at least ten thousand, but it was impossible to collect them into a single army.

When the American Revolution came, none of this had changed. Each colony still had its own militia—its home guard —but the thirteen colonies as a whole had no army. George Washington's first, and probably his greatest, achievement was somehow to create a Continental Army.

When Washington took command on July 3, 1775, all he had were some thousands of militiamen without uniforms, and without regular military training. It was no easy matter to create discipline. Washington tried to accustom American soldiers to having their officers appointed from above instead of being elected by the soldiers. Since each colony had its own officers, when Washington tried to combine these forces their officers constantly quarreled about who was over whom. In discouragement, Washington reported to the Continental Congress that he could not really say whether he had *"one* army, or *thirteen* armies." Sometimes he had neither and sometimes he had both!

But these crude, disorganized Americans had some special advantages. Of course it was hard to bring the militia together, but that was because they were already spread all over the continent. In vast and trackless America, that itself could be helpful. You did not have to transport all your soldiers. Wherever you were, or wherever the enemy was, a militia was always there.

The militia did not have any uniform. But the fringed hunting shirt of the American backwoodsmen could inspire terror in the regular British soldier. Many Americans used a new and distinctive American rifle which was in every way superior to the old-fashioned British musket. Their ragged costume became

a trademark of the crack shot. General Washington arranged an exhibition of markmanship by men in hunting shirts on Cambridge Common in August 1775, hoping that spies would carry the frightening word of their perfect aim back to the British troops. And he issued an order encouraging "the use of hunting shirts, and long breeches made of the same cloth . . . it is a dress justly supposed to carry no small terror to the enemy, who think every such person a complete marksman."

When the British sent a captured American rifleman back to England as a trophy of the war, his marksmanship actually discouraged recruiting for the war in America. The American militiaman became a legend.

The militiaman's unpredictable behavior made him all the more terrifying. According to the European rules for wars on open battlefields, masses of soldiers were arrayed opposite other masses of soldiers. The European muskets had such poor aim that it was hard for any soldier to pick off a particular opponent. But the sharpshooting Americans disregarded tradition. They aimed especially at the officers. They did not hesitate to use Indian tactics, to sneak up on their enemy, and to hide behind rocks and stumps—all of which was considered cowardly by the rules of the game.

The drab buckskin that Americans wore instead of the colorful uniforms of the British Redcoats made them less conspicuous as targets. Without the spit-and-polish that was the pride of European armies, the rough and ready Americans really did look crude. But they wore no shining brass buttons to reflect light and attract the enemy. Their weapons, which were not burnished for parade or for inspection, were much easier to hide in the woods.

All these peculiarities of the American militiamen helped Americans to haunt and taunt and terrify their better-organized enemy. But even if militia could keep an enemy from winning, could a militia army ever actually *win?* A militia was everywhere. But a militia was also nowhere. Of course, there were tens of thousands of militiamen sprinkled over the colonies. Each was ready to run quickly to defend his home. But where were the massed thousands you needed to repulse a massed British attack?

At the end of the war, George Washington wrote that people in future years would hardly believe that the Americans could have won. "It will not be believed that such a force as Great Britain has employed for eight years in this country could be baffled in their plan of subjugating it by numbers infinitely less—composed of men sometimes half-starved, always in rags, without pay, and experiencing at times every species of distress which human nature is capable of undergoing." Even today it is not easy to understand how the Americans managed to win.

It is easier to explain why the British lost. The British were separated from their headquarters by a vast ocean. Their lines of communication were long. The British government was badly informed. They thought the Americans were much weaker than they really were. And they expected help from uprisings of

The American militiamen soon won a world-wide reputation for marksmanship and hardiness. This is a German drawing of an American soldier wearing fringed buckskin and a hat embroidered with the word "Congress."

thousands of "Loyalists," their name for Americans who refused to join the Revolution. But these uprisings never happened.

The most important explanation was that the British had set themselves an impossible task. Though they had an army that was large for that day, how could it ever be large enough to occupy and subjugate a continent? The British knew so little of America that they thought their capture of New York City would end the war. After the Battle of Long Island in August 1776, General Howe actually asked the Americans to send him a peace commission, and cheerfully expected to receive the American surrender. But he was badly disappointed. For the colonies had no single capital, by conquering which the British could win.

During the first four years of the war, the British managed to capture and hold for some time every one of the four largest cities in the colonies: Boston, New York, Philadelphia, and Charleston. But to snuff out American resistance they would have to control them all at the same time, and then also occupy the stretches of wilderness in between.

It was a long, a very long, war. From the first shot fired at Lexington until the last shot fired at Yorktown, it was nearly eight years. That was almost twice as long as World War I, and a full year longer than World War II. It was a long, slow job to convince the greatest empire with the biggest navy in the world that it should give up.

American success was largely due to perseverance. George Washington was a man of great courage and good judgment. And Americans had the strengths of a New World—with a new kind of army fighting in new ways.

Before they were finished, the Americans did raise their own Continental Army, although there were probably never more than thirty thousand men serving at one time. It is doubtful if the Americans could have won without the aid of France.

Although many Americans opposed the Revolution, and some were lukewarm, it was still a people's war. As many as half of all men of military age were in the army at one time or another. Each had the special power and the special courage which came from fighting for himself, for his family, and for his home.

The very same reasons that made the colonists willing to revolt made them unwilling to unite. The people of Virginia were fighting to be free from a government in far-off London. Why should they submit to a government in far-off New York? The very same feelings that gave Americans strength, that explained why their scattered everywhere-army could not be defeated by a regular army of empire, also explained why it would be hard for them to become a nation. The task of making the nation had only begun.

CHAPTER 12
New States or a New Nation?

Independence had created not one nation but thirteen. At the time of the Declaration of Independence, when John Adams spoke of "my country" he meant Massachusetts Bay, and Thomas Jefferson meant Virginia. The resolution which announced independence on July 2, 1776, had proclaimed "That *these*

United Colonies are, and of right ought to be, free and independent *States*." The first heading at the top of the Declaration of Independence called it "The unanimous Declaration of the thirteen united States of America." They used a small "u" for united because it was still only a hope.

Each State called itself "sovereign," which meant that now it had all the highest powers of government. Each State had all the powers to levy taxes, to raise an army and build a navy, to enter into treaties, and to make war and peace. When Franklin was in Paris as a representative of the Continental Congress, trying to persuade the French to give war aid, he found "ambassadors" from three separate American States.

Americans like Washington and Madison and Hamilton had seen the troubles of waging a successful war with thirteen different governments. They began to wonder whether thirteen tiny quarrelsome States on the edge of a wilderness could ever prosper—even in peace. Under the so-called Articles of Confederation (in operation 1781–89) which the new States had formed to carry on the war, each State could keep out the farm produce and manufactured goods of its neighbors, much as the British Empire had kept out the products of the French. Instead of facing across the ocean one large power—the British government—hemming in their trade, each of the new little States now found itself surrounded right here in America by a lot of other annoying little States.

The thirteen new American governments had found it impossible to live with a strong London government. They

The New England town meeting, where common problems were discussed and voted on by adult men who owned property. In this way Americans grew accustomed to deciding things for themselves.

now found it almost impossible to live without it. Still nobody wanted to risk replacing the old British tyranny with a new American tyranny. What were they to do?

This was a great moment in history. A few men could shape the world for

After the Revolution each of the thirteen "Sovereign" States issued its own money.

Above: Rhode Island's 60-shilling note. Below: Georgia's 10-shilling note. Both are dated 1786.

centuries. Would America become another Europe? Would the New World become only a new battlefield for thirteen new little nations? Had they risked their "lives, their fortunes, and their sacred honor" only to make the continent into a sea of anarchy?

Wise men, then, dared not let this happen. Their children and their grandchildren, they said, would curse them if they threw away this opportunity to explore together and in peace the vast, mysterious, rich New World.

They decided to come together to talk about their problems. No one thought then of founding all at once a powerful continent-nation. Anyone who proposed that would have been called a silly dreamer. What was in their minds was simply how to prevent thirteen weak nation-states from committing suicide. And how to prevent each little nation-state from strangling the others in a misguided effort to save itself.

In the War of Independence, each colony was fighting to preserve its right to run its own show. When the colonies agreed to cooperate on the War of Independence, they had no idea of making a single new government for a single new nation. What they wanted (as the Governor of Rhode Island had explained) was a "Treaty of Confederation." They were an alliance of thirteen little nations that had come together only to fight the war. Many thought the alliance would disappear after the war was won.

The Continental Congress had begun the war and had declared independence. "The United States in Congress Assembled," which after 1781 carried on the war, was not a Congress of one nation. It was simply a meeting of ambassadors, like the Assembly of the United Nations. Each State had one vote. Every one of the thirteen States had to agree on anything important. Such an assembly of ambassadors could not force any State to support it with money and, of course, had no power at all over individual citizens. It was a miracle that this loose arrangement was able to run a war and force the British Empire to give up.

Then came bad years. As long as the war lasted there had been, as usual in wartime, a business boom. Goods were scarce. Anybody with something to sell found lots of buyers. After the Peace in 1783, Americans were still hungry for the things they could not buy during the war. Once again, they began importing from Great Britain. But they bought a good deal more than they could pay for. Each State issued its own paper money. Nobody knew precisely how much a New York dollar was worth, compared to one from Pennsylvania or Rhode Island. The more money there was, the less a dollar bought. For five long years after 1784 there was the worst business depression the colonies had ever suffered. It was one of the longest and deepest depressions in all American history.

In January 1786, Virginia sent an invitation to all the States to meet and discuss their problems. Nine States accepted the invitation, but only twelve men (representing only five States) actually came to the meeting at Annapolis, Maryland, that September. By then farm workers could barely support themselves on their declining wages.

Moneylenders were seizing farms. In Massachusetts a rebellion was brewing. It was led by Daniel Shays, a now-penniless farmer who had been a captain in the Revolution. To keep order the militiamen of Massachusetts were now being asked to fight against their fellow Americans.

With less than half the States represented at Annapolis there was not much they could do. Luckily, one of the twelve men there was the young, bold Alexander Hamilton. Born of an impoverished family in the Virgin Islands, he had attended King's College (later called Columbia University) in New York, until the Revolution came. During the war, Washington, recognizing Hamilton's brilliance, used him as his close adviser and gave him the job of organizing military headquarters.

Although in 1786 Hamilton was only about thirty years of age, he took the lead. He argued that the thirteen States would never prosper until they formed a strong union. He demanded that, then and there, they send out an alarm to all the States quickly to dispatch representatives to another, larger meeting to see what could be done. If Hamilton had never lived another day, his courage and vision on that occasion would entitle him to a place in American history.

Less than a year later, fifty-five delegates from twelve States met in the hot summer of 1787 in Independence Hall in Philadelphia. The thirteenth State, little Rhode Island (a Boston newspaper called her "Rogue Island"), simply ignored the Convention. It was not at all clear what the delegates were supposed to do. Unlike a convention that the people of Massachusetts had held back in 1780, this meeting had not been called to write a brand-new Constitution. But many members, including especially the two men from Massachusetts, must have remembered the Massachusetts experience. The invitation to this later meeting was vague. The object was somehow to remodel the Articles of Confederation and "to take into consideration the situation of the United States."

Among the many questions that bewildered the fifty-five men in the Convention, the very first was: What power did they really have? But the wiser men did not worry over technicalities. Instead they thought about the job they had to do—to make life better and to make business prosper.

Nothing was newer about the New World than that Constitutional Convention in Philadelphia. This was the first time that there had been a meeting quite like this. History gave them very little to go on.

Despite all the confusion, there was probably one fact on which nearly all the delegates agreed. Each of the States they represented was somehow a "Sovereign" State. That is, the people in each State had *all* the powers to run *all* their own affairs. The American Revolution had been fought to prove it. This was not a mere technicality. It was everybody's starting point. And it was what made the job of the Convention so hard.

What they really had on their hands, then, was a kind of problem in international relations. This was precisely what they meant when they said they wanted to make a new plan for their "federal" union.

In those days "federal" meant something different from what it means today. It was still commonly spelled "foederal," because it came from the Latin word *foedus*, which means "treaty." A treaty was, of course, an agreement made by a "Sovereign" State (or nation). And a "federal" union, then, would be a kind of international association held together by fully Sovereign States which had made treaties with one another. Of course, that would be a very different kind of thing, and would have much less power, than something like the government of England or of France. Could such a weak, loose international association of the thirteen new States do the job for America?

No! was the answer of many delegates to the Philadelphia Convention. Some of the most energetic men—like Alexander Hamilton of New York, James Madison of Virginia, and Gouverneur Morris of Pennsylvania—were sure that would not be good enough. To do the job, the government would have to be "national." That was the word they used, and by it they meant something more or less like the government of France or England.

A "national" union would not be merely a collection of different States, each with its own government. It would be something much stronger. It would actually make laws, have its own courts, levy its own taxes, control commerce, and have supreme power over all the people and all the States under it. Obviously, though, to make that possible, each of the "Sovereign" States would have to give up some of its "sovereign" powers.

It would not be easy to persuade people to this. You would have to ask the people in each State to take powers away from their own Massachusetts, or New Jersey, or Maryland, which the people in that State loved and still called their "country," and give those powers to some imaginary new nation that did not even exist. There were good reasons to fear a powerful new government with its headquarters far outside your State. The best reason of all was the recent bitter experience with King George III and with the British Parliament. But there were other very good reasons for these Americans who had just fought nearly eight years to defend their right to govern themselves.

The thirteen States were very different from one another. What was good for seafaring New England might be bad for tobacco-raising Virginia. And the States were very different sizes. There were vast States like Virginia and New York, which owned unmeasured stretches of wilderness reaching out to the west. And there were small states like Maryland and New Jersey and tiny Rhode Island, which were pushed up against the sea by powerful neighbors.

If under the new plan for a government the States were all to be equal, then the small poor States, with very little to lose, would lord it over the large rich States and make them share their wealth. Or, if the States were all to be

This float honored Alexander Hamilton, in a New York parade celebrating the ratification of the Constitution. Hamilton had represented New York at the Constitutional Convention, and his arguments for a strong central government in the Federalist Papers *helped persuade many doubting Americans.*

*un*equal, and each State had power in the central government proportioned to its own size or wealth, then what would happen to the little ones?

If any large number of delegates had stuck by their guns and demanded that everything go their way, there would never have been a Constitution. Luckily that did not happen. Although the Convention was held in Philadelphia, which was the headquarters of the uncompromising Quakers, what prevailed in 1787 was the practical spirit of compromise.

Before the Convention had any meetings it was plain that, if there was to be a new government at all, everybody would have to be satisfied with half a loaf. George Washington, who was the chairman of the Convention, was accustomed to bringing people together and solving insoluble puzzles. With the glory of the war behind him, he was able to keep order and keep people on the track. The good-humored Benjamin Franklin, already eighty-one years old, was able to keep people optimistic and keep them talking instead of fighting. Most of the men in the Convention were wise enough to distrust their own wisdom.

The delegates in Philadelphia debated for the whole hot summer of 1787. We do not know exactly what they said, for they had decided in advance to keep everything they said a secret. No complete record was kept. We have to depend on the private notes taken by a few members. But we do know what came out of their meetings. It was the same Constitution of the United States of America which (with only a few amendments) we live under today.

They were able to make a Constitu-tion only because they were ruled by the spirit of compromise. Everybody got something he wanted; nobody got everything he wanted. The big States got a House of Representatives where the big States had more delegates, according to their population; the small States got a Senate, where all States were equal. To satisfy those who wanted a union truly "national," the new government had the power to tax, to control commerce, to make war, to raise an army and a navy, and to carry on foreign relations. To satisfy those who wanted a union merely "federal," the Constitution left to each "Sovereign State" the power to make the laws controlling daily life, and all powers not given to the new central government.

This new government, as one member put it, was "partly national, partly federal." In the Constitution you will not find either the word "federal" or the word "national." The members of the Convention knew that each of these words would be a red flag to some members. They purposely took out these words, and left everybody to guess for himself how much the new government was either federal or national. That way each side could think it had won a little more than the other.

If they did not call the new arrangement either "federal" or "national" what would they call it? Their answer was very wise and very simple. Every time they mentioned the new government in the Constitution, they just called it "the United States."

It was a great enough achievement to make a Constitution that would work in those difficult times. But how can

Peter Lacour delin.   A. Doolittle Sculpt.

FEDERAL HALL
The Seat of CONGRESS

Six years after the end of the Revolution, Americans were united enough to inaugurate George Washington as their first President. The ceremony took place on the balcony of Federal Hall in New York City, then the national capital. An engraving by Amos Doolittle.

we explain the greater miracle, that the Constitution was able to live so long and serve so different an America? Today it is the oldest living written Constitution.

Although this success was miraculous, the explanation is not so difficult. Just as the members of the Constitutional Convention served the people of their own day by being willing to compromise, so they served all of us who came later by being willing to leave some things open. They knew they were building for the future, but they did not know what the future would bring. So they decided to let the future decide many things for itself.

They did this partly by keeping the Constitution short and not trying to list everything. And they purposely left many parts of the Constitution unclear. Precisely what powers would the central government have over the commerce of the States? Could the Supreme Court veto the laws passed by Congress if the Supreme Court thought they were against the Constitution? There is no way of answering these—or many other questions—from the brief few words in the brief Constitution. Let the future make its own definitions!

The members of the Convention were also wise enough to include in the Constitution itself instructions for changing the Constitution. Then, if the people in the future found they needed changes, they would not have to junk the whole Constitution and start all over again. They could keep the Constitution as a whole, while following the rules for making the few amendments they needed. This was a master stroke, and was as new as anything else they did.

When the fifty-five men in Philadelphia finished their work and voted to approve the Constitution, they sent it out to the States. Within less than a year, by June 21, 1788, when New Hampshire approved the Constitution, nine States had accepted. That was enough to put the new Constitution in force.

Since the Constitution was such a patchwork of compromises, we cannot be surprised that it was no easy matter to persuade all the States to adopt it. In every State there were some patriotic and intelligent men (like Patrick Henry in Virginia) who feared a strong new government more than anything else. These men therefore argued against adopting the Constitution. Rhode Island, which had not been represented at all in the Convention, at first refused to join the new government, and did not finally come in until nearly a year after the government was actually working.

The first capital under the new Constitution was New York City. There, on April 30, 1789, George Washington, standing on the balcony of Federal Hall, facing Wall Street, and looking down Broad Street, took his oath of office as the first President of the United States. The motley population of the city which watched him was full of uncertainty and promise and growth.

PART THREE

AMERICAN WAYS
OF GROWING

The new nation found its own ways of growing. Other nations had expanded by seizing territory from their rivals, or by sending citizens to far colonies overseas. This is how the great empires had grown. The people back home—in Britain, France, or Spain—added to their own wealth and their opportunities by lording it over distant colonists, making them serve the mother country. But Americans had a vast unsettled empire in their own backyard. Very early they devised a new plan for enlarging their nation by adding neighboring pieces of the continent. Their plan would not make the added people into "colonists," but instead allowed them to become full-fledged, self-governing Americans.

When other nations wanted to increase the population of their homeland, they had to wait for children to be born to the families who had already lived there for centuries. Englishmen were the sons and daughters of Englishmen, Frenchmen the sons and daughters of Frenchmen. But America was the world's leading importer of people. Americans were the sons and daughters of Englishmen, Frenchmen, Irish, Germans, Italians, Asians, and Africans. They were the children of the whole rest of the world. Except possibly for the American Indians, there were no "pure" Americans. The United States attracted its people from everywhere.

In the West before the Civil War, new American cities sprouted by the hundreds. The great European cities—London, Paris, Berlin, Rome, and others—grew gradually by adding to the old residents whose families had lived there for generations. People accustomed to the slow calendar of Europe were astonished to see that in America within only a few years the little raw Western villages had become buzzing metropolises. These instant cities, finding new, quick ways of constructing houses and of building communities, were inspired by extravagant new hopes.

CHAPTER 13

The Add-a-State Plan

Luckily for the nation, there had been two kinds of colonies—"haves" and "have-nots." There were seven "have" colonies: Massachusetts, Connecticut, New York, Virginia, the two Carolinas, and Georgia. Each of these owned vast lands reaching westward.

There was great confusion about some of these Western lands. Sometimes more than one colony thought it owned the very same land. Some had charters from the King giving them a slice of the whole continent all the way to the "Western Ocean," although nobody knew how far that really was. In 1763, the British government tried to take back some of these lands—to confine the colonists eastward of the Appalachian Mountains.

But Americans did not like to be fenced in, and this was one reason for the war.

The remaining six colonies were "have-nots." New Hampshire, Rhode Island, New Jersey, Pennsylvania, Delaware, and Maryland were all hemmed in by other colonies and by the ocean. After Independence they feared their "have" neighbors almost as much as they had once feared the British government. If these six joined a union of such unequal members, they might be bullied and overwhelmed. Weren't they *all* fighting the same war to win all Western lands from the British? And then wasn't it

only fair, as the people of tiny Maryland said, that *all* lands "wrested from the common enemy by blood and treasure of the Thirteen States, should be considered as common property"?

Maryland, leading the six "have-not" States, had first refused to join a Confederation with the seven "have" States. Before joining in, she demanded promises that they would all give up their unsettled Western lands. These would go into a treasury belonging to all thirteen States. Virginia began giving up her lands on January 2, 1781. When New York gave up hers two months later,

Jefferson's vision of an Add-a-State Plan (1784). His sketch map proposed 14 future States to be established west of the original 13. (There are now 10 States in this area.)

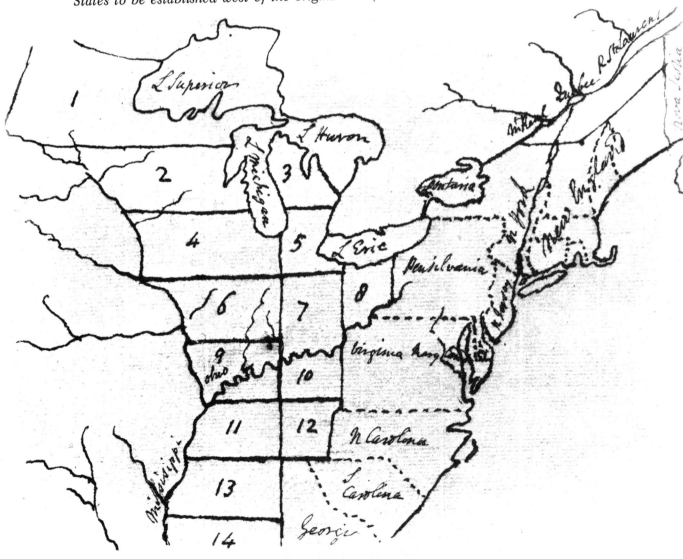

Maryland signed the Articles of Confederation. It was another twenty years before Georgia, the last of the "have" states, fulfilled her promise and put her lands in the common treasury.

Although this argument between the "have" and the "have-not" States was a nuisance at the time, in the long run it was lucky. If all the States had been more equal, each might have kept its own unsettled Western lands all for itself. Then America might have had a very different history. But because the "have" States needed the "have-not" States to help fight the War of Independence, the lands were given to the whole Union.

These Western lands became the treasury of the war. The loose league of States under the Articles of Confederation had no power to tax. Lands took the place of taxes. All the States together owned vast unsettled tracts (called the "public domain") larger than all the settled States put together. By selling the land, the weak new government could get money it could find in no other way. It could even pay the Revolutionary soldiers in land instead of money.

Just as important, the land—whether to be sold or to be governed—would give the new government an important peacetime job. No nation, new or old, had been blessed with such land-treasure in its own backyard. What should be done with it? This unsettled public domain, which belonged to all the States together, was then far larger than France or England or Spain or any other Western European nation.

The Confederation could have made that land into colonies. Just as the British government in London had sent out colonists, while Great Britain remained the mother country and planned the life of the colonies to serve herself, so the original thirteen States could have been a kind of mother country for some new Western colonies. The thirteen Atlantic States then could have used the inland Western colonies to serve them and to make themselves rich and strong.

But the makers of the new nation had seen enough of old-style empires. They preferred to make something quite new. If there was to be any American empire, let it be (in Jefferson's phrase) an "Empire for Liberty." Let it grow in a new way. Why not build this Empire for Liberty by adding one State after another? Each new State would be the equal of each older State. Nowadays this seems an obvious and sensible way for a nation to grow. But in those days it had never been heard of. It was a quite new, American way of growing.

When the seven "have" States began to give up their land, Jefferson began devising a plan. His plan finally became the "Northwest Ordinance." It was adopted by the old Congress of the Articles of Confederation in 1787 at the very time when the makers of a new Constitution were meeting in Philadelphia. This Northwest Ordinance set an American way of growing for centuries to come. It gave instructions for what we can call an Add-a-State Plan.

The plan was simple. Every part of the public domain would eventually become a full-fledged State of the Union, "on an equal footing with the original states in all respects whatsoever." This goal was reached by three simple stages, described in the Northwest Ordinance of 1787. First, when there were still almost no people in a territory it would have a Governor, a secretary, and three judges named by Congress. Then, as soon as there were 5,000 adult free men, there would be a legislature where the people of the territory could make laws for themselves. And finally, when the free population numbered 60,000, the people could apply for admission to the Union as a State.

How many new States should there be? It was anybody's guess. When Jefferson had first started working on his plan back in 1784, he took his map and drew off neat checkerboard squares. He sliced up all Western lands between the boundaries of the Atlantic colonies and the Mississippi River into fourteen new States. But his map was so inaccurate that it did not even have the Great Lakes in the right place! Therefore his plan made very little sense on the real land.

By the time of the Northwest Ordinance in 1787, a little more geography was known. But information was still crude. James Monroe (destined to be President as one of the Virginia Dynasty) took a quick trip out to the Northwest, and he hastily reported back that the land there was "miserably poor." Along the edges of the Great Lakes and around the shores of the Mississippi River and the Illinois River all he saw was vast swamps, separated by "extensive plains which had not had from appearances and will not have, a single bush on them, for ages."

If the land was so poor, then to support a respectable-sized population each new State would have to be much bigger

than Jefferson had planned. The Northwest Ordinance of 1787 therefore prescribed that in the area northwest of the Ohio River there should eventually be "not less than three nor more than five States."

The men who made the Constitution expected the nation to grow, and the States to multiply. They wrote into the Constitution: "New States may be admitted by the Congress into this Union."

In the Constitutional Convention, a few fearful men—Gouverneur Morris of Pennsylvania, Elbridge Gerry of Massachusetts, and some others—distrusted the future. They wanted to write into the Constitution some kind of guarantee that the thirteen old Atlantic States would *always* be more powerful in the government than all the new States put together. Fortunately, the men who looked for and hoped for change, and wanted to encourage new States, prevailed. In the Constitution they also included another promise: "The United States shall guarantee to every State in this Union a republican form of government." In this way they made it plain that the new Union would not be merely a mother country for new colonies.

They also expected people to move around. They were so convinced that this would happen that they actually put into the Constitution some machinery for measuring changes in population. This was the Census. It would keep the government up-to-date. Every ten years there would be a head count, and the number of Representatives of each State in Congress would be changed according to the latest figures. This was something new. It was needed in America if

Centers of population changed as thousands moved westward. This painting by Edward Hicks shows a thriving Quaker farm in western Pennsylvania soon after the Revolution.

the government was to remain really representative.

When the Constitution was adopted, Virginia had more people than any other State; therefore it had more Congressmen in the House of Representatives. But as people moved around and as more came from Europe, things changed. Fifty years later, New York had twice as many people as Virginia. By then Ohio (which did not become a State until 1803) and Pennsylvania each had a half-million more people than Virginia. Before the Civil War more than half the people of the United States were living in States that did not exist when George Washington became President.

In America, change was normal. The power to grow gave the nation the power to live.

After Washington was inaugurated and the new United States began, a procession of new States (in addition to the original thirteen) entered the Union— Vermont (1791), Kentucky (1792), Tennessee (1796), and then Ohio in 1803. All these were carved out of the lands which had belonged to the American colonies when they declared their independence. All were east of the Mississippi River.

Bold Americans like Thomas Jefferson imagined that some day the people of the United States might fill up all the lands between the Atlantic Ocean and the Mississippi.

But anyone who said that the United States would become a continent-nation, with States from ocean to ocean, would have been ridiculed.

CHAPTER 14

An Empire for Liberty

Could the United States remain fenced in forever by those old colonial boundaries? Would the new nation be only a new way of organizing those territories between the Mississippi River and the Atlantic Ocean long ago claimed by the British? Or would the new nation reach out on its own, to enlarge its new-style Empire for Liberty?

The answer came quickly enough— and in a surprising way. No one would have guessed that a New World could be born from the intrigues of the Old. Or that a still larger Empire for Liberty would be born from wars between the Empires of Emperors. But that is how it would happen.

The two leading figures in the story were Napoleon Bonaparte and Thomas Jefferson. Napoleon was a dictator (he called himself "Emperor") who had arisen out of a revolution that failed. Jefferson was a President who had arisen out of a revolution that succeeded. Who could have predicted that Napoleon's thirst for power and glory would give the American President Jef-

ferson his great opportunity to extend the American Empire for Liberty?

It all began because more and more Americans were settling between the Appalachian Mountains and the Mississippi River. They needed transportation. It seemed hopeless to carry produce overland. You had to carry it on your own back or on horseback or by wagon for hundreds of miles up and down the mountains before you could reach the cities on the Atlantic seacoast, where you could sell your crops or buy what you needed. Before the railroad the only cheap and easy transportation was by water.

Western Americans lived far from all the civilized conveniences. But luckily their West was a land of many rivers —the Wisconsin, the Illinois, the Kaskaskia, the Wabash, the Miami, the Ohio, the Cumberland, the Yazoo, and others. These rivers ran into the great Mississippi—"Father of Waters"—down to the Gulf of Mexico and into the ocean. For the Western Americans, these rivers were their highways to the world. But they could reach the outside world only if they had clear passage down and out the Mississippi. If any enemy held the mouth of the Mississippi, he could shut them off.

President Thomas Jefferson understood this very well. His own State of Virginia was a land of many rivers. Jefferson wanted Americans to move out west over the mountains and start new farms. He did not like cities or city life and he believed the Western lands would save America. But who would start a farm if he could not bring in what he needed and send out what he raised? The power to shut off the Mississippi highway was the power to destroy the American West. This worried Jefferson.

Outside the boundaries of the new United States, all the unsettled parts of America were still under the old system of empires. But for Jefferson and other Americans that West seemed a new kind of place—a place to move to, a place to live in, and a place for making a living. For the rulers of Spain and France, the settlers in their far-off American lands seemed nothing but chessmen in a great game of empire-building. The territory itself was for use in a game of diplomacy. They gambled with those American lands and the people on them as if they were not real lands and real people.

When one country won a war it would win another piece of America; if it lost a war it would have to give up a piece. Since the continent was still unexplored, all these bargains were pretty chancy. No king really knew what he was winning or losing, but anyway the game went on. Pieces of America were handed back and forth. When a country "owned"

a part of America, it could do whatever it pleased with the land and it had the power to govern everybody living there.

All America on the western side of the Mississippi River and all the parts around the entrance to the River were being used in this game of empire. Back in 1681, the French explorer La Salle had gone down the Mississippi River and claimed the surrounding territory in the name of King Louis XIV. Calling it after his King, he named it "Louisiana." La Salle claimed all lands drained by the Mississippi, but nobody knew exactly how far that reached.

Then, when the French were defeated by the British in 1763, they handed over to the British all of "Louisiana" east of the Mississippi. Meanwhile, in order to persuade the Spanish to join their war against the British, the French had handed over the rest of Louisiana to Spain. When Jefferson became President in 1801, he began to worry over how to keep open the Western Americans' highway to the world. It looked at first as though he would have to deal with Spain.

But that was not the whole story. Napoleon, who was now in charge of France, had some grand and complicated plans. He had a new scheme to build a French Empire in America. He actually persuaded the Spanish to give him back all of "Louisiana." For reasons of his own, this was done in secret. When word got out that the Mississippi River was no longer controlled by weak and decadent Spain but by the clever, powerful, and ambitious Napoleon, Americans were more worried than ever. And they had good reason. The French soon showed that they knew how to use New Orleans. They made this gateway to the Mississippi into a kind of tollgate. They could, and would, extract whatever they pleased as the price of admission to the Mississippi.

When President Jefferson heard of this he decided that he had to do something at once. He wrote to the American minister in Paris and then sent his friend James Monroe of Virginia as his special ambassador. Jefferson told them to buy from France the land at the mouth of the Mississippi or to find some other way to guarantee that Western Americans could come in and out of their river. If there was no other way, they were to buy New Orleans and all the lands on the east bank of the river (then called West Florida). For this little piece Congress provided two million dollars. But Congress told them they could pay up to ten million dollars if they had to.

Napoleon was a man who made up his mind quickly. He could change his mind just as quickly. Without telling anyone, he had suddenly decided to get rid of his American empire. When the Americans in Paris offered to buy that small piece of land around the entrance to the Mississippi River, they received a reply that astonished them. Napoleon would *not* sell or even rent them that little piece. But he *would* sell them the

In the world-wide scramble for empire, Louisiana was a prize. The popular English artist James Gillray showed the British Prime Minister (Pitt) and the French Emperor (Napoleon) greedily carving up the globe.

whole of Louisiana! How much would they offer?

This was the very last answer they expected. They were not prepared for it. Neither President Jefferson nor Congress had imagined it, nor told them what to do if anybody offered them half a continent! But they had to act quickly. Napoleon was a dictator. He did not need anybody's permission for anything. And he expected others to make up their minds just as quickly.

But, unlike Napoleon, the American minister Robert R. Livingston and Jefferson's messenger James Monroe of course had no power to make up their country's mind. What should they do? Should they simply tell Napoleon they could give no answer till they had instructions from the President and Congress back in Washington? That would take weeks —maybe months—and by then the changeable Napoleon might very well say it was all off. Or should they, for the sake of their country, do what they really had no power to do? Should they snatch up this amazing bargain and then pray that the people back home would support them?

This was one of the fateful moments of American history. It was not too remarkable that the dictator Napoleon had made a bold decision. But could Americans with their President and Congress match his boldness? Were the people of a republic doomed to be slow and timid?

Livingston and Monroe took the bold and dangerous way. They decided to take up Napoleon's offer. On their own responsibility they offered fifteen million dollars for all of Louisiana. And he

accepted. As soon as the deal was closed, they began wondering whether what they would have to share was praise or blame. It was some years before either of them dared claim any credit for the decision.

When the news finally reached America it was greeted by shock, delight, astonishment, and dismay. These two Americans, some complained, had been sent to Paris simply to buy a small piece of land to keep the riverways open in the West. Instead of doing that, they had allowed a whimsical dictator to trap them into buying half a billion acres of worthless wilderness! Napoleon was not known for his charities. He was a wily man and, people said, this must be a trick to make innocent Americans serve his evil schemes.

The opponents of President Jefferson (they called themselves "Federalists") said this Louisiana Purchase was typical of the reckless Virginian. They had often accused Jefferson of loving the French, and even of favoring the French Revolution. Now, they said, he was using Americans to help the French sell their undesirable real estate. This was one of the great tests of Jefferson's life.

Jefferson was on the spot. All his life he had been afraid of power and of men in power. He had demanded a bill of rights in the Constitution, to protect citizens from their government. And whenever any question came up, he had said that the central government should not be allowed to do anything that was not listed in the Constitution. If the government could do anything (even though it was not mentioned in the Constitution) simply because it seemed a good idea to the rulers at the time, then there would be no way of ever protecting the people. That was tyranny. That was the way the British tried to rule the colonies. That was precisely why the Revolution was fought, and why there had to be a Constitution in the first place.

But the Constitution said nothing at all about whether or how Congress could buy land from a foreign country. Again and again, in many other cases, Jefferson had argued that Congress had only those powers that the Constitution had given them in so many words. Maybe the power to buy land from foreign countries had been left out of the Constitution *on purpose*—to prevent the United States from playing the dangerous, old-fashioned game of empire. The people of the new United States had tried to escape from the ways of the Old World, where the rulers were in the habit of buying and selling, bartering and gambling faraway lands and unknown peoples.

Now would Jefferson go against everything he had been saying for years? If he had been a weak man he would have been afraid to change his mind. But he decided to show the same courage that had been shown by Livingston and Monroe in Paris. It was harder for him, because he had to stand up and change his mind in public. All his enemies were there to hoot at him. Still, Jefferson decided to go to Congress and ask them to buy Louisiana. He asked them to forget technicalities—"metaphysical subtleties" is what he called them—and instead to think of the future of the nation. He asked them to approve afterwards what they had not been wise enough to approve in advance.

After long and bitter debate, the Congress agreed. In 1803, the Senate approved the treaty with Napoleon. Louisiana became the property of the United States. Within a year, an American Governor was sitting in New Orleans, where he could see that the Mississippi River would stay open. Western Americans would have their highway to the world.

The Louisiana Purchase was a triumph in more ways than we can count. It was one of the first modern proofs that in a battle of wits between a dictator and a government of the people, the popular government does not need to lose. It showed that a people could have a Constitution to protect them against tyrants, and still make speedy decisions. If courageous men did what the nation needed, the people's representatives would approve.

And the Louisiana Purchase provided far more than a mere pathway from Western America to the world. It helped make the new nation itself into a new world. The Louisiana Purchase *doubled* the area of the United States. It made it possible for Americans to keep going west—far across the Mississippi River. It made it possible to carry the Add-a-State Plan westward to the Pacific. It made it possible to build a continent-wide Empire for Liberty. Some men from Eastern States had opposed Jefferson's purchase of Louisiana because they feared that too many new States might be carved out of the West. Then the United States would no longer be an Atlantic-seacoast nation. The original thirteen would no longer run the Union.

Before the nineteenth century ended,

Picturesque New Orleans, after many years under the French and Spanish flags, became even busier as a way station for the new millions in the West. The first State made from the vast Louisiana Purchase was the State of Louisiana, admitted in 1812.

thirteen new States and parts of States would be formed from the Louisiana Purchase. The timid Easterners were wrong in imagining what the United States ought to be. The first thirteen States were nothing but a beginning: a get-on-your-mark line for the spread over North America to the Pacific. There had been other one-ocean nations. Ours was to be a two-ocean nation.

The most wonderful feature of the Louisiana Purchase was the mystery of its boundaries. When we look at a textbook map we sometimes see the Louisiana Purchase clearly marked off. But when Jefferson made the Purchase in 1803, the boundaries were extremely vague. No one, not even Napoleon him-self or Jefferson, knew exactly how far Louisiana reached up north or out west.

Napoleon thought he was very clever to keep the boundaries of Louisiana so vague. Then he could pretend he was selling more than he really owned. Napoleon could not imagine that those uncertain boundaries would all be gateways for new States of the great new American Union. But in this way Napoleon provided Americans with expandable boundaries for their Empire for Liberty. The Louisiana Purchase freed Americans from the sharp, confining western boundary of the Mississippi River. The new nation would no longer be imprisoned in the outlines of the antique British Empire.

CHAPTER 15
America's Leading Import: People

With an empty continent to be filled, the United States was more than ever different from the crowded nations of Europe. The Louisiana Purchase itself was seven times the size of Great Britain, four times the size of France or Spain. Yet it had in it fewer people than a single big city of the Old World. During the eighteenth and early nineteenth centuries, European nations doubled their people. But how could they increase their land? The nations were jostling one another. Over there, any little piece of ground was a treasure to be fought over. Nations marked off their boundaries with forts and armies.

It was not surprising, then, that the United States became a nation of immigrants. While Europe became more and more crowded, America offered open air and cheap land. When a man in Europe could not find food for his family or a place for his children in school or as apprentices, he naturally thought of America. In Europe, too, it was an age of turmoil. Between the time of the American Revolution and the American Civil War, there were revolutions and dictatorships in France, Spain, Germany, Greece, Italy, and Belgium. And it was an age of floods and famine. There were lots of reasons why people in Europe might want to get *away from* their Old World. The disasters of Europe made refugees by the millions.

And there were plenty of reasons why someone would want to come *to* America. Of course, there were all the old legends started in the early advertising brochures which had brought people to the colonies. These still brought people to the new nation. Now there were lots of new legends—of rich land, undiscovered mines, and fast-growing cities. And there was the real-life romance of a new nation with its doors open and its people's eyes on the future.

When you had so little to lose, why not try America?

By now nearly fifty million people have crossed the oceans to settle in the United States. This is almost as large as the total number of people in Great Britain or France in our day.

It was lucky that the United States had so much unfilled land. The overflow of the Old World could find a place in the New. Peoples who did not know one another or who had fought against one another could now live side by side. America was called the "last best hope of mankind." The story of European hopelessness is a story of American hope.

In the years between the American Revolution and the Civil War, the two great sources of new Americans were Ireland and Germany. Events in those countries far across the Atlantic Ocean helped make the United States a world-nation.

In September 1845 a paper in Dublin, Ireland, gave its usual happy report of the harvest season. "The autumn is waning sunnily and cheerfully for the country. It is a busy and hopeful time. The husbandman is merrily at his toil, because it has rich promise; and the beautiful Giver of all good has, by a guarantee of abundance in the bad food of the poor, given assurance against famine."

Potatoes were the main food of the Irish poor.

One day the next month a young farmer in the north of Ireland said "he felt a peculiar smell. . . . It was the smell of the blight upon the potatoes." The terrible Irish famine was on its way. That year the blight spoiled a full third of the Irish potato crop. In 1846, the blight destroyed the whole crop all over the country. The potato blight continued until 1850.

"The hunger is upon us!" wailed the poor people of Ireland. Their misery, according to a Boston sea captain who visited Cork, was something "to harrow up your hearts." Everywhere was "the smell of the grave." A Quaker missionary found thousands on the northwest coast of Ireland "living or rather starving on turnip-tops, sand-eels, and sea-weed, a diet which no one in England would consider fit for the meanest animal which he keeps."

Tens of thousands died of starvation. Weakened by hunger, hundreds of thousands more died of disease. Typhus, relapsing fever (carried by ticks or lice), dysentery (from eating garbage), scurvy, and dozens of other ailments carried away many who did not die of hunger. Travelers reported that if you drove a cart down an Irish road at night and felt a bump, it was likely to be the dead body of a famine victim. Death haunted the land.

Ireland never was a rich country, and for centuries its produce had been drained off to England. Irish peasants were left just enough to keep them alive with strength enough to work the farms of the English. Most Irish peasants were Catholics, but the ruling British were Protestants and also persecuted them for their religion. The downtrodden Irish

---

The Irish famine, which drove families like this to desperate search for some shred of food, also prodded them to seek a new life in America. (London Illustrated News, 1849.)

tried to revolt time after time, but they were not able to throw off English rule. As the population of England grew, the English were more anxious than ever to have the Irish food for themselves.

Irishmen said, then, that Almighty God had sent the potato blight, but the English created the famine. Even while the poor of Ireland were dying of hunger for want of potatoes, there was food enough for the rich English landlords. Shiploads of wheat, oats, barley, flour, oatmeal, along with beef, pork, bacon, lard and butter that had been raised in Ireland, were sent across the narrow Irish Sea to feed the nearby people of England.

The poor people of Ireland were not even second-class citizens. They were more like slaves. Judges and sheriffs were Protestants. After 1829, when Britain passed a "Catholic Emancipation Act," the Catholics were still not really free. The theory was that now Catholics could vote. But woe to the Irishman who voted against the English landlord!

Again and again the desperate peasants organized for rebellion. They organized secret societies (some called themselves "Whiteboys," others "Terry Alts," "Hearts of Steel," or "Molly Maguires") to terrorize the worst landlords. But they made little headway. By the time of the Irish famine in 1845, the peasants of Ireland were still little better than slaves.

Even before the famine, Irish had been coming to America by the thousands. America, in the phrase of the time, was "a sort of half-way stage to Heaven." To many Irish it seemed almost as hard to get here as to reach heaven, because the cost of a steerage ticket across

the ocean (between $12.50 and $25.00) seemed so high. Letters written back to Ireland made everybody want to come. "This is the best country in the world," wrote one Irish girl from New York City in 1848. "It is easy making money in this country but hard to save it." One new arrival wrote back with glee that the Irish here "eat the pig themselves, and have plenty of bread to their potatoes." "Every day is like a Christmas Day for meat."

And now the Irish came by the hundreds of thousands. Through the port of New York City alone, between 1847 and 1860, from Ireland there came over a million. That was nearly half of all the Europeans who landed in New York in those years.

But once the Irish had landed in Boston or New York or some other port city, they had very little choice about where to go. Few had the money to move on. And few wanted to move to a lonely Western farm. The farming they knew in Ireland did not make them lovers of the land.

Many of those who moved westward in the early years used their strong arms and sturdy backs to dig canals and build railroads. The Erie Canal was a ditch 363 miles long, 40 feet wide, and 4 feet deep. It ran from Albany on the Hudson River to Buffalo on Lake Erie, and connected the growing West to New York City. When the digging began in 1817, there were not many Irish around, but before it was completed eight years later, the Irish were arriving by the thousands. On the canal they had a reputation for strength, courage, and willingness to work. Irish contractors organized teams

The Erie Canal in 1831.

of their fellow immigrants.

When the Erie Canal was finished in 1825, they moved on to help build other canals and then the railroads, which brought life to many instant cities. Soon people could say that "of the several sorts of power working at the fabric of the Republic—water-power, steam-power, and Irish-power," Irish-power had worked the hardest.

Those who stayed in the cities along the Atlantic were not always welcomed. In places like Boston they were kept out of the best jobs. Advertisements often ended: "No Irish Need Apply." The bewildered new arrivals needed help, and they received it mostly from Irishmen who had come before them. The Irish liked the sociable city life. They found a new use for what they had learned in Ireland while organizing secret clubs to fight unfair laws and English landlords. Democracy gave them their chance. Now, in New York City and Boston, they banded together to elect Irish aldermen to the city government.

The Irish alderman could help provide government jobs and money and advice. If a new arrival was arrested for a petty crime, the alderman helped him find a lawyer, or persuaded the judge to let him off. The alderman organized benefit dances. The money people paid for dance tickets would go to some Irish worker who had been crippled at his work, or to an Irish widow who had no way of supporting her children. The alderman found doctors for the sick, and brought groceries to the poor. He reached into his pocket to give a few dollars to needy orphans, or to men wanting a new start in business. He was a one-man Community Chest. No wonder the Irish in the Sixth Ward in New York City voted again and again for Dennis McCarthy (who had been a liquor dealer) or Thomas S. Brady (a lawyer) or Felix O'Neill (a grocer).

These men had a clear and simple idea of what politics was for. It was to help the needy Irish who had voted for them. They were not "statesmen." Sometimes they were not too honest, and kept a good share for themselves. But they had warm hearts and helped other newly arrived fellow Americans who had nowhere else to turn.

The Irish loved politics. They were good at it, and they loved the growing cities where they found their chance to be politicians. Their old Irish experience in the Whiteboys, the Terry Alts, and the Molly Maguires—when they had terrorized the tyrannic English—

The welcome to some Irish and German immigrants was a modern version of what the earliest settlers received from unfriendly Indians. Here we see a recent immigrant in Baltimore terrorized by members of a secret society who, because they refused to answer questions about themselves, were called "Know-Nothings."

was now a great help. In Boston and New York and other cities, if all other arguments failed, they were not afraid to use their fists.

Mike Walsh had been born in Ireland, and was brought here as a child. Wandering the streets of New York as a runaway apprentice, he learned the ways of the poor. In 1840 he organized his "Spartan Band" to take over the city's Democratic Party from an old political club which called itself "Tammany Hall." His Spartan Band was really a gang. They went into meetings, using fists instead of votes to defeat their enemies.

Walsh called his newspaper *The Subterranean.* It stood for the "subterranean democracy"—that is, the people who were underground or downtrodden. His motto was "Independent in Everything—Neutral in Nothing." He had a sense of humor. As a Congressman he made fun of stupid and wasteful projects by proposing to build a lighthouse on the Erie Canal. He liked to orate and knew how to stir up an audience. "I will yet ride over all this rotten opposition," he said, "like a balloon over a dunghill!"

Prizefighting was against the law but the Irish took the lead. One of their heroes was John "Old Smoke" Morrissey. He got his nickname during a barroom fight when a stove which had been knocked over set fire to his coattails. "Old Smoke" rose from the burning coals, and with his coattails flaming he scored a knockout. In 1853, when he was only twenty-two years old, he won the heavyweight championship from "Yankee" Sullivan in a fight that lasted thirty-seven rounds. Morrissey

was sometimes called the Irish Strong Boy.

In those days the fighters wore no gloves, but fought with bare knuckles. There were almost no rules, and fights went on as long as necessary, some lasting more than a hundred rounds. The Irish were the pioneers of prizefighting. After horse racing, it was the first important American spectator sport.

America, then, offered all sorts of new opportunities. People had a chance to discover that they could do new things. An Irish peasant, beaten down in the old country, here might become a prizefighter hero, or might help build canals and railroads, or might organize the government of cities.

The other large group of new arrivals in the years before the Civil War was the Germans. Nobody planned it that way, but whenever and wherever the people of Europe suffered, the United States somehow gained. Over there, 1816 was the terrible "year without a summer." Hail and sleet fell at all seasons. The Rhine River flooded, floating away barns and livestock. Autumn storms uprooted fruit trees. Hunger and misery cursed the land. We cannot be surprised, then, that during the following year about eight thousand Germans arrived in American ports. Again in 1829–30, the winter was one of the worst in the history of Europe. People froze because there was not enough wood to burn in fireplaces. Food was scarcer than ever, and prices went up.

By 1832, more than ten thousand Germans were coming to America in a single year. As suffering on the German countryside deepened, it became plain that

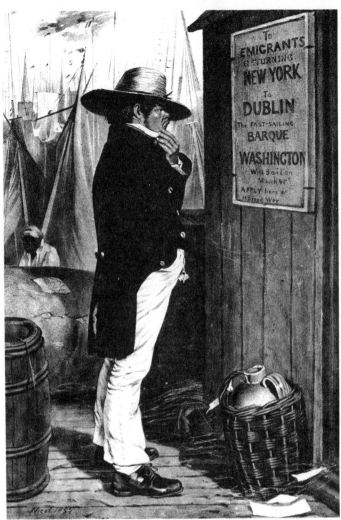

An Irishman who left home as a pauper (left) could hope to return as a rich man.

their governments were not going to help. Then Germans started coming to America by the tens of thousands. They continued to come in vast numbers till nearly the end of the nineteenth century. In 1854 alone (when Germans were half of all immigrants to the United States) they numbered nearly a quarter-million. The move to America became a craze. One night people would decide to leave Germany and they would leave the next morning. A thirteen-year-old boy with a pack on his back walked the three hundred miles to the French port of Le Havre in order to find passage for America.

Throughout these years, revolutions were brewing in Germany. Students formed secret societies and studied new constitutions, hoping to overthrow the government. Peasants gathered around "Liberty Trees." They refused to pay taxes and roughed up tax officials.

In Central Europe, Prince Metternich, the enemy of democracy, was in charge. He had seen the terror of the French Revolution of 1789, and he hated democracy, which he imagined was always government by a mob. He organized tyranny in Germany. But even Metternich could not prevent protests like that in May 1832 when 25,000 people gathered in a small German town to drink the health of Lafayette (the hero of the American Revolution) and to demand a republic.

Metternich's policies created a growing flood of refugees. By 1848, there was civil war and a full-fledged revolution in Germany. The country was in turmoil, and many revolutionaries had to flee.

These political refugees from Germany were not many—perhaps only a few thousand. But they included some, like Carl Schurz, who became eminent here and helped to build in America the democracy they could not build in Germany. When the German Revolution failed in 1852, Schurz came to the United States. His career covered the whole country. After becoming a lawyer in Milwaukee, he campaigned for Lincoln in 1860, fought as a general on the Northern side at Gettysburg and other battles. He was Minister to Spain, Senator from Missouri, and then served in the Cabinet as Secretary of the Interior. He was one of the leading Americans of his day.

Germany's loss was America's gain. New Americans from Germany built whole cities like Milwaukee, and helped make Milwaukee a center of American beer brewing. They spread all over the country, becoming farmers, teachers, professors, lawyers, doctors, newspapermen, and they built prosperous businesses. Many fought on the Union side in the Civil War.

The German passion for music showed in folk-singing clubs and in new symphony orchestras. The orchestra in Chicago was directed and manned by Germans for many years. They helped found American colleges and universities. The Germans brought with them some new ideas about schools. They believed in physical education and many early physical education teachers were German. They persuaded Americans to build gymnasiums attached to schools. Before the Germans came, it was not usual to send children to school before they were old enough to read. Then Germans brought over the *Kindergarten* (a German word meaning "garden of children") where children as young as four years old could learn by playing. The idea caught on, and soon there were American kindergartens everywhere.

In the half-century before the Civil War, although the largest numbers came from Germany and Ireland, immigrants

---

Instant Americans. Old friends talk German to an immigrant girl two weeks after her arrival from Germany. "You are mistaken," she replies haughtily. "I don't speak German."

were coming from other places, too. Thousands came from the Scandinavian countries, from the Netherlands, Belgium, Switzerland, France, and elsewhere. The nation was growing by a great migration.

CHAPTER 16

Instant Cities

In places where men still alive could remember the sound of the Indian war whoop and the shadow of the virgin forest, there sprouted cities.

On riverways and the joinings of riverways appeared Pittsburgh, Cincinnati, St. Louis, Louisville, Memphis, Minneapolis and St. Paul, Davenport, Des Moines, Omaha, and hundreds of others. On the Great Lakes and at the river entrances to the Lakes, men founded Rochester, Buffalo, Cleveland, Toledo, Detroit, and Chicago. Around the river entrances to the Gulf Coast appeared Mobile, Galveston, and Houston, in addition, of course, to New Orleans. And now on the far Pacific shores there were Portland, Seattle, San Francisco, and Los Angeles. An astonishing crop of cities to grow so quickly across a wilderness-continent!

When before had so many cities grown so fast? In America the moving spirit was in the air. In England or France, where families had lived in the same village for centuries, it took a lot of spunk to leave the old homestead and move to a new place. But over here were the children and grandchildren of people who had come from Europe, three thousand miles across an ocean. They did not think it so odd that they too should move on. Americans easily

took root in new places.

In the years between the Revolution and the Civil War, Americans went west to start new cities. Many hoped to make their living out of building them. Some hoped to make money out of selling the land. The wilderness was worth very little, but once a city was there, land became valuable. Then some people would want to buy land for houses, others for farms to raise vegetables and chickens and eggs nearby where there would be no problem of transportation.

Merchants came to open their stores. New towns were good for young doctors in search of patients, and for young lawyers looking for clients. Even if you were inexperienced and unknown, you could still get started, because everybody else there was also unknown. You did not have to take business away from old established firms, because there were none. But the value of your land and your business, whatever it was, depended on more people coming.

This was when the American businessman began. About 1830 in these new Western cities, the word "businessman" took a meaning it had never had before. A businessman was not just a merchant, trying to sell people something from his store. He was a man who had staked his living on a new town. He expected great

Big-city politicians provided useful services for new immigrants. Here, a magazine artist of 1856 shows members of New York's Tammany Hall helping immigrants from Europe, Africa, and Asia to become naturalized as American citizens. On election day these politicians expected the new citizens to remember their friends.

things, and tried his hand at all sorts of new enterprises. He prospered only when the town prospered. Naturally he was cheerful about the future.

The great cities of the Old World had been built on their rich past. To satisfy the many people who were already there, citizens had provided one thing after another—a newspaper to give them news, inns to house the travelers, theaters and opera houses to entertain the crowds, colleges and universities where the learned men could gather and the young could be educated. A European city grew up piece by piece, over decades and centuries. An older city had more to offer simply because it was

older. Over there the people had come first, and then the city was slowly built to meet their needs. This seemed an obvious and sensible way for a city to grow.

But that way was much too slow and haphazard for impatient, purposeful Americans. Western city-builders wanted their city first. They wanted to see it even *before* the people were there. If they already had a newspaper, hotel, theater, and college or university, then surely people would come. But if they waited, then some other city might provide all those attractions first. People would then go on to Cleveland instead of staying in Pittsburgh, or they would

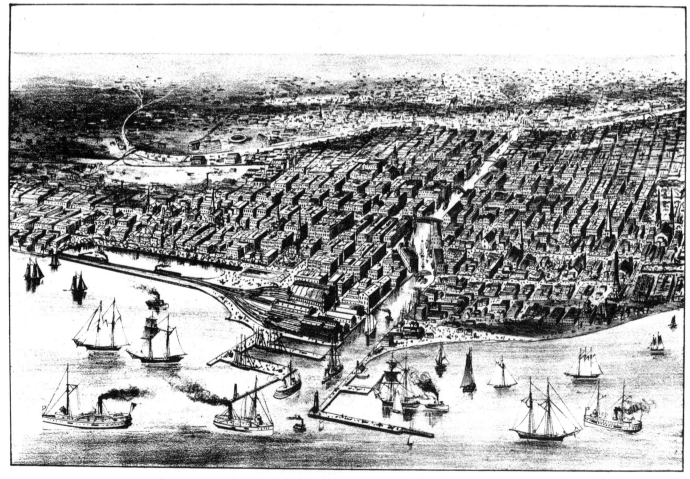

move on from Kansas City to Omaha, or from Omaha to Denver.

The men who went west in the early nineteenth century were often going to cities that did not yet really exist. To them a city was not just any place where lots of people happened to live. It was where people were building a community together. They built not for their needs but for their hopes.

For example, in Europe a city did not have a newspaper until it already had a large reading community. But in the American West, the newspaper actually arrived *before* the city. Your place might never even become a city unless you *started* with a newspaper.

To men of the Old World, it seemed foolish to start a newspaper in the wilderness. But Americans had strong imaginations. They imagined their great cities—Pittsburgh, Cleveland, Chicago, Kansas City—sprouting in the backwoods. To make their dreams come true, they first needed a newspaper. "The spirit of adventure," a pioneer St. Louis editor boasted, "thrust it forward ahead of the calaboose, the post office, the school, the church, and made it a symbol of conquest." Along with the axe and the musket, the newspaper press became a way of subduing the wilderness. Here was a new kind of pioneer—the newspaper-pioneer.

Along the Atlantic Coast in older American cities, newspapers had been more like those in England. They satisfied people who were already there. But in the new Western cities, at first newspapers were advertisements. Like the early colonial advertising brochures for Georgia and the other colonies, they aimed to attract people. Then their place would become as great as the writers pretended it already was.

Pittsburgh, west of the Alleghenies, was a tiny village with a population of only three hundred when the Pittsburgh *Gazette*, its first newspaper, appeared on July 29, 1786. A small press, together with type, ink, and paper, had been packed across the mountains. It was hard to get supplies. Once, when the outfit ran out of paper, they borrowed from Fort Pitt some cartridge paper that was supposed to be used for wrapping ammunition. Since there was no mail service, the editor delivered the papers himself, while at the same time he gathered news for the next issue. The main purpose of the newspaper was to advertise Pittsburgh and attract settlers there.

John Scull, who started that first Pittsburgh newspaper even before there was a city, became a leader of the city when it actually appeared. He became postmaster, president of a bank, a founder of the new University of Pittsburgh, and a member of the town council. Before Scull died in 1828, Pittsburgh was a thriving city of twelve thousand.

This same success story could be told again and again. To succeed with your newspaper, you had to be able to do many different things. It was not enough

Chicago was one of the most spectacular of the instant cities. Top: Chicago as a tiny settlement in 1820. Bottom: By about 1860 Chicago had become a thriving metropolis of more than 100,000 people. This is a print from the firm of Currier and Ives, whose scenes of American life were popular in the nineteenth century.

to be able to write. You had to be able to collect the news, to set the type, and then be willing yourself to do all sorts of chores, like delivering the paper.

There were many "Franklins of the West" who used their printing presses to build their cities. But there were risks. In the little village of Cincinnati (with a population of less than four hundred), when the first newspaper, called the *Centinel of the Northwestern Territory*, appeared in 1793 it warned of house burning and massacre by Indians. A "Public Notice" in that paper offered a

---

A hazard of journalism in the West. A reader "requests" a retraction of an uncomplimentary statement. This editor, like many others, also acted as postmaster. This gave him an opportunity—not quite legal —to gather news from incoming letters before they were delivered.

government reward of $168 for "every scalp, having the right ear appendant, for the first ten Indians" killed in the neighborhood.

By the middle of the nineteenth century there were cheap portable printing presses. One, called the "army press," was only a foot across and could be lifted by one man. With $150 you could set yourself up as a newspaperman. But you had to be energetic and willing to move around till you found the right place.

Young Robert Thompson Van Horn, who was destined to be the newspaper-pioneer of Kansas City, showed how to do it. Born in Pennsylvania in 1824, he tried his hand at teaching school and at being a lawyer. Then moving westward, he edited several papers. Everywhere he went his newspaper advertised some new city which still had to be built. "Standing around scratching heads," his newspaper warned an Ohio village in 1850, "will never make Pomeroy the city nature intended it to be." Disappointed with Pomeroy, he moved on to Cincinnati. When his printing plant there burned down, he took a job on a river steamboat.

"I am going out West, probably to Nebraska," Van Horn wrote his parents in 1854, "where I hope to retrieve my fortunes and kick up a dust generally among the natives." When he was working in St. Louis, a committee of businessmen from Kansas City went to ask him to come edit their newspaper. He took up their offer. Beginning with only $250 he became Kansas City's pioneer newspaperman.

The main problems of these newspaper-pioneers, one of them explained, were "to get paper, to get news, and to get paid." Cash was scarce, and editors had to be willing to be paid in produce. They even advertised that you could pay them in corn, molasses, potatoes, cabbage, flour, meal, fruit, or kindling wood. One editor announced that he would accept "any other variety of produce except babies."

In 1846, foreign travelers to western Tennessee, along the banks of the Mississippi River, were astonished to find there in a remote forest in the middle of nowhere a large and imposing hotel. Fronted by an elegant facade of tall white columns, it called itself the "Gayoso House." It was still three years before Memphis would be incorporated as a city, and ten years before there would be a railroad. Where were the guests? In the future, of course. The men who built the hotel expected the guests to come quickly enough. They were sure that Memphis would soon become a great city. *First* it needed a "spacious and elegant hotel." To Europeans, this seemed all topsy-turvy.

When the English novelist Anthony Trollope traveled across America in the 1860's, he noted:

Hotels in America are very much larger and more numerous than in other countries. They are to be found in all towns, and I might almost say in all villages. In England and on the Continent we find them on the recognized routes of travel and in towns of commercial or social importance. . . . But in the States of Amer-

An early passenger elevator of the kind first used in hotels.

ica, the first sign of . . . settlement is an hotel five stories high with an office, a bar, a cloak-room, three gentlemen's parlours, two ladies' parlours, a ladies' entrance and two hundred bedrooms. . . .

Whence are to come the sleepers in those two hundred bedrooms, and who is to pay for the gaudy sofas and numerous lounging chairs in the ladies' parlours? . . . When the new hotel rises up in the wilderness, it is presumed that people will come there with the express object of inhabiting it. The hotel itself will create a population, — as the railways do. With us [in Europe] railways run to the towns; but in the States the towns run to the railways. It is the same thing with the hotels.

Nearly everything about the American hotel was new. Even the word was new to the English language. "Hotel" was borrowed from the French language, where it meant a noble house or a city hall. The old English "inn" was a modest building with a few rooms where tired travelers could sleep. In England, "tavern" was the name for the place where you could get food or drink. The American "hotel" combined the services of the inn and the tavern.

The architecture was new. The American hotel was often the biggest and most imposing building in the wilderness place that hoped to become a city. It looked less like a modest English inn than like a great church or a palace. The St. Charles Hotel in New Orleans struck English visitors in 1846 by its "large and elegant Corinthian portico and the lofty swelling dome." American hotels were impressive public buildings. They came to be called "Palaces of the Public" or "People's Palaces." And they deserved the name. For they were the social centers where a democratic people could meet, just as European nobles had met in the lobbies and courtyards of their ruling princes.

Hotels were where all sorts of conveniences were first tried. Some of the first systems of central heating were in hotels. A furnace blew hot air through the public rooms so that visitors did not have to rely on a fireplace. The first public building in America heated by steam was the Eastern Exchange Hotel in Boston (1846). But it was a long while before it seemed worth the trouble to heat the bedrooms.

The Tremont House in Boston was probably the first large building in modern times to have extensive plumbing. One of its most famous features was a row of eight flush toilets (then called "water closets"). The bathtubs in the basement actually had running water, a curiosity at the time. In the Astor House, built in New York City in 1836, guests were astonished to find plumbing on the upper floors. Each floor had its own water closets and its own bathrooms, fed from a roof tank to which water had been raised by a steam pump.

The first passenger elevators (originally called "vertical railways") appeared in hotels. A passenger elevator was installed in the Fifth Avenue Hotel in New York in 1859. Until then the rooms on upper floors had been much cheaper. Who wanted to climb five or six flights of stairs? But when rooms on the top floor could be reached by an elevator, they actually had a special attraction. From a top-floor room, as one traveler suggested, a guest could "look down on surrounding buildings in the same manner as our most gracious English nobility look down on the peasants beneath them."

During a night in the city hotel many people became acquainted with conveniences which they then wanted for their own homes. Beds with springs were found in hotels long before people had them at home. People were still using oil lamps to light their homes when Boston's Tremont House in 1829 set a bright example with gas light in its public rooms. The Astor House in New York actually had its own gas plant.

It was in hotels that electricity was first used for bells and buzzers. Until then, when you wanted service in your room you shook a hand bell, incidentally waking up the other guests. One guest explained how the system worked: "One ring for ice-water, two for bell-boy, three for porter, four for chambermaid,—and not a darned one of them will come."

By the time of the Civil War, the hotels of the United States were already famous throughout the world. "The American hotel," a London newspaperman reported in 1861, "is to an English hotel what an elephant is to a periwinkle. . . . An American hotel is (in the chief cities) as roomy as Buckingham Palace, and is not much inferior to a palace in its internal fittings." When an English comedian stayed at the luxurious St. Nicholas Hotel in New York he was reminded of the Arabian Nights. He was afraid, he said, to leave his shoes outside the door to be shined (as was the custom in Europe) for fear someone would cover them with gold.

Hotels drew people together and became the centers of social life in the new Western cities. There the rich gave their parties. The lobby was the meeting place

Brown's Indian Queen Hotel, Washington, D.C., about 1832. This elegant building stood on Pennsylvania Avenue, about midway between the Capitol and the White House.

The expanding West: dream and nightmare. Unscrupulous land promoters were described by Charles Dickens in Martin Chuzzlewit *after his 1842 tour of the United States. Left: "The thriving City of Eden, as it appeared on paper." Right: "The thriving City of Eden, as it appeared in fact." (Illustrations by Phiz.)*

of leading citizens. Since Americans moved so freely around the country many who could afford it lived in hotels —until their own houses could be built, or until they decided where to settle. An American city was judged not by its cathedrals or by its government buildings, but by its hotels.

Yet it was risky business trying to build an instant city. We remember the successes, but there were many more failures. These became ghost towns. When we drive through the West today, we can see what is left of a few of them. Some, like the abandoned silver-mining towns of Aspen and Central City, Colorado, have been revived as curiosities, to serve for skiing resorts in winter and tourist centers for summer opera.

Most ghost towns have left no trace. When the mines ran out, or when neigh-boring farmers found the land would not grow crops, or when there was a drought, or when the hoped-for canal or railroad did not come, citizens left for some other, more promising town. We can never know exactly how many there were of these "melancholy deserted villages, monuments of blighted hopes." But there were thousands. In Iowa alone, between 1838 (when Iowa became a territory) and the early twentieth century, we can count over twenty-two hundred abandoned places. In Kansas there were even more than that number of ghost towns—towns whose people had walked away in the last half of the nineteenth century.

Sometimes, when people realized that a village would never become a city, they would actually take down the buildings to use the lumber in some other place where they had moved their hopes. Sometimes, when the people finally gave up, their town was already (in a Kansas phrase) "too dead to skin."

The glory of American cities was always in the future. Visitors from England were sometimes puzzled by the American language. Americans tended to confuse what had already happened with what they simply expected to happen. In England the word "city" had a very precise meaning. It was used only for a large and impressive place. A smaller place was called a "town," a "village," or a "hamlet." In England a city meant a place big enough to have a cathedral, which was the headquarters of a bishop. Englishmen would not call a place a city unless it was old and

thriving, with thousands of people.

Americans, though, looked ahead. They were so certain that their places in the wilderness would quickly become cities that they did not bother to wait. They preferred to call them cities right now. Then by a kind of magic, they thought, the name would attract people and help make the place become a real city. This amused foreign travelers. "In the course of the last two days," the Earl of Derby reported in 1826, "we passed several *cities*—some of them however almost invisible."

"It is strange that the name of city should be given to an unfinished log-house," the English Captain Marryat noted in 1834, "but such is the case in Texas!"

CHAPTER 17
Every Man His Own Carpenter

In their instant cities Americans needed houses. And they needed them quickly. There were no grandparents or other relatives to live with until you had a home of your own. There were no old houses to rent or to buy. And out in the West carpenters were scarce, or non-existent. If you wanted shelter you had to provide it yourself.

Americans, then, invented a new way of building. The novel idea was very simple.

In England, builders of houses had got into a rut. They believed there was only one right way to build a wooden house. You built it around a frame of heavy timbers. Each timber was about

a foot square. You held these heavy timbers together by cutting down the end of one into a tongue (a "tenon") which was then fitted into a hole (a "mortise") in the adjoining timber. When there was a pull on the joint you held the pieces together with a wooden peg

---

The old style of house building required that at each joint a "tenon" be carved so it would exactly fit into its "mortise." A wooden peg was inserted to hold the tenon in place.

Before the balloon-frame house was invented, the framework of a house was made of heavy timbers which might first be put together on the ground. Then a crew of men was needed to lift the cumbersome sections.

fitted into a hole that went through both the joined timbers. You rested your floors on these heavy supports, and closed in the sides with mud, plaster, or wood.

There were advantages to this kind of building. The weighty frame was not easily shaken or moved. But to make it required lots of skill. You had to be an experienced carpenter, clever with the crude tools of the day, to make mortise-and-tenon joints that fit tight. It took lots of time to square off the huge, cumbersome timbers and to carve the joints just right. In new Western towns like Cincinnati, Chicago, Omaha, and Denver, where carpenters were not to be found, the people themselves did not have the skill—much less the time—to build their own houses in the old style.

All these needs produced the "balloon frame." Nobody knows exactly who invented this new American type of building. But we do know that it began to appear in the Western instant cities. Probably the first was built in Chicago in 1833. The name "balloon-frame house" was used by respectable, old-fashioned builders because they thought the whole building was ridiculously light. The first wind, they said, would surely blow it away—just like a balloon. They could not believe that anything as quick and as light as the new Chicago construction could possibly hold up.

What was the balloon frame? The idea

is so simple that it is hard to believe it ever had to be invented. The first notion was to forget that you ever needed a frame of heavy timbers with their ends neatly carved to fit into one another. Instead make the lightest possible frame! Get a supply of long thin boards about two inches thick and four inches wide. Then buy some long heavy nails. Stand up some of the thin boards—say eighteen inches or two feet apart—and nail other thin boards across them to hold them together.

Once you have your frame up, cover it outside and in with thin wide clapboards or any other material you wish. Nothing could be simpler. About three-quarters of the wooden houses in the United States are now built this way.

Of course, to build a balloon frame you need plenty of nails. In the old days, nails had been extremely expensive, because each one was fashioned by hand. But by 1830 New England nail-making machines were turning out nails by the thousands, better and cheaper than before.

Anybody could build a balloon-frame

The construction of a balloon-frame house in 1855. The light boards of the frame are simply held together by nails.

house. You only had to be able to use a hammer. "To erect a balloon-building," someone explained in 1855, "requires about as much mechanical skill as it does to build a board fence." Clever carpenters and builders experienced in the old ways naturally could not believe that a sturdy house could be so simple to build.

The new way of building was speedy. It took less than half the time to build a balloon-frame house than one of the same size built in the old style. In Chicago, within one week in April, 1834, seven new buildings of this kind appeared. By mid-June there were seventy-five more. By October an additional five hundred were in use.

The balloon frame proved to have other advantages that nobody had counted on. It turned out to be even stronger and more durable than the old heavy-timbered construction. For moisture had tended to collect in the joints where the old heavy timbers were fitted together. Then the timbers would begin to rot. The beams were also weakened by the holes cut for tenons and drilled for wooden pegs. On the other hand, the balloon frame, which used lots of thin boards, did not weaken them with holes. It used the whole plank and the very grain of the wood so as to stand the most strain.

For Americans on the move, the balloon frame had still another great advantage. It could be taken apart easily and then set up again in some other place. The old heavy-timbered buildings had been made to stay forever in the same place. But the boards of a balloon frame were light and easy to carry. St. Mary's Church in Chicago, said to be the first balloon-frame building, within ten years of its construction was taken down, moved away, and reerected three times.

Ambitious Americans, always on the lookout for better opportunities in another place, might want to take their houses with them. In Omaha, General William Larimer in 1856 was living in a balloon-frame house that had first been set up in Pittsburgh, then knocked down and shipped out west by steamboat. When Omaha grew, he moved his house to another site.

As balloon-frame houses became popular and the demand increased, companies manufactured and sold them in large quantities. You could order your house from a catalog by mail, and the nails and the boards (cut to the right size) would be shipped out to you with some simple directions. You could put up your house, then, wherever you pleased, with the help of a few friends. By 1850, in New York alone, about five thousand such prefabs were being made to send out to relieve the housing shortage among Gold Rushers in California. One company shipped 100 portable wooden houses which were carried on pack mules across the Isthmus of Panama; another sent out 175 all the way by sea around Cape Horn.

Not only houses, but also churches and even hotels were commonly built with ready-made balloon frames. The spacious San Francisco Astor House, a three-and-a-half-story hotel 180 feet long, containing ten shops and a hundred rooms, was erected from a kit ordered by Westerners who needed shelter in a hurry.

PART FOUR

THINKING LIKE
AMERICANS

Americans were united by the new experiences they were sharing every day. By the time of the Civil War, there were clearly recognizable American ways of life and American ways of thinking. Americans devised new ways of making things—not only houses, but muskets and locks and clocks and nearly everything else. Americans, too, became more like one another simply because they had to do more things for themselves. In Europe many of their tasks would have been done for them by professionals, with their own ancient royal guilds and monopolies.

Americans were pushed together because, to cross the continent safely, they had to leave behind many of their belongings—together with old prejudices and snobberies. They learned to act more equal and more friendly.

Out of all this, too, grew new American kinds of political parties. In this new world, politics was not just for the few. The American party conventions became a popular entertainment, and election campaigns became a national circus with as many different circus rings as there were States.

The citizens of the new nation had begun thinking like Americans. Not so much because they were trying—but mostly because they could not help it. Living like Americans was what made Americans.

Here was being created a "nation of nations." Americans were united less by memories than by hopes, less by a shared past than by an exciting present and by dreams of the future.

CHAPTER 18

American Know-how

Back in January 1801, the American people were frightened. The French dictator Napoleon seemed out to conquer the world. He had overrun Egypt, as a step toward taking India away from the British Empire. He invaded Syria on the far edge of the Holy Land. In the opening year of the new century, he sent his troops in winter across the snowy Swiss Alps to occupy Milan. And now he was on his way to conquering Italy. After defeating the Austrians in a great battle at Hohenlinden he was master of Central Europe. He had even forced the Spanish to give him the vast American territory called Louisiana.

Americans yet had no inkling of the surprising events that were to make Louisiana part of the United States. Napoleon still seemed unbeatable. Would the United States be his next victim?

John Adams of Massachusetts, who was President, warned the country that it was no use trying to talk Napoleon out of his adventures. The new nation, young and weak, had to prepare for a French attack. America needed guns. And the worst of it was that America had very few gun-makers. There was still no such thing as a gun factory anywhere in the world, much less in primitive America. The muskets Americans had used in the Revolution twenty years before had come from France or elsewhere in Europe. Now, to keep the United States safe, guns had to be made within the country. There was no time to waste.

In those days in Europe a whole musket was made by one man. He was called a "gunsmith." (The word "smith" came from an older word meaning to shape or cut.) Just as a goldsmith shaped pieces of gold into jewelry, so the gunsmith actually shaped all the pieces of a gun to make them fit together. It seemed obvious, then, that unless the United States could import lots of gunsmiths, it would not have the guns it needed.

An American named Eli Whitney refused to see it that way. Whitney had a notion that there might be an entirely new way of making muskets. Born on a farm in Massachusetts, as a boy he had puttered around his father's machine shop, where he learned to use a mechanic's tools. He was so clever with his hands that he could make and repair violins. By the time he was fifteen years old he had hired helpers for his own business of manufacturing nails. Later he made hatpins.

At the age of twenty-three, he decided that he needed a college education after all. When he entered Yale College in 1789, he was eight years older than his classmates. After he graduated in 1792, he went down south to live with the family of the Revolutionary General Nathanael Greene, on their plantation outside Savannah, Georgia.

It was easy to grow cotton on plantations in the South. But there was no easy way of separating the fuzz attached to the cotton seeds from the seeds themselves. The cotton fuzz had to be separated so it could be twisted into cotton threads. In those days the seeds had to be taken out by hand one at a time. It was so much trouble that cotton was not a very valuable crop. When people in the neighborhood saw that Whitney was clever at repairing things about the plantation, they asked him to set his mind to making a machine to solve their great problem. And within ten days he had actually made a "cotton gin." ("Gin" was short for "engine.") His was an extremely simple machine. The worker turned a crank attached to combs that combed out the fuzz from the seeds. Now one man could clean fifty pounds of cotton in a day.

Suddenly cotton became a valuable crop. The South soon exported large

A cotton gin.

quantities of cotton up north and all over the world. In 1794, within two years after Whitney's invention, the South was exporting a million and a half pounds of cotton, the next year over six million pounds, and by 1800 cotton exports from the South reached nearly eighteen million pounds.

Whitney, without intending to, had changed the life of the South. But now the whole nation was in desperate need. Could he find a way of making guns without gunsmiths?

His idea again was very simple. Each musket was made of fifty different parts. For one man to make all these parts himself he had to be a skillful gunsmith, and had to know a great deal about guns. But suppose a man had to make only *one* of these parts. Suppose you gave the man a model of that one part and invented for him the right tools so he could quickly make lots of precise copies. That might be as simple as tracing out copies of a paper doll. Instead of tracing on paper, he would trace on sheets of iron. The man would not need much skill at all. You could quickly show him how to make a hundred copies of that one part in a single day. Then suppose you found forty-nine other men and trained each man to make lots of copies of another one of the parts.

When all the men had finished their day's work, you would have a hundred copies of each of the different parts in a musket. Of course you would have to be very careful about your measurements. But if you could make each copy exactly like every other copy of the same part, then any one part would fit together with any other. It would be easy to put the fifty parts of the musket together.

In this way you would have done a kind of magic. You would have made guns without a single skilled gunsmith! If your copy-making machinery was good, you could even make the guns much faster.

This was a neat trick. It was Eli Whitney's idea for supplying the nation's guns. But very few people believed it would work. It was too hard to imagine that good guns could be made without gunsmiths. Of course the leading "experts" on the question were the few gunsmiths in the United States at that time. They were harder to convince than anybody else. When the Secretary of War asked them whether Whitney's plan would work, they simply laughed. Whitney thought the best answer was a demonstration.

In the wintry January of 1801, Eli Whitney came to Washington for the climax of his years of work and planning. Three years before, in January 1798, when he had first begun to figure out his new plan, he had promised the government to make ten thousand muskets. That was a fantastic number. Whitney was not a gunsmith and had never made even one gun before. When he promised to make guns for the government, he had not even seen the gun he was going to make. Was the Secretary of War crazy to put the arming of the nation in the hands of an amateur?

But Whitney had faith in his new kind of mechanical magic. What he had in his mind was not simply a new way of making guns. It was a new way of making *anything!*

His idea was so new that the machinery for it did not yet exist. Before he could make any muskets in his new way, he had to make the machinery for making the muskets. He spent over two years inventing and perfecting the tools that would make precise iron copies of the single part which was used as a pattern. He made new kinds of measuring machines so the worker could be sure his part was precisely the right size. Since he had spent so much time making the new machinery, he had been able to make very few muskets. Even his friends began to wonder whether his system was only a pipe dream. Would it work at all?

Now he had a chance to show. He had an appointment with President John Adams, Vice-President Thomas Jefferson, the Secretary of War, the Secretary of the Treasury, and other members of the Cabinet. When they met he showed them one of his completed muskets. Then he laid out separate piles of the loose pieces. He told each man present to take one piece—any piece—from each pile and see how easily they all fitted together into a complete, working musket. They were astonished. Any one of the pieces actually fitted with all the others.

"He had invented," Jefferson reported, "moulds and machines for making all the pieces of his [flint]lock so exactly equal, that take 100 locks to pieces and mingle their parts and the hundred locks may be put together as well by taking the first pieces which come to hand . . . good locks may be put together without employing a [gun]smith."

The witnesses now had a new faith in Whitney and in his system. Not until 1809, ten years after Whitney began his assignment, did he finally deliver the last of the ten thousand muskets. For his work during all those years he made a profit of only $2,500. By then the United States had bought Louisiana and felt safer in the West. The menace of Napoleon was no longer so great. But the British were a new threat. They blocked American ships and seized American sailors. The United States might have to fight a second war for independence. Now the nation needed arms more than ever. Whitney was ready to help arm the nation.

Whitney's system soon was called the "Uniformity System"—because each part in one gun was uniform (precisely the same in shape and size) with that same part in another gun of the same design. Some called it the "Interchangeable System," because the parts of one gun were interchangeable with the parts from another.

The need for Whitney's system came from America's lack of skill. If we had had lots of trained gunsmiths here, he might never have thought of it. Yet to make his system work at all, his guns actually had to be better than those made altogether by an individual gunsmith. The parts from one gun would not fit another unless they were very precisely made. Whitney's enemies were surprised to find his guns even better than the imported guns made by trained craftsmen.

There were other advantages. In the old days, when a piece of your musket broke, you could not simply buy a new piece to put in its place. You had to take the whole musket to a gunsmith. He had

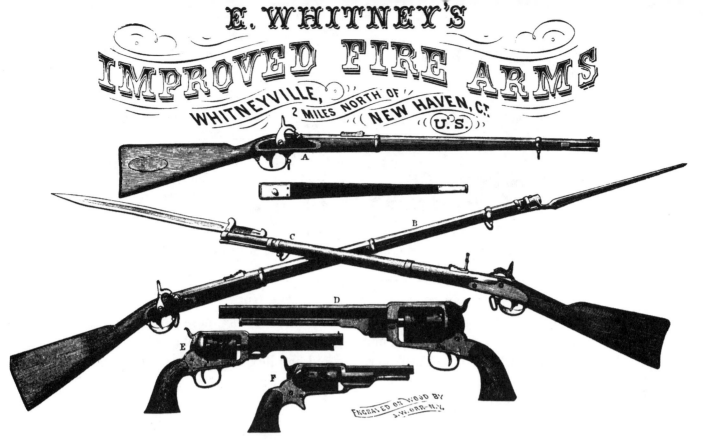

The "Uniformity System," turning out guns by the thousands, created the need and the opportunity for national advertising. This advertisement (about 1860) included a testimonial by the famous mountain man Kit Carson: "Whitney's Rifles are the best to cross the Plains with."

to manufacture a particular piece to fit that particular musket. Under the new Uniformity System all you had to do was buy the particular piece you needed, and you could be sure it would fit your musket.

Soon it was possible to make all kinds of complicated machinery much cheaper than ever before. Delicate machines could be made by the thousands, and without using expensive and highly trained workers. Even before the Civil War, locks and watches were cheaper in America (where they were made by the Uniformity System) than they were in countries where there were many skilled locksmiths and watchmakers.

This is what we mean by "mass production." It means producing lots of things of the same kind. It means, as Whitney explained, using the skill of the machine instead of the skill of the worker. When things were produced this way, they were much cheaper. More people could afford to buy. This in turn encouraged other people to make more cheap things to sell. The worker's time was worth a lot more. Now he could produce more of anything—guns or locks or watches—in a single day than ever before. The employer could afford to pay him more, and still make a profit.

All this changed the worker in America. In England, for example, a young man had to work for years as an apprentice before he finally became a master gunsmith. But in America a young man could work at making guns without

American factories like this one in a pleasant rural countryside startled Europeans, who were accustomed to find them in murky cities. A print by Nathaniel Currier.

even being an apprentice. He simply needed to learn how to run the machine that made one part of a gun. The American machines became more specialized. The American people were less specialized. Here it was more important that you have general intelligence so you could handle the expensive and complicated machinery. Here the worker had to be quick at learning new ways.

CHAPTER 19

Do-It-Yourself Doctors

The wound of an Indian's arrow or the bite of a rattlesnake called for speedy treatment. A man had to be his own doctor.

This was all very different from the way it was in England. Over there during the colonial period anyone who could afford it would call in a learned physician. The sign of a physician was his gold-headed cane. He was a dignified man who commonly wore a powdered wig, a coat of red satin or brocade, short breeches, stockings, and buckled shoes. This "Doctor of Physick" knew Latin and Greek and had been to the university, where he had acquired lots of technical terms. But, oddly enough, he was squeamish about the human body. He would not dirty his hands, much less let them be stained with blood. Of course he would not dress wounds or perform operations. He thought he was above all that, because he was a member of an exclusive guild. His monopoly was called the Royal College of Physicians, with headquarters in London.

Surgery—the performing of operations—was the job in England of quite another man, a member of the Guild of Barber-Surgeons. Since he dirtied his hands, he was a member of a lower class. Of course he was not supposed to know learned languages, or to read books, for he was simply a craftsman who knew how to carve and cut and sew up the human body. By the eighteenth century there was still another division of jobs between the barbers (who cut hair, trimmed beards, and pulled teeth) and the surgeons, who performed all other operations.

Pharmacy, the art of mixing medicines, was practiced by people who called themselves "apothecaries." Originally they were members of the grocers' guild, but in the seventeenth century they received royal permission for a guild of their own, and then grocers were forbidden to sell drugs. The midwife (usually a woman) was experienced in delivering babies. Any of these groups would not allow nonmembers to do their kind of work. The laws punished those who tried.

The physician, of course, lorded it over all the others. By the eighteenth century the Royal College of Physicians in London had become a snobbish social club. People were admitted because they had money and came from the "best" families, but they received almost no solid instruction. Very little practical medicine was taught at Oxford or Cambridge. What was taught in the universities was mostly grand theories about how the body was supposed to operate. But neither the professors of "physick" nor their students spent much time on the details of human anatomy. Dissecting dead bodies was still considered indecent or irreligious, and had to be done in secret when it was done at all.

In early New England, trained physicians with a university degree were scarcely to be found. Most doctoring was done by ministers and schoolmasters. John Winthrop, the first Governor of Massachusetts Bay Colony, was a leading medical adviser. His son, who became Governor of Connecticut, used to give medical advice by letter. The missionary John Eliot gave the Indians medical advice at the same time he tried to convert them. The two New Englanders who pioneered in preventing smallpox by inoculation—Cotton Mather and Zabdiel Boylston—had taught themselves all the medicine they knew.

In the South, on the remote and widely dispersed plantations, even if a trained doctor could have been found, the planter could not afford to summon him for all the ailments of his slaves. For medical treatment the owner relied on himself, his wife, or his overseer. George Washington commonly prescribed for the ills of his slaves. In his own last illness it was his overseer, not a doctor, who first treated him. When Thomas Jefferson returned to Monticello from the White House one summer, he himself gave smallpox inoculations to seventy or eighty people on his plantation, and he supervised his neighbors in inoculating another hundred. The planter's wife bore much of the burden of doctoring, for she delivered babies and was often awakened in the middle of the night to look after the dangerously ill in the slave quarters.

One of the commonest books in Virginia plantation libraries was *Every Man his own Doctor; or, the Poor Planter's Physician*. First published in 1734, it was printed and sold in large numbers by Benjamin Franklin in Philadelphia. The book offered "plain and easy means for persons to cure themselves of all, or most of the distempers incident to the climate, and with very little charge, the medicines being chiefly of the growth and production of this country."

These American amateurs often did not know what they were doing. But they had one great advantage. Unlike the English professionals, they had not been trained to use drastic and painful "remedies." Those dangerous treatments were called "heroic" remedies—perhaps because they made a hero out of the unfortunate patient. They included drinks of disgusting and indigestible concoctions (made of every conceivable substance, from urine and powdered insects to lead bullets), and "bleeding" the patient (letting blood out of his veins), which was supposed to relax him and cure almost any pain. Self-trained Americans tended to be more timid. Their treatments were at least less damaging.

Jefferson, like many other American amateur doctors, believed that when you did not really understand a disease, it was better to let nature take its course. From the beginning Americans had expected a great deal from nature. Many of the advertisements which brought them here told of the invigorating New England air, of the health-giving Virginia water, or of the magical Georgia climate.

The American belief in natural remedies encouraged Americans to learn from the long experience of the Indians. It also made them adventurous and resourceful—if sometimes overly optimistic—students of nature. Unlike the European woods, the woods of America had not been combed over by generations of botanists. Observant Americans might expect to discover wonderful new healing plants.

The gum of the white poplar tree,

they said, made a balm that would quickly heal deep wounds. They learned to make a refreshing tea from the sassafras bark. When the Indians taught them to smoke tobacco, the settlers praised it as a medicine which "purgeth gross humors, openeth all the pores and passages of the body," which prevented some ailments and cured many others—including the gout, hangovers, and fatigue. They came upon the Jamestown Weed, which today is still used as a narcotic. And they made medicines from the May apple and the witch-hazel shrub. One of their most remarkable finds was the so-called "Tooth-Ache tree," whose leaves, seeds, and bark were said to be used by the people along the Southern seacoast to cure toothache.

Of course, many of these cures were imaginary. But enough were real to encourage enterprising Americans to search their woods for balms and tonics and beverages.

One source of their extravagant hopes was the belief that God had always created a remedy for every disease and an antidote for every poison. For example, it was widely believed that, since the poisonous rattlesnake was found in America, there must be a remedy here for the rattlesnake bite. Sure enough, on the very terrain where they found the snake, they also found rattlesnake root, or rattlesnake master, plants supposed to counteract the snake's poison. "The bountiful Creator discovers his marvels in proportion to our wants," rejoiced an eighteenth century American minister-naturalist. "Every country has native remedies against its natural defects."

When the nation began to have a few

The rattlesnake, unknown in Europe, attracted special interest among travelers. Here it is drawn by Mark Catesby, an English botanist-artist who visited the southern colonies in the eighteenth century. Below: The "rattlesnake root" was so called because its resemblance to the rattlesnake led people to imagine that it had a peculiar power to cure the bite of this snake.

professionally trained doctors, these men also pioneered in botany and natural history. The study of a country's diseases and the study of its plants and animals naturally went together. Dr. Alexander Garden, who had a Scottish medical degree and practiced medicine in Charleston in the later eighteenth century, probably reported more new American plants and animals than anybody else of his time. The gardenia was named after him.

Americans learned their medicine not from classroom lectures but by working as apprentices. An American doctor would keep a young man in his house for seven years doing chores—as nurse, janitor, messenger, coachman, and assistant surgeon. The apprentice read a few medical books but learned mostly from his master. The young man's family paid tuition to the doctor.

The Old World differences between the physician, the barber-surgeon, and the others disappeared soon enough. When the Frenchman Marquis de Chastellux traveled through the country during the American Revolution, he called all medical men here by the name of "doctor"—"because the distinction of surgeon and physician is as little known in the army of Washington as in that of Agamemnon." The American doctor therefore had a wider experience than his English counterpart. Until well into the nineteenth century, the new nation was poor in its medical schools, and American doctors were not very learned. But even Europeans noticed that somehow the Americans were remarkably successful at curing people.

American doctors, partly because they had fewer theories, were more willing to learn from experience. "More is required of us," one of them said, "in this late settled world, where new diseases often occur." In the American West, people who faced emergencies had to act quickly and do the job themselves.

For example, on a Far West trail in the summer of 1826 a man traveling in a wagon train had his arm shattered by an accidental shot as he foolishly drew his rifle, muzzle first, from his wagon. The wound began to fester and the man was dying of gangrene. His companions in the wagon train—nothing but amateur doctors—were bold enough to save his life. They dared to amputate the arm from which the infection was spreading. One of them reported:

Their only "case of instruments" consisted of a handsaw, a butcher's knife and a large iron bolt. The teeth of the saw being considered too coarse, they went to work, and soon had a set of fine teeth filed on the back.

The knife having been whetted keen, and the iron bolt laid upon the fire, they commenced the operation: and in less time than it takes to tell it, the arm was opened round to the bone, which was almost in an instant sawed off; and with the whizzing hot iron the whole stump was so effectually seared as to close the arteries completely.

Bandages were now applied, and the company proceeded on their journey as though nothing had occurred. The arm commenced healing rapidly, and in a few weeks the patient was sound and well.

Again and again, ingenious Americans made medical history. The accidents of the backwoods, and the wounds which people suffered in their wars against the Indians, in the Revolution—and later in the Civil War—all gave medical students an opportunity to see the inside of the human body, as they never might have in a university.

William Beaumont was an army doctor trained entirely by the apprentice method. On June 6, 1822, while he was stationed at remote Fort Mackinac in northern Michigan, an employee of the American Fur Company out there accidentally received a load of buckshot in his left side. Beaumont did what he could to make the wound heal, but despite everything the hole in the victim's stomach remained open. He had the inspiration to take advantage of this rare opportunity to see directly through the unhealed opening exactly what went on in a man's stomach. He took the patient under his own roof and planned his observations.

Beaumont watched how the gastric juices worked, and then saw the effects of tea, coffee, and alcohol. The result of this was Beaumont's book, *Experiments and Observations on the Gastric Juice and the Physiology of Digestion* (1833). It laid the foundation for the study of digestion and the science of nutrition. If Beaumont had been near a city, with learned specialists to tell him that his study was impossible, would he have dared as he did?

CHAPTER 20

Wagon-Towns Moving West

When Americans decided to move farther west in the years after the Revolution, they seldom went by themselves. Sometimes, of course, there was a lone adventurer—an explorer, a priest, or a hunter. But that was rare. To survive and cover territory, even an explorer had to go with a large group. When Meriwether Lewis and William Clark were sent by President Thomas Jefferson to the Far Northwest in 1803 to find the riverways that poured into the Pacific and to explore the newly acquired Louisiana Purchase, they organized a group that numbered altogether forty-five men.

This was an old story. From the beginning, people came here in groups. You could not cross the ocean by yourself in a canoe. To lead men great distances into unknown territory, you had to be a good organizer. On his first voyage to America in 1492, Columbus took three ships with a crew of ninety men. When Captain John Smith landed on May 24, 1607, at Jamestown, 105 others landed with him. The crowded *Mayflower* which landed at Plymouth in 1620 carried 101 passengers.

Two hundred years later, in the early nineteenth century, Americans settling across the Mississippi traveled hundreds of miles into the great West and toward the Pacific. They also moved in groups. You might start out alone or with a few friends and family from the settled States on the Atlantic Ocean. But you were not likely to reach very far into the unknown West unless you soon joined with fifty or a hundred others.

Most of the West was still unknown. A few wagon ways had been marked off by earlier explorers, and they were the only paths through the wilderness. Nobody had put up signs telling you in which direction to go or how far you were from anyplace. If you were lucky you could find your way because so many other people and animals before you had worn a trail across the land.

The most important trails started from a little town called Independence over two hundred miles west of St. Louis, and just outside where Kansas City now stands. From there the California and Oregon Trail went up across the flat plains toward what is now Nebraska and

Emigrant families with covered wagons gathered here at Independence, Missouri, to form wagon trains for the long trip west.

Wyoming, took a famous pass through the Rocky Mountains (called the South Pass), then branched off into two paths. The Oregon Trail went up toward where Portland, Oregon, is now. The other, the California Trail, went down toward where we now find San Francisco. From Independence the Santa Fe Trail led through barren desert southwestward down to Santa Fe, then still deep in Mexican territory.

The busy little town of Independence was, as one traveler said in 1844, "the general 'port of embarkation' for every part of the great 'prairie ocean.'" At Council Grove, just outside Independence, astonishing things were happening. These did not look so unusual to Americans, but would have amazed people anywhere else in the world. People from all over, who had never seen one another

before, collected there because they all wanted to go west. Just as people in Chicago, Cincinnati, Denver, and in a hundred other places were quickly coming together forming their instant cities, so these people with wagons were forming their own kind of instant towns. These were wagon-towns, towns made to move.

It was not safe to travel alone. Indians were apt to attack a small party, but if you traveled in a large group, they might be frightened off. After General Anthony Wayne defeated the Indians at the Battle of Fallen Timbers in Ohio in 1794, Indian attacks were much rarer east of the Mississippi. Then it was less dangerous for men to travel with only their families in that part of the country. But on the other side of the Mississippi, travel in large groups kept on until after the Civil War.

With enough wagons in your party, you could make a kind of fort every night. At the end of the day's travel, the wagons would be formed into a hollow square. When wagons were arranged along the outside of a square, the space inside was like a small walled town. People were protected while they cooked their meals. They could sing and dance, or hold meetings to talk about the problems of the trip. If Indians attacked, women and children could be safe in the hollow square while the men and boys shot back at the Indians from behind the wall of wagons.

Since there was no other way of building a fence, the wagons also made a corral for the horses and oxen and other animals. If there were unfriendly Indians in the neighborhood, men were stationed on guard all night. Every man and boy had to take his turn. The more men and boys there were, the more time any one could sleep between his turns.

The covered wagon used for crossing the continent was about ten feet long, eight and a half feet to the top of the canvas. It was usually drawn, not by horses, but by three pairs of oxen. Even if two oxen were lost, the four that remained could still pull the wagon. When fully loaded, it could carry a ton.

Dragging this wagon up a hill was never easy. But it was much easier if you were in a large party. Then you could do what the Brown party did in 1846 at the head of the steep Goldstream Canyon in the Sierra Nevada Mountains. The whole party helped pull the first

---

"The Attack on an Emigrant Train" (1856) was the vivid recollection of a young painter who had known the Indians well. Carl Wimar had been born in Germany and moved as a boy to St. Louis in 1843, when the Indians still came there frequently to trade.

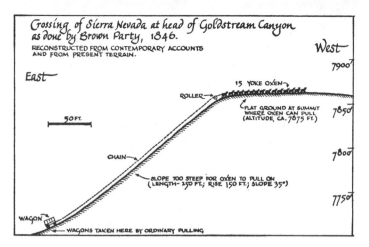

Crossing of Sierra Nevada at head of Goldstream Canyon
as done by Brown Party, 1846.
RECONSTRUCTED FROM CONTEMPORARY ACCOUNTS
AND FROM PRESENT TERRAIN.

West

7900'

East

15 YOKE OXEN
ROLLER
FLAT GROUND AT SUMMIT
WHERE OXEN CAN PULL
(ALTITUDE, CA. 7675 FT.)   7850'

50 FT.

7800'

CHAIN

SLOPE TOO STEEP FOR OXEN TO PULL ON
(LENGTH- 250 FT.; RISE 150 FT.; SLOPE 35°)   7750'

WAGON
WAGONS TAKEN HERE BY ORDINARY PULLING

From The California Trail *by George R. Stewart,
Copyright © 1962 by George R. Stewart. Used by
permission of McGraw-Hill Book Company.*

wagon up the hill. Then fifteen pairs of oxen were attached to a chain wound around a roller (the axle of a wagon) to make a windlass. At the top of the hill oxen turned the roller on the windlass, which hoisted the other wagons, one after the other, up the hill.

Going down a steep hill was also dangerous. The brakes on the wagons were primitive. If you let your wagon coast there was always a danger of tumbling or of breaking the legs of the animals. Trees were sometimes put through the spokes of the wheels or were dragged behind to slow the wagon down. But in some places there were no trees. It was better, if you had a big enough party, to set up a windlass and ease the wagons down the hill. One high place in the North Platte Valley was actually called Windlass Hill.

When your wagon stuck in the mud, other people's oxen were yoked together to pull you out. It was dangerous driving your wagon across swift, deep streams with soft bottoms. But if you could attach your wagon to a rope hauled by wagons on the other side, you were less apt to get into trouble. At the swiftest and deepest streams, the wheels were taken off one wagon and the wagon-box became a boat. It was pulled back and forth across the river till the whole party and all their baggage were over.

The trip across the continent was long and slow. From Independence on the lower Missouri River to Sutter's Fort in California, it was about two thousand miles on the wagon trail. The normal speed for a wagon was two miles an

A wagon train fording the Platte River in 1849.

hour. At that slow speed a wagon, even without springs, might not be too bumpy on flat ground. But when the trail was especially rough, or went up or down hill, the healthy passengers preferred to walk. Even with good luck, the wagon ride from Independence to the Pacific Ocean might take five months.

The first great westward party on the Platte Route, which followed the Platte River across Nebraska and Wyoming, was led by Colonel Stephen W. Kearny in 1845. Kearny's wagon train stretched out for three miles. When so many people lived together for so long, they had to be organized. They had to make rules for health and safety. They had to appoint judges, select juries, and punish criminals. They had to keep order, arrange marriages, and perform funerals. They felt all the needs of people in Cincinnati or Chicago or Omaha, and had additional problems, too. If the trip was not to take forever, they had to see that everybody kept moving. And they had to see that everybody did a fair share of the work and risked a fair share of the dangers.

At Council Grove, near Independence, in the 1840's and 1850's, you could see people forming these wagon-towns. People who had never known one another were now holding meetings, passing resolutions, and drawing up regulations. They made some rules before they left Independence, and the rest after they were out on the trail.

What they did was very much like what the Pilgrims on the *Mayflower* had to do two hundred years before. They were going "through a territory where the laws of our common country, the United States, do not extend their protection." They needed a government, so they made a government for themselves. Each wagon train, with its many passengers, was a kind of *Mayflower*. Like the first pilgrims, each wagon train made its Mayflower Compact. Each had its own do-it-yourself government. They wrote out their own laws, which everybody signed.

"In view of the long and difficult journey before us," the Green and Jersey company of emigrants to California, meeting not far from Independence on

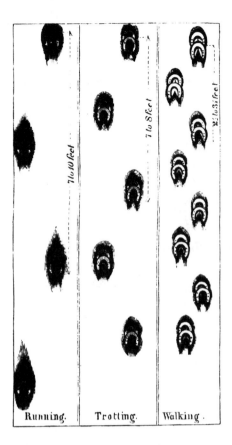

This illustration from Marcy's Prairie Traveler *showed how to judge the speed of an Indian pony ahead.*

May 9, 1849, adopted "strict rules and regulations to govern us during our passage."

And we do . . . pledge ourselves to each other, that we will abide by all the rules and regulations that may be made by a vote of the majority of the company . . . that we will manfully assist and uphold any authorized officer in his exertions to strictly enforce all such rules and regulations. . . .

And further, in case any members of the company, by loss of oxen or mules, by breaking of wagon, robbery by the Indians, or in fact from any cause whatever beyond their control, are deprived of the ability to proceed with the company in the usual manner, we pledge ourselves never to desert them, but . . . to support and assist them to get through to Sutter's Fort, and in fact, we pledge ourselves to stand by each other . . . to the death.

Each wagon train had a captain, usually elected by a vote of the majority. Before the election there were often speeches. Since most of the people did not know one another, they could not always pick the best man. But the captain of the wagon train, like the captain of a ship, had an important job. He had to assign tasks and settle quarrels. The fate of the whole wagon train might depend on his good humor and good judgment. If the people did not like him, they could vote him out and elect someone in his place.

Many companies used a book of instructions written by Captain Randolph B. Marcy, who had battled Indians in Michigan and Wisconsin, had fought in Texas, and once commanded a hundred men on a thousand-mile march across the Rocky Mountains in winter. His book, *The Prairie Traveler, A Hand-Book for Overland Expeditions* (1859), put out by the War Department, offered lots of good advice. "First business," he said, "should be to organize . . . into a company and elect a commander. The company should be of sufficient magnitude to herd and guard animals, and for protection against Indians." He explained how to handle oxen, how to repair a wagon, and how to cross rivers. Everyone should put in some money to buy extra animals to help anyone whose animals died on the way. It was one for all and all for one!

Impatient travelers would abandon one wagon train and join another, just as people might leave Kansas City for Omaha, or Omaha for Denver, when the prospects looked better in the other place. Young James A. Pritchard and seven companions set out on April 10, 1849, from a little town in Kentucky with their mules and wagons. They took a steamer up the Mississippi to St. Louis, then went overland to Independence, where they arrived on April 22. There they spent two weeks preparing to "bid adieu to homes, friends, and happy Country." When they happened to meet a Captain Fash from Indiana, they joined his party of seventeen wagons and sixty men. But Fash's party was too slow for them. Taking four wagons from Fash's party they made up their own wagon train.

By mid-May they were deep in Indian country. But the party did not have enough wagons to make a big hollow square, and did not properly guard their animals at night. At ten o'clock on the night of May 17 a large mountain wolf began prowling around the camp. Everyone was awakened by "those hideous howls that will startle one from the profoundest sleep—and make him think that one of the fiends of the infernal regions was standing before him. And away went picket ropes and pins, at a single dash about 40 of the mules were loosed."

They decided that at last they had to organize. Three men were nominated for captain, an election was held, and Pritchard received 38 of the 40 votes. After his acceptance speech, "one universal shout rose from the crowd." They then made some laws. But Pritchard was not a successful captain. He could not keep the wagons in line. The party split again, and some of his wagons joined other parties passing on the trail.

The best organizers were the best captains of wagon trains. The Mormons were remarkably successful. With their new American religion they were looking to the west for their Promised Land. They set up instant cities of their own in Ohio and Indiana. When the Mormons prospered, their envious neighbors believed all kinds of strange stories about them, and destroyed their towns. The Mormons had to move on. In February 1846, their able leader Brigham Young began taking them across Iowa toward Utah. They built their own roads and bridges as they went. They even planted seeds along the trail so that Mormon wagon trains the next season could harvest the crops for food as they went by. One wagon train that reached Utah in October 1847 brought 1,540 Mormon emigrants in 540 wagons, together with 124 horses, 9 mules, 2213 oxen, 887 cows, 358 sheep, 24 hogs, and 716 chickens.

The Mormons were held together by their religion, which was based on *The Book of Mormon*. According to Joseph Smith, the founder of the religion, who had been raised in poverty on a farm in upstate New York, an angel Moroni had come to him in 1827 and told him where to find certain gold tablets. Then, seated behind a curtain and using magic spectacles, he deciphered the inscriptions and translated them into English. He said that the gold tablets were lost before anyone else could see them.

But the Mormons were not the only ones who expected to find a Promised Land in the unknown West. Hundreds of other wagon-towns were held together by their own vague hopes of a great future.

CHAPTER 21
Haste Makes Democracy

People who wanted to travel fast and far had to travel light. The guidebooks, like Marcy's *Prairie Traveler*, told you to take only food, clothing, tools, and weapons needed for the trip. You could not bring along your family's heavy carved furniture, or fancy hats and coats and shoes, or the elegant silverware you inherited from your grandfather. Yet all these—together with the landed estates and mansions which of course also had to be left behind—were the very things that separated the rich from the poor. Out west people made a fresh start.

Going across the desert or up and down the mountains, you might have to abandon even the few things you had brought along. James Abbey, a young man who left Indiana for California in April 1849, wrote in his diary what happened as his party crossed the desert approaching the Sierra Nevada Mountains:

August 2nd.—Started out by four o'clock this morning; at six stopped to cook our breakfast and lighten our wagons by throwing away the heavier portion of our clothing and such other articles as we can best spare. We pushed on to-day with as much speed as possible, determined, if possible, to get through the desert, but our cattle gave such evident signs of exhaustion that we were compelled to stop.

Being completely out of water, myself, Rowley, and Woodfill bought two gallons from a trader (who had brought it along on speculation), for which we paid the very reasonable price of one dollar per gallon. The desert through which we are passing is strewed with dead cattle, mules, and horses. I counted in a distance of fifteen miles 350 dead horses, 280 oxen, and 120 mules; and hundreds of others are left behind, being unable to keep up. Such is travelling through the desert. . . . A tanyard or slaughterhouse is a flower garden in comparison. . . .

Vast amounts of valuable property have been abandoned and thrown away in this desert—leather trunks, clothing, wagons, etc., to the value of at least a hundred thousand dollars, in about twenty miles. . . . The cause of so many wagons being abandoned is to endeavor to save the animals and reach the end of the journey as soon as possible by packing through; the loss of personal goods is a matter of small importance comparatively.

The American love of speed—the desire to get there first—was born in this race to and through the West. To float quickly down the Ohio, the Missouri, or the Mississippi, you put together enough rough timbers to make a crude flatboat and then let the strong current carry you. When you reached New Orleans you took the boat apart and used the lumber to build your house.

Going upstream was more difficult. By the 1820's Americans had developed a new type of steam engine to drive their boats against the current. It was called a high-pressure engine and was built less for safety than for speed. The pioneer maker of these engines was Oliver Evans, from the neighborhood of Philadelphia, who was a genius at labor-saving devices. He made a flour mill that used chutes and moving belts in place of man-power. And he actually had a plan for a steam-driven carriage that might have been a pioneer automobile. At first people said he was crazy. Then when his ideas worked they began stealing them.

The high-pressure engine was faster than anything known before. It burned lots of wood to keep up the steam, but that was not a serious objection in the virgin forests of the West. With a full head of steam the boilers in these engines sometimes exploded. But still Americans were willing to risk anything to get there first. The American motto was "Go ahead anyhow."

On these speeding Western steam-boats, the accidents were appalling. Without safety valves on the crude boilers, unlimited speed meant unlimited disaster. "The democrats here never like to remain behind one another," a traveling German nobleman reported from the West about 1840. "On the contrary, each wants to get ahead of the rest. When two steamboats happen to get alongside each other, the passengers will encourage the captains to run a race. . . . The races are the causes of most of the explosions, and yet they are still constantly taking place. The life of an American is, indeed, only a constant *racing*, and why

A scene in 1849 on one of the Western trails. If emigrants had not started out traveling light, they soon learned on the trail.

Scene on the Emigrant Trail, near settlements, Nov. 1849.

should he fear it so much on board the steamboats?"

Captains and firemen on the Mississippi sneered at the eastern slowpokes. "It don't take no spunk to navigate them waters. . . . But I tell you stranger, it takes a man to ride one of these half alligator boats, head on a snag, high pressure, [safety] valve soldered down, 600 souls on board and in danger of going to the devil."

These Western racers, called "brag" boats, lived a short, fast life. Of all the steamboats built before mid-nineteenth century, nearly a third were lost in accidents. The main cause was explosions, which killed scores of passengers with bursts of flying wreckage, floods of steam, and scalding water. Some steamboat owners sent the passengers who had not yet paid their fares to the back part of the vessel. There, in case of explosion, they would be less likely to be killed, and the owner could still collect his fares from them.

When the railroad came, it was the same story all over again. Cautious European railroad builders, who came over here in the 1840's and fifties and sixties to see how Americans managed to lay tracks so fast over such vast distances, were horrified. Americans laid single sets of tracks, which saved time and money but of course increased the danger of collisions. Unlike European railroaders, Americans commonly did not trouble to level off hills or to lay tracks into long gentle curves or to cut tunnels. They did not bother to lay solid foundations for embankments.

All this increased the chance of speeding trains going off the rails as they tried to maneuver sharp curves, or came rocketing down steep hills. In some places hasty American railroad builders, anxious to keep working all through the winter, laid tracks right on the snow— with disastrous consequences when the spring thaws came.

American railroad builders had good reasons to hurry. State legislatures and the Congress rewarded the builders of the first railroads with big loans of money and valuable grants of land. In 1866, the self-confident leaders of the Central Pacific Railroad, which had started building from the West, actually persuaded Congress to make the laying of the transcontinental tracks into a race. The Union Pacific was building out from the East. The company that built more mileage would receive that much more money. Each company was racing against the other. They both were naturally tempted to put fast construction above everything else.

By 1850 the wrecks on the instant railroads of the West were as common as steamboat explosions had been. Experienced travelers rode in the middle cars rather than at front or back. In those days before seat belts, prudent passengers braced themselves by holding onto the seat in front of them, and they sat diagonally so they would not receive the collision shock directly on their knees. Fast American trains of the mid-nineteenth century gave you the excitement of a roller-coaster, but they were a good deal less safe.

Still the American quest for speed did have some good effects. The heavy, rigid English locomotives could not manage the sharp curves and steep in-

On hastily built American railroad bridges, accidents were common.

clines. And weak embankments and flimsy trestles sagged under their enormous weight. The famous *Stourbridge Lion,* imported from England, was the first working, steam-powered locomotive to run on American rails. It had only a short demonstration run in 1829. When it was found to be ill-suited for the American tracks, it was left on a siding to rust. A few pieces of it can be seen in the National Museum in Washington. America needed a new kind of locomotive that put less strain on the tracks and could speed around sharp curves without going off the rails.

The answer was simple enough as soon as one stopped thinking in the old European ways. English locomotives usually had only four wheels. These were big and heavy and were mounted rigidly on axles like those of the old horse carriage. They were all right on a sturdy roadbed and on a straight road. But they could not follow sharp curves. John Bloomfield Jervis, a self-taught engineer from New York, had seen the troubles with the *Stourbridge Lion.* He had very little education but lots of experience building canals and roads. He designed a new kind of railroad car. His idea, like many revolutionary innovations, was simplicity itself.

Why, Jervis asked, must we rest the whole enormous weight of the locomotive only on those four big wheels? Why must the construction be so rigid? Instead he made a separate little truck (called a "bogie") with four low wheels and put it under the front end of the locomotive. It was arranged on a swivel,

Some of the earliest American passenger cars (shown here) followed the English plan of mounting carriage bodies on a frame with railroad wheels. The large rigid front wheels of this English-style locomotive could not always hold the track in America.

---

so it could follow even a sharply curving track. Since the bogie wheels were low and small they were not so apt to derail. But Jervis still kept the big wheels under the rear end of the locomotive. Now the locomotive had more wheels. This spread the locomotive's weight over more points on the track. Then even badly built track was less likely to sink and bridges were less likely to sag.

In 1832 Jervis made a locomotive by this design, and he called it the "Experiment." This came to be called the "American-type locomotive" and has been the plan for locomotives ever since. Since you could now spread out the weight, with Jervis' plan you could make locomotives even longer and more

powerful and speedier than ever before.

People in a hurry—whether traveling by steamboat or by railroad—had to be willing to be jammed together. There was not the space to give everybody a private compartment. Any snob who was anxious to keep his proper distance from the common herd had better not go at all. On a Western steamboat the so-called "cabin" passengers included a wide range of people—from the rich and famous to those who could barely afford the extra fee to avoid being carried "deck" (or steerage) with the cattle. Among the cabin passengers, the comforts were assigned on the basis of first-come-first-served. After sleeping on the open deck or in dormitories, passen-

---

To help locomotives hold the track on the sharp curves and steep grades of American railroads, Jervis invented the "bogie truck" of low wheels which could swivel. Americans also simplified the railroad car, making it a single long box with entrances at either end.

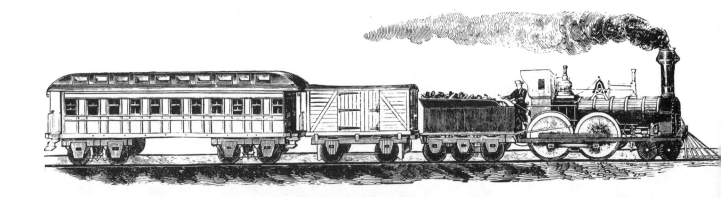

gers ate together family style at long tables. It did not matter whether you liked your fellow passengers. You still had to sleep in the same bedroom with them and eat at the same table.

The American railroad car, like the Western steamboat, was newly designed for quick construction, speed, and long distances. It also pushed people together in the new democracy of haste. The English passenger car had been made by mounting the bodies of several horse carriages on a single long frame—making a lot of separate closed compartments. The entrances, like those on the carriages, were still from the sides. You sat closely confined with six or eight other passengers who were all traveling the same "class" (first, second, or third) until the trip was over. The earliest American-type passenger cars were *one* class. Their new American design did not follow that of the old horse-carriages. Instead each American passenger car was a single, long, open, box-like compartment. You could not enter from the sides but had to enter from either end.

Like the hotel lobbies in the new cities, these spacious American passenger cars became democratic mixing places. Passengers did not sit primly in their own seats, but made themselves comfortable by removing their shoes or outer garments. They wandered about, introducing themselves, conversing, playing games, and cracking jokes. By the end of several days' journey through the vast Western spaces, they knew one another quite well.

Upper-class Europeans were embarrassed. They said Americans were always putting their noses into other peoples' business. The Viscountess Avonmore, as late as 1874, reported her annoyance at traveling with "thirty or forty human beings . . . boxed up together for seven days and nights, crammed close to each other all day, sleeping on shelves at night and in the same atmosphere."

She was shocked by the forced intimacy with so many vulgar persons. One of her fellow passengers each morning took from her pocket a set of false teeth which, she insisted on explaining, she did not sleep in because they were so expensive and she hated to use them up. The lavatory of the car could not be made private. "You cannot even tuck up your hair or roll up your sleeves," the Viscountess complained, "but some gentleman or conductor is sure to pounce upon you and remark, 'Very refreshing to get a good wash.'"

This new kind of train was perfect for the restless American. He could wander through the train, passing out the door at the end of his car and crossing the open platform into the next, where he could mingle with those passengers too. The danger of being crushed between cars or of being jolted off the train was so great that one company painted a tombstone on the doors at the ends of each car. But fidgety Americans wanted to know they were on the move. They walked on until the last car where they could admire the receding view.

When you ate in a hurry you did not have time to be upper-class or elegant. The differences between passengers with polished manners and those who had never used a napkin quickly disappeared. From time to time, the train stopped—but only for a few min-

"Ten Minutes for Refreshment," an advertisement for A&P tea and coffee. A sign by the door said: "The bell rings 2 minutes before the train starts."

utes—to feed the passengers. If you did not want to go hungry, you had better run out and grab what you could.

"The cars stop," recorded the British naval captain Frederick Marryat in 1839, "all the doors are thrown open, and out rush all the passengers like boys out of school, and crowd round the tables to solace themselves with pies, patties, cakes, hard-boiled eggs, hams, custards, and a variety of railroad luxuries too numerous to mention. The bell rings for departure, in they all hurry with their hands and mouths full, and off they go again until the next stopping-place." The dining car did not come into use until 1863.

The "lunch counter"—in a railroad station or elsewhere, where people in a hurry could grab a bite—was an American invention of this period. Europeans complained that it was actually designed to keep a person so uncomfortable that he would eat quickly to make way for another customer. The surest way to indigestion, they said, was an American train trip!

CHAPTER 22
Political Parties for All

Newcomers were nearly everywhere after about 1820. Only the old seaboard South failed to attract them in large numbers. The cities on the Atlantic began to fill up with immigrants—especially Irish and Germans. In Kansas City, Chicago, Omaha, Denver, and in other Western cities, everybody was a newcomer. Out there you could hardly respect a man because his grandfather was rich or famous—for the simple reason that you did not know his grandfather. Every man had to stand on his own feet. And every man wanted to vote.

The old cozy rule by a few gentlemen was out. It had worked in colonial Virginia only because there were enough well-to-do families who had lived in that same colony for many years. George Washington was the great-grandson of John Washington, who had come to Virginia back in 1657. Jefferson was the great-grandson of a Thomas Jefferson who was living in Virginia in 1677.

The aristocrats of Virginia were respected partly for their ancestors. Much of their wealth and power came from relatives. They lived in mansions like Mount Vernon or Monticello, where they presided over large plantations. In the days of the Virginia Dynasty political parties had resembled clubs more than ways of grouping all Americans. And they tended to be run in private by their few aristocratic leaders.

A new American politics grew in the new cities, and in the older cities now overflowing with newcomers. Fed by every conceivable means of transportation—wagon trains, canals, transatlantic steamers, Western steamboats, and railroads—American cities multiplied and grew. When George Washington was inaugurated there were only *five* American cities of more than ten thousand people, and the largest city in the United States still had a population of less than fifty thousand. By the time of the Civil War, there were to be nearly *one hundred* American cities with a population of more than ten thousand each. By then the largest American city, New York, had over a million people. And even Philadelphia, with over half a million, was ten times the size of the biggest city in 1790.

More cities meant more politics—and a new kind of politics. People sprinkled around on farms found it hard to come together for meetings. News traveled slowly. But city people could meet at a moment's notice. They found it easy to organize, to talk with candidates, to discuss policies, to arrange debates and parades and demonstrations. Long before the Civil War it was plain that American political parties and campaigns and elections were going to be quite different from those anywhere else in the world.

Under the Constitution each State could decide for itself which of its citizens could vote. You might be a respectable farmer or an honest businessman, but you still could not vote by the laws of your State if you did not own quite enough property. Then, in the early nineteenth century, in the Age of Newcomers, one State after another changed its laws. By 1850 nearly every adult white man could vote. Most Negro Americans were still slaves, and even those who were free were rarely allowed to vote. Women would not have the vote until the Nineteenth Amendment to the Constitution in 1920.

Some of the first States to open up voting were in the West. In Ohio, for example (which in those days was still "West"), there were no "old families." The Ohio Constitution of 1802 gave the vote to almost all adult white men. And so did the constitutions in other new Western States—Indiana (1816), Illinois (1818), and Alabama (1819)—and the new Eastern State of Maine (1820).

Meanwhile, in the older States, the pressure was on to make voting more democratic. Many of the original thirteen States revised their constitutions. Connecticut (1818), Massachusetts (1821), and New York (1821) gave up the property requirement for voting. In some older States there was a bitter struggle. John Adams—who had helped write the Declaration of Independence, had been a leader in the Revolution, and was founder of a "Massachusetts Dynasty"— was chairman of the Constitutional Convention in Massachusetts in 1820. He warned of anarchy and mob rule if Massachusetts put the vote in the hands of men who had no property.

In aristocratic Virginia, change was slow. Madison, Monroe, and Chief Justice John Marshall—all members of the Virginia Dynasty—wanted to keep the property qualification. Even after the new Virginia Constitution of 1831 about one-third of the adult white men (about eighty thousand people), and all the Negroes, still were not allowed to vote. It was 1851 before Virginia abolished the property requirement. But Virginia was an exception. By 1828 about twice as many Americans could vote as could vote twenty years before.

At the same time the power to choose delegates to the Electoral College (in other words, to decide who would be President of the United States) was given to the voters themselves. By 1828, there were only two States in the Union (South Carolina and Delaware) where the delegates to the Electoral College were still chosen by the State legislature.

There was a change, too, in the way people cast their ballots. In colonial Virginia (and in some other colonies, too), a man voted by announcing his choice aloud to people standing around the village green. This way of voting, which had been brought over from England, continued in some States even after the Revolution. It was surely not the way to guarantee a poor man his right to vote for anyone he really wanted. In some States soon after the Revolution, people began writing their votes on a paper ballot. Since there were no printed ballots, the voter had to write out for himself all the names of the people he wanted to vote for. In the Pennsylvania election of 1796, for example, even if you had the right to vote, the only way you could vote for President of the United States was to write down the names of fifteen different electors on your ballot.

Someone tried printing "tickets" with

the names of his party's candidates, and then gave these to voters so they could copy the names on their ballots. In some States the government itself began printing ballots with all the candidates' names already on them. Massachusetts, for example, began this in 1830. Then all the voter had to do was put a mark beside the names of the candidates of his choice and put the ballot in a sealed box. This way of voting was much more private than the old Virginia way of announcing your choice out loud. People who were not educated enough to spell a lot of names now could vote without making mistakes.

A "party ticket" was the new name for the list of candidates supported by a political party. "Ticket-making" became a popular pastime. But who would make up the official party "ticket"? The old "caucus" where a few leaders got together and privately chose the candidates would no longer do. Everybody wanted his say—not only about who was elected, but even about who was nominated.

To do this new job of ticket-making, the parties began to hold conventions. Members of the party in each county met to choose delegates to a State Convention. There the delegates would meet

"The Verdict of the People" shows an election day in Missouri in 1854. The painter, George Caleb Bingham, had been born in Virginia but as a child had moved west to Missouri with his family. An active politician himself, he liked to paint political scenes.

to make up their party ticket. They listed their candidate for Governor and for all the other offices in the State—and they chose a candidate for President of the United States.

The State Conventions were great fun. In the days before movies or radio or television, and when other public entertainment was scarce, farmers and villagers were delighted to have an excuse to visit the big city. A State Convention was less like a solemn committee meeting than like a church picnic or a State fair. People exchanged jokes and gossip, and enjoyed plenty of refreshments. Incidentally, of course, delegates gave orations about their candidates, talked about party politics, and gave three cheers for the party. By the late 1820's and the 1830's State Party Conventions were being held all over the country.

In 1840 the Whigs pretended that their candidate was a simple man of the people.

HARRISONIAN

BALL ROLLING.

WILLIAM HENRY HARRISON · THE FARMER OF NORTH BEND.

KEEP THE

RALLY!

A General Meeting

Will be held at the Old COURT ROOM, [Riey's building]

American politics was beginning to be nearly everybody's hobby.

The next step, of course, was the National Party Convention. In the presidential election of 1832, for the first time, National Nominating Conventions were held by all the major parties that offered candidates.

The spacious new American-style hotels—"Palaces of the Public"—were convenient headquarters for candidates and for parties at their conventions. One reason why so many early National Conventions were held in Baltimore was that city-boosters there had built one of the grandest hotels in the country. Barnum's City Hotel was an elegant six-story building with two hundred apartments.

These National Party Conventions were even livelier and more festive than the smaller State Conventions. They provided a larger audience for rousing speeches by famous men. They whipped up enthusiasm for the party platform and for the party's candidates.

The colorful State Conventions and the wild celebrations at the National Conventions—all vividly reported in the newspapers—prepared people for a rip-roaring campaign.

Here was a new and very American public entertainment. It was a kind of national circus, far bigger than a county fair or a State fair. There were brass bands, barbecues, and lots of jokes and talks and stunts. Never anywhere else in the world had there been anything quite like an American national campaign.

Of course the national campaign had a serious purpose—to elect a President of the United States. When they created the office of President of the United States, the men who wrote the Constitution had, without ever intending it, paved the way for the new American party system. For the President was supposed to speak for *all* the people. Since he had to be elected every four years, this offered one regular occasion when the whole country had to worry about the same question: Who was the *man* best qualified to lead them?

On this question everybody could have an opinion. For everybody, whether or not he can read, or whether or not he is interested in politics, has an opinion about other men. As American politics became more and more democratic, as more and more people could vote, the personality of leaders became more and more important. A new type of man was put up for President.

The aristocratic members of the Virginia Dynasty—Washington, Jefferson, Madison, and Monroe—did not like to shake hands or kiss babies. Washington was a solemn man with a quick temper. He was not a good public speaker. Even his Farewell Address had not been spoken by him, but had been printed in a newspaper. Jefferson also was a poor speaker. John Adams and his son John Quincy Adams—of the Massachusetts Dynasty—were also aristocratic, dignified men who did not like crowds.

After 1828, when many more people had a voice in politics, men like these were no longer the best presidential timber. To sell a man to the American voters, he had to be popular. Or at least you had to be able to make him popular.

Andrew Jackson, who was elected in 1828, was the first of this new type of President. His father had come over from Ireland only two years before Andrew was born. Both his parents as well as his two older brothers had died before he was fifteen, and he never went to college. He was a self-made man. Settling in the fast-growing Western town of Nashville (even before Tennessee became a State), Jackson grew up with the place. He helped write the first Constitution of the State in 1796, then he represented Tennessee as Congressman and as Senator, and was a judge of the Supreme Court of the State. In 1804, with an impressive public career behind him, he "retired" to private life at the age of thirty-seven.

In the second war against Great Britain, the War of 1812, Jackson became a general. He was hailed as a hero when he defeated the British at New Orleans on January 8, 1815. This did not have any effect on the outcome of the war because two weeks before (although Jackson did not know it) a peace treaty had already been signed at Ghent in Belgium.

Jackson transformed American politics. Unlike Jefferson, who was a man of learning and who liked to speak of the international Republic of Letters, Jackson was proud of not being literary. He was not good at spelling, and once even said that he had no respect for a man who could think of only *one* way to spell a word!

Although Jackson was the first new-style President, the first campaign in the new style was the presidential election of 1840. When the Whig Party

The candidate Harrison, widely advertised as a simple backwoods farmer, actually lived in this grand mansion with a thousand acres of land. His father had been a Governor of Virginia.

held its National Nominating Convention in Harrisburg, Pennsylvania, on December 4, 1839, it passed up the able Senator Henry Clay of Kentucky because he had made too many enemies. Instead the Whigs chose a general, William Henry Harrison, although he had been nominated by them four years before and had lost. They thought he could win this time. His main qualification was that he had won a couple of battles against the Indians, and that he had very few enemies.

Since the Whigs had a reputation for being conservative and upper-crust, they had to make a special effort to appeal to the common people. For this purpose, Harrison was a good candidate. He had lived in the West a good deal, and had helped pass a law which gave land to Western farmers. The Whigs then nominated John Tyler of Virginia for Vice-President.

Against Harrison, the Democratic Party (the old party of Andrew Jackson) in their convention renominated Martin Van Buren of New York. Van Buren was a lawyer and an extremely clever politician, who had been Andrew Jackson's right-hand man. He was Vice-President under Jackson, and then served as President after defeating General Harrison in the election of 1836.

Oddly enough, the keynote of the campaign of 1840 was set by an anti-Harrison newspaper in Baltimore. What Harrison really wanted, they sneered, was not to be President at all, but simply to have a barrel of hard (alcoholic) cider to get drunk on, and a log cabin to live in. The Whigs now had their clue. They eagerly took up the cry: Hurrah for the log cabin and hard cider! Being an ordinary man who lived in a log cabin and liked to drink cider, they said, was no disgrace! On the contrary, that proved Harrison was a real man of the people.

They held a great rally in Baltimore on May 4, 1840. It opened with the firing of cannon. The Whigs boasted that 25,000 people marched in their parade and 75,000 stood by to watch. Eight log-cabin floats pulled by horses moved in the endless procession. Out of one log-cabin chimney came smoke (supposed to show that a squirrel was roasting inside) while several supporters kept drinking hard cider from the barrel at the cabin door. "An army of banners" waved in honor of Harrison. Thousands wore campaign buttons with Whig and Harrison slogans.

The log-cabin idea had great appeal. General Harrison had really been born of an old, well-to-do Virginia family, and he lived in a mansion. But his supporters soon invented a log cabin that he was supposed to have been born in.

Instead of arguments, Whig supporters of General Harrison shouted songs and slogans. The General had supposedly won his greatest victory against the Shawnee Indians at the Battle of Tippecanoe (a small creek that ran into the Wabash River). "Tippecanoe and Tyler Too!" became their battle cry. This was the most popular song of the campaign (sung to the tune of "Little Pig's Tail"):

The new style in Presidential campaigns (Baltimore, 1840).

What has caused the great commotion,
    motion, motion
  Our country through?
  It is a ball a rolling on.
For Tippecanoe and Tyler too—Tippe-
    canoe and Tyler too,
And with them we'll beat little Van, Van,
    Van,
Van is a used up man,
And with them we'll beat little Van.

Parading along while they sang this nonsense-song, men pushed huge balls—taller than a man. Sometimes a crowd would push their ball long distances, just to prove there *was* a ball "rolling on" for their hero. At the Harrison rally in Baltimore a crowd arrived with an enormous ball they had pushed with their own hands for over a hundred miles—all the way from Allegheny County in far western Maryland! Rallies all over were celebrated with tasty barbecues, washed down from free-flowing barrels of intoxicating cider.

Voters could not resist these appealing arguments. Harrison was elected, but he caught pneumonia within a month of his inauguration and died. Many people said the strain of the campaign had been too much for him.

These political high jinks looked pretty silly to people who came from countries where politics was the solemn preserve of the respectable few. Was this the curse of democracy? Or was it simply that a democratic country had to have its democratic politics? The people shared a good-natured enthusiasm for their country, for their party, and for their leaders. If they were not so solemn, they also were not so angry at their political opponents. If politics was a game, then both winners and losers were more likely to be good sports. The future of the nation, the prosperity of workers and businessmen, and the issues of peace and war might depend on who won or lost. But good-humored politics could remind all Americans of how much they had in common.

After Jackson, candidates for President were usually "men of the people." Often they were popular because they were military heroes. After "The Hero of New Orleans" there was General Harrison ("Hero of Tippecanoe"), General Zachary Taylor ("Hero of Buena Vista"), and General Franklin Pierce, who had led volunteers in Mexico. A Presidential candidate now was supposed to be an everyday man, as common as an old shoe. He might be "Old Hickory" (Andrew Jackson), or "The Farmer of North Bend" (Harrison), or "Old Rough and Ready" (Taylor), or "The Rail-Splitter" (Lincoln). If you expected your party to win, you had better choose someone whom you could imagine being born in a log cabin.

The ideal candidate did not always make an ideal President. The problems of the nation by 1828 were deep and complicated. Although there were many ties to hold people together, the United States was really beginning to come apart at the seams. The seams were the boundaries of the States. The new issues were too deep to be wished away with songs and slogans or to be washed away in hard cider. The campaign might be jolly. But worrisome problems faced a new President when he finally reached the White House. It would take more than songs and slogans to hold the young nation together.

PART FIVE

THE ROCKY ROAD

TO UNION

As the United States sprawled across the continent, the nation did not grow all in the same way or at the same pace. While some cities—Chicago, Omaha, Denver, and San Francisco—grew fast and prospered, others were left behind. They became ghost towns, or disappeared without a trace. The different States and different regions flourished or languished in various ways. Some people dreamed of gold and found it. Others found only rocks and disappointment. Some tried to raise crops which the soil would not nourish or where the rain did not come.

By the time of the Civil War, some regions of the United States were as different from others as, a century before, life in crowded, civilized Great Britain had been different from life in the far-off American colonies. Boston, New York, and Philadelphia already had universities and libraries and museums and a culture run by Cabots and Lawrences and Lowells and Peabodys and Livingstons and Rushes—proud "old" families. Life in the crude mining camps of Dead Man's Gulch or Virginia City was as different as possible from the ways of the elegant town houses of Charleston or New Orleans, or of the planters' mansions in Virginia.

Texas was actually a separate nation from 1836 to 1845. California, also, was briefly independent. The lonely wheat farmer or cattleman of the Great Plains of Nebraska or Iowa felt the hundreds of miles separating him from the lively crowds of Pittsburgh, Chicago, Milwaukee, or Omaha. There were many different American ways.

Could the Constitution that had been made to hold together thirteen seaboard States now bind a continent? Was it possible for a whole nation to be dedicated to the proposition that all men are created equal?

CHAPTER 23

Slavery Conquers the South

The Civil War was both the simplest and the most complicated event in American history. It was the simplest because the real issue can be summarized in one word: slavery. But it was the most complicated because, as Southerners still say, it was a "War Between the States."

The eleven seceding States, which made up the Confederate States of America, contained nine million people. On both sides there were many different kinds of people and many ways of life.

In the North there were many who did not want to abolish slavery, and in the South there were many who did. In the North were many people who did not care about slavery one way or another, and in the South were many people who did not own slaves and did not make their money from slavery.

Slavery did not belong in the United States. The puzzle, then, is not why there was so much trouble over slavery. The real puzzle is how slavery became so strong, and how some white Southern Americans (even if they did not themselves own slaves) came to believe it was the very foundation of their life. If we can understand this, then we may understand why there had to be a war against slavery in order to save the Union.

In ancient times slavery was found everywhere. When one people defeated another in war, the losers, instead of being massacred, were often enslaved and made to serve the winners. In the Middle Ages, too, slavery was widespread in Europe. But beginning in the sixteenth and seventeenth centuries, out-and-out slavery was gradually displaced. Twenty years before the Pilgrim Fathers sailed, an English judge said that "England was too pure an air for slaves to breathe in."

But slavery was destined to have a new life in the New World. For many white Europeans, America meant a new freedom. For many others—especially for Negroes brought from Africa—America meant a new slavery. Under the old system of empires, as we have seen, the European mother country wanted from her colonies the things she could not produce herself. In addition to gold and silver, these were products like tobacco, rice, indigo (a plant of the pea family that made a deep blue dye), cotton, and sugar cane—crops which grew only in a warm climate.

The climate of the new colonies in South America and the Caribbean was ideally suited for these tropical crops. But these particular crops needed lots of labor. Hard work in the hot sun did not appeal to men who had left Europe for a better life. It was not easy to find workers. The Portuguese in Brazil and

Loading plan for a ship which carried slaves from Africa to America.

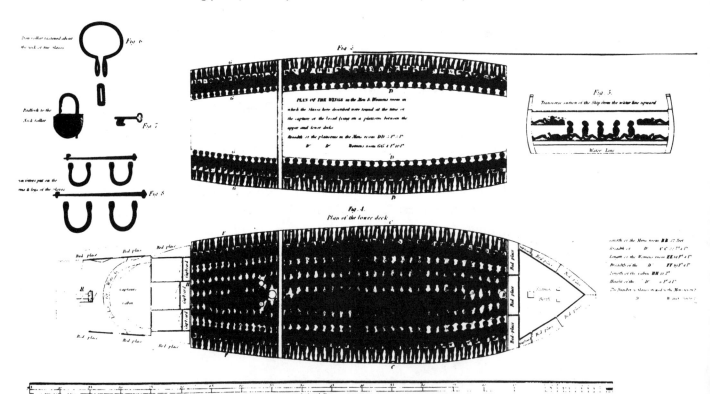

other colonists in Latin America solved their problem for a while by making slaves of the Indians. But there were not enough Indians. Harsh treatment, exhausting work, and diseases imported from Europe killed off many of them.

The Portuguese looked for other sources of labor. They began importing from Africa Negroes who had been sold into slavery by their tribal chiefs or who were captured by slave catchers. These unfortunate Negroes were stowed like livestock in ships which brought them across the Atlantic. Their misery was beyond our imagining, but since profits were high, the slave traders brought over these prisoners by the thousands. A full century before Captain John Smith landed at Jamestown in Virginia, there were parts of Brazil where there were twenty Negro slaves for every white worker.

The first Negroes, unwilling immigrants, were brought to Virginia from Africa in 1619. By the early eighteenth century Negro slaves were being imported into Virginia by the thousands. Year by year slavery was becoming more important in the life of the colony.

Thoughtful Southerners began to worry. Thomas Jefferson was especially concerned. When he made up the list of George III's crimes against mankind for the Declaration of Independence, the final item—the worst crime of all—was that the King had encouraged the slave trade. "He has waged cruel war against human nature itself, violating its most sacred rights of life and liberty in the persons of distant people who never offended him, captivating and carrying them into slavery in another hemi-sphere, or to incur miserable death in their transportation thither." But in order not to hurt the feelings of Southern slave owners or of Northern slave traders, this item was taken out before the Continental Congress adopted the Declaration.

Jefferson continued to worry about what slavery did to the slaveholder. He explained in his *Notes on Virginia* (1783) that every slaveholder became a tyrant, and his children learned bad habits. "The parent storms, the child looks on . . . puts on the same airs in the circle of smaller slaves, gives a loose to the worst of passions, and thus [is] nursed, educated, and daily exercised in tyranny." In Virginia, Jefferson already saw "an unhappy influence on the manners of our people produced by the existence of slavery among us."

After Eli Whitney made his simple new machine in 1793 for separating the cotton fuzz from the cotton seeds, cotton became the great crop of the South. The more important cotton became, the more important was slavery. Slaves were used to plant and cultivate and pick cotton, and to work the cotton gins. Now planters aimed "to sell cotton in order to buy Negroes—to make more cotton to buy more Negroes."

Southerners soon began to say, "Cotton is King." And Cotton was a very whimsical King! For the price of cotton depended not only on the weather and the size of the crop. It also depended on how much the cotton-cloth manufacturers in Birmingham, England, or in Lowell, Massachusetts, were willing to pay. People in the South could not imagine a world without cotton. It also

Abolitionists argued that slavery destroyed civilization by leading men to treat their fellows as if they were mere things. This advertisement for a Southern raffle announced that the prizes were a horse and a 20-year-old slave girl.

By 1831 so many people in Virginia were worried about slavery that the new Governor, who himself owned twelve slaves, tried to persuade the State legislature to make a plan for gradually abolishing slavery. The Virginia State legislature held a Great Debate on slavery, which lasted most of the month of January 1832. They offered arguments, for and against. All sorts of suggestions were made on how to abolish slavery or how to lessen its evils. On January 25 the legislature voted: 58 for abolishing and 73 for keeping slavery. It was a narrow margin. And it was a tragic mistake. It meant that if slavery was to be abolished in Virginia, it would have to be by force from the outside.

The importing of slaves from abroad had been prohibited by Congress beginning in 1808, the earliest time allowed by the Constitution. The British had abolished the slave trade all over their empire in 1807, and then abolished slavery itself in 1834. But slave trading still flourished inside the South.

Foreign travelers who came to the United States were shocked. In the "Land of the Free" there were more slaves than in all Europe. How could a free people tolerate a tyranny which the Old World had left centuries behind?

During the generation following the American Revolution, slavery had been abolished in most Northern States. Into his draft that later became the basis of the Northwest Ordinance of 1787, Jefferson had put a law forbidding slavery northwest of the Ohio River. In 1830, of the two million Negro slaves in the United States, nearly all were in the South. There they made up more than a

became harder and harder for them to imagine a world without Negro slaves.

Every year the Negro population in the South increased. In cotton-growing regions, Negroes began to outnumber whites. For example, in Tidewater Virginia east of the Blue Ridge Mountains, in 1830 the Negroes were in the majority by 81,000. When people in the South began to think about this, it terrified them. Wise men like Jefferson and Madison were convinced that in the long run you could not have a decent life for *anybody* where anybody else was not free. The American Colonization Society, headed by ex-President Madison, aimed to rid the country of slavery by gradually exporting all Negroes to Africa.

third of the population. Slavery, then, was mainly a Southern problem.

Why did not people in the South settle the problem for themselves? Ever since the American Revolution, some leading Southerners—like Jefferson and Madison and Chief Justice John Marshall—had seen that slavery was a dangerous evil. "I tremble for my country," warned Jefferson in 1783, "when I reflect that God is just; that his justice cannot sleep forever . . . the way [is] I hope preparing, under the auspices of heaven, for a total emancipation . . . with the consent of the masters, rather than by their extirpation."

Why didn't it happen that way, "with the consent of the masters"? There are a number of reasons. Southerners became accustomed to slavery. Most— perhaps as many as three-quarters—of the white people of the South never themselves owned a slave, and were not even members of a slave-owning family. But nearly everybody got tangled in the web of slavery.

Free white men did not want to work alongside slaves. Hard labor came to be "slave labor." Work took on the stigma of the slave. While cities sprouted elsewhere, the South for the most part remained a land of farms and plantations. Partly because there were fewer cities, opportunities were scarcer in the South. Very few new immigrants came from abroad to settle there. Because the South lacked immigrants, it lacked new ideas. It was often immigrants who wanted to shake things up, so they could have their chance. But no one shook up the South.

CHAPTER 24

The Splitting of the Nation

We will never know whether the South would have done its own job of housecleaning, whether it would have abolished slavery on its own. For things were happening outside the South which made it hard for Southerners to keep their heads.

After the Revolution, groups in Northern cities, especially in New England, formed clubs to fight slavery. They called themselves "abolitionists." They collected lots of unpleasant facts about slavery, put them in books and pamphlets and magazines, and sent them all over the country. Of course, there were plenty of unpleasant facts to be told— about the mistreatment of individual slaves, and the separation of Negro families.

Theodore Dwight Weld, a New England minister, started his career on a crusade against alcohol. Then, inspired by English abolitionists, he began to fight slavery. In 1839 he published *Slavery As It Is: Testimony of a Thousand Witnesses*, put together from items he had sifted from twenty thousand newspapers.

The book was a chamber of horrors. His purpose, Weld wrote, was to "see the inside of that horrible system of oppression which is enfibred with the heart strings of the South. In the advertisements for runaways we detect the cruel whippings and shootings and brandings, practiced on the helpless slaves. Heartsickening as the details are, I am thankful that God in his providence has put into our hands these weapons [these facts] prepared by the South herself, to destroy the fell monster."

Nearly everybody likes to read horror stories. The book sold for only 37½¢ a copy and nearly everybody could afford one. There was a bargain price of $25.00 per hundred for people who wanted copies to give away. The book spread all over the North. Within the first four months it sold 22,000 copies, within a year more than 100,000. Northerners now began to get their picture of the South from Weld's book and from others like it. When Charles Dickens, the English novelist, wrote his book about America he copied his stories about the South from *Slavery As It Is.*

In Weld's book Harriet Beecher Stowe found much of the ammunition for her own anti-slavery novel. While she was writing *Uncle Tom's Cabin,* she said, she used to sleep with Weld's book under her pillow. *Uncle Tom's Cabin* came out in March 1852. In the story the Christ-like Negro, Uncle Tom, finally is flogged to death by the brutal slave dealer, Simon Legree, because he won't give away the hiding place of two escaped slaves.

The book quickly sold more than 100,-000 sets of an expensive two-volume edition. When it too was put out in a single cheap volume for 37½¢, within a year it sold more than 300,000 copies. It was made into plays and musical comedies.

Uncle Tom side shows at fairs and circuses played up the scene of "Eliza Crossing the Ice" with her baby in her arms, and had Little Eva yanked up to heaven by pulleys. "Uncle Tom's Cabin played here last night," said one newspaper. "The bloodhounds were good." The book sold enormously in England. It was quickly translated into French, Italian, Dutch, Swedish, Danish, Flemish, Polish, and Magyar. In the German language alone there were more than forty different translations. *Uncle Tom's Cabin* became America's all-time, world-wide best seller.

Mrs. Stowe gave one of the first copies to her Congressman one day as he was about to board the train for Washington. He started reading the book on the train. The story was so sad that he began to cry. He attracted the attention of the other passengers as he wiped the tears from his face and blew his nose. To avoid embarrassment, he got off the train at the next stop, where he rented a hotel room and sat up all night finishing the book. There, in the privacy of his room, he could weep to his heart's content. Many other people, too, reported that the book had upset them, and there must have been thousands of tear-stained copies of *Uncle Tom's Cabin.*

It is possible that, without this book, Lincoln could never have been elected President. During the Civil War, Mrs. Stowe went to see President Lincoln. "Is this the little woman," Lincoln asked her, "whose book made such a great war?"

Many abolitionists were devout Christians. They believed that Jesus hated slavery. "Do unto others as you would have others do unto you." You do not want to be a slave yourself. What right, then, do you have to enslave others? Christianity, they said, was the religion of love—love for all your fellow men. The abolitionists wanted to preach love. But before very long they were also preaching hate.

It was easy enough to go from hating slavery to hating slaveholders. And easy enough, too, to go from hating slaveholding Southerners to hating all Southerners. Since abolitionists were more interested in horror stories than in statistics, they did not advertise the fact that most white Southerners were not slaveholders, and that many slaveholders were not cruel. Their picture of the South had no bright spots in it. If there was any virtue in the South, why had not Southerners already abolished this monstrous evil for themselves?

Beginning in the 1830's a rising flood of abolitionist literature covered the country. It awakened Northerners to the evils of slavery. It made them hate slavery. It made them hate slaveholders. It also made them lump together all people in the South as if all Southerners wanted slavery. More and more people in the North began to hate the South and to hate Southerners.

As Northern propagandists became more and more violent, more and more unreasonable, Southerners too became more and more unreasonable. As Northerners began to attack things about the South that were not really evil, Southerners replied by defending things about the South that were not really good. Instead of worrying over how to get rid of slavery, more Southerners began to worry over how to defend slavery, and the South and themselves, against outside attack. They stopped apologizing for slavery. They stopped saying that slavery was only a "necessary evil."

Leaders in the South began to change their tune. "Slavery is not an evil," declared the Governor of South Carolina in 1829. "On the contrary, it is a national benefit." A professor at the College of William and Mary wrote an influential book putting together the best arguments in favor of slavery.

One of the strongest supporters of slavery was Senator John C. Calhoun of South Carolina. He had been Secretary of War under Monroe, then was Vice-President of the United States, and was now the leading Southern thinker. "Many in the South," he said, "once believed that it [slavery] was a moral and political evil; that folly and delusion are gone; we see it now in its true light, and regard it as the most safe and stable basis for free institutions in the world."

Calhoun was supported by many others when he called slavery a "positive good." Southern ministers said the Bible required that the Negroes be slaves. Southern "scientists" said the Negroes were an inferior race—the product of a "separate creation" that God made in the beginning on the African continent. Southern historians said that the glories of Ancient Greece were possible only because the Greeks had lots of slaves. Astonishing nonsense was written by otherwise sane people—all to show that slavery was the greatest thing that had ever happened to the human race.

The most brilliant and most extreme of these defenders of slavery was a

Virginia lawyer, George Fitzhugh. Having traveled through the North, where he saw some miserable factory workers, Fitzhugh returned South a convinced pro-slavery man.

In his curious book, *Cannibals All!, or Slaves without Masters* (1857), he went even further than those who only said that slavery was a "positive good." According to him any "free" society—that is, any society without slaves—was evil, precisely because it did *not* have slaves. Factory owners in the North were "Cannibals All." That is, they ate up the lives of poor workers, who labored long years and then were thrown away when old or sick. For all practical purposes, according to Fitzhugh, Northern workers too were slaves, but they were "slaves without masters." Nobody was required to look after them, to see they were fed and clothed.

Slaves in the South, Fitzhugh said, were more lucky. They were slaves *with* masters. They had the best kind of social security. Whatever happened, it was not their worry. They did not have to pay any bills. They had no problem of unemployment. Slavery, as Fitzhugh described it, was a kind of socialism, where all property was put in the hands of the people (the white people) best qualified to use it, for the benefit of everybody, whites and Negroes. Three cheers for slavery!

Southerners now showed they were

Negro field hands as they were: A photograph on a South Carolina plantation, 1862.

just as clever as the Northerners in the great national competition in name-calling. When Northerners called all Southerners torturers and monsters in human form, Southerners answered by calling all Northerners cheating, stingy, money-grubbing Yankees. A Yankee, they said, was a man without a heart—or rather his heart was in his pocketbook. He understood nothing but money.

A pamphlet that circulated in the South after 1832 told about a Yankee who was sent to Hell. Before letting the Yankee in, the Devil put him on trial, and accused him of the following crimes: (1) cheating people by selling 497,368 wooden nutmegs, 281,532 cigars made of oak leaves, and 647 wooden clocks with no works in them, (2) stealing an old grindstone, smearing it over with butter, and then selling it as cheese, (3) selling to a pious old lady a worn pair of shoes represented to be the shoes of Saint Paul. The Yankee replied that in New England where he came from these were considered "the cutest tricks." They had delighted his father, who said they proved his son a genius. Even the Devil was disgusted! And he said that Yankees were a bigger nuisance than all the rest of the world put together.

Of course, both Northerners and Southerners were wrong when they said the people in the other region were evil. But they were right when they said that the United States was being separated

Negro slaves in the idealized view of an unidentified pro-slavery artist.

into two different nations.

There were really many Souths. There was the "Old South," including six States (Delaware, Maryland, Virginia, North Carolina, South Carolina, and Georgia) of the original thirteen. And then there was a newer South of nine other States where slavery was also permitted. Among these Florida, which for centuries had belonged to Spain and was finally admitted as a State in 1845, was a peculiar place. It had lots of jungles and everglades, where Indian tribes still roamed. The other new Southern States —Kentucky (admitted 1792), Tennessee (1796), Louisiana (1812), Mississippi (1817), Alabama (1819), Missouri (1821), Arkansas (1836), and Texas (1845)— were as much West as South. Situated on the western side of the Appalachian Mountains, they looked away from the Atlantic Ocean. Their superhighway was the Mississippi River. They were the goal of many new settlers, and they had much of the Western spirit.

The dignified old families of Virginia and the Carolinas looked down their noses at the crude backwoodsmen of Kentucky, Tennessee, and Alabama. In the Old South, gentlemen settled their quarrels in well-mannered duels arranged by seconds and held according to elaborate old rules, under the traditional Dueling Oaks. In the newer South, life was rough. Quarrels there were more likely to be settled by a free-for-all with the Bowie knife.

One thing drew all these States together. It was not so much that they were Southern States, but that they were *Slave* States. As Southerners began to boast of slavery, slavery began to dominate everything. To avoid the word "slavery," which freedom-loving men everywhere hated, Southerners began to call it their "Peculiar Institution." The Peculiar Institution was really making the South into a peculiar place.

To keep out abolitionist books and magazines, Southern States began stopping the United States mails. If a professor was suspected of not supporting slavery enthusiastically enough, he was fired. To prevent slave uprisings, Southerners wanted to arm every white man. Military academies flourished, but other kinds of schools and colleges and universities did not. Southerners began to be afraid of their own shadows. If you did not proclaim the virtues of slavery, you were probably an enemy or a traitor.

Southerners began to think they were a separate nation—which would stand or fall with slavery. Anyone who attacked slavery, they said, was attacking all the Southern people. Southerners became angrier and more passionate. Hate was brewing on all sides. Southerners began to shout: "Death to Abolitionists!"

Elijah Parish Lovejoy was a New Englander who studied to be a Presbyterian minister at Princeton, and then in 1833 settled in St. Louis, Missouri, where he began publishing a religious newspaper. Lovejoy was a fanatic. He was against lots of things—including alcoholic drinks, the Catholic Church, and slavery. He wrote strong words in his newspaper, which he sent down the Mississippi from St. Louis, Missouri, to serve the cause of abolition. But Missouri itself was a Slave State. In order to find a safer place for his newspaper, in 1836 he moved twenty-five miles up the river to Alton, Illinois, where slavery was not allowed. But the pro-slavery forces even reached up over the border. Lovejoy was in for serious trouble.

One Sunday morning his press, which had been brought up the river from St. Louis, arrived on the dock in Alton. Lovejoy was so religious that he would not do any work on Sunday, and he left the press unguarded on the river bank. That Sunday night somebody dumped it in the river. The decent citizens of Alton gave their own money to replace the press. But pro-slavery mobs destroyed Lovejoy's press again—and again.

Finally, on November 7, 1837, word spread that the Ohio Anti-Slavery Society had sent Lovejoy another press which had just arrived. Sixty young abolitionists from nearby towns gathered to defend the press. Merchants, expecting trouble, closed their stores and begged Lovejoy to leave town. He refused, saying he preferred to be a martyr. That night there was a battle at the warehouse where Lovejoy's new press was stored. An armed mob of pro-slavery men gathered, but the abolitionists' guard held them back. Then the pro-slavery forces began to set the warehouse on fire. When Lovejoy leaped out to prevent them, he was shot dead.

For abolitionists everywhere, Elijah Parish Lovejoy became a martyr. Pro-slavery men said he merely got what was coming to him.

Both sides were collecting their heroes and martyrs. It was becoming harder and harder to imagine that the peoples of the North and the South could be kept within a single nation.

CHAPTER 25

A National Tug-of-War

The powers of the national government were increasing. And the Slave States feared that those powers might be used to destroy slavery. The very same Northwest Ordinance of 1787 which had set up the Add-a-State Plan also had prohibited slavery in all the new States that would be carved from the territory northwest of the Ohio River.

When the Louisiana Purchase in 1803 added lands as large as the whole area of the original thirteen States, nervous Southern slave owners had more reason than ever to be fearful. What would happen when *those* lands were sliced up into new States? Would those States, too, be set up under some law that forbade slavery? If that should happen, then the Slave States which had once dominated the Union would become only a small minority. Then surely the new-style national government in Washington would no longer understand the South and its problems. Perhaps it would even launch a crusade against slavery and destroy the Peculiar Institution inside the original Southern States.

The only way to avoid this danger, Southern statesmen believed, was to be sure that the new States carved out of the West were equally balanced between Free and Slave. Then it would not matter so much how unevenly the population grew or how many more new Northern Congressmen might come into the House of Representatives. In the Senate, where each State had its two votes—no more and no less—Slave States still would be able to block any threatening laws. In this way the South could actually use the Add-a-State Plan to preserve slavery.

The story of how new States were added in the early nineteenth century reads like a tug-of-war. Each side added one whenever the opposite side added one. By the end of 1819, there were twenty-two states in the Union, and the sides were precisely even—eleven Slave States against eleven Free States. The population of the whole country had grown to nearly ten million. Since the North was growing faster than the South, there were about a half-million more people in the North. This meant that in the House of Representatives the North had 105 members against only 81 for the South. But in the Senate, of course, the two sides were still even.

When the Territory of Missouri applied to Congress for Statehood in 1819, the South held its breath and prepared for its first great struggle to defend slavery. Louisiana, admitted as a State in 1812, had been the first one carved out of the Louisiana Purchase. But Louisiana, where slavery had long existed, was plainly Southern. There was no question about its being a Slave State. Missouri, now, was quite another matter. For Missouri was located squarely in the middle, halfway between the north-

ern and the southern boundaries of the newly purchased West. Was Missouri to be Slave or Free?

In Congress, then, the battle lines were drawn. Some Southerners already believed they were in a life-and-death struggle. If they let Missouri go Free, the Union would surely be flooded by still more and more Free States. Then it was only a question of time until the national government would abolish slavery everywhere. A new bitterness entered the halls of Congress. Northern Congressmen argued that to allow slavery into the West would be a national disgrace. As the debate went on, it simply confirmed the fears of Southerners that the Free States were out to destroy slavery, and with it the South.

The "Missouri Compromise," which Congress passed in 1820 after a whole year of debate, was not so much a compromise as a stalemate. Following the rules of the North-South tug-of-war which had already been going on for at least twenty years, each side added one State to its team. Missouri was admitted as a Slave State, while, to balance it, Maine was admitted as a Free State. At the same time the law drew a line through all the rest of the lands of the Louisiana Purchase (at 36° 30′, extending the southern boundary of Missouri) and declared that slavery would be *excluded* north of that line.

Although people at the time called it a compromise, it was not really like the compromises made by the framers of the Constitution in 1787. Those earlier compromises—for example, the one between the large and small States—were designed to give each side on every question part of what it wanted, so that everybody could consider that question settled and move on to other things. But slavery was a different kind of question. For both sides it was all-or-nothing. Both sides were simply biding their time.

Far-sighted men saw that the Missouri Compromise was nothing more than a truce which announced the opening of a fight to the finish. The aged Thomas Jefferson, retired at Monticello on his Virginia mountaintop, was saddened. It was, he said, "a fire-bell in the night . . . the [death] knell of the Union." John Quincy Adams saw it as "a title-page to a great tragic volume."

If the nation had not been growing and moving west so fast, the truce between North and South might have lasted longer. The next crisis came over Texas. Stephen Austin started an American settlement out there in the year after the Missouri Compromise. He was so successful that he soon attracted thousands of immigrants from the United States to settle in this Mexican territory. Austin was a versatile young man who had been born in Virginia, had attended Transylvania College in Lexington, Kentucky, and had lived in Missouri, Arkansas, and Louisiana. He had run a store, had directed a bank, edited a newspaper, and officered the militia, and he was a good-natured dictator.

The House of Representatives in 1822, as painted by the versatile Samuel F. B. Morse (who besides being a notable artist also invented the telegraph and the Morse Code). Here were heard some of the bitterest debates over slavery.

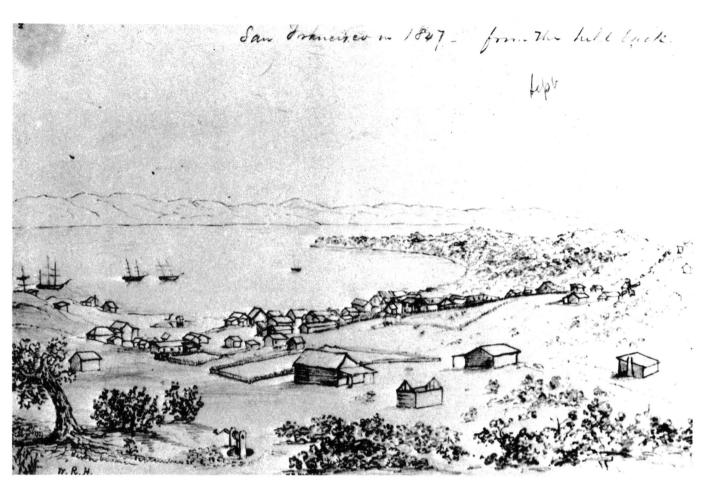

In 1847, before the Gold Rush, San Francisco was a mere village.

But he was a pro-slavery man, and he protected slavery in Texas.

Then in 1836, after their valiant defense of the Alamo and a victory at San Jacinto where they captured the Mexican general, the people of Texas declared their independence from Mexico. Now that Texas, on the very border of the United States, was an independent country settled and run by people from the United States, it was only a question of time until its people asked to join the Union. Texas was so big that there was no telling how many new States might be carved from her territory. And all Texas was slave country. It is not surprising, then, that when the people of Texas asked to become part of the United States and the proposal came up in Congress, Northerners again and

again voted it down. Texas, they said, was nothing but a slave-owners' clever plot to smuggle a lot of new Slave States into the Union.

For years the Northern States managed to keep Texas out of the Union. Texas was drawing the country's energy away from all other questions. At the time of the presidential election of 1844, the Texas question was more alive than ever. The popular desire for compromise was so great that the Democratic Party actually refused to nominate their best-known leader, Martin Van Buren, who had already been President once. For Van Buren had said he was against annexing Texas.

Instead, for the first time in American history, a party nominated a "dark horse," a man who was not nationally known and whom few had imagined as a candidate. He was James K. Polk, once governor of Tennessee, and a loyal Democrat. The Whigs, running the famous Henry Clay as their candidate, ridiculed the Democratic choice of a man who was unknown. It happened that earlier that year the polka had become the most popular dance in Washington. "The *Polk*-a dance," they said, "will now be the order of the day. It means two steps *backward* for one in advance."

But the Whigs were wrong, and Polk carried the day. Polk had a formula for compromise. His word was: *Expansion!* To annex Texas all by itself seemed a menace—at least to the North. But if at the same time you annexed the vast Oregon Territory, which stretched far up into the Northwest, you had something to give the North in return. That was Polk's platform. Expand everywhere at once, and then there would be something for everybody. Anyway, the very thought of stretching the nation all the way to the Pacific was exhilarating. Perhaps the nation could be united simply by marching westward together. In a divided nation, growth itself could be a kind of compromise.

And so it happened. In 1845, Texas finally was admitted as a State of the Union. The law also provided that, with the consent of Texas, not more than four additional States might some time be carved from her territory, and that the Missouri Compromise line would extend north over Texas. That was something for the South. Later that year, living up to his campaign promise, Polk claimed for the United States the whole vast Oregon Territory, which we had been sharing with Great Britain. That was something for the North.

Polk at first demanded a stretch which reached all the way up to the borders of Alaska (then owned by Russia), but he finally settled on the forty-ninth parallel, which simply extended to the Pacific the northern boundary of the rest of the nation. Now both North and South had gained large territories. New States out there would eventually add to the strength of both sides.

But for those who wanted to cement the nation and to quiet the conflict between North and South, Polk's program actually created some new problems. Mexico considered the annexation of Texas (which she said was still a part of Mexico) to be an act of war by the United States, and anyway she disputed the boundary of Texas.

Meanwhile, a new trouble spot had developed in California (still part of Mexico), where settlers from the United States were beginning to move in. The Mexican government wanted to keep all Americans out of California, for fear that it would go the way of Texas. Mexico threatened war. But Northerners feared that victory over Mexico might secure still more territory to make new Slave States in the Southwest. Over Northern opposition, Polk led us into war against Mexico.

Northern fears proved to be well founded. In 1848, after United States forces had captured Mexico City (as was expected), the helpless Mexican government gave up all claims to Texas and agreed that Texas belonged to the United States. And that was only a beginning. Before the war, Mexico had owned all the land in the Far West that reached up to Oregon from the present Mexican border, and all the lands between the Pacific Ocean and Texas. The defeated Mexico now handed all that vast tract over to the victorious United States. That included the present California and New Mexico, and most of the present States of Utah, Nevada, Arizona, and Colorado.

These lands (including Texas) were larger than the whole Louisiana Purchase or all the original United States when the Constitution was adopted. This should have satisfied any American's yen for expansion. Yet when President Polk asked the Senate to approve the Mexican treaty that gave the United States all this, a dozen Senators voted against it because they wanted to annex the *whole* of Mexico! But the treaty passed.

It took no prophet to predict that more Western lands spelled more trouble. Every new acre was a new subject for a debate—or rather, for a quarrel. Southerners did not bother to study whether these new lands were really places where slavery and the plantation system would flourish. They were thinking only about spreading the Slave Power.

In the bitterly divided nation, every stroke of national good luck became a new cause of discontent. Each section was afraid the other would somehow gain more.

By an astonishing coincidence, gold was discovered in California in the very same year when Mexico handed over

---

The discovery of gold in northern California in 1848 drew settlers by the thousands, so that California was ready for Statehood two years later. This print shows San Francisco in 1851.

California to the United States. Gold-rushers flocked to California by the tens of thousands. These people, too, would soon want to come into the Union as a State. But in 1849 there were thirty States altogether, and the national score-card showed fifteen Slave States against fifteen Free States. To admit the State of California, as its people requested in 1850, would break the tie.

How long could the national balancing act go on? The United States was now stretched from ocean to ocean. The boundaries on the north and the south with Canada and Mexico were now substantially settled. The slavery issue could no longer be indefinitely postponed by promising outside neighboring territory to the North or to the South. Now the conflict had to take place *inside* the established boundaries of the nation.

Early in 1850, when the Senate met to decide the future of the territories taken from Mexico, the air was more than ever charged with fear and hate. Senator Calhoun from South Carolina made impossible demands. He actually had prepared a fantastic constitutional amendment providing for the election of two Presidents—one from the Slave States and one from the Free States. Senator Seward of New York called all compromise "essentially vicious," and refused even to appeal to the Constitution. He preferred a "higher law."

Leading the forces of conciliation was the energetic Senator Henry Clay of Kentucky, who had a plan. By nature a compromiser, he had the half-hearted support of lots of people, and the enthusiasm of very few. The bundle of laws which later became the "Compromise" of 1850 was sponsored by this man whom the nation had already three times defeated for its President. He offered something for everybody, but he left the main question unanswered. California was to be admitted as a Free State (something for the North). A strong Fugitive Slave Act would protect the right of Southern slaveowners to recapture slaves who had escaped to the North (something for the South). The slave trade was abolished in the District of Columbia, where the city of Washington was located (something for the North). But slavery was still protected there (something for the South).

The biggest question—whether all the rest of the vast new areas taken from Mexico would be Free or Slave—was left unsettled. Clay's compromise postponed the answer. He provided that the people of those States should in the future decide that for themselves when they applied to join the Union. This scheme was called "popular sovereignty" by those who admired it, and "squatter sovereignty" by those who did not. It held the seeds of civil war.

Short-sighted optimists called this a "final" settlement. But a second look showed that it only put off the evil day. As usual in the years before a war, each side accused the other of acts of aggression.

Both sides were right. Both freedom and slavery *were* aggressive. The champions of each rightly believed that each must expand or die. Pro-slavery forces in the South would not leave well enough alone. They had lost California, but that simply stirred them to push harder on

"Border Ruffians" was the name given to pro-slavery men like these who invaded Kansas from Missouri in order to vote illegally or to terrorize the anti-slavery settlers.

the next round.

The next round came sooner than most people expected—in 1854. People had been moving into the lands left over from the Louisiana Purchase. It was time for them to become Territories, and to provide for their eventually becoming States. Would they be Free or Slave? Senator Stephen A. Douglas of Illinois took the lead. He argued that it was best for Congress to refuse to answer the most difficult question. He argued that the idea of "popular sovereignty" should extend even into those northern regions. Let slavery be decided "democratically" —by the people who actually lived

there at the time they applied to become States.

Douglas, who was a clever politician, actually managed to get his Kansas-Nebraska Bill passed in 1854, after months of debate. It *seemed* to keep an even balance between Slave and Free by allowing future new States to decide for themselves. Actually it was a great victory for the South. For the whole Kansas-Nebraska Territory was north of the old freedom-line drawn in the Missouri Compromise back in 1820. "Popular sovereignty" now opened those lands to slavery.

If Senator Douglas thought his plan

could somehow settle the slavery issue and hold the Union together, he was soon proved wrong. His Kansas-Nebraska Act aroused a strong new political force, organized in that same year of 1854. It was called the Republican Party. And it drew together people who opposed allowing slavery into the new West.

Senator Douglas had simply marked off a new battleground. This was no longer a battleground of mere words. New Englanders formed Emigrant Aid Societies and collected money to send large numbers of anti-slavery people into Kansas to keep it a Free State. Southerners sent in their pro-slavery settlers. "Popular sovereignty" became an invitation to civil war. Kansas soon had two rival governments, one anti-slavery and the other pro-slavery.

By mid-1856, American citizens in Kansas were killing one another over slavery. On May 21, pro-slavery forces, led by the Southern Colonel Jefferson Buford and his Kickapoo Rangers, captured, sacked, and burned the anti-slavery town of Lawrence, Kansas. Then John Brown, who believed he had been sent by God to destroy slavery and slave

A constitutional convention in Kansas Territory in 1855. The temper of the times is symbolized by the rifles close at hand.

CONSTITUTIONAL CONVENTION, KANSAS TERRITORY. [SEE PAGE 14.]

owners, took revenge with his four sons and other anti-slavery men. In another Kansas town, Brown's party executed five pro-slavery men in the Massacre of Pottawatomie. Now less than ever could the Congress of the United States escape the great issue.

When the question came up of admitting Kansas as a State, there was not *one* Kansas government but *two!* Each claimed to be the true and only government of Kansas. Kansas would not finally be admitted as a Free State until 1861 when the whole nation was preparing for war. Back in 1856 no one was sure whether it would be Free or Slave. But everyone called it "Bleeding Kansas."

The spirit of violence reached into the very halls of the Senate. While the Kansas issue was debated, Senator Charles Sumner of Massachusetts attacked the South and several of its Senators with every insulting word he could command. Representative Preston S. Brooks of South Carolina (the nephew of a Senator from that State who had been insulted) avenged the honor of the South—not with words, but with a cane. On May 22, 1856, Brooks came up to Senator Sumner while he was seated in the Senate Chamber and beat him senseless. Brooks was reelected by his constituency, and became a Southern hero. Senator Sumner never regained his health. He became a Northern martyr, and for several years his empty seat in the Senate was a vivid symbol that many Northern and Southern leaders were no longer on speaking terms.

We can easily be misled if we think that the years from 1820 to 1860 were years of compromise. The Missouri Compromise (1820), the Compromise of 1850, and the Kansas-Nebraska Act (1854)—none of these was truly a compromise. Each was a truce in a war to the death. The issue was not to be settled by words and votes. The fate of slavery would be settled on the battlefield.

CHAPTER 26

The First Shot Is Fired

As late as 1860, some people thought the nation might avoid a civil war. Even if Americans could not agree on the issues, maybe they still could agree on a man. Maybe an American President— one man elected by all the people and speaking for all the people—could save the day. Maybe the right man could hold the Union together.

Until then the political parties had, on the whole, been *national.* The old Federalist Party of George Washington and the Republican Party of Thomas Jefferson had both drawn supporters from all parts of the country. The new Democratic Party which had elected Presidents Jackson and Van Buren and Polk, and the Whig Party which had elected Presidents William Henry Harrison and John Tyler and Zachary Taylor—both these parties, too, gathered votes from North, South, East, and West.

When the Presidential election year of 1860 approached, the Democratic Party was still a national party. The tug-of-war was going on *inside* the party, but the Democrats still had support all over the country. If the political battles could only be fought out *inside* the parties! Then the compromises would be made at the Party Conventions. And then perhaps the politicians from the North and the South could be held together (as politicians often are) simply by hope for the rewards of a political victory. Maybe the game of politics, which Americans had learned to play so good-naturedly, might take the place of the bloody game of war.

When the political parties met in their National Conventions during the spring and summer of 1860, it quickly appeared that politics was not the road to reunion. As soon as the Democratic Party opened its regular convention at Charleston, South Carolina, Southerners demanded that the party should favor protecting slavery in the territories. When Northerners voted them down at this point, delegates from eight Southern States left the convention. Even then, and after fifty-seven ballots, the convention still could not agree on a candidate for President. The convention broke up, and after

A cadet dance at West Point in September 1859. A year and a half later these young officers would be facing their classmates across the trenches.

FREE SPEECH, FREE HOMES, FREE TERRITORY.

PROTECTION TO AMERICAN INDUSTRY

FOR PRESIDENT
ABRAHAM LINCOLN
OF ILLINOIS

FOR VICE PRESIDENT
HANNIBAL HAMLIN
OF MAINE

A handsome, clean-cut Lincoln with his running mate, Hamlin of Maine. Lincoln did not grow his familiar beard until after his election as President. He said it was to please a certain little girl, but it may have been to give him the feel and the look of mature wisdom.

a month it met again (without the delegates of the eight Southern States). Then yet another group of Southerners withdrew. What was still left of the Democratic Party, of course, was not a national party at all. It nominated Senator Stephen A. Douglas of Illinois.

The Southern Democratic seceders gathered at Richmond, Virginia. There they named their own candidate, John C. Breckenridge of Kentucky, who was then Vice-President of the United States. He believed in protecting slavery, and he thought States had a right to secede. The damage was done! Even "national" political parties were no longer national.

The other main party in the election of 1860 was only six years old. The Republican Party had been founded for the very purpose of opposing the spread of slavery. It was the anti-slavery party of the West and the North. Still vainly hoping for some national appeal, the new Republicans named one of the most conservative men they could find in their party. He had not made any radical statements, and he sounded like the soul of easygoing common sense. His nickname was "The Rail-Splitter" and his name was Abraham Lincoln, of Illinois.

It was a stroke of rare good luck that Lincoln happened to be there at that moment. There had never been a better symbol of all America. Lincoln's own life was a capsule history of the whole nation. His restless family had come from England to New England and then to Pennsylvania. Lincoln's great-grandfather had lived in Virginia, where he had five sons. Four of these moved on to Kentucky, Tennessee, and Ohio. In 1782, Lincoln's own grandfather had gone west to Kentucky where, four years later, he was killed by Indians while clearing his farmland in the forest. There Abraham's father was raised and there the future President was born in 1809.

Unlike other "log-cabin" candidates before him, Lincoln really was born in a log cabin. When he was only seven his family moved again—on to Indiana. And when he was twenty-one he moved with them once more, still farther west, to Illinois. Working his way up in the world, he did a little of everything. He built a flatboat and navigated it down the Mississippi to New Orleans. He did a little surveying, managed a mill, ran a country store, served as a village postmaster, and was elected captain of the militia that chased Chief Black Hawk and his Indians back into the Wisconsin wilderness.

Lincoln educated himself, and made himself into a lawyer who was especially successful before juries. But his political career had been brief and not impressive. After serving in the Illinois legislature he had one term in Congress, where he opposed the Mexican War. Then he was defeated for the United States Senate by the much better-known Stephen A. Douglas.

Lincoln had a magic in his speech. With his slow backwoods drawl, using the simple words of the Bible, he uttered the wisdom of a cracker-barrel philosopher. He sometimes told slightly vulgar jokes, and yet he had the uplift-power of a first-class preacher. He spoke the way the average man could imagine himself speaking.

On the slavery issue Lincoln was firm, but he was no fire-eater. He was no abolitionist. In his debates against Douglas, when both were running for the Senate in 1858, he showed that he was about as conservative as an anti-slavery man could be. He tried to narrow down the whole slavery question simply to preventing slavery from spreading westward into the territories. The Founding Fathers, he explained, in their Northwest Ordinance of 1787 had prohibited slavery in what was then *their* West. Now, he said, to be true to their ideals, Americans must also keep slavery out of the newer West.

Himself of Southern ancestry, he did not hate the South. He believed in making every possible concession—short of allowing the spread of slavery. If anyone could have held the Union together, it would have been Lincoln. If an Abraham Lincoln—with Lincoln's shrewdness, with Lincoln's charity, with his generous understanding of the South and its problems, with his feeling for compromise—could not do it, the Union was surely beyond the help of politics.

The fateful presidential election of November 1860 confirmed widespread suspicions that there were no longer *national* parties. It convinced the South that their hope was not in words but in weapons. From ten Southern States, Lincoln received not a single electoral vote. In the Electoral College, Lincoln

A Southern view of Lincoln aided by the Devil. Even Lincoln's desk has cloven hoofs, and Lincoln himself is casually using the Constitution for a footstool.

carried all eighteen Free States, Breckenridge carried eleven Slave States, Douglas carried only Missouri (and also received a minority of New Jersey's split votes), and John Bell, a compromise candidate from Tennessee, carried three border Slave States. Although Lincoln easily won in the Electoral College (with 180 votes against 123 for all the others), he was not the choice of the majority of the American people. Lincoln received less than 40 percent of the popular vote. The other candidates all together had received nearly a million votes more than Lincoln. Lincoln had won, but the Union was in new peril.

When word of Lincoln's election reached South Carolina, the State seceded from the Union. She was quickly joined from the lower South by six other States: Mississippi, Florida, Alabama, Georgia, Louisiana, and Texas. Each declared its own independence. Then their delegates met in Montgomery, Alabama, in February 1861, even before Lincoln was inaugurated. They wrote a new constitution for the Confederate States of America and elected Jefferson Davis their first President.

For them, the United States was now

a foreign nation. The seceded States therefore could no longer allow the United States to keep its arsenals and forts inside their borders. Using their own State troops, they at once began seizing federal posts. To avoid bloodshed, the United States troops withdrew to one of their strongest positions, a place in Charleston Harbor called Fort Sumter.

As soon as Lincoln was inaugurated on March 4, 1861, he had to make one of the great decisions in American history. Should he let the South take Fort Sumter and go its own way? That would mean no civil war. But it would also mean the end of the Union. Or should he reinforce the federal forts in the South, prepare for war, and lead a fight that might go on for years to keep all the States inside one great nation?

Lincoln decided to stand firm for the Union. He would fight if necessary, but he would let the South fire the first shot. He notified South Carolina that he was sending supplies to Fort Sumter. South Carolina then decided to take the fort before it was reinforced. At 4:20 A.M. on April 12, 1861, Confederate General P. G. T. Beauregard, a West Point graduate who had once fought for the Union in the Mexican War, began bombarding Fort Sumter from the Charleston shore batteries. At 2:30 P.M. the next afternoon Major Robert Anderson, also a West Point graduate who had fought alongside Beauregard in Mexico, surrendered the fort. No one had been wounded, but war had begun. The first, the quickest, and the most bloodless battle of the war was over. But it was no fair sample of what was to come.

CHAPTER 27

Everybody's War ᘒᕲᘒᕲᘒᕲᘒᕲᘒᕲᘒᕲᘒᕲᘒᕲᘒ

This American Civil War was not quite like any war that had ever happened before. Half a nation fought against the other half over the freedom of a small minority. This itself was something new. It was as new, as strenuous, and as unpredictable as everything else in America. Leaving over 600,000 dead, the Civil War would be the bloodiest in all American history—and the bloodiest war in the whole world during the nineteenth century. Of every ten men who fought, four became casualties. No other modern nation paid so high a price to hold itself together.

Southerners did not see themselves simply as slave owners fighting to preserve their property, or as rebels trying to tear the Union apart. Instead they imagined they were fighting the American Revolution all over again. White Southerners, they said, were oppressed by Yankee tyrants. Men of the South were now playing the role of the gallant American colonists. Northerners were the oppressive British, and Abraham Lincoln was another George III. If the British government had no right to force American colonists to stay inside their empire, why did the United States government have any right to force Southern States to stay inside the Union?

Southerners said they were fighting for self-government. One flaw in this argument was that it left out the whole question of slavery. Self-government—*for* whom, and *by* whom? In 1860 there were nearly four million slaves in the Southern States. White Southerners who said they were fighting for their own right to govern themselves were also fighting *against* the right of Negroes to govern themselves. Of course, Fitzhugh and Calhoun and other defenders of slavery had not seen it quite that way. The Negro, they said, had no right to govern himself. Self-government was for white people only.

When Southerners said that all they wanted was to secede from the Union, they also gave themselves a military advantage. To win their point all they had to do was to declare their independence and to go their own way. On the other hand, the North would have to *force* the Southern States to obey the Union. The North would have to invade the South, occupy it, and subjugate it. The North had to attack.

At the beginning, many Northerners hopefully called it "the six months' war." They expected it to be over in short order. For the North seemed stronger in every way. Also they had been taught that the attacking army always had a great advantage. The textbooks the generals had studied when they were cadets at West Point explained that the way to win a war was to concentrate your forces on one or two points, and attack. Meanwhile the defenders would be weaker, because they would have to spread out

their forces to protect against lots of possible assaults.

The old-fashioned weapons gave almost no advantage to the defenders. For the old smoothbore flintlock musket (which was standard equipment in the British army during the Revolution and in European armies even afterward) was inaccurate, it had a short range, and it was slow to reload. That meant that the attacking forces could come very close before the defenders could shoot them down, and most of them would get through before they could be hit. If, as Northern generals at first imagined, the North could only keep the advantage of the attack, they could win a few decisive battles, capture the enemy capital, and then the war would be over.

These generals were wrong. The war lasted four blood-soaked years. This new warfare would be as different from earlier American wars as an elephant is different from a mosquito.

A number of great changes made the difference. During the American Revolution, as we have seen, while the standard British weapon was the flintlock musket, many American backwoodsmen had begun using the rifle. But it was not until the Civil War that the rifle became the standard American army weapon. The textbooks which the Civil War generals had read at West Point came from the earlier age of the smoothbore flintlock.

The rifle was so called because the inside of its barrel was "rifled"—cut with spiral grooves. Then when the bullet was pushed out it was set spinning. This gave it a longer range (500 yards instead of 50 yards) and a much more accurate aim. Another improvement was the "caplock," which used a new chemical (fulminate of mercury) enclosed in a cap to make the explosion that sent the bullet. The caplock was reliable even when the old flintlock—which struck a piece of flint against steel to make a spark—would not have worked because of wet weather. Also the old muskets had been "muzzle-loaders," but the new rifle was a "breech-loader." This meant it loaded from the back near the trigger, which was much more convenient and quicker. There were even some rifles which were automatic. A single clip of bullets would fire many shots.

These new weapons gave a great new advantage to the defenders. In the old-fashioned war, a soldier was expected to carry on him all the ammunition he could use in a battle. The old muskets were so slow to load that it took some time before he could use up his ammunition. But with the fast-loading new rifles, the soldier could not keep shooting very long unless new supplies were being constantly brought up to him. This made some troublesome new problems—especially for the generals on the attack. To move ammunition became as important as to move men.

Now the defenders, with their accurate long-range rifles, sat protected behind battlements in well-supplied forts. Now they could pick off the attackers before these even came close. They could fire quickly again and again. But the attacking force was on the move. If they stopped to reload they were sitting ducks.

No more would armies confront each other in solid ranks. Everybody had to

VOLUNTEERS WANTED!

AN ATTACK UPON WASHINGTON ANTICIPATED!!

THE COUNTRY TO THE RESCUE!

A REGIMENT FOR SERVICE

UNDER THE FLAG  OF THE UNITED STATES

IS BEING FORMED IN JEFFERSON COUNTY.

☞ **NOW IS THE TIME TO BE ENROLLED!**

Patriotism and love of Country alike demand a ready response from every man capable of bearing arms in this trying hour, to sustain not merely the existence of the Government, but to vindicate the honor of that Flag so ruthlessly torn by traitor hands from the walls of Sumter.

RECRUITING RENDEZVOUS

Are open in the village of WATERTOWN, and at all the principal villages in the County, for the formation of Companies, or parts of Companies. ☞ Officers to be immediately elected by those enrolled.

WATERTOWN, APRIL 20, 1861. WM. C. BROWNE, Col. Comd'g 35th Regiment.

Ingalls, Brockway & Beebee, Printers, Reformer Office, Watertown.

A Northern recruiting poster dated only eight days after the firing on Fort Sumter.

take cover. Attackers had to spread out into small parties of skirmishers to make more dispersed targets. Now the "Indian" tactics, which Americans had tried against the British in the Revolution, would become common. But attacking soldiers now made instant fortifications—of logs, bales of hay, rocks, anything in sight—so they could pile their ammunition beside them and get some of the advantages of defenders.

Most important, they learned to make the earth itself into a fort by using the spade. This was the beginning of modern trench warfare. In the old days, generals thought it was cowardly for a

Federal troops destroying a Southern railway bridge.

soldier to hide in a hole in the ground. Now the soldier had no choice. When General Robert E. Lee ordered his men in the Army of Northern Virginia to work hard at digging trenches, at first they laughed at him as their "King of Spades." But they soon thanked him for giving them protection against enemy rifles. The axe and the spade were now as important as the gun. One man in a hole with an artillery battery behind him was worth three in the open.

The attacking army, then, had to carry enormous supplies of ammunition and had to build its own fortifications as it advanced. The railroad, which had never been used much in wars before, was now a great help. But once the supplies left the rails, they still had to be carried by horse or mule over bumpy roads and through mud.

In this kind of warfare, railroads were life lines. They were slow and hard to build, but quick and easy to cut. If you could cut the enemy's rails, he would eventually have to stop shooting. The Civil War therefore became more and more a war aimed at the enemy's communication lines. The first Battle of Bull Run (July 1861) was still very much like the old-fashioned warfare, with solid lines of soldiers standing up against each other to fight a "decisive" battle. By the time of the Battle of Petersburg three years later, the Union army was aiming at the Confederate railroads.

The new kind of warfare was a war of exhaustion. It was not enough to cut off the enemy's supplies by railroad. You also had to prevent his bringing in supplies by water. The South, as we have seen, was blessed with many rivers. At first it seemed that the Mississippi would be a God-given supply line behind the whole South.

But early in the war this hope was blasted when a bold move by the astonishing David Glasgow Farragut captured New Orleans for the Union. Farragut, the son of a naval officer, had been commissioned a midshipman at the age of nine, and had seen action in the War of 1812 when he was only eleven. His orders commanded him first to capture the two forts at the mouth of the Mississippi which protected New Orleans. But he disregarded orders and at one blow seized New Orleans itself by racing past the two forts (losing only three of his seventeen ships). Farragut took the city on April 26, 1862, almost before anyone knew he was in the neighborhood. Now the South could not bring in supplies from the Gulf of Mexico for its troops in the West.

The ocean and the Gulf of Mexico surrounded the Southern States. With several other good ports besides New Orleans, the South still had highways to the world. The North therefore had to block up the other Southern ports if the South was to be strangled. The South did wonders with its few ships by shielding them with iron and equipping them with steam-driven propellers. These had an advantage against old wooden sailing vessels similar to that which the new firearms had against the old. The new ironclad ships gave a great new advantage to the defense. Still the scores of Northern ships offshore harassed merchant vessels and kept them from reaching Southern ports.

The war of exhaustion hit everybody in the South, civilians as well as the military. The same ships that would have brought arms and ammunition to the armies also would have brought machinery for the factories and food and clothing and medical supplies for all. The Northern blockade against the South worked slowly but it worked surely. People called it the "Conda" after the Anaconda, the huge boa constrictor snake that kills its prey by squeezing.

The war of exhaustion was slow. It was not won by a few knockout blows like the Battle of Waterloo, but by deprivation and strangulation and starvation. As the struggle dragged on into its fourth year, European experts, who had never seen this kind of war before, began to think it was not war at all. One Prussian general sneered that he would not even study the battles of the war because they were nothing but "the combats of two armed mobs." Another Old World critic compared the North and South to two lunatics playing chess—both knew a few moves, yet neither understood the game.

But this kind of war was no longer a game. The old rules of war which the generals had learned at West Point were no longer of much use. It was everybody's war, with no holds barred. The winning generals turned out to be those, like U. S. Grant, who had never believed the old rules, or those, like William T. Sherman, who were good at forgetting them.

The long war was enough to try anybody's patience. Northern generals devised shortcuts. Of course, you could exhaust your enemy by cutting off his supplies, by wearing him down in one place after another. And that was Lincoln's large strategy. Surround the South, cut off the South from the world and the world's supplies, and then the South could not live. You could exhaust your enemy, too, simply by destroying him—by burning his crops and houses and destroying his factories, by tearing up his railroads and blowing up his bridges. Impatient Northern generals tried precisely this.

On May 7, 1864, Union General William T. Sherman set out southeastward from Chattanooga, Tennessee, on a march of destruction. Going through Georgia his army traveled light. He told his men to carry only their arms, for he figured that they would loot food and supplies along the way. This too would help exhaust the enemy, while it solved the problem of supply. He ordered them to move fast, without waiting to protect their rear. Sherman's army left a path of devastation three hundred miles wide all across Georgia. What was not worth carrying away they burned, what they could not burn they smashed.

Later General Sherman explained that what many people called "humanity" had no place in modern war. In the long run, so his argument went, the only way

The Civil War provided a vast variety of subject matter for a new generation of realistic artists. This engraving of a Northern sharpshooter was made from a sketch by Winslow Homer, the young artist-correspondent for Harper's Weekly.

to be humane—to get the war over—was to be cruel. The Confederate General Lee had warned his men that they should never hurt civilians. But modern war could not be won that way. The only up-to-date strategy, according to the brilliant Northerner Philip H. Sheridan whose victories had made him a general when he was barely thirty, was to punish every enemy—man, woman, and child. Leave them "nothing but their eyes to weep with." That was the new path to victory in the new kind of warfare.

It took four full years to exhaust the South. If the North had not been so much the stronger, it might have taken much longer. With twenty-three States against the South's eleven, with 22,000,000 people against the South's 9,000,000, the North had a big advantage. The North had more and better railroads, more ships, and more factories.

Also, while the North had lots of labor-saving devices like the reaper to free men for the army, the South depended for its labor on Negro slaves. These might any moment turn out to be a "fifth column"—an enemy force behind Southern lines—because they had very good reasons of their own for helping the enemy. Every third Southerner was

The war also provided rich, horrendous materials for pioneers in the new art of photography. This photograph shows a soldier killed at the Battle of Gettysburg.

a Negro. Southerners therefore lived in fear of a civil war all their own—if the Negroes ever decided to take up arms. Meanwhile, after the North finally decided in December 1862 to accept Negroes in its armed forces, it was strengthened by more than 180,000 Negroes fighting on its side. The North grew lots of different crops, while the South was glutted with a few staples—tobacco, cotton, and rice—which it had to export in order to obtain anything else.

Worst of all, the South suffered from delusions which prevented her seeing facts. Southerners were still astonished that any power on earth dared make war on the world's greatest producer of cotton. They had long told themselves: "Cotton is King." They imagined too that only Southerners were civilized, and that one Southerner "could whip a half-dozen Yankees and not half try." The South's grandiose dreams turned into nightmares.

In the North, too, it was everybody's war. There, too, nearly every family lost a soldier. And in quite new ways the gore was brought into everybody's home. For the first time in history, the battles were thoroughly covered by newspaper correspondents who telegraphed back eyewitness accounts so that civilians could read the horrors next morning at breakfast.

The New York *Herald* alone once had forty correspondents in the field, and spent a half-million dollars on them. Northern correspondents, who would have been shot as spies if discovered, smuggled themselves behind Southern lines disguised as women or as Confed-

erate soldiers. When Albert D. Richardson of the New York *Tribune* traveled through the South in 1861, he sent back his dispatches through a New York bank in code. General William T. Sherman was so irritated at the crowd of correspondents around his headquarters that he threatened to shoot them. General Grant was more amiable and used the correspondents to give people the news he wanted them to believe. When some generals objected that the newspapers were giving away valuable information to the enemy, the New York *World* protested that this was a "people's war."

The pioneer photographer Mathew Brady and his large crew, at the risk of their lives, sent photographs back home to show everyone the battle action. Soldiers sometimes ran away from Brady's camera because they had never seen a camera before, and imagined it to be a new kind of gun. Brady's photographic buggy, which soldiers called the "What-Is-It?," was a conspicuous target. On several occasions, Brady barely escaped being killed. After the first Battle of Bull Run, Brady was lost for three days before finding his way back to Washington. There he quickly secured new equipment and rushed back to the battlefield.

In the "people's war" women played a new, important part. Dorothea Dix, the courageous New Englander who had braved public opinion to prevent cruelties to the insane, now followed the example of the Englishwoman Florence Nightingale. Miss Dix became the first Superintendent of Army Nurses. She was a strict manager and enlisted only women who were strong and not too good-looking. In those days, it took

"Our Women and the War," another view of the varied American scene by Winslow Homer.

gumption to find any place for women in the army, and she was the pioneer. Women were so anxious to do their part that some four hundred of them pretended to be soldiers until they were discovered.

Although it was everybody's war, the leaders did much to turn the tide. If Jefferson Davis had been President of the United States and Lincoln had been President of the Confederacy, would the North still have won?

Lincoln was a stronger leader. As a politician, he knew how important it was, in everybody's war, to keep everybody's support. At the beginning of the war, in order to keep the support of the border Slave States—Delaware, Maryland, Kentucky, and Missouri—Lincoln had refused to emancipate the slaves. But in late 1862, when the war was going badly for the North, he felt the time had come to show the great moral purpose of the war, and to try to secure foreign support. On January 1, 1863, he issued the Emancipation Proclamation. It freed the slaves, but only in the States that were rebelling against the United States. The freeing of all the slaves would have to wait until after the war.

Just as the Declaration of Independence had helped unite the colonists and

Lee, Grant, and their staffs at Appomattox.

helped persuade the world, so the Emancipation Proclamation did its work. "Mr. Lincoln's cause," wrote an English merchant on hearing of the Proclamation, "is just and holy, the cause of truth, and of universal humanity." English workingmen held mass meetings to support the Union. Now there was little danger that the British government would recognize or support the Confederacy. This was not merely a war for Union, but a war against slavery.

Lincoln was not afraid of new ideas. He tried one general after another until he found U. S. Grant. Of course, it was partly good luck that Grant happened to be there. But Lincoln was willing to try his luck on a general who usually looked a mess and who did not insist on

waging war according to the textbooks he had studied at West Point. Lincoln believed that a new world needed new ideas. General Grant agreed. He had a notion of how new the new warfare had become. And he had the advantage that he was a hard man to predict.

After General Sherman's march of devastation through Georgia and the Carolinas, the South was still not quite defeated. But she was exhausted. She had no strength to go on. Then at last when the railroad to the Confederate capital of Richmond was cut, Richmond had to be abandoned. In a final battle at Appomattox, General Grant overwhelmed Lee's force.

On the afternoon of April 9, 1865, the Confederate General Lee, accompanied only by his military secretary, rode his horse to a little white house in the town of Appomattox Court House on the Appomattox River in central Virginia. He went to arrange his surrender. There occurred one of the most remarkable, and one of the most encouraging, episodes in American history. It would show that, despite the monstrous indecencies of war, the respect of one American for another had not been destroyed.

Grant, who had just come in from the field, was dusty and even more unkempt than usual. Confronting him in the living room of the house he had taken for his headquarters was General Lee—handsome, erect, in a spotless uniform, and wearing his dress sword. The men sat down and then exchanged recollections of their fighting together twenty years before in the Mexican War. The two great generals talked to each other with calmness, courtesy, and respect.

Now that the fighting was over, it seemed that humanity had suddenly returned. Lee heard Grant's terms of surrender. Grant was more generous than he needed to be. He allowed Southern officers to keep their swords—the symbols of their honor—and he allowed officers and men to keep their horses, so they could go home and plant their crops. Lee was touched. "This," he said, "will have a very happy effect upon my army."

A renewed nation, fused in the fires of war, would now seek its destiny in peace.

APPENDIXES

The Declaration of Independence

When in the Course of human events, it becomes necessary for one people to dissolve the political bands which have connected them with another, and to assume among the powers of the earth, the separate and equal station to which the Laws of Nature and of Nature's God entitle them, a decent respect to the opinions of mankind requires that they should declare the causes which impel them to the separation.

We hold these truths to be self-evident, that all men are created equal, that they are endowed by their Creator with certain unalienable Rights, that among these are Life, Liberty and the pursuit of Happiness. That to secure these rights, Governments are instituted among Men, deriving their just powers from the consent of the governed, That whenever any Form of Government becomes destructive of these ends it is the Right of the People to alter or to abolish it, and to institute new Government, laying its foundation on such principles and organizing its powers in such form, as to them shall seem most likely to effect their Safety and Happiness. Prudence, indeed, will dictate that Governments long established should not be changed for light and transient causes; and accordingly all experience has shewn, that mankind are more disposed to suffer, while evils are sufferable, than to right themselves by abolishing the forms to which they are accustomed. But when a long train of abuses and usurpations, pursuing invariably the same Object evinces a design to reduce them under absolute Despotism, it is their right, it is their duty, to throw off such Government, and to provide new Guards for their future security. Such has been the patient sufferance of these Colonies; and such is now the necessity which constrains them to alter their former Systems of Government. The history of the present King of Great Britain is a history of repeated injuries and usurpations, all having in direct object the establishment of an absolute Tyranny over these States. To prove this, let Facts be submitted to a candid world.

He has refused his Assent to Laws, the most wholesome and necessary for the public good.

He has forbidden his Governors to pass Laws of immediate and pressing importance, unless suspended in their operation till his Assent should be obtained; and when so suspended, he has utterly neglected to attend to them. He has refused to pass other Laws for the accommodation of large districts of people, unless those people would relinquish the right of Representation in the Legislature, a right inestimable to them and formidable to tyrants only.

He has called together legislative bodies at places unusual, uncomfortable, and distant from the depository of their public Records, for the sole purpose of fatiguing them into compliance with his measures.

He has dissolved Representative Houses repeatedly, for opposing with manly firmness his invasions on the rights of the people.

He has refused for a long time, after such dissolutions, to cause others to be elected; whereby the Legislative powers, incapable of Annihilation, have returned to the People at large for their exercise; the State remaining in the mean time exposed to all the dangers of invasion from without, and convulsions within.

He has endeavoured to prevent the population of these States; for that purpose obstructing the Laws for Naturalization of Foreigners; refusing to pass others to encourage their migrations hither, and raising the conditions of new Appropriations of Lands.

He has obstructed the Administration of Justice, by refusing his Assent to Laws for establishing Judiciary powers.

He has made Judges dependent on his Will alone, for the tenure of their offices, and the amount and payment of their salaries.

He has erected a multitude of New Offices, and sent hither swarms of Officers to harass our People, and eat out their substance.

He has kept among us, in times of peace, standing Armies without the Consent of our legislatures.

He has affected to render the Military independent of and superior to the Civil power.

He has combined with others to subject us to a jurisdiction foreign to our constitution, and unacknowledged by our laws; giving his Assent to their Acts of pretended Legislation:

For Quartering large bodies of armed troops among us:

For protecting them, by a mock Trial, from punishment for any Murders which they should commit on the Inhabitants of these States:

For cutting off our Trade with all parts of the world:

For imposing Taxes on us without our Consent:

For depriving us in many cases of the benefits of Trial by Jury:

For transporting us beyond Seas to be tried for pretended offences:

For abolishing the free System of English Laws in a neighbouring Province, establishing therein an Arbitrary government, and enlarging its Boundaries so as to render it at once an example and fit instrument for introducing the same absolute rule into these Colonies:

For taking away our Charters, abolishing our most valuable Laws, and altering fundamentally the Forms of our Governments:

For suspending our own Legislatures, and declaring themselves invested with power to legislate for us in all cases whatsoever.

He has abdicated Government here, by declaring us out of his Protection and waging War against us.

He has plundered our seas, ravaged our Coasts, burnt our towns, and destroyed the Lives of our people.

He is at this time transporting large Armies of foreign Mercenaries to compleat the works of death, desolation and tyranny, already begun with circumstances of Cruelty & perfidy scarcely paralleled in the most barbarous ages, and totally unworthy the Head of a civilized nation.

He has constrained our fellow Citizens taken Captive on the high Seas to bear Arms against their Country, to become the executioners of their friends and Brethren, or to fall themselves by their Hands.

He has excited domestic insurrections amongst us, and has endeavoured to bring on the inhabitants of our frontiers, the merciless Indian Savages, whose known rule of warfare, is an undistinguished destruction of all ages, sexes and conditions.

In every stage of these Oppressions We have Petitioned for Redress in the most humble terms: Our repeated Petitions have been answered only by repeated injury. A Prince, whose character is thus marked by every act which may define a Tyrant, is unfit to be the ruler of a free people.

Nor have We been wanting in attentions to our Brittish brethren. We have warned them from time to time of attempts by their legislature to extend an unwarrantable jurisdiction over us. We have reminded them of the circumstances of our emigration and settlement here. We have appealed to their native justice and magnanimity, and we have conjured them by the ties of our common kindred to disavow these usurpations, which, would inevitably interrupt our connections and correspondence. They too have been deaf to the voice of Justice and of consanguinity. We must, therefore, acquiesce in the necessity, which denounces our Separation, and hold them, as we hold the rest of mankind, Enemies in War, in Peace Friends.

We, therefore, the Representatives of the united States of America, in General Congress, Assembled, appealing to the Supreme Judge of the world for the rectitude of our intentions, do, in the Name, and by Authority of the good People of these Colonies, solemnly publish and declare, That these United Colonies are, and of Right ought to be Free and Independent States; that they are Absolved from all Allegiance to the British Crown, and that all political connection between them and the State of Great Britain, is and ought to be totally dissolved; and that as Free and Independent States, they have full Power to levy War, conclude Peace, contract Alliances, establish Commerce, and to do all other Acts and Things which Independent States may of right do. And for the support of this Declaration, with a firm reliance on the protection of divine Providence, we mutually pledge to each other our Lives, our Fortunes and our sacred Honor.

John Hancock

Button Gwinnett	James Wilson
Lyman Hall	Geo. Ross
Geo Walton.	Caesar Rodney
Wm. Hooper	Geo Read
Joseph Hewes,	Tho M:Kean
John Penn	Wm. Floyd
Edward Rutledge.	Phil. Livingston
Thos. Heyward Junr.	Frans. Lewis
Thomas Lynch Junr.	Lewis Morris
Arthur Middleton	Richd. Stockton
Samuel Chase	Jno Witherspoon
Wm. Paca	Fras. Hopkinson
Thos. Stone	John Hart
Charles Carroll of Carrollton	Abra Clark
George Wythe	Josiah Bartlett
Richard Henry Lee	Wm: Whipple
Th: Jefferson	Saml. Adams
Benja. Harrison	John Adams
Thos. Nelson jr.	Robt. Treat Paine
Francis Lightfoot Lee	Elbridge Gerry
Carter Braxton	Step. Hopkins
Robt. Morris	William Ellery
Benjamin Rush	Roger Sherman
Benja. Franklin	Saml. Huntington
John Morton	Wm. Williams
Geo Clymer	Oliver Wolcott
Jas. Smith.	Matthew Thornton
Geo. Taylor	

The Constitution
of the United States of America

PREAMBLE

We the People of the United States, in Order to form a more perfect Union, establish Justice, insure domestic Tranquility, provide for the common defence, promote the general Welfare, and secure the Blessings of Liberty to ourselves and our Posterity, do ordain and establish this Constitution for the United States of America.

ARTICLE I.

SECTION 1. All legislative Powers herein granted shall be vested in a Congress of the United States, which shall consist of a Senate and House of Representatives.

SECTION 2. The House of Representatives shall be composed of Members chosen every second Year by the People of the several States, and the Electors in each State shall have the Qualifications requisite for Electors of the most numerous Branch of the State Legislature.

No Person shall be a Representative who shall not have attained to the Age of twenty five Years, and been seven Years a Citizen of the United States, and who shall not, when elected, be an Inhabitant of that State in which he shall be chosen.

[Representatives and (direct Taxes) shall be apportioned among the several States (which may be included within this Union,) according to their respective Numbers, which shall be determined by adding to the whole Number of free Persons, including those bound to Service for a Term of Years, and excluding Indians not taxed, three fifths of all other Persons.][1]

---

1. Changed by section 2 of the Fourteenth Amendment.

The actual Enumeration shall be made within three Years after the first Meeting of the Congress of the United States, and within every subsequent Term of ten Years, in such Manner as they shall by Law direct. The number of Representatives shall not exceed one for every thirty Thousand, but each State shall have at Least one Representative; and until such enumeration shall be made, the State of New Hampshire shall be entitled to chuse three, Massachusetts eight, Rhode-Island and Providence Plantations one, Connecticut five, New-York six, New Jersey four, Pennsylvania eight, Delaware one, Maryland six, Virginia ten, North Carolina five, South Carolina five, and Georgia three.

When vacancies happen in the Representation from any State, the Executive Authority thereof shall issue Writs of Election to fill such Vacancies.

The House of Representatives shall chuse their Speaker and other Officers; and shall have the sole Power of Impeachment.

SECTION 3. The Senate of the United States shall be composed of two Senators from each State, [chosen by the Legislature thereof,][1] for six Years; and each Senator shall have one Vote.

Immediately after they shall be assembled in Consequence of the first Election, they shall be divided as equally as may be into three Classes. The Seats of the Senators of the first Class shall be vacated at the Expiration of the second Year, of the second Class at the Expiration of the fourth Year, and of the third Class at the Expiration of the sixth Year, so that one third may be chosen every second Year; [and if Vacancies happen by Resignation, or otherwise, during the Recess of the Legislature of any State, the Executive thereof may make temporary Appointments until the next Meeting of the Legislature, which shall then fill such Vacancies.][2]

No Person shall be a Senator who shall not have attained to the Age of thirty Years, and been nine Years a Citizen of the United States, and who shall not, when elected, be an Inhabitant of that State for which he shall be chosen.

The Vice President of the United States shall be President of the Senate, but shall have no Vote, unless they be equally divided.

The Senate shall chuse their other Officers, and also a President pro tempore, in the Absence of the Vice President, or when he shall exercise the Office of President of the United States.

The Senate shall have the sole Power to try all Impeachments. When sitting for that Purpose, they shall be on Oath or Affirmation. When the President of the United States is tried, the Chief Justice shall preside: And no Person shall be convicted without the Concurrence of two thirds of the Members present.

---

1. Changed by section 1 of the Seventeenth Amendment.
2. Changed by section 2 of the Seventeenth Amendment.

Judgment in Cases of Impeachment shall not extend further than to removal from Office, and disqualification to hold and enjoy any Office of honor, Trust or Profit under the United States: but the Party convicted shall nevertheless be liable and subject to Indictment, Trial, Judgment and Punishment, according to Law.

SECTION 4. The Times, Places and Manner of holding Elections for Senators and Representatives, shall be prescribed in each State by the Legislature thereof; but the Congress may at any time by Law make or alter such Regulations, except as to the Places of chusing Senators.

The Congress shall assemble at least once in every Year, and such Meeting shall be [on the first Monday in December,][1] unless they shall by Law appoint a different Day.

SECTION 5. Each House shall be the Judge of the Elections, Returns and Qualifications of its own Members, and a Majority of each shall constitute a Quorum to do Business; but a smaller Number may adjourn from day to day, and may be authorized to compel the Attendance of absent Members, in such Manner, and under such Penalties as each House may provide.

Each House may determine the Rules of its Proceedings, punish its Members for disorderly Behaviour, and, with the Concurrence of two thirds, expel a Member.

Each House shall keep a Journal of its Proceedings, and from time to time publish the same, excepting such Parts as may in their Judgment require Secrecy; and the Yeas and Nays of the Members of either House on any question shall, at the Desire of one fifth of those Present, be entered on the Journal.

Neither House, during the Session of Congress, shall, without the Consent of the other, adjourn for more than three days, nor to any other Place than that in which the two Houses shall be sitting.

SECTION 6. The Senators and Representatives shall receive a Compensation for their Services, to be ascertained by Law, and paid out of the Treasury of the United States. They shall in all Cases, except Treason, Felony and Breach of the Peace, be privileged from Arrest during their Attendance at the Session of their respective Houses, and in going to and returning from the same; and for any Speech or Debate in either House, they shall not be questioned in any other Place.

No Senator or Representative shall, during the Time for which he was elected, be appointed to any civil Office under the Authority of the United States, which shall have been created, or the Emoluments whereof shall have been encreased during such time; and no Person holding any Office under the United States, shall be a Member of either House during his Continuance in Office.

---

1. Changed by section 2 of the Twentieth Amendment.

SECTION 7. All Bills for raising Revenue shall originate in the House of Representatives; but the Senate may propose or concur with Amendments as on other Bills.

Every Bill which shall have passed the House of Representatives and the Senate, shall, before it becomes a Law, be presented to the President of the United States; If he approve he shall sign it, but if not he shall return it, with his Objections to that House in which it shall have originated, who shall enter the Objections at large on their Journal, and proceed to reconsider it. If after such Reconsideration two thirds of that House shall agree to pass the Bill, it shall be sent, together with the Objections, to the other House, by which it shall likewise be reconsidered, and if approved by two thirds of that House, it shall become a Law. But in all such Cases the Votes of both Houses shall be determined by Yeas and Nays, and the Names of the Persons voting for and against the Bill shall be entered on the Journal of each House respectively. If any Bill shall not be returned by the President within ten Days (Sundays excepted) after it shall have been presented to him, the Same shall be a Law, in like Manner as if he had signed it, unless the Congress by their Adjournment prevent its Return, in which Case it shall not be a Law.

Every Order, Resolution, or Vote to which the Concurrence of the Senate and House of Representatives may be necessary (except on a question of Adjournment) shall be presented to the President of the United States; and before the Same shall take Effect, shall be approved by him, or being disapproved by him, shall be repassed by two thirds of the Senate and House of Representatives, according to the Rules and Limitations prescribed in the Case of a Bill.

SECTION 8. The Congress shall have Power To lay and collect Taxes, Duties, Imposts and Excises, to pay the Debts and provide for the common Defence and general Welfare of the United States; but all Duties, Imposts and Excises shall be uniform throughout the United States;

To borrow Money on the credit of the United States;

To regulate Commerce with foreign Nations, and among the several States, and with the Indian Tribes;

To establish an uniform Rule of Naturalization, and uniform Laws on the subject of Bankruptcies throughout the United States;

To coin Money, regulate the Value thereof, and of foreign Coin, and fix the Standard of Weights and Measures;

To provide for the Punishment of counterfeiting the Securities and current Coin of the United States;

To establish Post Offices and post Roads;

To promote the Progress of Science and useful Arts, by securing for limited Times to Authors and Inventors the exclusive Right to their respective Writings and Discoveries;

To constitute Tribunals inferior to the supreme Court;

To define and punish Piracies and Felonies committed on the high Seas, and Offenses against the Law of Nations;

To declare War, grant Letters of Marque and Reprisal, and make Rules concerning Captures on Land and Water;

To raise and support Armies, but no Appropriation of Money to that Use shall be for a longer Term than two Years;

To provide and maintain a Navy;

To make Rules for the Government and Regulation of the land and naval Forces;

To provide for calling forth the Militia to execute the Laws of the Union, suppress Insurrections and repel Invasions;

To provide for organizing, arming, and disciplining, the Militia, and for governing such Part of them as may be employed in the Service of the United States, reserving to the States respectively, the Appointment of the Officers, and the Authority of training the Militia according to the discipline prescribed by Congress;

To exercise exclusive Legislation in all Cases whatsoever, over such District (not exceeding ten Miles square) as may, by Cession of particular States, and the Acceptance of Congress, become the Seat of the Government of the United States, and to exercise like Authority over all Places purchased by the Consent of the Legislature of the State in which the Same shall be, for the Erection of Forts, Magazines, Arsenals, dock-Yards and other needful Buildings;—And

To make all Laws which shall be necessary and proper for carrying into Execution the foregoing Powers, and all other Powers vested by this Constitution in the Government of the United States, or in any Department or Officer thereof.

SECTION 9. The Migration or Importation of such Persons as any of the States now existing shall think proper to admit, shall not be prohibited by the Congress prior to the Year one thousand eight hundred and eight, but a Tax or duty may be imposed on such Importation, not exceeding ten dollars for each Person.

The Privilege of the Writ of Habeas Corpus shall not be suspended, unless when in Cases of Rebellion or Invasion the public Safety may require it.

No Bill of Attainder or ex post facto Law shall be passed.

No Capitation, or other direct, Tax shall be laid, unless in Proportion to the Census or Enumeration herein before directed to be taken.

No Tax or Duty shall be laid on Articles exported from any State.

No Preference shall be given by any Regulation of Commerce or Revenue to the Ports of one State over those of another: nor shall Vessels bound to, or from, one State, be obliged to enter, clear, or pay Duties in another.

No Money shall be drawn from the Treasury, but in Consequence of Appropriations made by Law; and a regular Statement and Account of the

Receipts and Expenditures of all public Money shall be published from time to time.

No Title of Nobility shall be granted by the United States: And no Person holding any Office of Profit or Trust under them, shall, without the Consent of the Congress, accept of any present, Emolument, Office, or Title, of any kind whatever, from any King, Prince, or foreign State.

SECTION 10. No State shall enter into any Treaty, Alliance, or Confederation; grant Letters of Marque and Reprisal; coin Money; emit Bills of Credit; make any Thing but gold and silver Coin a Tender in Payment of Debts; pass any Bill of Attainder, ex post facto Law, or Law impairing the Obligation of Contracts, or grant any Title of Nobility.

No State shall, without the Consent of the Congress, lay any Imposts or Duties on Imports or Exports, except what may be absolutely necessary for executing it's inspection Laws: and the net Produce of all Duties and Imposts, laid by any State on Imports or Exports, shall be for the Use of the Treasury of the United States; and all such Laws shall be subject to the Revision and Controul of the Congress.

No State shall, without the Consent of Congress, lay any Duty of Tonnage, keep Troops, or Ships of War in time of Peace, enter into any Agreement or Compact with another State, or with a foreign Power, or engage in War, unless actually invaded, or in such imminent Danger as will not admit of delay.

ARTICLE II.

SECTION 1. The executive Power shall be vested in a President of the United States of America. He shall hold his Office during the Term of four Years, and, together with the Vice President, chosen for the same Term, be elected, as follows

Each State shall appoint, in such Manner as the Legislature thereof may direct, a Number of Electors, equal to the whole Number of Senators and Representatives to which the State may be entitled in the Congress: but no Senator or Representative, or Person holding an Office of Trust or Profit under the United States, shall be appointed an Elector.

[The Electors shall meet in their respective States, and vote by Ballot for two Persons, of whom one at least shall not be an Inhabitant of the same State with themselves. And they shall make a List of all the Persons voted for, and of the Number of Votes for each; which List they shall sign and certify, and transmit sealed to the Seat of the Government of the United States, directed to the President of the Senate. The President of the Senate shall, in the Presence of the Senate and House of Representatives, open all the Certificates, and the Votes shall then be counted. The Person having the greatest Number of Votes shall be the President, if such Number be a Majority of the whole Number of Electors appointed; and if there be more than one who have such Majority, and have an equal Number of Votes, then the House of Representatives shall immediately chuse by Ballot one of them for President; and if no Person have a Majority, then from the five highest on the List the said House shall in like Manner chuse the President. But in chusing the President, the Votes shall be taken by States, the Representation from each State having one Vote; A quorum for this Purpose shall consist of a Member or Members from two thirds of the States, and a Majority of all the States shall be necessary to a Choice. In every Case, after the Choice of the President, the Person having the greatest Number of Votes of the Electors shall be the Vice President. But if there should remain two or more who have equal Votes, the Senate shall chuse from them by Ballot the Vice President.][1]

The Congress may determine the Time of chusing the Electors, and the Day on which they shall give their Votes; which Day shall be the same throughout the United States.

No Person except a natural born Citizen, or a Citizen of the United States, at the time of the Adoption of this Constitution, shall be eligible to the Office of the President; neither shall any person be eligible to that Office who shall not have attained to the Age of thirty five Years, and been fourteen Years a Resident within the United States.

[In Case of the Removal of the President from Office, or of his Death, Resignation, or Inability to discharge the Powers and Duties of the said Office, the Same shall devolve on the Vice President, and the Congress may by Law provide for the Case of Removal, Death, Resignation or Inability, both of the President and Vice President, declaring what Officer shall then act as President, and such Officer shall act accordingly, until the Disability be removed, or a President shall be elected.][2]

The President shall, at stated Times, receive for his Services, a Compensation, which shall neither be increased nor diminished during the Period for which he shall have been elected, and he shall not receive within that Period any other Emolument from the United States, or any of them.

Before he enter on the Execution of his Office, he shall take the following Oath or Affirmation:—"I do solemnly swear (or affirm) that I will faithfully execute the Office of President of the United States, and will to the best of my Ability, preserve, protect and defend the Constitution of the United States."

SECTION 2.   The President shall be Commander in Chief of the Army and Navy of the United States, and of the Militia of the several States, when called into the actual Service of the United States; he may require the Opinion, in writing, of the principal Officer in each of the executive Departments, upon any Subject relating to the Duties of their respective Offices,

---

1. Superseded by the Twelfth Amendment.
2. Modified by the Twenty-fifth Amendment.

and he shall have Power to grant Reprieves and Pardons for Offenses against the United States, except in Cases of Impeachment.

He shall have Power, by and with the Advice and Consent of the Senate, to make Treaties, provided two thirds of the Senators present concur; and he shall nominate, and by and with the Advice and Consent of the Senate, shall appoint Ambassadors, other public Ministers and Consuls, Judges of the supreme Court, and all other Officers of the United States, whose Appointments are not herein otherwise provided for, and which shall be established by Law: but the Congress may by Law vest the Appointment of such inferior Officers, as they think proper, in the President alone, in the Courts of Law, or in the Heads of Departments.

The President shall have Power to fill up all Vacancies that may happen during the Recess of the Senate, by granting Commissions which shall expire at the End of their next Session.

SECTION 3.   He shall from time to time give to the Congress Information of the State of the Union, and recommend to their Consideration such Measures as he shall judge necessary and expedient; he may, on extraordinary Occasions, convene both Houses, or either of them, and in Case of Disagreement between them, with Respect to the Time of Adjournment, he may adjourn them to such Time as he shall think proper; he shall receive Ambassadors and other public Ministers; he shall take Care that the Laws be faithfully executed, and shall Commission all the Officers of the United States.

SECTION 4.   The President, Vice President and all civil Officers of the United States, shall be removed from Office on Impeachment for, and Conviction of, Treason, Bribery, or other high Crimes and Misdemeanors.

ARTICLE III.

SECTION 1.   The judicial Power of the United States, shall be vested in one supreme Court, and in such inferior Courts as the Congress may from time to time ordain and establish.   The Judges, both of the supreme and inferior Courts, shall hold their Offices during good Behaviour, and shall, at stated Times, receive for their Services, a Compensation, which shall not be diminished during their Continuance in Office.

SECTION 2.   The judicial Power shall extend to all Cases, in Law and Equity, arising under this Constitution, the Laws of the United States, and Treaties made, or which shall be made, under their Authority;—to all Cases affecting Ambassadors, other public Ministers and Consuls;—to all Cases of admiralty and maritime Jurisdiction;—to Controversies to which the United States shall be a Party;—to Controversies between two or more States; between a State and Citizens of another State;—between Citizens of different States—between Citizens of the same State claiming Lands under Grants of different States, and between a State, or the Citizens thereof, and foreign States, Citizens or Subjects.

In all Cases affecting Ambassadors, other public Ministers and Consuls, and those in which a State shall be Party, the supreme Court shall have original Jurisdiction. In all the other Cases before mentioned, the supreme Court shall have appellate Jurisdiction, both as to Law and Fact, with such Exceptions, and under such Regulations as the Congress shall make.

The Trial of all Crimes, except in Cases of Impeachment; shall be by Jury; and such Trial shall be held in the State where the said Crimes shall have been committed; but when not committed within any State, the Trial shall be at such Place or Places as the Congress may by Law have directed.

SECTION 3. Treason against the United States, shall consist only in levying War against them, or in adhering to their Enemies, giving them Aid and Comfort. No Person shall be convicted of Treason unless on the Testimony of two Witnesses to the same overt Act, or on Confession in open Court.

The Congress shall have Power to declare the Punishment of Treason, but no Attainder of Treason shall work Corruption of Blood, or Forfeiture except during the Life of the Person attainted.

ARTICLE IV.

SECTION 1. Full Faith and Credit shall be given in each State to the public Acts, Records, and judicial Proceedings of every other State; And the Congress may by general Laws prescribe the Manner in which such Acts, Records and Proceedings shall be proved, and the Effect thereof.

SECTION 2. The Citizens of each State shall be entitled to all Privileges and Immunities of Citizens in the several States.

A Person charged in any State with Treason, Felony, or other Crime, who shall flee from Justice, and be found in another State, shall on Demand of the executive Authority of the State from which he fled, be delivered up, to be removed to the State having Jurisdiction of the Crime.

[No Person held to Service or Labour in one State, under the Laws thereof, escaping into another, shall, in Consequence of any Law or Regulation therein, be discharged from such Service or Labour, but shall be delivered up on Claim of the Party to whom such Service or Labour may be due.][1]

SECTION 3. New States may be admitted by the Congress into this Union; but no new State shall be formed or erected within the Jurisdiction of any other State; nor any State be formed by the Junction of two or more States, or Parts of States, without the Consent of the Legislatures of the States concerned as well as of the Congress.

---

1. Superseded by the Thirteenth Amendment.

The Congress shall have Power to dispose of and make all needful Rules and Regulations respecting the Territory or other Property belonging to the United States; and nothing in this Constitution shall be so construed as to Prejudice any Claims of the United States, or of any particular State.

SECTION 4.   The United States shall guarantee to every State in this Union a Republican Form of Government, and shall protect each of them against Invasion; and on Application of the Legislature, or of the Executive (when the Legislature cannot be convened) against domestic Violence.

ARTICLE V.

The Congress, whenever two thirds of both Houses shall deem it necessary, shall propose Amendments to this Constitution, or, on the Application of the Legislatures of two thirds of the several States, shall call a Convention for proposing Amendments, which, in either Case, shall be valid to all Intents and Purposes, as Part of this Constitution, when ratified by the Legislatures of three fourths of the several States, or by Conventions in three fourths thereof, as the one or the other Mode of Ratification may be proposed by the Congress; Provided that no Amendment which may be made prior to the Year One thousand eight hundred and eight shall in any Manner affect the first and fourth Clauses in the Ninth Section of the first Article; and that no State, without its Consent, shall be deprived of it's equal Suffrage in the Senate.

ARTICLE VI.

All Debts contracted and Engagements entered into, before the Adoption of this Constitution, shall be as valid against the United States under this Constitution, as under the Confederation.

This Constitution, and the Laws of the United States which shall be made in Pursuance thereof; and all Treaties made, or which shall be made, under the Authority of the United States, shall be the supreme Law of the Land; and the Judges in every State shall be bound thereby, any Thing in the Constitution or Laws of any State to the Contrary notwithstanding.

The Senators and Representatives before mentioned, and the Members of the several State Legislatures, and all executive and judicial Officers, both of the United States and of the several States, shall be bound by Oath or Affirmation, to support this Constitution; but no religious Test shall ever be required as a Qualification to any Office or public Trust under the United States.

ARTICLE VII.

The Ratification of the Conventions of nine States, shall be sufficient for the Establishment of this Constitution between the States so ratifying the Same.

Done in Convention by the Unanimous Consent of the States present the Seventeenth Day of September in the Year of our Lord one thousand seven hundred and Eighty seven and of the Independence of the United States of America the Twelfth In Witness whereof We have hereunto subscribed our Names,

G? Washington—Presid?
and deputy from Virginia

The Word, "the," being interlined between the seventh and eighth Lines of the first Page, The Word "Thirty" being partly written on an Erazure in the fifteenth Line of the first Page, The Words "is tried" being interlined between the thirty second and thirty third Lines of the first Page and the Word "the" being interlined between the forty third and forty fourth Lines of the second Page.

Attest William Jackson Secretary

DELAWARE
Geo: Read
Gunning Bedford jun
John Dickinson
Richard Bassett
Jaco: Broom

MARYLAND
James McHenry
Dan of St Thos. Jenifer
Danl Carroll

VIRGINIA
John Blair—
James Madison Jr.

NORTH CAROLINA
Wm. Blount
Richd. Dobbs Spaight
Hu Williamson

SOUTH CAROLINA
J. Rutledge
Charles Cotesworth Pinckney
Charles Pinckney
Pierce Butler

GEORGIA
William Few
Abr Baldwin

NEW HAMPSHIRE
John Langdon
Nicholas Gilman

MASSACHUSETTS
Nathaniel Gorham
Rufus King

CONNECTICUT
Wm. Saml. Johnson
Roger Sherman

NEW YORK
Alexander Hamilton

NEW JERSEY
Wil: Livingston
David Brearley
Wm. Paterson
Jona: Dayton

PENNSYLVANIA
B Franklin
Thomas Mifflin
Robt Morris
Geo. Clymer
Thos. FitzSimons
Jared Ingersoll
James Wilson
Gouv Morris

IN CONVENTION MONDAY
SEPTEMBER 17th 1787.

PRESENT
THE STATES OF

New Hampshire, Massachusetts, Connecticut, Mr. Hamilton from New York, New Jersey, Pennsylvania, Delaware, Maryland, Virginia, North Carolina, South Carolina and Georgia.

Resolved,

That the preceeding Constitution be laid before the United States in Congress assembled, and that it is the Opinion of this Convention, that it should afterwards be submitted to a Convention of Delegates, chosen in each State by the People thereof, under the Recommendation of its Legislature, for their Assent and Ratification; and that each Convention assenting to, and ratifying the Same, should give Notice thereof to the United States in Congress assembled. Resolved, That it is the Opinion of this Convention, that as soon as the Conventions of nine States shall have ratified this Constitution, the United States in Congress assembled should fix a Day on which Electors should be appointed by the States which shall have ratified the same, and a Day on which the Electors should assemble to vote for the President, and the Time and Place for commencing Proceedings under this Constitution.

That after such Publication the Electors should be appointed, and the Senators and Representatives elected: That the Electors should meet on the Day fixed for the Election of the President, and should transmit their Votes certified, signed, sealed and directed, as the Constitution requires, to the Secretary of the United States in Congress assembled, that the Senators and Representatives should convene at the Time and Place assigned; that the Senators should appoint a President of the Senate, for the sole Purpose of receiving, opening and counting the Votes for President; and, that after he shall be chosen, the Congress, together with the President, should, without Delay, proceed to execute this Constitution.

By the unanimous Order of the Convention

G? WASHINGTON—Presid!.

W. JACKSON Secretary.

AMENDMENTS TO THE CONSTITUTION OF THE UNITED STATES OF AMERICA

ARTICLES IN ADDITION TO, AND AMENDMENT OF, THE CONSTITUTION OF THE UNITED STATES OF AMERICA, PROPOSED BY CONGRESS, AND RATIFIED BY THE SEVERAL STATES, PURSUANT TO THE FIFTH ARTICLE OF THE ORIGINAL CONSTITUTION.

AMENDMENT I.[1]

Congress shall make no law respecting an establishment of religion, or prohibiting the free exercise thereof; or abridging the freedom of speech, or of the press, or the right of the people peaceably to assemble, and to petition the Government for a redress of grievances.

AMENDMENT II.

A well regulated Militia, being necessary to the security of a free State, the right of the people to keep and bear Arms, shall not be infringed.

AMENDMENT III.

No Soldier shall, in time of peace be quartered in any house, without the consent of the Owner, nor in time of war, but in a manner to be prescribed by law.

AMENDMENT IV.

The right of the people to be secure in their persons, houses, papers, and effects, against unreasonable searches and seizures, shall not be violated, and no Warrants shall issue, but upon probable cause, supported by Oath or affirmation, and particularly describing the place to be searched, and the persons or things to be seized.

AMENDMENT V.

No person shall be held to answer for a capital, or otherwise infamous crime, unless on a presentment or indictment of a Grand Jury, except in cases arising in the land or naval forces, or in the Militia, when in actual

---

1. The first ten Amendments (Bill of Rights) were ratified effective December 15, 1791.

service in time of War or public danger; nor shall any person be subject for the same offence to be twice put in jeopardy of life or limb, nor shall be compelled in any criminal case to be a witness against himself, nor be deprived of life, liberty, or property, without due process of law; nor shall private property be taken for public use without just compensation.

AMENDMENT VI.

In all criminal prosecutions, the accused shall enjoy the right to a speedy and public trial, by an impartial jury of the State and district wherein the crime shall have been committed; which district shall have been previously ascertained by law, and to be informed of the nature and cause of the accusation; to be confronted with the witnesses against him; to have compulsory process for obtaining witnesses in his favor, and to have the assistance of counsel for his defence.

AMENDMENT VII.

In Suits at common law, where the value in controversy shall exceed twenty dollars, the right of trial by jury shall be preserved, and no fact tried by a jury shall be otherwise re-examined in any Court of the United States, than according to the rules of the common law.

AMENDMENT VIII.

Excessive bail shall not be required, nor excessive fines imposed, nor cruel and unusual punishments inflicted.

AMENDMENT IX.

The enumeration in the Constitution of certain rights shall not be construed to deny or disparage others retained by the people.

AMENDMENT X.

The powers not delegated to the United States by the Constitution, nor prohibited by it to the States, are reserved to the States respectively, or to the people.

AMENDMENT XI.[1]

The Judicial power of the United States shall not be construed to extend to any suit in law or equity, commenced or prosecuted against one of the United States by Citizens of another State, or by Citizens or Subjects of any Foreign State.

---

1. The Eleventh Amendment was ratified February 7, 1795.

AMENDMENT XII.[1]

The Electors shall meet in their respective states, and vote by ballot for President and Vice President, one of whom, at least, shall not be an inhabitant of the same state with themselves; they shall name in their ballots the person voted for as President, and in distinct ballots the person voted for as Vice-President, and they shall make distinct lists of all persons voted for as President, and of all persons voted for as Vice-President, and of the number of votes for each, which lists they shall sign and certify, and transmit sealed to the seat of the government of the United States, directed to the President of the Senate;—The President of the Senate shall, in the presence of the Senate and House of Representatives, open all the certificates and the votes shall then be counted;—The person having the greatest number of votes for President, shall be the President, if such number be a majority of the whole number of Electors appointed; and if no person have such majority, then from the persons having the highest numbers not exceeding three on the list of those voted for as President, the House of Representatives shall choose immediately, by ballot, the President. But in choosing the President, the votes shall be taken by states, the representation from each state having one vote; a quorum for this purpose shall consist of a member or members from two-thirds of the states, and a majority of all the states shall be necessary to a choice. [And if the House of Representatives shall not choose a President whenever the right of choice shall devolve upon them, before the fourth day of March next following, then the Vice-President shall act as President, as in the case of the death or other constitutional disability of the President—][2] The person having the greatest number of votes as Vice-President, shall be the Vice-President, if such number be a majority of the whole number of Electors appointed, and if no person have a majority, then from the two highest numbers on the list, the Senate shall choose the Vice-President; a quorum for the purpose shall consist of two-thirds of the whole number of Senators, and a majority of the whole number shall be necessary to a choice. But no person constitutionally ineligible to the office of President shall be eligible to that of Vice-President of the United States.

AMENDMENT XIII.[3]

SECTION 1. Neither slavery nor involuntary servitude, except as a punishment for crime whereof the party shall have been duly convicted, shall exist within the United States, or any place subject to their jurisdiction.

---

1. The Twelfth Amendment was ratified June 15, 1804.
2. Superseded by section 3 of the Twentieth Amendment.
3. The Thirteenth Amendment was ratified December 6, 1865.

SECTION 2. Congress shall have power to enforce this article by appropriate legislation.

AMENDMENT XIV.[1]

SECTION 1. All persons born or naturalized in the United States and subject to the jurisdiction thereof, are citizens of the United States and of the State wherein they reside. No State shall make or enforce any law which shall abridge the privileges or immunities of citizens of the United States; nor shall any State deprive any person of life, liberty, or property, without due process of law; nor deny to any person within its jurisdiction the equal protection of the laws.

SECTION 2. Representatives shall be apportioned among the several States according to their respective numbers, counting the whole number of persons in each State, excluding Indians not taxed. But when the right to vote at any election for the choice of electors for President and Vice President of the United States, Representatives in Congress, the Executive and Judicial officers of a State, or the members of the Legislature thereof, is denied to any of the male inhabitants of such State, being twenty-one years of age, and citizens of the United States, or in any way abridged, except for participation in rebellion, or other crime, the basis of representation therein shall be reduced in the proportion which the number of such male citizens shall bear to the whole number of male citizens twenty-one years of age in such State.

SECTION 3. No person shall be a Senator or Representative in Congress, or elector of President and Vice President, or hold any office, civil or military, under the United States, or under any State, who, having previously taken an oath, as a member of Congress, or as an officer of the United States, or as a member of any State legislature, or as an executive or judicial officer of any State, to support the Constitution of the United States, shall have engaged in insurrection or rebellion against the same, or given aid or comfort to the enemies thereof. But Congress may by a vote of two-thirds of each House, remove such disability.

SECTION 4. The validity of the public debt of the United States, authorized by law, including debts incurred for payment of pensions and bounties for services in suppressing insurrection or rebellion, shall not be questioned. But neither the United States nor any State shall assume or pay any debt or obligation incurred in aid of insurrection or rebellion against the United States, or any claim for the loss or emancipation of any slave; but all such debts, obligations and claims shall be held illegal and void.

SECTION 5. The Congress shall have power to enforce, by appropriate legislation, the provisions of this article.

---

1. The Fourteenth Amendment was ratified July 9, 1868.

AMENDMENT XV.[1]

SECTION 1. The right of citizens of the United States to vote shall not be denied or abridged by the United States or by any State on account of race, color, or previous condition of servitude.

SECTION 2. The Congress shall have power to enforce this article by appropriate legislation.

AMENDMENT XVI.[2]

The Congress shall have power to lay and collect taxes on incomes, from whatever source derived, without apportionment among the several States, and without regard to any census or enumeration.

AMENDMENT XVII.[3]

The Senate of the United States shall be composed of two Senators from each State, elected by the people thereof, for six years; and each Senator shall have one vote. The electors in each State shall have the qualifications requisite for electors of the most numerous branch of the State legislatures.

When vacancies happen in the representation of any State in the Senate, the executive authority of such State shall issue writs of election to fill such vacancies: *Provided,* That the legislature of any State may empower the executive thereof to make temporary appointments until the people fill the vacancies by election as the legislature may direct.

This amendment shall not be so construed as to affect the election or term of any Senator chosen before it becomes valid as part of the Constitution.

AMENDMENT XVIII.[4]

[SECTION 1. After one year from the ratification of this article the manufacture, sale, or transportation of intoxicating liquors within, the importation thereof into, or the exportation thereof from the United States and all territory subject to the jurisdiction thereof for beverage purposes is hereby prohibited.

SECTION 2. The Congress and the several States shall have concurrent power to enforce this article by appropriate legislation.

SECTION 3. This article shall be inoperative unless it shall have been ratified as an amendment to the Constitution by the legislatures of the several

---

1. The Fifteenth Amendment was ratified February 3, 1870.
2. The Sixteenth Amendment was ratified February 3, 1913.
3. The Seventeenth Amendment was ratified April 8, 1913.
4. The Eighteenth Amendment was ratified January 16, 1919. It was repealed by the Twenty-first Amendment, December 5, 1933.

States, as provided in the Constitution, within seven years from the date of the submission hereof to the States by the Congress.]

AMENDMENT XIX.[1]

The right of citizens of the United States to vote shall not be denied or abridged by the United States or by any State on account of sex.

Congress shall have power to enforce this article by appropriate legislation.

AMENDMENT XX.[2]

SECTION 1.   The terms. of the President and Vice President shall end at noon on the 20th day of January, and the terms of Senators and Representatives at noon on the 3d day of January, of the years in which such terms would have ended if this article had not been ratified; and the terms of their successors shall then begin.

SECTION 2.   The Congress shall assemble at least once in every year, and such meeting shall begin at noon on the 3d day of January, unless they shall by law appoint a different day.

SECTION 3.   If, at the time fixed for the beginning of the term of the President, the President elect shall have died, the Vice President elect shall become President. If a President shall not have been chosen before the time fixed for the beginning of his term, or if the President elect shall have failed to qualify, then the Vice President elect shall act as President until a President shall have qualified; and the Congress may by law provide for the case wherein neither a President elect nor a Vice President elect shall have qualified, declaring who shall then act as President, or the manner in which one who is to act shall be selected, and such person shall act accordingly until a President or Vice President shall have qualified.

SECTION 4.   The Congress may by law provide for the case of the death of any of the persons from whom the House of Representatives may choose a President whenever the right of choice shall have devolved upon them, and for the case of the death of any of the persons from whom the Senate may choose a Vice President whenever the right of choice shall have devolved upon them.

SECTION 5.   Sections 1 and 2 shall take effect on the 15th day of October following the ratification of this article.

SECTION 6.   This article shall be inoperative unless it shall have been ratified as an amendment to the Constitution by the legislatures of three-

1. The Nineteenth Amendment was ratified August 18, 1920.
2. The Twentieth Amendment was ratified January 23, 1933.

fourths of the several States within seven years from the date of its submission.

AMENDMENT XXI.[1]

SECTION 1.   The eighteenth article of amendment to the Constitution of the United States is hereby repealed.

SECTION 2.   The transportation or importation into any State, Territory, or possession of the United States for delivery or use therein of intoxicating liquors, in violation of the laws thereof, is hereby prohibited.

SECTION 3.   This article shall be inoperative unless it shall have been ratified as an amendment to the Constitution by conventions in the several States, as provided in the Constitution, within seven years from the date of the submission hereof to the States by the Congress.

AMENDMENT XXII.[2]

SECTION 1.   No person shall be elected to the office of the President more than twice, and no person who has held the office of President, or acted as President, for more than two years of a term to which some other person was elected President shall be elected to the office of the President more than once. But this Article shall not apply to any person holding the office of President when this Article was proposed by the Congress, and shall not prevent any person who may be holding the office of President, or acting as President, during the term within which this Article becomes operative from holding the office of President or acting as President during the remainder of such term.

SECTION 2.   This article shall be inoperative unless it shall have been ratified as an amendment to the Constitution by the legislatures of three-fourths of the several States within seven years from the date of its submission to the States by the Congress.

AMENDMENT XXIII.[3]

SECTION 1.   The District constituting the seat of Government of the United States shall appoint in such manner as the Congress may direct:

A number of electors of President and Vice President equal to the whole number of Senators and Representatives in Congress to which the District would be entitled if it were a State, but in no event more than the least populous State; they shall be in addition to those appointed by the States,

---

1. The Twenty-first Amendment was ratified December 5, 1933.
2. The Twenty-second Amendment was ratified February 27, 1951.
3. The Twenty-third Amendment was ratified March 29, 1961.

but they shall be considered, for the purposes of the election of President and Vice President, to be electors appointed by a State; and they shall meet in the District and perform such duties as provided by the twelfth article of amendment.

SECTION 2. The Congress shall have power to enforce this article by appropriate legislation.

AMENDMENT XXIV.[1]

SECTION 1. The right of citizens of the United States to vote in any primary or other election for President or Vice President, for electors for President or Vice President, or for Senator or Representative in Congress, shall not be denied or abridged by the United States or any State by reason of failure to pay any poll tax or other tax.

SECTION 2. The Congress shall have power to enforce this article by appropriate legislation.

AMENDMENT XXV.[2]

SECTION 1. In case of the removal of the President from office or of his death or resignation, the Vice President shall become President.

SECTION 2. Whenever there is a vacancy in the office of the Vice President, the President shall nominate a Vice President who shall take office upon confirmation by a majority vote of both Houses of Congress.

SECTION 3. Whenever the President transmits to the President pro tempore of the Senate and the Speaker of the House of Representatives his written declaration that he is unable to discharge the powers and duties of his office, and until he transmits to them a written declaration to the contrary, such powers and duties shall be discharged by the Vice President as Acting President.

SECTION 4. Whenever the Vice President and a majority of either the principal officers of the executive departments or of such other body as Congress may by law provide, transmit to the President pro tempore of the Senate and the Speaker of the House of Representatives their written declaration that the President is unable to discharge the powers and duties of his office, the Vice President shall immediately assume the powers and duties of the office as Acting President.

Thereafter, when the President transmits to the President pro tempore of the Senate and the Speaker of the House of Representatives his written declaration that no inability exists, he shall resume the powers and duties

---

1. The Twenty-fourth Amendment was ratified January 23, 1964.
2. The Twenty-fifth Amendment was ratified February 10, 1967.

of his office unless the Vice President and a majority of either the principal officers of the executive department or of such other body as Congress may by law provide, transmit within four days to the President pro tempore of the Senate and the Speaker of the House of Representatives their written declaration that the President is unable to discharge the powers and duties of his office. Thereupon Congress shall decide the issue, assembling within forty-eight hours for that purpose if not in session. If the Congress, within twenty-one days after receipt of the latter written declaration, or, if Congress is not in session, within twenty-one days after Congress is required to assemble, determines by two-thirds vote of both Houses that the President is unable to discharge the powers and duties of his office, the Vice President shall continue to discharge the same as Acting President; otherwise, the President shall resume the powers and duties of his office.

AMENDMENT XXVI.[1]

SECTION 1.   The right of citizens of the United States, who are eighteen years of age or older, to vote shall not be denied or abridged by the United States or by any State on account of age.

SECTION 2.   The Congress shall have power to enforce this article by appropriate legislation.

---

1. The Twenty-sixth Amendment was ratified July 1, 1971.

INDEX

THE LANDMARK HISTORY OF THE
AMERICAN PEOPLE

VOLUME 2
From Appomattox to the Moon
NEWLY REVISED AND UPDATED

BY DANIEL J. BOORSTIN
With Ruth F. Boorstin

Illustrated with prints and photographs

Sonlight Curriculum Ltd.

Author's Acknowledgments

This book has benefited from the suggestions of many friends and fellow historians, especially those at the University of Chicago and the Smithsonian Institution. At Random House, Janet Finnie proposed the book to me and helped shape it; Karen Tobias helped find and select the illustrations. Janet Schulman of Random House suggested the new edition and with the assistance of Kate Banks helped guide the updating and revisions.

PICTURE CREDITS: Bethlehem Steel Company, 32; The Bettmann Archive, 3, 4, 7; Black Star (Eugene Anthony), ix, (Fred Ward), 135, (John Bennewitz), 167, (James A. Sugar), 187; Brown Brothers, 11, 41, 54, 56, 59, 60, 69, 83, 91, 120, 124, 132 left, 162, 180; Camera 5 (Ken Regan), 185; Culver Pictures, 6–7 margins, 12, 14, 16, 18, 21, 23, 27, 29, 33, 35, 39, 45, 49, 51, 62, 64, 66, 70, 71, 74, 76, 81, 82, 113, 117, 121, 129, 131 both, 132 right, 144, 149 top, 149 bottom, 151; Defense Department photo, Marine Corps, 169; DeWys Inc., vi; Drake Well Museum, 9; Richard Erdoes, 128; Library of Congress, front endpaper, 36, 37, 42, 79, 98, 103, 104, 111, 123, 126, 173, 174; Magnum, Inc., back endpaper; Montgomery Ward Catalog (1895), 18, 30; Museum of the City of New York, 73, 100 both; National Aeronautics and Space Administration, 141, 182; New-York Historical Society, cover, 1, 24–25 top, 57, 65, 67, 84, 114; New York Public Library, Picture Collection, 28, 53; Pictorial Parade, 139; Pix (James Pickerelle), 170, (Charles Simonpietri-Gamma), 171; courtesy Joseph Pulitzer, Jr., 145; Radio Corporation of America, 176; Remington Art Memorial Museum, 146; courtesy Epes Winthrop Sargent (from *Queen of Populists*, by Richard Stiller), 107; Sears Roebuck Catalog (1897), 20; Smithsonian Institution, 31, 88, 92, 94, 95, 96, 101, 108, 109, 154, 159; Union Pacific Railroad Company, 77; United Press International, reverse of front endpaper, 119, 138, 165, 178; official United States Air Force photo, 164; Wide World Photos, 136, 155, 160, 186.

First published by Random House, Inc.
Current edition published by Sonlight Curriculum, Ltd., 1996, by arrangement with the author.
Library of Congress Cataloging-in-Publication Data:
Boorstin, Daniel J. (Daniel Joseph), 1914—   .
    The landmark history of the American people.
    Includes bibliographies and indexes.
    Contents: v. 1. From Plymouth to Appomattox—
v. 2. From Appomattox to the moon.
    1. United States—History—Juvenile literature.
[1. United States—History]   I. Boorstin, Ruth Frankel.
II. Title.
E178.1.B717   1987   973   87-9603
ISBN 1-887840-02-8

Manufactured in the United States of America   3 4 5 6 7 8 9 0

*Dedicated with love
to our grandchildren,
Julia, Eric, Adam, and Ariel*

CONTENTS

Prologue: A World Transformed

Part One: The Go-Getters

Part Two: People on the Move

Part Three: Bringing People Together

Part Four: Champions for the People

Part Five: To This Whole World—and Beyond

PROLOGUE
A World Transformed

For the American people, everyday life changed in the century following the Civil War more than the life of earthlings had changed in the thousand years before.

As millions from everywhere became Americans, they invented a new Way of Life. And they gave a new meaning to almost everything.

Americans, for example, changed the meaning of day-and-night. Indoors, after sundown, could now be brighter than during the day.

Americans changed the meaning of the seasons. Wherever they lived, with central heating and air conditioning, they could be warm in winter and cool in summer. Foods of all seasons could be eaten any time. The United States became the land of strawberries in winter.

Americans changed the meaning of country-and-city. Every day the farmer, like the city man, could read his city newspaper. He wore city-made clothes and he bought city-made furniture in the latest styles—delivered right to his door.

Americans changed the meaning of distance. Faraway events were heard and seen in everybody's living room. Now millions could afford to go out by jet plane to Paris or Rome or Tokyo and see the world for themselves.

Americans even changed the meaning of the earth. Ever since the beginning of history this had been a lonely planet. The heavens were where living men could never go. Now, once again, Americans accomplished the "impossible." They walked on the moon and planned trips to Mars and beyond.

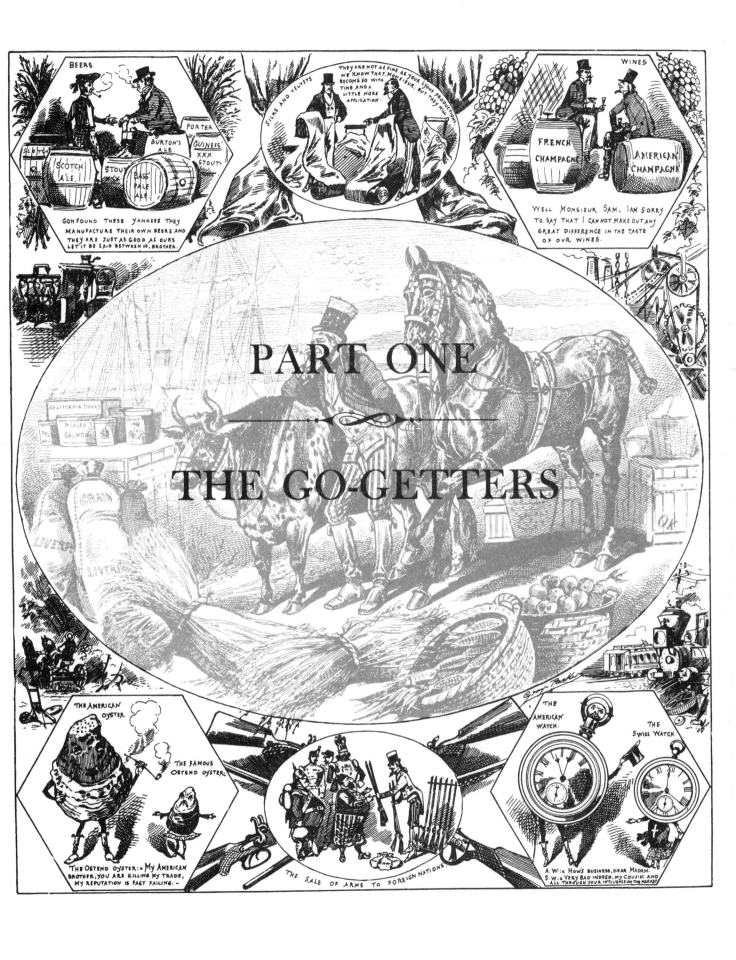

PART ONE

THE GO-GETTERS

THE GO-GETTERS

By the time of the Civil War, Americans had only begun to discover America. The land was still half-explored. The highest mountains were still unclimbed and the swiftest rivers still unmapped. Nobody had yet reached the top of Long's Peak or Mount Whitney. The Colorado River, which began somewhere high in the Rockies, had not been traced in its dangerous meanders. The shores of the Great Lakes were still a mystery. The bayous of Louisiana and the everglades of Florida seemed dark and threatening.

The Gold Rush to California in 1849 was only a first finding of the treasures in mountain streams and deep under the earth. America was full of secret resources.

A new kind of American, the Go-Getter, helped discover these treasures. Just as the nation was founded by people with assorted dreams and hopes, so a new American Way of Life was invented by a wide assortment of Go-Getters.

Some were outdoor men riding the range, leading thousands of cattle on new trails. Some were adventuring miners, risking fortunes to drill deep in search of mysterious new minerals. Some were businessmen—new-style storekeepers finding ways to make the whole nation their customers. Some were engineers and inventors, anxious to build bigger engines than the world had ever seen, and machines which could turn out things by the millions.

E Pluribus Unum was the Latin motto of the young nation. It meant "one made from many." The Go-Getters were experts at bringing people together. Just as earlier Americans had organized thirteen new colonies and a new nation, so now the Go-Getters brought later Americans together in their cattle-trains and oil companies and department stores, and in thousands of other new enterprises. The new American Way of Life was designed for everybody.

America would be not merely a democracy of people but also a democracy of things. It would be a long time —maybe forever—before no one was poor. But after the Civil War it became easier for more and more Americans to share the good things of life. The Go-Getters, without even intending it, were bringing the whole nation together.

Some of the Go-Getters were more honest than others. Some made their fortunes by new ideas, by hard work, by being clever. Some were simply lucky. All prospered from the continent's hidden wealth.

The Go-Getters were not satisfied with the slow pace of the Old World. They wanted to see things happen fast. And by the early years of the twentieth century they had helped transform American life.

CHAPTER 1

Cattlemen and Cowboys

About the time of the Civil War, the Western cattle trade became big business. The men who made money from it were as different as possible from the European peasant who kept his few cattle at night in the room where he slept. The peasant could keep only a few because his house was small, and he had to feed his animals by hand in winter.

The Western cattleman numbered his stock by the thousands. He did not have to give them a roof, for Western cattle were tough enough to look after themselves on the range. And on the great Western plains there grew "buffalo grass" which survived drought and provided free food right on the ground throughout the winter.

Western cattlemen were bold and adventurous, willing to take big risks in a wild country. In the Old World, the expression "Man on Horseback" meant a military man, a commander of troops which he might use to take over the government. But in the American West the "Man on Horseback" was a cowboy. And the Western cattleman was a Go-Getter on horseback.

One of the first and most energetic of these was John Wesley Iliff. His father, an Ohio farmer, had offered him $7,500 if he would settle nearby on a respectable Ohio farm. But in 1856 he heard of the fortunes farther west. Young Iliff, who wanted adventure, told his father he would be satisfied with $500 if he could use it to make his start out there.

A cowboy and his horse, working together, could rescue a Longhorn from the mud. In the days before the camera could take action pictures, the artist Frederic Remington became famous for his drawings and sculptures of men and horses in action.

A cowboy in his "uniform," fully equipped with lariat and six-shooter. A drawing by C. M. Russell, who was born in St. Louis and went to Montana as a cowboy at the age of sixteen.

Iliff did not find gold in the Colorado mountain streams. But he did find it in the cattle that came there with Americans pushing westward.

During the Colorado Gold Rush the thousands of covered wagons that arrived near Denver—just before the climb into the mountains—wanted to lighten their load. They shed most of their belongings, so they could go ahead on foot or with a few pack mules. They were glad to sell to Iliff the footsore oxen that had pulled their wagons across the plains.

He fed these cattle free on the open range that belonged to everybody. He began breeding a herd. When the animals were fattened, Iliff sold them either to butchers in the mining camps or to travelers returning east who needed oxen to pull their wagons.

Of course there were risks, especially from winter weather and from Indian attack. Iliff became friendly with a man named Gerry, a pioneer fur trader who had married the twin daughters of Chief Swift Bird of the Oglalas. Using the information from his wives, Gerry warned Iliff whenever the Indians were about to attack, so that Iliff's cattle could be moved to a safe place.

For a Go-Getter like Iliff, even the Indians became a source of profit. He made a small fortune supplying meat to the remote western outposts where troops had been sent to fight the Indians. At the same time he sold beef to government officials so they could feed the Indians on reservations.

When railroads—promoted by Eastern Go-Getters—pushed West, they opened another new market. Now Western beef could be shipped to the growing Eastern cities. At the same time, hard-working crews building the railroads had to be well fed, and what they most wanted was meat. Iliff agreed to deliver cattle by the thousands to the Union Pacific Railroad construction gangs and to the troops guarding them against the Indians.

This was easier said than done. He had to find more beef than anyone had ever yet seen in one place. And he had to bring it to the middle of nowhere, where railroads were still to be built.

Iliff was helped by still another brand of Go-Getter, the Western Trailblazer.

One of the oldest of them was a remarkable man with the unlikely name of Charles Goodnight. His family had taken him to Texas when he was a boy of nine. In 1868 Goodnight agreed to deliver to Iliff's camp near Cheyenne, Wyoming, forty thousand dollars worth of cattle from Texas.

When Americans had come to Texas in the 1830's thousands of Longhorn cattle were running wild. These were the great-great-grandchildren of a few animals brought over by Spanish explorers in the sixteenth century. To get your herd all you had to do was to hunt and capture. Hunting wild cattle became a prosperous business. But it was not child's play. For the wild cattle of Texas, one hunter reported, were "fifty times more dangerous than the fiercest buffalo." Armed with sharp horns that they were not afraid to use, these bold beasts could not be managed by men on foot. They made the Texas cowboy get onto his horse, and they kept him there.

It was a thousand miles from the cattle country of central Texas to Goodnight's promised delivery point in southeastern Wyoming. You had to cross some of the driest, most unfriendly land in the whole continent—what maps before the Civil War called the "Great American Desert." In all that country there was no town worthy of the name. There was not even any trail. To deliver his cattle, Goodnight had to find his own way.

It would be a risky business. But it seemed worth trying, when a steer bought for four dollars in Texas sold for forty dollars in Wyoming. Multiply that by three thousand (the number of cattle Goodnight hoped to take on each

trip) and it added up to a handsome profit.

The Texas Longhorns were well equipped for long trips. Their sense of smell, the cowboys said, was as much superior to that of an ordinary Eastern cow as the bloodhound's was to that of a parlor poodle. Where water was hard to find, the Longhorn's nose for water could make the difference between life and death. Cowboys who let the leading steer act as guide sometimes found remote lakes they had never seen before.

The real problem was how to keep all those three thousand cattle together and moving at just the right speed. If they were allowed to stop or dawdle, they might never reach their goal. But if they were allowed to trot they might get out of control or exercise off the weight that was worth money in Wyoming.

Stationed at the front, or "point," of the herd were two of the most experienced men, called "pointers." They navigated for the whole herd, following the course set ahead by the foreman. Bringing up the rear were three steady cowboys whose job it was to look out for the weaker cattle—the "drags." To prevent the herd from straggling out for miles, the whole party moved no faster than the weakest "drags" at the rear. The rest of the cowboy crew were stationed along the sides to keep the herd compact and all the same width.

Every herd of cattle on the trail needed its own herd of horses to give the cowboys fresh mounts for their tricky jobs. To feed the men you needed a chuck wagon which the cook would drive fast ahead of everybody else. His job was to have food ready as soon as the weary cowboys arrived.

Communication between the front and rear of the herd was difficult. The rumbling of hoofs smothered words. The cowboys, then, borrowed a clever system of hand signals from the Plains Indians.

Apart from Indians, the greatest peril was a stampede. Suddenly at night the three thousand cattle, which a moment before had been quietly dozing, might rouse into a thundering mass. To stop a stampede, experienced cowboys made a circle to keep the animals churning and circling, always round to the right. Then by tightening their circle they squeezed the stampeding cattle tighter and tighter together till they had no place to run. The milling herd was forced to halt.

If the encircling tactic failed, all was lost. The stampede would get out of control. Then the cattle would fly out like sparks into the night, and they might never be seen again.

The cowboys had their own trail-tested ways of preventing stampedes by soothing the jumpy Longhorns. At night the men guarding the herd would sing and whistle while they made their rounds. The purpose of this "serenading," the veteran cowboy Andy Adams explained, was "so that the sleeping herd may know that a friend and not an enemy is keeping vigil over their dreams."

The cowboys called these songs "hymns" because they were sung to tunes which the cowboys remembered from their mothers' songs in childhood or from church services. But the words the cowboys sang usually were not church-words. What they sang might have shocked or startled the cattle if they could have understood. For these cowboy songs told the exploits of famous horse races and notorious criminals, or they repeated advertising texts from coffee cans or whiskey bottles, or they recited profanity sprinkled between nonsense syllables.

At the end of the Long Drive came the "Cow Town," which was as American as the cowboy. It was simply another smaller kind of "instant city" like those already dotted over the West. The Cow Town was where cowboys delivered their herd to the cattle dealers and the railroads. There, after long lonely weeks on the trail, cowboys enjoyed the company of strangers, bought liquor, and gambled away their money.

Go-Getting cattlemen made these instant towns prosper. One cattleman, Joseph G. McCoy, picked a place along the Kansas Pacific Railroad. In 1867, when he first made his plans for Abilene, it was (as he later recalled) "a very small, dead place, consisting of about one dozen log huts, low, small rude affairs, four-fifths of which were covered with turf roofing; indeed, but one shingle roof could be seen in the whole city. The business of the burg was conducted in two small rooms, mere log huts, and of course the inevitable saloon, also in a log hut, was to be found."

Within sixty days the place was transformed. As if by magic, Abilene had a shipping yard for three thousand head of cattle, besides a large pair of Fairbanks Scales to weigh the cattle on, a big barn and office, and of course "a good three-story hotel." The idea was to ship out thousands of cattle from Abilene to Chicago and other big cities.

Texas cowboys trying to end a stampede of Longhorns frightened by thunder (1881). In the margin of this and the facing page are cattle brands.

On September 5, 1867, when the first shipment (twenty carloads of cattle) left Abilene, the Chicago stockmen had come there to celebrate. In tents specially erected for the occasion, they feasted, drank wine, sang, and listened to bombastic speeches. Before the end of that year Abilene shipped out 35,000 head of cattle.

The Go-Getting McCoy had paid only $2,400 for the whole Abilene townsite. Before long he was offered more than that for a single city lot. He received from the Kansas Pacific Railroad a commission of one-eighth of the freight charges on every carload of cattle. Before the end of the second year,

the railroad company owed McCoy a quarter of a million dollars.

Soon there were other prospering Cow Towns sprinkled all over the West: Schuyler and Fort Kearney and North Platte and Ogallala and Sydney in Nebraska, Pine Bluffs and Rock River and Rock Creek and Laramie and Hillsdale and Cheyenne in Wyoming, Miles City and Glendive and Helena in Montana.

The Cow Towns did not suffer from modesty. More than one boasted that she was the "Queen of Cow Towns." But Dodge City, in Kansas, and others competed for the title of the "Wickedest Little City in America."

While town-building was profitable

and exciting, prosperous cattlemen still fondly remembered their days on the trail. "All in all, my years on the Trail," Charles Goodnight remembered on his ninety-third birthday, "were the happiest I ever lived. There were many hardships and dangers, of course, that called on all a man had of endurance and bravery; but when all went well there was no other life so pleasant. Most of the time we were solitary adventurers in a great land as fresh and new as a spring morning, and were free and full of the zest of darers."

Western cattlemen and cowboys were among the first and bravest of the Go-Getters. They tried the impossible and succeeded in making something from nothing. They captured wild cattle that belonged to nobody. Then they fed the cattle on buffalo grass that nobody even imagined could be food, and grazed them on range that belonged to everybody and nobody. And they finally transported the cattle on their very own feet for thousands of miles to places where they could become beef.

Who could have imagined that the "Great American Desert" would become the greatest beef factory in the world?

CHAPTER 2

Rock Oil to Light up the World

The Indians had taught the early settlers how to raise new crops like corn and tobacco, and how to find new medicines in the forests and underground. One of these medicines was a curious black oily substance that the Seneca Indians of upstate New York saw floating on ponds. They laid their blankets on top of ponds where the oil was floating, until the blankets had soaked up the oil. Then they wrung the oil out of the blankets into a bowl. They treasured the oil as an ointment, which they thought would cure all sorts of ills.

Before the end of the eighteenth century, the American colonists had learned to use this oily medicine, and it became an item of trade with the Indians. It was called "Seneca Oil" after the Indians who sold it.

Down in Kentucky in the 1830's, when a salt well was ruined by the oil which bubbled into it, the owners discovered that the black stuff was really Seneca Oil. They stopped selling salt, and instead went into the medicine business. They put the stuff in bottles, called it "Rock Oil" or "American Oil," and sold it as a remedy for rheumatism and nearly everything else. They sold these bottles by the hundreds of thousands.

Other salt manufacturers, who found this black stuff ruining their salt wells, also went into the medicine business. One of them, Samuel Kier, put out leaflets boasting of his Rock Oil's "wonderful curative powers" for rheumatism, chronic cough, ague, toothache, corns, neuralgia, piles, indigestion, and liver ailments. He printed advertisements in

A bottle and wrapper for Kier's "Genuine Petroleum" which he sold as medicine. The scene from the Biblical story of the Good Samaritan (who helped his suffering fellowmen) was supposed to show what Kier's Genuine Petroleum could do for you.

the shape and size of paper money. These featured the number 400—the number of feet below the earth's surface from which the oil was drawn—as if every drop of the oil was worth its weight in gold.

To attract customers, Kier sent salesmen out over the countryside in circus wagons. They played music, sang songs, displayed animal freaks, and used every possible means to attract attention and sell their magic fluid. Within a few years, Kier had disposed of a quarter-million half-pints of his wonderful Rock Oil at a dollar a bottle.

But Kier's wells gushed out even more than his clever salesmen could sell. What could be done with the rest?

About the same time that Kier and other salt manufacturers found themselves flooded with Rock Oil, there was a growing need for some inexpensive kind of lighting. In those days before electric lights, home lighting came from tallow candles and oil lamps, not much different from the ones used in ancient Rome. A wick made from a twisted rag burned in a dish of fish oil or animal oil or vegetable oil. That weak flickering light of burning oil was all that people

had to read and play and work by after sundown.

But oil was expensive. So most homes were usually not lit at night. And people went to bed when the sun set.

In the years before the Civil War, American cities were growing. Homes built close together lacked sunlight. At the same time city people wanted to get together more in the evenings. New factories and railroads also required more and better artificial light. As early as 1830, gas (manufactured from coal) was used to light a few streets and public buildings in Baltimore, Boston, and New York. But gas was not yet used in houses.

Some help came when Isaiah Jennings invented a new lamp oil, which he called "camphene." He used American turpentine—the yellowish sticky fluid that seeped out of holes made in certain pine trees. When this sticky stuff was heated and the product was mixed with alcohol, it made an excellent lighting fluid. It was much cheaper than the other lighting oils, and when it burned it gave a brighter, whiter light. But it had an unpleasant smell and it gave off explosive gases.

Nearly everybody agreed that American homes would not be bright at night until there was a safer inexpensive lamp oil. Where could it be found?

A hint of the great new source came when a clever Canadian doctor, Abraham Gesner, in 1850 found a way to make lighting oil from coal. He called his new product "kerosene" (from *keros,* the Greek word for wax). It had an unpleasant odor, but it could be used without danger of explosion. Doctors who had warned against the "horrors of burning fluid" now urged people to fill their lamps with the safe new "coal oil." Before the end of 1859 nearly two million coal-oil lamps had been sold. But since there were about thirty million people in the United States, the country was still a long way from the goal of "a lamp in every room."

Dr. Gesner had showed that lamp oil could be made not only from plants and animals but also from coal, which was a *mineral.* Was it possible that the new mineral product, Rock Oil, could also be used for lighting?

About this time a New Haven businessman, George H. Bissell, formed the Pennsylvania Rock Oil Company to buy lands in western Pennsylvania, where Rock Oil was found floating on ponds. He hired a famous Yale professor of chemistry, Benjamin Silliman, Jr., and agreed to pay him $500 to find out what the Rock Oil was good for.

Professor Silliman's report opened a new age for Rock Oil. He discovered that Rock Oil—by now also called "petroleum" from *petrus,* Latin for rock, and *oleum* for oil—would make an excellent oil for lamps. His process was cheap. He simply distilled the Rock Oil

—that is, heated it and collected the gas that came off. When the gas cooled down into a liquid, it was lamp oil. This, he discovered, was a new way to make kerosene that was just as good as kerosene made from coal. Kerosene made from Rock Oil also gave a bright, white light, with almost no smoke, and would not explode.

The Rock Oil itself also had wonderful lubricating powers. It would keep the wheels and gears of machines from wearing out and would make them run quiet and smooth.

Rock Oil, with these valuable uses, could surely be sold in large quantities. But until then the only known way to collect it was to find it on the surface or accidentally in a salt well. Sometimes people would dig a shallow ditch to increase the flow where it was already bubbling up.

Then one day, the story goes, Bissell saw one of Kier's advertisements. It was the sheet printed to look like paper money that featured the numeral 400. "A.D. 1848," it read. "Discovered in *boring* for salt water . . . about FOUR HUNDRED FEET below the Earth's surface." Boring! If oil could be obtained when you bored for salt water, why not simply bore for the oil?

"Oil coming out of the ground!" exclaimed a friend. "Pumping oil out of the earth the way you pump water? Nonsense! You're crazy."

But Bissell and the other Go-Getting businessmen in the Pennsylvania Rock Oil Company decided to try. From New Haven they sent Edwin L. Drake out to the oil fields. One reason they picked him was that since he had been a railroad conductor, he still had a free pass on the railroads. He could go out to western Pennsylvania without it costing anybody anything.

When Drake reached Titusville, the town closest to the biggest finds of surface oil, he decided to drill for oil. But at first he could not find a driller willing to do the job. The drillers all thought that boring for oil was silly.

Then, luckily, he found an old salt driller, "Uncle Billy" Smith, who was also a skilled blacksmith and knew how to make drilling tools. Uncle Billy began drilling in June 1859. But after he reached bedrock thirty-two feet down,

Uncle Billy could drill no more than three feet each day. Drake thought that to find oil they might have to drill a thousand feet.

On Saturday, August 29, 1859, the hole still reached down less than seventy feet. When Drake and Smith came back on Monday morning the hole was full of oily black stuff.

"What's that?" Drake asked.

Uncle Billy replied, "That's your fortune!"

Soon there was an oil mania. Everybody wanted to get rich from oil. The map of northwestern Pennsylvania was

The first oil well, Titusville, Pennsylvania. The pointed wooden structure held a derrick for pulling up the drilling tools.

Barrels of oil being loaded on flat-bottomed barges for shipment by water. Shallow boats like these had to navigate the torrents of the Pond Freshet.

dotted with such new names as Oil City, Oleopolis, and Petroleum Center.

Like the instant Cow Towns, these instant Oil Towns boomed. They were good places for salesmen and for swindlers. Some well drillers began "doctoring" their wells. They would pour buckets of oil into their holes at night to trick buyers who came to look the next morning.

When Drake's first well began to gush oil, the oil was put into old whisky barrels, washtubs, and any other container in sight. But since the oil was inflammable, it was dangerous to store in the open. The oil was usually sealed in barrels before being loaded on wagons to

be hauled to the railroad or to docks on the nearest rivers. As roads were poor, the best way to move the oil barrels was on flatboats. But in the streams nearest the oil wells the water was too low to float the loaded flatboats.

The clever oilmen then invented their own way of filling the creeks with water to float their oil barrels to market. The name for their system was the "Pond Freshet" ("freshet" meant a sudden flood of water). For example, on Oil Creek, each oilman made his own artificial pond held back by a dam. Then, at a signal, each quickly opened the dam of his own artificial pond. This suddenly flooded the creek.

Only a few minutes before, the creek was much too shallow for the big flatboats. Now this man-made wave floated down the stream. All the flatboats along the way were alert and ready. At just the right moment, each oilman pushed his loaded boats into the flood, which carried them quickly down to the railroad center.

Just after a successful Pond Freshet, as an oilman recalled, the Oil Town was very much like a Cow Town after the arrival of a large Texas herd.

Shippers are busy paying off the boatmen, the citizens of the creek are laying in a stock of the necessaries of life, and all is bustle and business. You see men dripping with the oleaginous product. Our hotels are filled to repletion with these greasy men who are supplying light for the world. Oil is the only topic of conversation, and the air is redolent with its sweet perfumery.

The great success in oil—one of the most spectacular of all American Go-Getters—was John D. Rockefeller. He was not an inventor or an explorer. He was an organizer. His talent was like that of Charles Goodnight, who had collected thousands of cattle for the Long Drive.

Young Rockefeller went to school in Cleveland, but he never went to college. His father, who traveled through the West selling patent medicines, left young John in charge of the family long before he was grown. John D. Rockefeller was ambitious. "I did not guess what it would be," he recalled. "But I was after something big."

Even as a boy he was systematic and well organized. While still struggling to make his way, he gave one-tenth of his income to the Baptist Church and to charities. But when it came to organizing his oil business, he did not always use Sunday School methods.

Cleveland was a good place to organize "something big" in the oil business. At the receiving end of two railroads which came from the western Pennsylvania oil fields, Cleveland was also on a lake big enough for large ships. Rockefeller determined to make Cleveland the center of the oil business, and from there to command the biggest oil company in the world. Beginning with a small sum he had made in a grain-trading business, in 1865 he bought his first Cleveland refinery. There crude oil from the fields was made into kerosene for lighting and oil for lubricating. Then he bought up the smaller refineries in Cleveland and many oil wells in western Pennsylvania.

As other oilmen went out of business, the railroads needed Rockefeller's freight more than ever. He was clever at making the two Cleveland railroads compete for his business. He bargained with one railroad by threatening to give all his business to the other. And he finally forced them to charge him lower prices than they charged anybody else. He did this by secret arrangements so other customers of the railroad could not know for sure what was happening. He pretended to pay the same prices the railroad charged everybody else. Then the railroads secretly gave him back a "rebate"—a refund on each barrel of his oil that they had hauled.

After he perfected these tactics he went to the small refiners in other parts of the country and asked them to sell to him. "If you don't sell your property," he would say, "it will be valueless, because we have advantages with the railroads."

"But we don't want to sell," they would say.

"You can never make money," Rockefeller would reply. "You can't compete with the Standard Oil Company. We have all the large refineries now. If you refuse to sell, it will end in your being crushed."

He would then offer a price far below what the owners thought their refineries were worth. But they usually sold because they realized that Rockefeller could drive them out of business.

When it became cheaper to pump oil through pipelines instead of carrying it in barrels, Rockefeller organized his own pipeline. Then, when a different kind of oil was found in Ohio, Rockefeller hired chemical engineers to invent new kinds of refineries.

Rockefeller's Go-Getting business reached around the world. To the Chinese, his Standard Oil Company sold inexpensive lamps by the millions—and then sold the oil to fill them. Before long, people on all continents were

---

A magazine cartoon published two years after Drake's first oil strike. Whales (whose blubber had been an important source of lamp oil) had good reason to celebrate the discovery of "mineral oil." As the new oil industry prospered, the whaling industry declined.

VANITY FAIR. [APRIL 20, 1861.

GRAND BALL GIVEN BY THE WHALES IN HONOR OF THE DISCOVERY OF THE OIL WELLS IN PENNSYLVANIA.

using lamp oil from American wells. Between the Civil War and 1900 over half the American output went abroad. In those years the giant Go-Getter, John D. Rockefeller, helped light up the world. Now Americans could afford a lamp in every room.

In the twentieth century, Rockefeller's business would grow in ways even he had never imagined. After the automobile was invented, petroleum was refined into gasoline—and Rock Oil made it possible for a whole nation to move on wheels.

CHAPTER 3

City Goods for Country Customers

During the colonial years, an American farmer made for himself almost everything he needed. He built his own house (with the help of a few neighbors) and he made his own furniture. His wife and daughters spun the thread, wove the cloth, and then made the family's clothes. The pots and pans and metal tools which he could not make for himself he would buy from a peddler. But he bought very few things. There were not many ready-made things for him to buy.

Then, in the years before the Civil War, American know-how built on ideas from Europe's Industrial Revolution to develop a new kind of manufacturing. Lots of new things were produced in vast new quantities. The new American System of Manufacture, which Eli Whitney and Samuel Colt had organized to make guns and revolvers, also turned out clocks and locks, and countless other items—both better and cheaper. Now farmers could afford to buy them.

But when a farmer wanted any of these things he had to go to the nearest village and visit the general store.

Children loved the place because it was where you could buy candy and toys. Since the storekeeper kept a good fire in his stove, the store was where you could stay warm in winter. Year round it was where you could meet friends and exchange ideas.

But it was no place for bargains. The country storekeeper, who bought only a little bit of everything, could not command the best wholesale prices from the big-city manufacturers. Each item had to be hauled by wagon over bumpy backwoods roads. Things would get dusty and out-of-date before they could be sold.

Soon after the Civil War an energetic young salesman, who had covered the West selling goods to the owners of general stores, began to think of a new plan. His name was A. Montgomery Ward. He had done all sorts of things, from working in a barrel factory and in a brickyard to selling drygoods. Often in his travels he had heard farmers complain about the small choice of goods and the high prices.

Young Ward's idea was to sell goods

An old general store with the village post office. The storekeeper often doubled as postmaster.

in an entirely new way. Instead of the old general store which stocked only a few of each item, Ward imagined a mail-order store. The storekeeper would stay in the big city where it was easier to collect a large stock of all sorts of goods. He would send out to farmers lists of his goods with descriptions and pictures. The farmer would not need to come to the store because the store—in the form of a catalog—would go to the farmer. And the farmer would order by mail, picking out whatever he wanted from the catalog. Then the storekeeper would mail the farmer his goods.

If this new scheme worked, the store-keeper would be selling not only to the few customers in one particular village. He could sell to farmers all over America—to anyone within reach of a mail-box.

The possible customers of this new kind of store would not be just a few hundred, they might be millions! And then Ward could buy his goods from the manufacturer by the hundreds and thousands. The manufacturer could afford to give him a lower price.

For the customer, too, there were advantages. He had a much wider selection of goods. And he paid a lower price since the mail-order storekeeper, with so many more customers, could take a smaller profit on each item and yet would make more money in the long run.

Young Montgomery Ward had lost nearly all his savings in the Chicago fire of 1871, but in the very next year he managed to scrape together enough to make a start with his new idea. He put in $1,600 and a partner added $800. They rented a small room over a stable, and started modestly. Their single price-sheet listed the items for sale and told how to order. Within two years Ward was issuing a 72-page catalog with illustrations. By 1884 the catalog numbered 240 pages and listed nearly ten thousand items. Within another thirty years it was over a thousand pages and included every conceivable object for animals or men.

One way Ward rounded up customers was to get himself appointed the official supplier for the "Grange." This was one name for a large farmers' club, the Patrons of Husbandry, founded just after the Civil War. By 1875 its members numbered 750,000 and all these were likely customers. Ward offered Grange members a special discount. He stocked the official Granger hat and in his catalog printed recommendations from Grange officers. This encouraged other farmers to trust Ward's.

Trust was the most important thing for a mail-order store. If you bought in a general store you were buying from a storekeeper you knew. You could see the goods and handle them to satisfy yourself. But when you bought from a mail-order store you had to trust somebody you had never seen. You had to believe that the storekeeper would really send you the exact thing described in the catalog.

Ward was a spectacular success. The first secret of his success was not a secret at all, but simply to be honest, give good value, and always let the customer be the judge. On everything Ward's gave an ironclad guarantee. "Satisfaction or your money back!" If a customer did not like the goods when they arrived, he could always return them. If something arrived damaged, he could send it back to Ward's to be replaced. The company paid the postage both ways.

Of course there had to be trust on the company's side, too. The company had to be willing to cash the customer's checks, to believe his complaints, and to replace damaged goods without a lot of investigating. Ward was willing to do this, and to take the risks.

The catalog showed pictures of Ward himself, of the other executives, and of the men in charge of the different departments. This was to convince the customer that he was dealing with real people. Some customers wrote in to say how pleased they were to deal with such "fine looking men." Some even named babies after Ward, and said he would be an inspiration to their children.

Ward saw that their letters were promptly answered—even if they were not ordering goods but only asking advice. One customer asked how to find a baby to adopt. Others tried to sell Ward their secondhand furniture or their livestock. Parents asked help in finding boys who had run away from home. They wanted to know how to handle disobedient children. Some wrote him simply because they were lonely and had nobody else to write to.

SHOPPING by CATALOG

From the Montgomery Ward catalog, 1895. At that time both wages and prices were much lower than today. A typical workingman earned about $500 a year.

Children's Suits.

32434 Boys' Shirt Waists, striped cotton cheviot, light ground, double ruffle down front, sailor collar with 1 inch ruffle.
Each $0.30
Per dozen 3.24

32436 Boys' Shirt Waists, light ground striped chambray, double ruffle down front, sailor collar, turned over cuffs with ruffle. Each $0.45
Per dozen $4.86

32438 Boys' Shirt Waists, indigo blue, fancy figured penang; double ruffle down front, sailor collar, turned over cuffs with ruffle, pleated front and back. Each $0.55
Per dozen 5.94

32434 to 32440

32440 Boys' Shirt Waists, medium heavy stripe, cotton cheviot, double ruffle down front, sailor collar with ruffle, pleated front and back.
Each $0.60

Spinning Wheels.

39583
39583 Quill or Spooling Wheel, like cut. Each. $3.60
39585 German or Flax Spinning Wheel, with foot power.
Price, each $4.00

39585

Bathing Suits.
ONE-PIECE SUITS.

Knit goods, very elastic, not cloth goods. Button well down to the front, making them easy to get on or off. Extra, by mail, 5 to 10 cents. Give chest measure.

	Each.
49150 Cotton, striped	$0.75
49151 Cotton, navy blue	1.50
49152 Cotton, fast black	1.50
49153 Cotton, navy with stripes	1.25
49154 Worsted, navy blue	2.90

TWO-PIECE SUITS.

Consisting of quarter sleeve shirts and knee pants.

	Per Suit.
49155 Cotton, striped	$1.00
49156 Cotton, navy, with stripes	1.50
49157 Worsted, navy blue	2.40
49158 Worsted, black	2.40
49160 Best Worsted, striped	5.25

Extra, by mail, 15 to 20 cents.

Style N2. Case only. 14k filled $8.80

36570 Child's Lawn Hat, extra shirred brim. Colors: Cardinal, white, pink or light blue.
Each $0.45
Per dozen 5.00

36571 Child's Shirred Hat, made of Swiss embroidery shirred brim, trimmed all round with embroidered edging
Each $0.50
Per dozen 5.50

5704 Ladies' Newport Suit, same style as 5700, made of heavy all-wool storm serge, trimmed with two rows of folded satin rhadame on collar, cuffs and bottom of skirt. Colors: Black or navy blue only. A stylish and splendid wearing suit. Per suit $5.95

5705 Ladies' Newport Suit, same style as 5700, made of heavy English whip cord, trimmed in narrow folds of satin. Navy blue or black only. Very serviceable and elegant. Per suit. $7.50

5708 Ladies' Newport Suit, same style as 5700, made of fine all wool broadcloth, high finished; collar, cuffs and bottom of skirt trimmed with narrow fold of moire silk, very elegant. Colors: Black, brown, light or dark navy blue.
Per suit $8.50

5709 Ladies' Newport Suit, made of all wool cheviot serge in navy blue; new organ pipe skirt, double breasted jacket, double stitching around skirt and jacket, immense sleeves, made in first-class style. Per suit $8.75

5711 Ladies' Newport Suit, made of stylish tweed suiting, in light brown and white mixture. Very neat and serviceable, will not show dust or wear. Same style as 5709. Per suit $9.00

The Razor Toe.
Weight 15 ounces.

52034 This style shoe is becoming very popular on account of the long narrow toe, and patent tip, which has a tendency of giving the foot a very graceful appearance. The stock is a very soft dongola, with light flexible soles and medium but slightly concave; for a neat stylish dress boot, it has no equal and for the quality, compares favorably with many of the three dollar and a half grades now on the market. Sizes, 2½ to 7 widths, C, D, E and EE.
Per pair $2.50

5709

Just as the colonial tobacco planter might ask his London agent to send him whatever he needed, now the lonely farmer asked Ward's. One customer wrote:

Please send me a good wife. She must be a good housekeeper and able to do all household duty. She must be 5 feet 6 inches in height. Weight 150 lbs. Black hair and brown eyes, either fair or dark. I am 45 years old, six feet, am considered a good looking man. I have black hair and blue eyes. I own quite a lot of stock and land. I am tired of living a bachelor life and wish to lead a better life and more favorable.

Please write and let me know what you can do for me.

Ward's answered that it was not a good idea to select a wife by mail. "After you get the wife and you find that she needs some wearing apparel or household goods," Ward's added, "we feel sure we could serve both you and her to good advantage."

Some felt that Ward's would be disappointed at not hearing from them.

I suppose you wonder why we haven't ordered anything from you since the Fall. Well, the cow kicked my arm and broke it, and besides my wife was sick, and there was the doctor bill. But now, thank God, that is paid, and we are all well again, and we have a fine new baby boy, and please send plush bonnet number 29d-8077.

This friendly customer received a friendly reply. Ward's said they were sorry about his arm, glad that his wife was better, and sent congratulations on the son with hopes he would grow up to be a fine man. The order for the bonnet was acknowledged. Then, finally, Ward's asked whether the customer had noticed that there was an anti-cow-kicker for sale in the catalog.

It is not surprising that the mail-order store was a roaring success. Of course, in an age of Go-Getters, Ward was not the only man who tried his hand at building a mail-order store. One of the cleverest of these others was a young railroad station agent, Richard Sears. When a stray package of watches arrived at his station in North Redwood, Minnesota, the Chicago watch company offered to sell them to Sears at $12 apiece. Sears bought the watches and then sold them by mail to other agents along the line for $14 apiece.

Sears was in business. By selling watches to other station agents, Sears made five thousand dollars in six months, gave up his railroad job, moved to Chicago, and began selling other jewelry by mail. He found a partner in Alvah Curtis Roebuck, a watchmaker who ran a print shop where they could turn out their catalogs.

Sears was a clever man, and a near-genius at selling by mail. One of his schemes was a club plan for selling watches. He persuaded men to form a "Watch Club" of thirty-eight members. Every week each member would pay the Club one dollar. And every week when the members drew lots, one of them would win a watch. At the end of thirty-eight weeks, every club member had a watch. And they had bought all thirty-eight watches from Sears!

Of course, Sears could not have succeeded for long in the mail-order business unless he, like Ward, had been honest. He too gave good value for the money, and let customers return any goods they did not like.

But Sears was not afraid of a good joke. He knew that lonely farm families were glad to be entertained. In a rural weekly newspaper in 1889 he made an "Astonishing Offer." It was illustrated by a drawing of a sofa and two chairs, all of "fine, lustrous metal frames beautifully finished and decorated, and upholstered in the finest manner with beautiful plush." Sears offered to ship all this furniture "as an advertisement only" and "for a limited time only" for the ridiculously low price of ninety-five cents.

The customers who sent in their money really were astonished. They received a set of doll's furniture, made exactly according to the description. They had not noticed in the first line of the advertisement, in tiny print, the word "miniature."

There were lots of stories about how clever Sears was. One of his advertisements offered a "sewing machine" for a dollar. When the customer sent in his

dollar, he promptly received by return mail a needle and thread. But Sears used such stunts only to attract attention.

Like Ward, Sears actually built his business on trust and on the personal touch. After the typewriter first came into general use, about 1900, some farmers still preferred to get a letter written by hand. Sears still went to the trouble of hiring people to write out handwritten letters for the company. Then farmers would not have their feelings hurt by receiving a letter that was "machine-made."

Sears knew that his catalog was both his shopwindow and his salesman. And he invented schemes for getting his catalogs around. He would send them in batches of twenty-four to people who had agreed to distribute them. But how could he be sure that the distributors would give their catalogs to the people most likely to be good customers? Sears kept a record of purchases by the new customers to whom each distributor had given his catalogs. The distributor then received a prize in proportion to the amount of money spent by his new customers. When, for example, total orders from his new customers amounted to $100, the distributor was awarded a bicycle, a sewing machine, or a stove.

Sears was constantly improving his catalog. He developed a new quick-drying ink, new systems of color printing, and thinner paper that would take color but was cheaper to mail. He found, for example, that four pages of

A four-passenger surrey advertised in 1897 by Sears Roebuck for $44. The buyer also needed a horse.

advertisements in color would sell as much of the same goods as twelve pages in black and white. His improvements were widely copied by other advertisers and by publishers of newspapers and magazines.

As Sears's catalog grew bigger and bigger it also reached more and more customers. He sent out two big catalogs a year, one in the spring and one in the fall. By 1904 each of these had a circulation of over one million. By the 1920's the figure was seven million. And it kept on rising.

As the mail-order catalog reached more and more people on remote farms, it became more and more important in their daily lives. While the farmer kept his Bible in the living room, he kept his Sears or Ward catalog in the kitchen. That was where he really lived.

There were all sorts of stories about how much faith people put in this big book. When one little boy was asked by his Sunday School teacher where the Ten Commandments came from, he said he supposed they came from Sears.

Just as Puritan boys and girls in colonial times had studied the New England Primer with its stories about God and the Devil, now Americans on farms studied the Sears catalog. In country schoolhouses, where there were few textbooks, teachers made good use of the catalog. They used it to teach reading and spelling. For arithmetic, pupils filled out orders and added up items. And they learned geography from the catalog's postal-zone maps.

In a school that had no other encyclopedia, pupils used a Ward or Sears catalog. It had a good index, it was

COMBINA-TION OF LACE, JET, IMPORTED ROSES AND FINE RIB-BON.

Price, $3.95

Ladies' hats, like this one advertised in the Sears catalog of 1910, offered the latest fashions for the farmer's wife—and for his daughter's paper dolls.

illustrated, it told you what things were good for, what they were made of, how long they would last, and even what they would cost. Mothers gave the catalogs to children to keep them occupied. When a new catalog arrived, the old one would be given to the girls, who cut it up for paper dolls.

Nothing did more than the new mail-order stores to change life on the farm —and to make life in America something new. Before the twentieth century most Americans still lived on the farm. Now that the American farmer could order from Ward's or Sears, his life became increasingly different from that of a European peasant. His view of the good things in the world was no longer confined to the shelves of the little village store. The up-to-date catalogs brought news of all kinds of new machines, new gadgets, and new fashions. Now American farmers could buy big-city goods at prices they could afford and from someone they could trust.

CHAPTER 4

One Price for Everybody!

Meanwhile other Go-Getters were inventing ways to attract the new millions of city customers. The big stores which now grew up in American cities were as different from the little shops in London's West End as the grand new American hotels were different from the modest Old World inns.

The new American hotels were People's Palaces. Anybody could meet his friends in the elegant lobby or, if he had the money, could entertain in a dining room with a crystal chandelier. The new department stores were Buyers' Palaces. And they, too, were democratic.

In London, nobody was admitted to the elegant shops unless he looked like a "gentleman" or a "lady." Unless the shopkeeper knew who you were, he would not let you in. You had to be a "person of quality" (as the upper classes were called) to see "goods of quality."

Department stores changed all this. Suddenly there were vast Buyers' Palaces, some large enough to fill a whole city block—specially designed to display goods of every shape, price, and description. Anybody could walk in. Now everybody could have a close look at elegant jewelry, clothing, and furniture of the kind once reserved for rich men's eyes.

Like many other American achieve-

ments, this happened quickly. English ways of selling had not changed much in five hundred years. But this department-store revolution, which began shortly before the Civil War, changed the lives of American customers within a few decades.

Stewart's Cast Iron Palace, completed in 1862 in New York City, was one of the first big department stores. It was the product of two different kinds of Go-Getters—a businessman and an inventor.

A. T. Stewart, the merchant who built up the business, came to the United States from Ireland at the age of seventeen. He started by selling the Irish laces he had brought with him. But he soon branched out into all kinds of goods. He was a bold, ambitious businessman. And he decided to spend a fortune on an enormous building in an entirely new style. When Stewart decided to build his grand new store he picked an inventing genius who was sure to try something new.

James Bogardus, the man Stewart chose, had started as a watchmaker's apprentice in upstate New York. He first became famous by his new design for an eight-day clock. Then he invented all kinds of new machines—for making cotton thread, for mixing lead paint, for grinding sugar, for metering gas, and for engraving postage stamps. He patented a metal-cased pencil with a lead that was "forever pointed."

His most important new idea was to construct buildings of cast iron. Bogardus' own five-story factory, built in 1850, was probably the first cast-iron building in America. The building Bogardus built for Stewart overwhelmed everybody at the time by its height—eight stories. It quickly became famous as the biggest store in the world.

Bogardus used cast iron to make an impressive Buyers' Palace. The outside looked palatial and dignified. Graceful columns which held up thin beams made a neat repeating pattern like that found in Old World palaces. The molded iron panels between columns were painted to resemble stone. Fancy cast-iron shapes decorated the window frames.

On the ground floor the outside walls no longer needed to be thick—as they had to be when a tall building was made of stone. Now there could be larger windows on every floor. Slender iron columns held up the high ceiling of display rooms a city-block wide. The ground floor was made even more palatial by a grand central staircase and a great rotunda reaching up the full height of the building, topped by a glass roof down which the sunlight streamed. You could enjoy long indoor vistas of appealing merchandise—gloves, umbrellas, suitcases, coats, furniture, all kinds of things in all shapes and sizes and colors. All the people busy looking, buying, and admiring helped make a splendid spectacle.

Naturally the Go-Getting department-storekeepers wanted to display their

A London furrier giving personal attention to upper-class customers. Only select "gentlemen" and "ladies" would be shown the elegant stock.

goods to everybody who walked down the street. The thin cast-iron building frames made this easier, but it would not have been possible without a new kind of window. Before the age of the department store, glass was expensive. Windows had to be small. They were made to admit a little daylight or to look *out of.*

Then, not long before the Civil War, an Englishman invented an inexpensive way of rolling out glass in large sheets. These large sheets of glass now at last made possible the "show window." Americans invented this new expression for the new kind of window that was made to look *into.* Now the goods could advertise themselves.

In a store where thousands of customers were buying and hundreds of people were selling, other things had to

"Buyers' Palaces"—open to all—were soon found in the larger American cities. A cutaway view of Abraham & Straus department store in Brooklyn about 1892.

change. The old way of selling goods was for the storekeeper to bargain with each customer separately. He did not mark a price on the goods. Instead he asked from each customer the highest price he thought he could get. This price depended upon how rich he thought the customer was, on how much he thought the customer wanted the goods, and on how anxious he was to make a sale at that time. You could never be sure in advance how much you would have to pay. If you were a good bargainer, you could always get it for less. But bargaining took time. It did not suit Americans in a hurry.

The big department store brought the age of the "fixed price." A. T. Stewart's Cast Iron Palace employed two thousand people. Stewart himself could not know all his salesmen. How could he let them bargain for him? At Stewart's, then, everything carried a price tag. Everybody could see the price, and it was the same price for all.

When you went shopping now, you could no longer get your fun from bargaining. But you got better value, and there were new experiences to enjoy— like looking at all the elegant things you could not afford. The department store was a new, very American, and very democratic kind of entertainment where the admission was always free.

CHAPTER 5

A Democracy of Clothing

At the outbreak of the Civil War in 1861 the government had to provide hundreds of thousands of uniforms for men in the army. This was the first time in American history that so much clothing had been required all at once. During the American Revolution the colonial army had been relatively small, and most soldiers brought along their own clothing. In the later wars too—the War of 1812 and the Mexican War—

the armies were only a few thousand strong.

So in 1861 there was no large ready-made clothing industry. The simple explanation was that it had always been the custom for each family to make its own clothes. Just as the meals that American families eat today are usually made at home, so it used to be with coats, suits, socks, and nearly everything else a person wore. Only the rich few, who could afford to look elegant, would hire a skilled tailor.

In New England in the early nineteenth century there were a few shops that sold ready-made clothing. But these offered only the cheapest grades. In New Bedford, Massachusetts, for example, sailors who had just returned from a three-year whaling voyage needed new clothing quickly. Other sailors who had just signed on for a new voyage hastily had to collect supplies for their months at sea. The stores that sold them their clothing were called "slopshops" because the clothing they sold was sailors' "slops." ("Slop" was an Old Norse word for the sailors' wide-bottomed trousers.) What sailors bought there they put on board ship in their "slopchests." Slopshop clothing was of poor quality, and the customer did not expect a good fit.

In the South, too, some plantation owners bought cheap ready-made clothing for their slaves. In Western mining towns the men who had quickly joined the Gold Rush had usually left their families behind. There were too few women to provide homemade clothing, and not enough rich people to support a tailor. Miners had to go to a store. "Store-boughten" clothing was better than nothing.

People took it for granted that if you bought ready-made clothing from a store, it could not possibly fit you well. They believed that everybody was a quite different size. Therefore, they said, the only way to make clothing fit was to have it made specially (either at home or by a tailor) to your very own measurements. How could a manufacturer possibly turn out thousands of suits, each a different size, for thousands of different people? A suit you bought in a store would surely be too loose in some places and too tight in others. Manufacturers—without even trying—had given up the effort to provide sizes that would really fit.

Take shoes, for example. Before the mid-nineteenth century, even after shoemaking machinery had been invented, the shoes you could buy ready-made in a store were usually "straights." That meant there was actually no difference between the shoe sold for the right foot and for the left foot. If you really wanted your shoes to fit, you had to hire a shoemaker to make a pair especially for you.

The uniform-makers in the Civil War learned a lesson. They found that if they made quite a few different sizes they could provide almost everybody with a reasonably good fit. They noticed that certain combinations of measurements were more common than others. For example, lots of men with a 36-inch waist also had a 30-inch trouser length. They kept track of the sizes of the uniforms they made.

When the War was over in 1865 and hundreds of thousands of veterans suddenly needed civilian clothes, the United States actually had a clothing industry. Manufacturers had learned so much about the commonest measurements of the human body that they could produce ready-made suits which fitted better than most homemade suits and almost as well as the best tailor-made. Merchants now began to open clothing stores for everybody because their assortments of sizes would fit any customer. Americans of all classes and occupations were glad to buy their clothes ready-made.

The age of statistics—a new age of careful measurement—had arrived in the world of clothing. A statistically-minded tailor named Daniel Edward Ryan, after years of collecting facts, in 1880 published *Human Proportions in Growth: Being the Complete Measurement of the Human Body for Every Age and Size during the Years of Juvenile Growth.* The new Science of Sizes gave clothing manufacturers a scientific guide for customers of all ages.

To put this new science to use, and to stock clothing stores with all the different sizes, there had to be a whole factory full of new machinery. The old tedious way of making garments—cutting cloth for one suit at a time and then sewing each seam by hand—was not good enough.

Most of the labor went into sewing. So the most important new machine would be a sewing machine. In 1831 a Paris tailor had made a workable sewing machine, and had begun to use it making uniforms for the French army. But Paris tailors, afraid that they would lose their jobs, smashed the machines and drove the inventor out of the city. Soon afterward, several Americans made sewing machines.

Walter Hunt was one of the most ingenious inventors of the age. Once when he needed money to pay a debt, within the space of only three hours he invented the safety pin, made a model of it, and sold the idea for $400. But he was more interested in making inventions than in making money. Among his new devices were a knife sharpener, a stove to burn hard coal, an ice plow, a repeating rifle, a street-sweeping ma-

chine, and paper collars. The vast new department stores and the catalogs of the new mail-order firms offered ways to show and sell such gadgets to Americans wherever they lived.

Most inventors who tried to make a sewing machine had not got very far, because they tried to make their machines imitate hand sewing. So they put the point of the needle at one end, and the eye, or hole, of the needle at the other. Hunt was more original. He put the hole at the pointed end. The thread was attached there. Then the other end of the needle was attached to a machine that simply pushed it up and down while another thread was thrust through the loop underneath the cloth. Using this original idea, by 1832 he had perfected a machine that sewed a lock stitch which would not unravel. But Hunt was not at all a businessman, and he did not even bother to patent his invention.

A few years later Elias Howe, who had been raised on a Massachusetts farm and then worked as apprentice to a scientific instrument maker in Cambridge, made the same invention on his own. He patented his machine in 1846.

The sewing machine that Howe patented in 1846. The spool at the left held the thread.

Before Thomas Edison brought electricity into homes, some people used small steam engines (fired by the kitchen stove) to run their sewing machines.

To prove that his machine really worked, Howe staged a public sewing race at the Quincy Hall Clothing Manufactory in Boston. He challenged five of the speediest seamstresses. Ten seams of equal length were prepared. One was given to each seamstress, and five were given to Howe at his machine. To everybody's amazement, before any of the seamstresses had finished her one seam, Howe had finished his *five*. His sewing machine was declared the winner.

But people feared that the sewing machine would put needy seamstresses out of work. As late as 1849 the sewing machine was still so rare that a man carried one around western New York State charging an admission fee of 12½ cents to see "A Great Curiosity!! The Yankee Sewing-Machine." Ladies took home specimens of machine sewing to show their friends.

Not for long would machine sewing remain a curiosity. For a remarkable Go-Getting salesman and organizer had become interested. When Isaac Merrit

Singer saw his first sewing machine in 1850 his main aim—like that of Henry Ford after him—was to make machines so cheap that he could sell them by the hundreds of thousands. When he used Howe's patented designs without permission, the courts eventually made him pay for the right to use Howe's design. But in 1856 Singer persuaded Howe to join a great Sewing Machine Combination to make machines with all the latest improvements.

Singer's dream came true, for by 1871 more than a half-million sewing machines were being manufactured each year. The combination of Howe design and Singer salesmanship sent American sewing machines all over the world. "Every nook and corner of Europe," the advertisements boasted, "knows the song of this tireless Singer."

The women who still had the job of making all the family's clothes were, of course, happy to have a machine to ease their work. And the sewing machine was only one of the first of many new machines—washing machines for clothes and dishes, vacuum cleaners, mixing machines for the kitchen, and many others—which would make the life of the twentieth-century American family both easier and more complicated.

Next to sewing the seams, what took most time in a man's coat or suit was cutting the cloth to the pattern. To cut heavy cloth for one suit at a time was tedious. But it was hard to make a knife that would cut through thick piles of cloth. The knife tended to twist the cloth so that the bottom pieces came out a different shape. This problem was solved in the 1870's when new high-speed, steam-powered cutting machines sliced neatly through twenty or more thicknesses. In the 1880's a Boston inventor perfected a machine that saved more hours by automatically cutting and finishing buttonholes.

Each factory-produced suit had to be neatly pressed. But the old heavy pressing iron (called a "goose" because it was so large and had a long awkward handle) was slow. A clever apprentice, Adon J. Hoffman, who was using a "goose" in a tailor shop in Syracuse, New York, dislocated his shoulder so that he could not handle the cumbersome iron. So he invented a presser he could operate with his feet. A foot pedal controlled the steam pressure which pushed down the top pad. All the operator had to do with his hands was to lay the garment between the pads. Within a few years Hoffman had become rich by selling thousands of his new steam pressers.

As the population grew and the American worker prospered, the demand for good ready-made clothing went up. At the same time, too, near the end of the nineteenth century, the flood of immigrants from Germany, Russia, and Poland included many who had been tailors over there. They naturally went to work in clothing factories here. But the new sewing machine was mak-

In their slum apartment a whole immigrant family (crowded together with their sewing machine) worked at making garments.

ing the tailor's skill less needed than ever. In the new clothing factories, the wives and children of these immigrants found quick employment.

Some of these factories became "sweatshops," where women and children worked long hours in stuffy rooms for low wages. But soon new laws required the children to stay in school. Meanwhile labor unions, led by enterprising immigrants, organized the clothing workers to demand better wages and shorter hours. Eventually the unions themselves would become rich enough to provide hospitals, clubhouses, and scholarships for their members.

By the end of the nineteenth century the United States saw a revolution in clothing. Here for the first time in history there was beginning to be a democracy of clothing. Here you did not have to be rich to dress well. A new industry was finding ways to make a stylish suit that any man could afford. Before 1900 nine-tenths of the men and boys in the

This fashionable man's suit was offered by Montgomery Ward (in 1895) for $7.50. For $2.25 his son could have a suit with extra pants and a cap.

United States were wearing ready-made clothing that they had bought in a store. Even the rich who once hired a tailor found a ready-made suit to fit. Americans dressed more like one another than people in any Old World nation. The new immigrant could go into a clothing store and buy a ready-made outfit that made him an instant American.

CHAPTER 6

Things by the Millions

On July 4, 1876, the nation celebrated its hundredth birthday with a Centennial Exposition held at Philadelphia. On the fairgrounds there were no rifle ranges or roller coasters or freak shows. There was no need for any. American products of all shapes and sizes—from shiny new bicycles to a new machine that sent your voice over a wire—were

themselves quite enough to entertain and amaze.

Visitors from Europe were astonished at how fast the United States had moved ahead. One hundred years before, the country had been thirteen weak and separate colonies—of a few towns and many scattered farms. Even twenty-five years before (when the Great Exhibition

The festivities at the Centennial Exposition in Philadelphia in 1876 included concerts like this one, held in the Music Pavilion.

had been held in London) England was plainly the leading manufacturing nation in the world. But now the United States was already threatening to take her place.

At this Philadelphia Fair, Machinery Hall, which drew the biggest crowds, was dominated by the gigantic Corliss Steam Engine. The largest ever, it was forty feet high, weighed seven hundred tons, and produced over two thousand horsepower.

George H. Corliss, the man who made the great engine, showed how to combine the Go-Getter spirit with American know-how. When timid businessmen would not buy his improved steam engine, he offered it to them free—in return for the money his engine would save them by using less coal. From one engine alone he received in five years nearly twenty thousand dollars, which was several times what the engine cost him to make.

But it was not only size and quality that impressed visitors from the Old World. They were astonished by how cheaply Americans could make so many different things. Early in the nineteenth century one ingenious Connecticut manufacturer, Eli Terry, had already managed to turn out new clocks that sold for so little it was not worth having an old one repaired. Even before the Civil War, American clocks sold for less than fifty cents apiece, and New England factories were producing a half-million clocks each year.

Now in 1876, Europeans who saw the Philadelphia exhibits were convinced that Americans would change the world. The American machines, one Swiss engineer predicted, would "overwhelm all mankind with a quantity of products which, we hope, will bring them blessing."

To make things by the millions, Americans first had to create whole new industries and whole new ways of thinking. Newest and most essential was the industry for making machine tools. Machine tools were the parent machines—the machines for making the sewing machines, the gun-making machines, the clock-making machines, and all the rest. Since all these machines themselves were made of metal, machine tools were mostly metal-cutting tools.

In the early nineteenth century, a number of clever British machinists perfected the art of metal cutting. They invented a new measuring tool called a "micrometer" (from the Greek *meter* for measure and *micro* for small) which could measure thousandths of an inch.

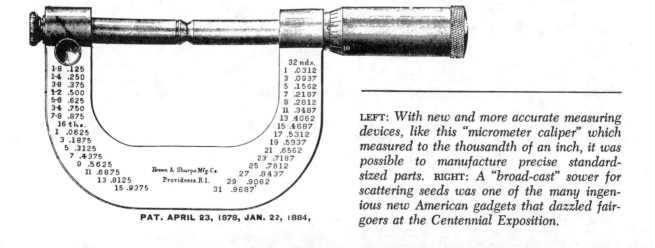

PAT. APRIL 23, 1878, JAN. 22, 1884,

LEFT: *With new and more accurate measuring devices, like this "micrometer caliper" which measured to the thousandth of an inch, it was possible to manufacture precise standard-sized parts.* RIGHT: *A "broad-cast" sower for scattering seeds was one of the many ingenious new American gadgets that dazzled fairgoers at the Centennial Exposition.*

The Englishmen had a head start. But England was an old country, with many craftsmen skilled at making things the old way. In America there were fewer skilled craftsmen, and few craft traditions. Workers here were more willing to try new ways. Soon after the Civil War ingenious Americans were making and improving their own machine tools.

One of the most remarkable of the American machine-tool makers was William Sellers of Philadelphia. By the time of the Centennial Exposition his work was already famous. He had invented machines that could measure and cut metal at the same time. These were essential for making standard-size screws.

And now screws were more important than anyone could imagine before. The millions of metal parts of the new machines were held together by metal screws. In the old days nobody could make one screw exactly like another. Each screw had been specially made to go into one particular hole in one particular machine. Then if you took a piece of machinery apart you had to label each screw so you could put it back in the same place.

Now that would not do. What good was it to make guns or clocks with standard-size parts unless you could hold them together with standard-size screws?

In his *System of Screw Threads and Nuts* (1864), William Sellers offered his own standard designs for the tiny grooves. After that, if you said your machine used a "Sellers Number 6" screw, then everybody knew exactly what you meant. The United States Government officially adopted Sellers' system in 1868. Before the end of the century an international congress in Switzerland made it the standard for Europe too.

Sellers was also interested in the appearance of the large new machines. Earlier machines had been decorated like fancy furniture. They were painted red and green and purple and were prettied up with iron beads and carvings. To Sellers, this made no sense. A machine, Sellers said, ought to look like a machine. He began painting his machines "machine gray"—not for decoration but to prevent rusting and to make cleaning easier. He took off the gimcracks and set the modern machine style which lasted into the twentieth century.

While Sellers was pioneering in new shapes and colors, other Americans were inventing a whole new way of thinking about factories. In the old days, the individual craftsman in his shop would simply do things the way they had always been done before. This was called the "rule-of-thumb." You did the job in a rough, practical way, using your thumb instead of a precise measure.

But the new American factory could not be run that way. If the old gunsmith was crude or inefficient, it meant simply that he made less money, or that people stopped buying guns from him. But in a factory where thousands of men worked elbow-to-elbow, everybody suffered if one man blundered. If your work was not precise, your mistakes were carried all over the country in the thousands of misshapen parts that came off your machine.

Now there was need for a new science —a science of avoiding waste. "Efficiency" was another name for it. The Go-Getting engineer who invented it called it the "Science" of Management.

The efficiency pioneer, Frederick W. Taylor, was born in 1856 in Philadelphia. His mother, a passionate abolitionist, was determined to liberate men from slavery. Taylor hoped to liberate men from waste. He was astonished that people who worried about conserving forests and water power and soil and minerals paid so little attention to conserving human effort.

He believed that there was one best way to do anything. But the one way that was most economical and least wasteful was not necessarily the way it had always been done.

Early in life he experimented to find the most efficient way to walk. He counted his steps and measured his stride. Then he figured out the best way to walk at different times and to different places. He did not drink alcoholic beverages or tea or coffee, and he did not smoke. He said these wasted human energy.

Taylor loved sports and thought they were important in education, not so much because they were fun as because they helped to give a man endurance for his productive work. He designed his own tennis racket, with a curved handle that made it look like a spoon. People laughed at him—until 1881 when Taylor and his partner (with Taylor using his spoon-handle racket) won the United States doubles championship.

The Bethlehem Iron Company hired Taylor to help make their enormous plant more efficient. Every year millions of tons of coal and iron ore were shoveled into furnaces. Paying the men to shovel was one of the largest expenses of making iron. Each man brought his own shovel and shoveled any way he wanted. But wasn't it possible, Taylor asked, that there was actually only one best way to shovel?

Taylor and his crew went into the factory and wrote down exactly what the men were already doing. Each worker was using his one favorite shovel no matter what kind of coal he was shoveling. A shovelful of the extremely light "rice coal" weighed only 3½ pounds, but a shovelful of the heavy iron ore weighed 38 pounds.

"Now," Taylor asked, "is 3½ pounds the proper shovel-load or is 38 pounds the proper shovel load? They cannot both be right. Under scientific management, the answer to the question is not a matter of anyone's opinion; it is a question for accurate, careful, scientific investigation."

Taylor counted the number of shovelfuls of the heavy ore that one man handled in a day. He found that with 38 pounds of ore in each shovel-load, a man in one day handled about 25 tons. Then Taylor cut off part of the metal scoop on the man's shovel so it would hold only 34 pounds. He discovered that this same man now managed to shovel *more* ore in the same length of time. Now the worker handled 30 tons. Yet the worker was less tired. Day after day Taylor kept cutting off a little bit of the shovel.

He found that when the shovel carried 22 pounds in each load, the man moved the most ore in one day.

Taylor had discovered a Science of Shoveling! He designed several different shapes and sizes of shovels and then tested each one to see that it was best suited to the stuff it had to carry. His small flat shovel was for the heavy ore and his immense scoop was for light rice coal. Soon there were 15 kinds of shovels in the Bethlehem tool room. Instead of the 600 men needed to do the shoveling before, with Taylor's Science of Shoveling the same work was done by only 140. Taylor had abolished the waste.

This system, according to Taylor, made it possible to pay each shoveler 60 percent more in wages. The wages of workers actually were increased. But,

naturally enough, many workers were afraid they would lose their jobs. Others were afraid that, even if they kept their jobs, they would have to work harder. Many were afraid they would be regimented. They liked their own shovels. They did not like anybody telling them how to do their simple job.

Still, all over the country, "Scientific Management" became more and more popular with employers. They discovered that by making a science of the simplest jobs, they usually could find a better way.

In an astonishingly short time, the American factory took on a new look. Scientific management engineers invented a whole new way of organizing a factory. Instead of having the worker walk around to pick up parts and bring them to his workbench, the manage-

One of the last steps in the Ford assembly line. The body (assembled on the second floor) was dropped down onto the chassis and motor (assembled on the ground floor), to be attached and fitted by alert mechanics.

ment engineers designed a workbench that moved. Then each worker could stay in one place and keep his mind on his proper job. The bench (now a moving belt) would carry along the heavy parts from one worker to another.

This new kind of moving workbench was called an "assembly line," because on it the whole machine was put together or "assembled."

In early April 1913 a bold mechanic named Henry Ford decided to try an assembly line for making automobiles. He wanted to make automobiles so cheaply that he could sell them by the millions. He made some improvements of his own in the assembly line. For example, he arranged the moving belt so that it

When Edison's new phonograph was still rare, this man made money by giving programs of recorded music and talk. Here he holds one of his cylinder-shaped records, chosen from a case decorated with Edison's photograph.

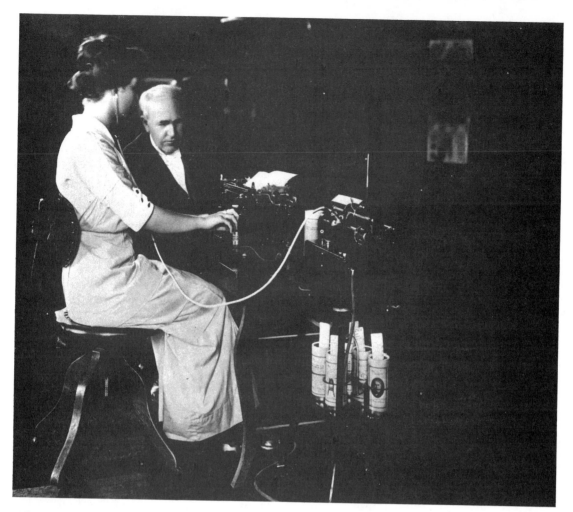

Edison's main interest in the phonograph was not for music but for office use. In this picture Edison watches while a secretary listens to the recorded voice of her employer and copies the words on a typewriter. Like the typewriter and the telephone switchboard, the new device helped to open a whole new world of office work to American women.

would always be "man-high." He changed the height according to the job so that nobody had to waste energy bending down or reaching up.

Ford also varied the speed of the belt. He explained:

The idea is that a man must not be hurried in his work—he must have every second necessary but not a single unnecessary second. . . . The man who puts in a bolt does not put on the nut; the man who puts on the nut does not tighten it. On operation number 34 the budding motor gets its gasoline. . . . On operation number 44 the radiator is filled with water, and on operation number 45 the car drives out.

In the early years when Henry Ford had been trying to perfect a gasoline-driven motor, many people laughed at him. They put him in the same class with crackpots who tried to make perpetual-motion machines. It was hard to imagine a self-propelled machine that would run not on steam but on a liquid fuel.

Luckily, in 1897, Ford met the already famous Thomas A. Edison. Some of Edison's own friends had been working on an electric automobile which worked on storage batteries that had to be recharged frequently. When Ford explained his "gas car," Edison cheered him on. "Young man, that's the thing!

You have it! The self-contained unit carrying its own fuel with it. Keep at it." Edison said the fuel could be a "hydrocarbon"—a chemical name for fluids like gasoline. Although Ford then did not even know the meaning of "hydrocarbon," he was encouraged and later said that the talk with Edison was a turning point in his life.

Ford and Edison became best friends. Even before they had met, Edison (who was sixteen years older) had been an inspiration to Ford, as he was to many other inventors.

Edison had invented a new kind of factory—an "invention factory." It's purpose actually was to invent new kinds of things to make. In the 1870's Edison set up his first "invention factory" with $40,000 he received from his own early inventions.

To his "invention factory" he brought the most ingenious men he could find. He inspired them with loyalty and hope, and built them into a team. Following the example of earlier Go-Getters like Benjamin Silliman and others who had found ways to make "Rock Oil" into fuel to light American homes, these men tried to find new uses for old materials, and also to invent new machines for all sorts of purposes.

Edison and his associates were tireless testers and imaginative mechanics. One of their first feats was to help make electric lighting possible. The most difficult problem had been to find a thread, to put inside the bulb, that would give light when electricity was sent through it and yet would not quickly burn out.

They tried all sorts of materials—carbon, bamboo, hair, platinum, copper, and scores of other substances. They finally discovered that a filament of charred paper served well if it was in a vacuum. This made possible the commercial production of light bulbs, which soon replaced Rockefeller's oil lamps.

Edison and his fellow inventors, looking for a way to record the human voice, invented the phonograph. They worked on a way to use the new art of photography to show "moving" pictures. In 1891 Edison patented a "kinetoscope"— a kind of peep show which showed moving pictures inside a box.

Edison's own ingenuity seemed endless. But he was also a great organizer, and when he could not make an invention of his own to solve a problem, he bought up the patent rights of others. Then he found ways to manufacture the new products cheaply and efficiently. He was most interested in the improvements in daily life that could reach everybody.

Edison fired the imagination, not only of Henry Ford, but of the whole American people. He was nicknamed the "Wizard." When Congress awarded him a special gold medal in 1928 it was announced that his inventions had been worth $15,599,000,000 to humanity! But this was only to say that there really was no way of measuring his enormous contribution to American life. By the time of his death at the ripe age of 85, in 1931, he had become an American hero —a truly democratic hero, because his work benefited every living American.

PART TWO

PEOPLE ON THE MOVE

PEOPLE ON THE MOVE

Americans were people on the move. There would have been nobody here except the Indians unless Old World millions had been willing to cross the ocean. The United States might have been only a string of seaboard farms and cities if brave new Americans had not then been willing to risk the move farther west. Going into the half-mapped continent was, of course, traveling into the unknown. But Americans were willing—even eager—to risk new places.

The Civil War, too, meant the moving of peoples. Great battles were fought by thousands of men in armies on the move. The fortunes of war brought Virginians to Gettysburg in Pennsylvania and sent Massachusetts volunteers deep into Georgia. Even while the armies of General William T. Sherman cut their bloody swath through the South, the Union men could not help seeing the beauties of the Southern land. They discovered that Southerners were not so different from themselves. Thousands of Americans pried into far corners of their country.

After the war, many soldiers returned to their old homes. A few stayed where they had fought, and found wives and homes in the new places. Some Northerners went south to teach school or help in the Freedmen's Bureau. From the burnt-over south, hopeful Southerners went north or west in search of opportunity. Negroes, at last free to leave the old plantation, for the first time were able to move about like any other Americans.

"Go-Ahead" became an American motto. Of course, Go-Getting Americans were eager to move up in the world. But they were just as eager to move around. The same spirit that before the Civil War had led Americans to move westward in wagon-towns, that had led them to build railroads even before there were cities to go to, now led Americans to move and keep moving.

After the Civil War, brave and needy men and women were still risking the ocean to come fill the land and crowd the cities. From impoverished European farms, many were drawn by extravagant promises. And thousands already here, who were disappointed by the American land, moved hopefully to the cities.

The Americans already here kept telling themselves: "Go ahead. Move on. Try to find a better place."

As Americans churned about the vast continent, they came to know their land —and to know one another. Most nations of the Old World were rooted to the same spot. Their people were held together because their ancestors had so long lived inside the same boundaries. It was unusual for them to move. They learned to be satisfied with their place.

But Americans would not long let themselves be confined anywhere. Americans were held together by their ways of moving and by their shared desire to move. And the freedom to move to a better place helped build the nation.

CHAPTER 7

To Punish—or to Forgive?

Lee's surrender to Grant at Appomattox brought peace to the nation. But peace brought new problems. How to find jobs for the million men who left the Union and Confederate armies? How to change factories from making cannon and rifles and ammunition to making harvesters and sewing machines?

When the South agreed to unconditional surrender, they put themselves at the mercy of the North. This gave Northerners their most difficult problem —what to do with the South.

Was it more important to punish the former rebels, to teach them a lesson they would never forget, so they never again would try to break up the Union? Or was it better to forgive the rebels, to welcome them back into the Union, so they would feel at home and never again want to leave?

Of course the South had already been punished. A quarter-million Southerners had died in the war. The Confederacy was a land of cinders and desolation —of charred plantation houses, broken bridges, twisted railways, and desecrated churches. An Englishman who traveled halfway across the South said he did not see a single smiling face. But

---

Ruins of Charleston, South Carolina, by the pioneer Civil War photographer, Mathew Brady. For many people in the South, "Reconstruction" after the Civil War meant clearing away rubble and rebuilding cities.

Thaddeus Stevens, Congressman from Pennsylvania (from an old and damaged photograph).

the North had also suffered, with its own quarter-million dead. And for Northerners who had lost fathers, sons, or husbands, no punishment of the South would be enough.

Yet this was not just a question of feelings. Unless the North wanted to feed and house millions of Southerners, it was important to get the South back into working order. This meant getting crops planted, factories built, railroads running, and pupils and teachers into schools. It also meant getting the Southern States organized to govern themselves, to collect their own taxes, to keep the peace, and to protect life and property.

But it was not easy to get people to agree on how to revive the Southern States. There was wide disagreement on what the war had really meant. What the North called "The War of the Rebellion" in the South was still called "The War between the States." The

Southerners argued that their State governments had never been destroyed. Once a State always a State!

Lincoln himself had almost agreed with the Southerners on this point. He also believed, Once a State always a State! But for Lincoln this meant that the Southern States had no power to secede. And if the Southern States had never really seceded, then even after the Civil War the Southern States were still within the Union.

Naturally, once the war was over, Southerners wanted to agree with Lincoln. They said they still had their States and therefore could still run their own affairs. The most, then, that the victorious North could properly ask was that some Confederate leaders be barred from office.

But on the other side were the Northern Avengers. The most powerful of them were in a group of Northern Senators and Congressmen called Radical Republicans. They were bitter against the Southern rebels. They remained suspicious of all white Southerners. They did not want to forgive and forget, but instead wanted to rub salt in Southern wounds. The Southern States, said the Radical Republicans, had actually "committed suicide." By trying to rebel, they had not only violated the Constitution but actually destroyed their own States. They were no longer States at all.

People who thought like this believed that after the war the Southern "States" could claim *no* rights under the Constitution. They had no right to govern themselves or to be represented in the Senate or the House of Representatives. They were nothing but so much territory

—like parts of the sparsely settled West. And, like those Western territories, they could be governed in any way Congress decided.

Congress could treat them as "conquered provinces." They could be ruled by military governors—generals of the Union army. When, if ever, they would be allowed to govern themselves and take part in the national government— this would depend on how they behaved themselves and what the victorious Congress wanted. This offered anything but a cheerful prospect for the Southerners.

The leader of the Radical Republicans was one of the strangest men in American history. Thaddeus Stevens was sometimes called "a humanitarian without humanity." For he seemed to use up all his good feelings on large noble causes and then he had very little left for individuals. Stevens was a sour man. Just as Lincoln inspired love and respect, Stevens inspired fear.

Very early in life he took up the great cause of abolishing slavery. He never gave it up, nor did he ever forgive men who had ever held slaves or who had been entangled in the web of slavery. After Appomattox, Stevens made it his purpose in life to punish all "traitors." Old age never mellowed him. At the age of seventy-five he boasted that he would spend his remaining years inventing new ways to make the Southern rebels suffer.

During the Civil War, Lincoln had shown his greatness—and his forgiving spirit—by his plan for bringing Southerners back to the Union. He was less interested in the past than in the future. Back in December 8, 1863, in his Proc-

lamation of Amnesty and Reconstruction, he had explained his plan. He would pardon almost all Southerners, even if they had fought against the Union.

All Lincoln asked was that Southerners take a solemn oath to support the Constitution of the United States in the future. As soon as enough citizens of a Southern State took the oath, Lincoln would recognize the government of that State and let the people govern themselves. Of course they must agree to abolish slavery. It would be enough, Lincoln said, if a number equal to only one-tenth of the voters in the last election took the oath.

This plan did not satisfy the Radical Republicans. They were busy in Congress making a plan of their own. During the war they concocted their Wade-Davis Bill in quite another spirit. They could not take their eyes off the past. Under their plan each Southern State was to make a list of all its white men. The State could not be recognized or given the power to govern itself until a *majority* of the people on that list took a new oath to support the Constitution. Then (since these Radicals believed that the old Southern States had committed suicide) there would have to be an election to call a convention to make an entirely new constitution for each Southern State.

No one could even vote in that election, much less be a delegate to help make the new constitution, unless he took the "ironclad oath." This oath was not merely a promise of future loyalty but was also an oath of past purity. You had to swear that you had never held office under the Confederacy or fought in the Confederate army. By the end of the war, most white men in the South could not honestly take such an oath.

Under the Radicals' scheme it would be years before any Southern State could set up a majority government for itself. It would have to wait until the whole Civil War generation was dead. But that did not bother the Radical Republicans. They were quite willing to keep the Southern States under military rule by Northern generals. They said they were in favor of liberty, but they were not willing to give it to white Southerners.

This was the Wade-Davis Bill, which passed Congress on July 2, 1864. It could not be law unless Lincoln signed it. What would Lincoln do?

Lincoln refused to sign the bill. But he was shrewd. Instead of attacking it, as he might have, for being evil and vengeful—or instead of saying simply that the plan for the South was the business of the President and not of Congress—he issued a new proclamation. He would not sign the Wade-Davis Bill into law, he said, because he did not think it should be the *only* way a Southern State could get back into working order. Any "seceded" Southern State that wanted to follow the Wade-Davis plan should feel free to do so.

But there were now, Lincoln said, two possible paths. Any Southern State could choose between Lincoln's one-tenth plan and the Radicals' majority-ironclad-oath plan. In the long run, of course, no Southern State would prefer the vengeful Radical plan. But still Lincoln had done his best to avoid a head-on clash with Congress.

On April 14, 1865, Lincoln called his Cabinet together to explain his policy to them. He urged them to use charity. He begged them to help bring the wartime spirit to an end.

That very night when President Lincoln and his wife went to Ford's Theater in Washington to attend a play, there occurred one of the great disasters of the Civil War era—and of all American history. It was less than a week after Lee had surrendered to Grant at Appomattox. The demented actor John Wilkes Booth rushed past the Secret Service men guarding the President's box and shot President Lincoln. The President died the next morning.

We cannot be sure what would have happened if Lincoln had lived. But we do know that Lincoln's combination of qualities was extremely rare. He was, of course, a strong man who would fight for what he believed. Yet he was also a simple, gentle man who understood other people. And, most important for a President, he was a clever politician. He knew how to give up less important things in order to persuade people to support him on what was more important.

Andrew Johnson, the new President, was in many ways like Lincoln. With no schooling, he began as a poor tailor. He, too, was a self-made man. Like Lincoln, he had been born in the South. And though he came from Tennessee, he had been against secession. When he was the Democratic Senator from Tennessee he was the only Southern Senator to support the Union after the Confederates fired on Fort Sumter.

Still, in some important ways, Johnson was no Lincoln. He was not good at persuading. He did not know how to use a joke to make a serious point. Just as Lincoln was gentle, generous, and compromising, so Johnson was crude and obstinate. His weaknesses would not have been serious in an ordinary citizen. But they were disastrous in a President.

When Lincoln was assassinated in April 1865, Congress was not in session. Many Republicans distrusted Johnson because he had been a Democrat. They had added him to the Republican ticket as their candidate for Vice-President in 1864 in the hope that he might draw the seceded States back into the Union.

Now, when the death of Lincoln had brought Johnson to the White House, the Radical Republicans wanted President Johnson to call Congress into special session to make new rules for the South. But he refused. President Johnson would follow the rules already declared by Lincoln. And *he* alone would decide when the Southern States had satisfied Lincoln's requirements so they could govern themselves.

Lincoln's requirements were not too hard for the Southern States to satisfy. By December 1865, when President Andrew Johnson made his first report to Congress, every one of the old Confederate States (except Texas, which soon came along) had done what Lincoln asked for. Each of these now had its own State government in working order. President Johnson reported happily that the Union was restored.

When the Congressmen from these "restored" Southern States came to take their seats in Congress, they were shut out. The Radical Republicans who controlled the House of Representatives told them that they were not really Congressmen at all—because the Southern States were not really States at all. Even if the Confederate States had followed

President Andrew Johnson, who had no Vice-President. If he had been removed from office, a Member of Congress (the Speaker of the House) would have become President.

the President's rules, the Radicals said, the President had no power to make the rules. Only Congress (by which they meant, of course, the Radical Republicans themselves) had that power. Their Punishing Bill—the Wade-Davis Bill—had declared what Congress wanted. The South would have to be "restored" by Congress or not at all.

Congress set up its own Committee on Reconstruction led by the Radical Avenger, Thaddeus Stevens, to make its own plan. The watchword of Stevens' Congressional plan was, Force! The South, he said, was a "conquered province" and nobody would be allowed to forget it. Northern troops would be sent to occupy the South.

The committee divided the old Confederacy into five military districts. The boundaries of the eleven seceded States were not to be respected. Each of the five districts would be ruled by a Northern general. The Northern Radical Republicans in Congress laid down new rules for building new Southern States. They wished to see the new States designed so as to keep political control in Republican hands.

Some of the Radical demands, such as abolishing slavery and giving civil rights to Negroes, were of course just and necessary. But others were not.

Worst of all was the Radical refusal to forgive. They denied many leading citizens in the Old South the right to vote, or even to work at their regular jobs. Hungry for power, the Radicals wanted to rule the South through a small group of their puppets. Anxious to hold their Republican majority in Congress, they were afraid the new Southern Congressmen might be against them. Although they said they loved liberty, they really were afraid of it. They were afraid to give political liberty to their old enemies.

What was President Johnson to do? Under the Constitution he was supposed to enforce the laws of Congress. Though he believed these laws unwise, he tried to enforce them. But the Radicals were out to "get" Johnson. They could not bear the idea of a President who was not in their pocket. They passed laws taking away powers which the Constitution had given to the President. For example, even though the Constitution made the President the Commander in Chief of the Army, the Radicals passed a Command of the Army Act taking away his power to command.

They were spoiling for a fight, hoping to tease the President into violating one law so that they could have him removed from office. They hoped that then they could seize the powers of the President.

But Johnson was careful to obey every law, to follow all the instructions of Congress.

Still there was a limit to his patience. When the Radicals passed the Tenure of Office Act which took away the President's control over his own Cabinet, that was too much. Secretary of War Stanton, whom Johnson had inherited in the Cabinet from Lincoln, had become Johnson's enemy and was actually plotting against him. So the President fired Stanton to test the Tenure of Office Act, which he believed to be against the Constitution. This was a small thing, but enough to give the Radicals their chance. They took it.

The framers of the Constitution, being wise men, had provided a way to remove a criminal President. But they saw that if they made it too easy to remove a President, opponents would be tempted to use it to get rid of any President they could not beat at the polls. Then every President would live in terror—afraid to do his duty, for fear some political enemy would make a crime out of it.

The Constitution said (Article II, Section 4) that the President could not be removed except "on Impeachment for, and Conviction of, Treason, Bribery, or other high Crimes and Misdemeanors." First the House of Representatives would have to "impeach" the President. This meant a majority vote to support a list of accusations. Then the President would actually be tried by the Senate. The Chief Justice of the United States would preside. But to remove a President a mere majority of the Senate was not enough. The framers showed their special wisdom when they required a vote of *two-thirds* of the members present.

When the Senate met on March 30, 1868, to try President Andrew Johnson on the impeachment brought by the House of Representatives, the nation was in breathless suspense. Few really believed that Andrew Johnson had been guilty of "Treason, Bribery, or other high Crimes and Misdemeanors."

Johnson, like Lincoln, was a man of rock-ribbed honesty. No one could prove otherwise. Earnestly he had followed his inaugural oath "to preserve, protect, and defend the Constitution of the United States, against all enemies foreign and domestic." Perhaps he had sometimes lost his temper, had shown bad judgment, or had used language that a President should not use. But these were not crimes. His only "crime" had been that he believed it *his* duty to obey the Constitution. And he was determined to follow a policy of forgiveness. He could not have satisfied the Radicals without surrendering all the powers of the Presidency into their hands.

On May 16, 1868, when the vote of the Senate was finally taken, 35 Senators voted "guilty" and 19 voted "not guilty." This was a big majority. But, luckily, it was *one* vote less than the two-thirds which the Founding Fathers required. Andrew Johnson remained President.

CHAPTER 8

A Two-Nation South

Peace and reunion brought an end to slavery. But the roots of slavery ran deep. They reached into every nook and cranny of Southern life.

One of its roots was racism—the belief that one race was naturally better than another. This belief had helped keep slavery alive. At the same time slavery had kept racism alive. Under slavery, nearly all the Negroes in the South did lowly tasks. Therefore, it was easy for white people—and sometimes even for Negroes themselves—to believe that God had meant it that way.

Slavery could be abolished simply by changing laws. But it was much harder to abolish the belief that one race was better than another. Many generations of Southerners had taught that to their children. After the war it was still rooted in their minds and hearts.

And after the war it became clearer and clearer that the South was still split into two "nations." There was a White South and a Negro South. Much of the time these two "nations" lived at peace.

Some of the time they lived in a nervous truce. Occasionally they were actually at war. Obviously the United States could not be truly united until the South ceased to be divided.

Lincoln and Johnson had their eyes mainly on the abolition of slavery. The future they looked to—a South without slavery—seemed not too hard to accomplish. Stevens and the Radicals also wanted to abolish slavery. But for them, abolishing slavery was not enough. They believed that slavery would not really be abolished until the Negro was treated as the equal of the white man. Their hopes were wider and deeper—and much harder to accomplish—than the hopes of Lincoln or of Johnson.

The Radical Republicans saw the wickedness of slavery. But they did not really see its full tragedy. Part of the tragedy was that the roots of slavery could not be removed in a year or two— nor perhaps even in a generation. The Radical Republicans were right when they said that the problem was not *only* slavery. But they were violent and impatient men.

For the deep problem they had no deep solution. They knew what they wanted, but they did not know how to get it. To transform the life of the South, to bring equality to the Negro, to cure both the white man and the Negro of the disease of racism, would take a patience and a charity and a wisdom which the Radicals lacked. They were wrong when they believed that the old cancer of slavery could be ripped out quickly and by force.

The Thirteenth Amendment to the Constitution, which abolished slavery, was proclaimed on December 18, 1865.

But when the legislatures of the Southern States (under the Lincoln-Johnson one-tenth plan) had their first meetings, they promptly adopted "Black Codes." These were supposed to provide for the new situation of the Negro now that he was no longer a slave. They provided, for example, that now the Negro could own property, and they gave him certain other rights.

But, under the Black Codes, the freedom of the Negro was still strictly limited. He could not vote. He was not allowed to marry a white person. He could generally be a witness only in trials against other Negroes. He could not leave the land where he had been a slave. He could not look for a new job. In Mississippi, for example, if a Negro was convicted of being a "vagrant"—a wandering person without a job—he could be fined $50. If he could not pay the fine, he could be hired out against his will to anybody who would pay the fine in return for his labor.

Had Northerners died in a Civil War merely to preserve slavery under a new name?

The Radical Republicans in the North, who anyway expected the worst from the Old Confederates, were not taken by surprise. Even before the war was over they had set up the Freedmen's Bureau. Its purpose was to help war refugees, to get Southern farms back in working order, and to help Negro freedmen make their new start in life.

The Freedmen's Bureau did a great deal of good work that nobody else could do. It handed out millions of free meals to Negroes and to white refugees. It built hospitals. And it brought thousands of Southerners back onto farms

A school for freedmen, Vicksburg, Mississippi, in the year after Appomattox. For the first time, many Negroes had a chance to learn to read.

where they could make a living again. The Bureau also helped Negro freedmen find jobs, and helped protect them against a new slavery.

The Bureau's most important work was in building schools and in providing teachers—to give Negroes the education they had been denied under slavery. Howard University, Hampton Institute, Atlanta University, and Fisk University were set up for Negro students of college age. A quarter of a million Negro children were sent to school for the first time.

Few white Southerners were grateful for this help. They were worried that Negroes were no longer being kept in their "place." And they were especially annoyed at this interference by "outsiders."

It took courage to go south to teach for the Freedmen's Bureau. One young lady teacher who went to North Carolina reported that while the men who passed her on the street only rarely lifted their hats, "the ladies almost invariably lift their noses."

Northern teachers in the South found it hard to survive. In South Carolina, for example, grocers charged them especially high prices hoping to starve them out. One Southern farm woman said she "would not sell milk to Yankees to save her life, she hated the very ground they trod." Some Yankee teachers were afraid to buy the food anyway, because they thought it might be poisoned. Some found that no one would rent them a room to live in. Even in church they were shunned and insulted.

The South was now at war with itself. Many Southerners said they were only fighting against meddling "outsiders." But they were really fighting their fellow Southerners—Negroes who wanted to be free and equal.

Before long, the Old Confederates in the South had organized a secret army. Its purpose was really to carry on the Civil War under another name. Although slavery was abolished by law, the Old Confederates still desperately hoped to preserve as much as possible of their old Southern Way of Life.

Late in 1865 a half-dozen ex-Confederate soldiers in Pulaski, Tennessee, founded an odd new club. It was the first unit in this secretly revived Confederate army. It called itself the Ku Klux Klan—nobody knows exactly why. Soon many branches appeared all over the South.

Almost everything about the Ku Klux Klan was peculiar, and many of its features were ridiculous. Its members met in secret and tried to keep everything about it a mystery to outsiders. Each member swore never to reveal the names of other members—nor even to admit that he was a member himself. At the initiation of a candidate the Grand Cyclops ordered, "Let his head be adorned with the regal crown, after which place him before the royal altar and remove his hoodwink." The "royal altar" was a big mirror, and the "regal crown" was a high hat sprouting donkey's ears.

According to the Klan's constitution:

The officers of this [secret lodge] shall consist of a Grand Wizard of the Empire and his ten Genii; a Grand Dragon of the Realm and his eight Hydras; a Grand Titan of the Dominion and his six Furies; a Grand Giant of the Province and his four Goblins; a Grand Cyclops of the Den and his two Night Hawks; a Grand Magi, a Grand Monk, a Grand Exchequer, a Grand Turk, a Grand Scribe, a Grand Sentinel, and a Grand Ensign.

No wonder some people thought this was only a "hilarious social club."

But there was nothing funny about the Klan's activities. The Klan actually pretended to be (as it said in its constitution) "an institution of Chivalry, Humanity, Mercy and Patriotism." It pretended to protect the weak and the innocent, and to support the Constitution of the United States. It soon became a weapon of violence and terror.

Klan members traveled the countryside flogging, maiming, and sometimes killing Negroes who tried to vote or who in other ways presumed to be the white man's equal. The Klan uniform was a pointed hat with a white hood to conceal the face, and a long robe, either white or black.

In the beginning, Klan members included some respectable citizens. A famous Confederate cavalry general, Nathan Bedford Forrest, was the Grand Wizard. But the Klan's "Invisible Empire" also included many hoodlums. They wanted to frighten Negroes into *not* claiming their rights under the Constitution. The object of these Klan members was to keep the South separated into two *un*equal nations. They could not do their work except by blackmail and bloodshed. In 1869 when the crimes of the Klan became too scandalous, General Forrest resigned as Grand Wizard and pretended to "dissolve" the organization. The Klan then simply went underground.

Nobody knows exactly how many people joined the Klan. In 1868, General Forrest said the Klan had forty thousand members in Tennessee alone and a half-million in all the South. Scores of other organizations joined in the bloody work—the Tennessee Pale Faces, the Louisiana Knights of the White Camelia, the North Carolina White Brotherhood, the Mississippi Society of the White Rose, the Texas Knights of the Rising Sun, the Red Jackets, and the Knights of the Black Cross. In 1871 alone, in a single county in Florida, 163 Negroes were murdered, and around New Orleans the murders came to over 300. Thousands of Negroes were driven from their homes, maimed, or tortured.

Under pressure from Northern Radical Republicans, some Southern State governments passed laws against these crimes. On December 5, 1870, President U. S. Grant—who as general had commanded the Union forces to victory—delivered a special message to Congress. "The free exercise of franchise," he warned, "has by violence and intimidation been denied to citizens of several of the States lately in rebellion." Congress then passed the Ku Klux Klan Acts to outlaw these organizations and to protect the rights of all citizens. But these laws had little effect.

For the State governments set up in the South by the Radical Republican Congress were being replaced by old-fashioned Southern State governments. Confederate heroes were back in charge. The land and the factories were still owned by white Southerners. The last few Northern troops were not withdrawn from the South until 1877. But by 1875—within ten years after Appomattox—eight of the eleven old Confederate States had already come back under rule of Old Confederates.

The work which only a few years before had been done by disreputable terrorists was now being done "legally" by the State governments. Although the Southern States had approved the Civil War Amendments (Thirteenth, Fourteenth, and Fifteenth) to the Constitution, although they had abolished slavery and their laws "guaranteed" the Negro his rights, all these proved to be

Members of the Ku Klux Klan, hooded and armed, 1868.

mere technicalities. Before long it was pretty plain that slavery itself was just about the only thing the Civil War had abolished.

Thaddeus Stevens died in 1868, and soon enough his avenging spirit—along with his special concern for the Negro's rights—was dead. Now more and more Northerners were anxious to "leave the South alone." In practice this meant putting the South back in the hands of white Southerners. And the South then remained divided into the same two nations—a "superior" race and an "inferior" race.

The South would not really become united with the rest of the United States until the South itself had become one. And this would take time.

The Two-Nation South was a One-Party South. When the Old Confederates came back into charge of the Southern States, they had no love for the Republican Party. That was the party of the Yankees, the party that had made war on the South and had then held the South under military rule. By keeping their control of the State governments, the Confederate heroes also kept those governments under the control of the new Democratic party. And the Negro was to have no voice in Southern politics for many years.

A divided South remained afraid of equality, afraid of change. This was at the very time when the American people —and newcomers from the whole world —were filling up the land and churning about the rest of the country faster than ever before.

CHAPTER 9

Filling the Land

From the earliest colonial days, America's leading import had been people. Before the Civil War nearly all immigrants arriving in New York or other American ports had come by sail. The passage from the Old World to the New had been a risky adventure lasting as long as two or three months. Sailing vessels depended on the wind, and the old sailing routes went only to certain places. Built mainly for cargo, these vessels stowed their poorer passengers like cattle.

Within a decade after Appomattox nearly all immigrants from across the ocean were arriving by steam. They were coming more speedily and in larger numbers than ever before. During the Civil War the need quickly to import supplies had encouraged the development of steamships. After the war the nation was eager to renew a free-flowing commerce with the world.

Steamships, unlike sailing vessels, could run on a reliable timetable. The uncertainty of the winds was replaced by a ten-day transatlantic schedule. The new steamships were actually planned for passengers. They were a good deal less uncomfortable—even for those who

Waiting room of the Union Pacific Railroad in Omaha, Nebraska, in 1877. Here immigrants from many countries, lured by promises of choice land advertised by the States and the railroad companies, could stock up for the journey farther west.

came most cheaply in steerage. Steamships could now pick up new thousands of immigrants in remote ports of the eastern Mediterranean and of Asia.

German and French and Italian and other steamship lines competed for passengers, offering lower rates, better accommodations, and a new easy system of prepaid passage. Prosperous immigrants who had already settled in the United States could pay in advance for the tickets of friends or relatives who wanted to come. The steamship companies opened offices all over the United States. By 1890 the Hamburg-Amérika Line had three thousand of these. More than one-quarter of the immigrants in that year came on tickets that someone in the United States had paid for in advance.

Before the Civil War, revolutions in France and Germany and Italy and

famines in Ireland prodded Europeans to leave. So too, in the later years of the nineteenth century, multiplying miseries drove out European peasants by the thousands.

Many of those peasants in western Europe who were lucky enough to own a few acres of land were losing their ancestral plots. The price of wheat in their home countries went down as the new railroads and cargo steamers brought wheat from the United States, from Russia, and even from India. A strange disease (phylloxera) was killing the grapevines in the Balkans. When Americans began raising their own oranges and lemons in the 1880's and when the French began keeping out Italian wines, Italian farmers with orchards and vineyards found themselves on the edge of starvation.

The Jews of Russia were being bar-

barously persecuted, and whole villages were murdered for their religion. Turks were slaughtering Syrian Christians.

Once again, there was plenty to get away from. And now that the United States was at peace, this country seemed more attractive than ever.

To generations of European peasants, owning a piece of land had been the sign of dignity, the beginning of freedom.

When President Lincoln signed the Homestead Act on May 20, 1862, America seemed to offer everybody the chance to be a landowner. The whole American West was begging for people. All you had to do was come. You only needed to be twenty-one years of age and to say that you intended to become a citizen. Then you picked a 160-acre plot of "homestead" land somewhere on the vast Public Domain that belonged to the United States government. If you simply lived on it and cultivated a part, then the whole 160 acres would be yours at the end of five years. You paid nothing but a small registration fee.

This was an Old World dream come true. Every man a landowner!

Before the Civil War, the Southern States had opposed this Homestead Act. They were afraid it would strengthen the anti-slavery forces by increasing the population of the Free States. As soon as the Slave States left the Union it was possible to pass the Act through Congress. Lincoln's simple aim was "settling the wild lands into small parcels so that every poor man may have a home."

But the "free" land was not really as free as it seemed. In the Western plains where most of the best homesteads were found, it cost labor and money to make wild land into a farm. Before anything could be planted, the ground had to be broken. The prairie grass had roots that grew in thick mats, unlike anything known in Europe. The familiar Old World plow would not cut through but was quickly twisted by the heavy sod.

The Oklahoma "Land Rush" which began at noon, April 22, 1889. At the firing of a starter's gun and the sound of a bugle, more than 20,000 people rushed in to stake their claims. Oklahoma was then still called "Indian Territory" because it was supposed to be reserved for Indians removed from the East.

It was slow work to plow up enough land to support a family and it was expensive to hire a man with the right tools to do the job.

Then you needed to find water. Where streams and springs were rare, the only answer was to dig a well. And to pump up the water you had to build a windmill. On the treeless plains you had to buy the lumber for your house. Posts and barbed wire for fencing had to be brought from great distances. All this added up. You needed about $1,000 to make your homestead livable. That was a big fortune for a landless peasant.

Still, if you were healthy, willing to work year round, and not afraid to shiver for a few winters in a crude house of earth or sod, you might manage. The Homestead Act allowed you to be away from your land for six months each year without losing your claim. Some energetic homesteaders used this time to earn money by working as lumberjacks in the pine forests of Minnesota, Wisconsin, and Michigan. Others helped build the short "feeder" railroads that branched off through the countryside. Or they worked as farm laborers for their more prosperous neighbors.

Even if life was hard on the "free" lands of the West in the post-Civil War years, it still was not so bad by comparison with peasant life in Europe. What had been little trickles of immigrants from faraway places now became wide fast-flowing streams. For example, the old Austro-Hungarian Empire in eastern Europe, which had sent only seventeen thousand in 1880, sent over one hundred thousand in 1900, and seven years later, over a third of a million.

Americans worked hard at finding ways to attract the dissatisfied peoples of the world—to persuade them to come here instead of going to those English, French, or German colonies in Africa, South America, or the South Pacific which also wanted new settlers. Even before the Homestead Act, Western States sent their agents abroad. They helped immigrants with information and with loans.

More people in Wisconsin, for example, would mean more business for everybody there. Everybody's land would be more valuable. The State of Wisconsin therefore appointed a commissioner of immigration in 1852. He enlisted the aid of the United States consul in Bremen, Germany, and of other consuls elsewhere. He advertised in European newspapers and in a single year distributed 30,000 pamphlets about the glories of Wisconsin.

The Americans used the empty lands of their vast Public Domain to help pay for building the first railroads here. These were the lands that belonged to the United States government—land given to the new nation by the States at the time of the Revolution, land acquired from Napoleon in the Louisiana Purchase in 1803, land taken from Mexico in 1848.

After all, the government land might be worth very little if there was no way to reach it. The railroad companies would give the land value—in two ways. While they provided the transportation to open up the West, they would also be working as real-estate salesmen.

So the federal government assigned large tracts of land to the States with the understanding that the States would grant these lands to the companies that

A sod house of the type common in the early West. This family was fortunate to have glass for a window. The teen-age daughters had perhaps been ordering the latest fashions from a mail-order catalog.

built railroads. And the federal government also granted some of its land directly to the railroad companies. These companies suddenly found themselves in the real-estate business.

Like the State governments, the railroad companies themselves became colonizers. They sent their own agents to Europe to attract immigrants to live along their tracks. These agents, too, helped with information and with loans. Sometimes they actually provided newcomers with a house while they were getting settled.

Often the railroad builders were granted the best lands in the West. And, anyway, once the railroads were built, the land near the tracks—since there were no automobiles and few roads— would be the most valuable. While railroad lands sold at higher prices, they were usually much more attractive than the more remote lands left over for dis-

tribution under the Homestead Act.

Land grants to the railroads finally amounted to about 150 million acres— an area almost as big as the whole State of Texas. Nine-tenths went to the companies that built railroads west of the Mississippi.

The first railroad company to receive a land grant from the federal government was the Illinois Central. The land along its future track was divided into a checkerboard pattern extending six miles from the track on each side. Each "section" in the checkerboard was one mile square (640 acres). The railroad was given every other square all along the way. The squares in between were kept by the federal government.

The Illinois Central Railroad extended four hundred miles from Chicago, the whole length of the State of Illinois. When it was completed in 1856 it was the longest railroad in the world.

And the company paid for the construction mainly by selling its two and a half million acres.

"Homes for the Industrious," the Illinois Central land salesmen announced, "in the Garden State of the West!"

There is no portion of the world where all the conditions of climate and soil so admirably combine to produce those two great staples, Corn and Wheat, as the Prairies of Illinois. . . . Nowhere can the industrious farmer secure such immediate results for his labor as upon these prairie soils, the fertility of which is unsurpassed by any on the globe.

The railroad printed brochures, bought space in newspapers and magazines, and hired "runners" in New York City to mingle with arriving immigrants.

To Norway and Sweden, the railroad sent a super-salesman. Oscar Malmborg was a Swedish immigrant who had succeeded. After serving in the Mexican War, he had helped build the railroad in Illinois. From personal experience he could convince people that the railroad lands were really fertile. He sang the praises of Illinois Central land from Gothenberg at one end of Sweden through all the big cities to Bergen at the other end of Norway. He published 2,500 brochures in Swedish and a thousand in Norwegian. He planned meetings at churches and country fairs until he had covered the countryside of both nations.

Swedish farmers began to fear he would lure away all their laborers. To keep their laborers at home they invented horror stories. The Swedes who

Advertisement by the Illinois Central Railroad to attract settlers to its lands.

arrived in New York, they warned, would be shipped to Siberia or sent as slaves to the Southern States. But in 1861, after Malmborg's successful campaign, nearly ten thousand Norwegians —a third more than in any earlier year —were planning to leave for America. The Swedish exodus was just as large. Even before the end of 1862 substantial new communities of Swedes and Norwegians had taken root near Chicago.

Scandinavia was only one of the immigrant sources. The Illinois Central hired the best-known German-born citizen of Illinois, Lieutenant Governor Francis Hoffmann, to cover Germany with a crew of salesmen. Within four years he settled Germans on eighty thousand acres of Illinois Central land.

To attract settlers from nearby Canada, an Illinois Central booklet claimed that while Canadian farms "are covered with huge boulders of granite, the summers are very hot, and the mosquitoes abound," the Illinois Central lands were a cool, mosquito-free earthly paradise. Colonies of hopeful Canadians were soon settled along the Illinois tracks.

CHAPTER 10

Crowding the Cities

Within the United States during these same years after the Civil War, there was another great movement of peoples —from the country to the cities. When the Civil War began, only one American in five was living in a city. By 1915, cities held half of all Americans. And this was only a beginning.

They came from everywhere. First of all they came from the countryside. While the railroad builders sent abroad their super-salesmen boasting the wonders of American farms, many American farmers were actually moving to the city. Older sections of New England offered visitors the sad spectacle of farms that had lost their farmers.

Many deserted farm villages seemed relics of a departed civilization. A traveler to one such village saw an abandoned church and a school half taken apart for its lumber. There were only two inhabitants, one living on each side of the broad street. Some of these farmers had gone west, but most had gone to the cities. By 1910 more than a third of all people who were living in American cities had moved in from American farms, many from the rural South.

Of the twenty-five million immigrants who came to the United States between the Civil War and World War I, most stayed in the cities. Outside of cities many of them would have felt lonely and lost. They loved the friendly bustle and wanted to be close to people like themselves. And some of them had no choice. They had spent everything to cross the ocean and had no money left for the trip west.

Within the big American cities there grew little immigrant cities. By 1890 New York City held twice as many Irish as Dublin, as many Germans as Hamburg, half as many Italians as Naples. And besides, there were large numbers of Poles, Russians, Hungarians, Austrians, Norwegians, Swedes, and Chinese. Four out of every five New Yorkers either were born abroad or were the children of foreign parents. The Germans and Irish who had come before 1880 were found nearly everywhere in the United States. There were also lots of Canadians in Boston and Detroit, Poles in Buffalo and Milwaukee, Austrians in Cleveland, and Italians in New Orleans.

Crowded Hester Street, on the lower East Side of New York City (shown here about 1900), was where many immigrants settled on their arrival. Some who later became famous department-store owners started by selling from pushcarts like these.

In a public school like this, the children of immigrants from many lands learned to speak and read English—and also learned American ways.

Cities were sometimes called the nation's "melting pots." Perhaps they should have been called "mixing bowls." The individual adult immigrant sometimes became Americanized only slowly. But very quickly his whole colony found its special place in American life. Just as the new United States had first been made from thirteen different colonies, now a great nation was being made from countless colonies of immigrants.

In New York City, for example, there were separate colonies from different parts of Italy. Italians from Naples and Calabria lived around Mulberry Bend, those from Genoa had settled in Baxter Street, and Sicilians clustered about Elizabeth Street.

Wherever you came from, you could find a neighborhood in New York or in the other big cities where you could feel at home. Whether you were from Germany, Italy, Hungary, or Poland, you could shop in your own old-country language, buy familiar old-country foods, and attend a church offering your old-country services. By 1892 nearly a hundred newspapers in German were published in American cities. And there were dailies in French, Italian, Japanese,

Polish, Yiddish, and a dozen other languages.

In the making of Americans nothing was more important than the public schools. They were free, and the States passed laws requiring all children to attend. There the children of Irish, German, Italian, and all sorts of other families learned and played—and sometimes fought—together. They came to know one another better than their parents knew people from other countries.

At home many families spoke only Polish or Italian, but in school everybody spoke English. Even if the parents spoke English with a foreign accent soon the children sounded like all other Americans. And the children taught their parents. They not only taught them English, but all sorts of American customs. One little girl in New York City who had learned to use a toothbrush brought it home from school. She showed it to her mother, who had been born in a peasant hut in Poland and had never seen such a thing. Her mother, too, was soon brushing her teeth like an American.

Although these immigrant colonies tried to keep separate, they could not stay separate forever. People from the different colonies became more and more alike. Children who stopped speaking their parents' language sometimes stopped going to their parents' church. They were afraid to seem foreign. Then, too, a young man from the Italian colony might marry a girl whose parents spoke German. In the city, people could not help feeling closer to one another.

If the crowds were the joy of the city, crowding was the curse. Old World cities had grown mostly by children being born to the people already living there. The parents put a cradle in the room with the other children. As the family grew larger everybody was more crowded.

The American city was different. It grew by adding not just new children but whole new families.

In the crowded cities after the Civil War land was expensive. Unless you were rich you could not afford a private house. Still the thousands who came pouring in had to be put somewhere.

New York—the nation's biggest city and busiest seaport and the magnet of the world's immigrants—was where the problem was worst. And in New York, American know-how, which at the same time was building grand cast-iron palaces for department stores, produced another, but unlucky, American invention. This was the "tenement house."

New Yorkers, of course, did not invent the slum. European cities had their streets of ancient rickety buildings and evil-smelling hovels where the poor were tumbled together. But in the years after the Civil War, New York City produced a new kind of slum—the tenement-house slum.

Most newcomers to the city could not afford to pay much rent. Back in the early years of the nineteenth century the poorer people of New York had lived in shacks on the swamps at the edge of Manhattan Island. But as the island filled with people, specially designed buildings went up for the city's new poor. A tenement house was a building six or seven stories high designed to hold the largest possible number of families. They were solid blocks of deep buildings whose inside rooms had no windows or ventilation. There were also helter-skelter buildings of many other kinds.

Then in 1878, to help find something better, *The Plumber and Sanitary Engineer*, a builders' magazine, announced a contest for architects. The editors offered a $500 prize for the best plan for tenement apartments for the poor.

The winning plan was the "dumbbell" tenement. The floor plan of the whole building, looked at from above, had the shape of a dumbbell. And it had a good deal to be said for it compared with some of the flimsy firetraps that were common before. The dumbbell tenement, built of brick, was meant to be fireproof.

It was specially designed to fit on a narrow lot twenty-five feet wide and a hundred feet deep. It was six or seven stories high, with the stairway running up the middle. On each floor were four sets of apartments—two in front and two in back. The front and back rooms got some light and air from their windows on the street.

What was new about the plan was that the inside rooms were also supposed to get some light and air. The building was slightly narrower in the middle.

Although the prizewinning tenement design was supposed to provide "light, air, and health" for working people, actually whole families (like this mother and six children) were crowded into little rooms. The new art of photography made it easier for reformers like Lewis W. Hine (who took this picture) and Jacob Riis (who took the picture on page 59 above) to awaken the conscience of other Americans.

When another tenement like it was built alongside, between them there was a narrow air shaft on which each inside room had a window. This became the standard plan for tenements.

By 1900 the island of Manhattan alone had over forty thousand buildings of this type, holding over 1,500,000 people. A prizewinning plan had produced the world's prize slum!

The air shaft between the buildings was only twenty-eight inches wide—so narrow that it did not really bring in light. Instead the foul air brought up smells from the garbage accumulating at the bottom. If there was a fire, the air shafts became flues which quickly inflamed all the rooms around. Up the air shaft resounded the noise of quarreling neighbors. There was no privacy.

The primitive plumbing in the hallway on each floor was shared by four families. It bred flies and germs. Sometimes the toilets became so disgusting that the tenants would not use them, but depended on the plumbing at work or at school. There were no bathtubs with running water. Nearly every one of these tenement houses had at least one sufferer from tuberculosis, and in some there were twenty or more.

When Theodore Roosevelt was Governor of New York, he appointed a commission in 1900 to report on the tenement-house slums. They were not at all surprised that these buildings festered with poverty, disease, and crime. But they were surprised that in spite of it all, so many of the people raised there managed to become decent and self-respecting. And they reported that the slums were even worse than they had been fifty years before.

Slum neighborhoods were given names like "Misery Lane" and "Murderers' Alley." This was hardly the America that the thousands of hopeful immigrants were looking for.

CHAPTER 11

Whose Country? Oldcomers and Newcomers

The bulging cities and bustling factories were full of men and women who had been raised in the quiet American countryside—or of European peasants who had come across the ocean with high hopes. Here, they had been told, anybody could succeed, if only he was honest enough and worked hard.

But many honest, hard-working immigrants found that they could not get ahead. These disappointed new Americans would not take their disappointment lying down. The United States was the land of help-yourself. It is not surprising, then, that the post-Civil War years became a time of conflict. Workingmen were organizing into labor unions. Their aim was a better life—shorter hours, higher wages—but peaceful means did not always seem strong enough.

Beginning in the 1870's labor battles

became more common. In 1872, nearly a hundred thousand builders and mechanics in New York City went on strike. They refused to work longer than eight hours in any one day. After several months, they won their point.

Miners in the eastern Pennsylvania coal fields organized a secret society called the "Molly Maguires." In 1875, on flimsy evidence that private detectives had gathered for the employers, ten Molly Maguires were hanged for murder. Then in 1877 a railroad strike, beginning with workers on the Baltimore and Ohio, spread across the country. It brought death to nine persons in West Virginia and to twenty-six in Pittsburgh.

In 1886 came the so-called Haymarket Massacre when a bomb killed seven policemen and wounded seventy after they tried to break up a meeting of anarchists and communists. In a fight at the steelworks at Homestead, Pennsylvania, in 1892, seven were killed. The Pullman Strike in 1894 again tied up the railroads. This became a minor civil war when Federal troops began fighting against workers.

A conservative and law-abiding organization of trade unions, the American Federation of Labor, became strong among skilled workers. The Federation's aim was simply better wages and shorter hours. Meanwhile a small number of radicals called "Wobblies," who aimed to take the factories away from their owners, started the International Workers of the World.

All over the country crime showed an alarming increase. In 1890 the prisons held 50 percent more criminals than ten years before. And the murder rate in the United States, already twice the rate in England or in Germany, was going up every year. National crime "rings" used hideouts in Chicago, Boston, Philadelphia, Detroit, and scores of other cities to help their members escape the police. The city crowds—at the Philadelphia Centennial Exposition of 1876, at the Chicago Columbian Exposition of 1893, and every day on streetcars or in department stores—were a pickpocket's paradise. Young hoodlums terrorized San Francisco with knives and six-shooters.

New expressions had to be invented to describe the assorted new criminals. There were "badger-game experts" and "knock-out drop" artists. "Green-goods" men tricked innocent farmers into exchanging their real money for large bundles of counterfeit. In 1880 one Go-Getting criminal from Springfield, Illinois, went to New York where he made a fortune selling "gold bricks." Before he was killed by a fellow thief,

Two Molly Maguires on trial, 1875.

IF 100 BULLETS WONT FINISH YOU 1000 WILL

A WARNING

Police firing on strikers in East St. Louis during the railroad strike that began in 1877.

he actually had taken in over a quarter-million dollars from the lead bricks which he had painted gold before he sold them to gullible country boys. Stores with fancy goods on display naturally attracted shoplifters.

A ring working out of New York managed one of the biggest bank robberies in history. In 1878 from a single job they had planned for three years, they got three million dollars.

Meanwhile newspapers, anxious to sell more copies so they could attract more advertising, became more sensational than ever. They found that it paid to feature the worst crimes and to glamorize the worst criminals.

In business and in government too there were notorious scandals. Beginning soon after the Civil War, President U. S. Grant made a bad start. He was so honest himself that he did not know a crook when he saw one. Some found their way into his Cabinet, and then used their position in the government to make a fortune for their railroads or their banks.

All decent Americans had reason to be worried. Was this the best that could be expected from what Jefferson had so hopefully called an "Empire for Liberty?"

The early American frontier had been a line on the outer edge of settlements. Beyond was the no-man's land where Indians had not yet given up and where settlers had not yet conquered. Out there a man could make a fresh start. In the Centennial Year of 1876, the defeat of Chief Sitting Bull and Chief Crazy Horse and their braves marked the last great battle between the Indians and

Sensational magazines like the Illustrated Police News *attracted their readers by playing up stories of crimes, such as the Indiana train robbery shown here.*

---

the invading settlers. Fifteen years later, the Superintendent of the Census reported that the wilderness-frontier had come to an end.

By the end of the nineteenth century, then, the New World had lost much of its newness. One bright young historian, Frederick Jackson Turner, who had been raised in the backwoods of Wisconsin, proposed the theory that this disappearance explained many of the country's troubles.

According to Turner, what had made America the Land of Promise was not its cities but its frontier. The free land out west, he explained, had also been a safety valve. In earlier times if a man in an Eastern city wanted a second chance, he could move to the West. But now that the country was being filled up it was no longer possible to find your second chance by going out to the edge of civilization. If you were unlucky enough to be a newcomer in a slum, there seemed to be no escape. Was it surprising, then, that so many Americans were unhappy? And that so many felt that

they had to fight for a better life?

For a while it seemed that the country might be divided between Oldcomers and Newcomers. Oldcomers themselves, of course, came from immigrant families originally, but their families had been here for a long time. Among them were the rich and famous. Few of them were crowded into slums.

In the older Eastern States that still controlled Congress, the Oldcomers were in charge. They were most of those who had money and education and power. But the Oldcomers did not agree on how to cure the country's ills. Some were simply frightened. They wanted to keep the country the way it was. They blamed the troubles on the Newcomers. Their answer was to slam the door. Simply because *their* families had been here longer they thought the whole nation belonged to them.

At Harvard College, a group of New England bluebloods thought that their world was coming to an end. Three young men in the graduating class of 1889, Charles Warren, Robert De Courcy Ward, and Prescott Farnsworth Hall, had been taught by their professors that there was an "Anglo-Saxon" race superior to all others. The race was supposed to be separated from other races not by color but by what countries the people had come from. The "superior" people were supposed to come from England and Germany. And that just happened to be where Warren's and Ward's and Hall's families had come from.

These young men had been raised near Boston. Their parents were horrified by the hordes of "vulgar" immigrants and especially by those with unfamiliar ways—from Ireland and from southern and eastern Europe. The New England aristocrats said the nation's problems could be solved by keeping out all people who were not like themselves.

Five years after their graduation, Warren and Ward and Hall formed the Immigration Restriction League to persuade Congress to pass laws to keep out all "undesirable" immigrants. In their League they enlisted famous professors and writers. Their real object was to keep out the "new" immigrants—the Newcomers. These "new" immigrants, they argued, were the main cause of the increasing crime, the strikes, and most of the troubles of the country.

To keep out "undesirables" they pro-posed a "Literacy Test." According to their proposed law anyone over fourteen years of age who wanted to come into the United States would have to prove that he could read and write. He did not have to know English, provided he could read and write the language of the country he came from.

At first sight the test seemed harmless enough. Actually it was aimed against the Newcomers from certain countries, such as Italy and Greece, where poor peasants had no chance to go to school. The Boston bluebloods believed that because Newcomers from such countries were not "Anglo-Saxons" they must be "inferior."

But in their proposed law they did not dare list particular countries. There

---

Poor Newcomers arriving in America while rich Oldcomers (with their governess) leave for a vacation in Europe. A magazine illustration by Charles S. Reinhart (1878).

already were many people in the United States from those countries. They would be insulted—and they, too, elected members of Congress.

Year after year the Immigration Restriction League tried to persuade Congress to pass a Literacy Test. But even when they finally pushed their bill through Congress, they did not manage to make it into a law. One President after another vetoed the bill. President Grover Cleveland called the law "underhanded," because it did not say what it really meant. President William Howard Taft said the United States needed the labor of all immigrants and should teach them to read. President Woodrow Wilson agreed.

All three Presidents said the law was un-American. The United States had always been "a nation of nations." It made no sense to keep out people simply because they had been oppressed. America was a haven for the oppressed. Here the starving could find bread and the illiterate could learn to read.

In 1917, however, when the war in Europe was frightening Americans, the Literacy Test finally had enough votes in Congress. The law was passed, over the strong objections of President Wilson, who had already vetoed it twice.

Out on the West Coast, Oldcomers feared Newcomers from Asia. They worried about imaginary hordes that might come across the Pacific. And they had persuaded Congress to pass a Chinese Exclusion Act in 1882. Then, in 1907, President Theodore Roosevelt persuaded the Japanese government to stop their people from emigrating. For some odd reason, this was called a "Gentlemen's Agreement." This became the slang expression for any agreement to discriminate against people on account of their race when you were ashamed to admit what you were really doing. Since there were so few Chinese-American and Japanese-American voters among the Newcomers, the fearful few among the Oldcomers found it easier to have their way.

CHAPTER 12

Reformers and Self-Helpers

Not all the Oldcomers were frightened. Some became Reformers. If the whole country had troubles, they said, it was everybody's fault. If the country had too many strikes and too much crime, it could hardly be blamed on those who had just arrived.

It was mainly the fault, they said, of the Americans who had been here long-

est and who had had the most chance to make the country better. Who had built the very cities and constructed the very slums where the poor were condemned to live? Who were the Congressmen and Senators and businessmen and policemen? It was not the immigrant's fault if the nation was not prepared to receive him.

One of the most remarkable of the Reformers and one of the most original Americans of the age was Jane Addams. She was born with a deformity of the spine which made her so sickly that after graduating from college in 1882 she had to spend two years in bed. Her wealthy family sent her to the best schools and colleges, she traveled abroad whenever she wished. One evening in Spain after watching a bullfight—"where greatly to my surprise and horror, I found that I had seen, with comparative indifference, five bulls and many more horses killed"—she suddenly decided that she could waste her life no longer.

The trouble with people like her, Jane Addams decided, was that they had been caught in "the snare of preparation." To become leaders they needed long years of education. But this meant that they were kept out of action at the very time when they were most anxious to rebuild the world. Jane Addams knew that she and her friends needed more education than they could find in books.

In June 1888, she stopped in London to visit the famous Toynbee Hall. There in the poorest section of the city lived a group of Oxford and Cambridge graduates while they tried to help the people of the neighborhood. She decided to try starting something like it in the United States.

Jane Addams' plan was simple. In the poorest, most miserable city slum she would settle a group of educated young men and women from well-to-do families. Like Toynbee Hall, the place would be called a "settlement house." And the well-bred young men and women newly "settled" in the midst of

A young woman settlement-house worker with girls of the neighborhood.

a slum reminded her of the early colonial "settlers" who had left the comforts of English life to live in an American wilderness.

The young men and women who came to live in the slum, seeing the struggles of the poor, would learn things they could never learn from books. At the same time, the people of the slum would use the settlement house as a school, a club, and a refuge.

With her purpose clearly in mind, she acted quickly. Since she knew Chicago she decided to do her work there. She looked for the neediest neighborhood. And she persuaded the owner of a large old house to let her have it free. She opened her settlement house between an undertaker's parlor and a saloon. She called it "Hull-House" after the man who had built it for his home years before.

In the neighborhood of Hull-House there were Newcomers from all over Europe—Italians, Germans, Polish and Russian Jews, Bohemians, French Cana-

Jane Addams (right) in a parade supporting votes for women. The Nineteenth Amendment to the Constitution, prohibiting the States from depriving women of the vote, was finally ratified in 1920.

dians, and others. For the young, Jane Addams set up a kindergarten and a boys' club. And she paid special attention to the very old people whom nobody else seemed to care about.

One old Italian woman was so delighted at the red roses which Jane Addams displayed for a Hull-House party that she imagined they must have been brought all the way from Italy:

She would not believe for an instant that they had been grown in America. She said that she had lived in Chicago for six years and had never seen any roses, whereas in Italy she had seen them every summer in great profusion. During all that time, of course, the woman had lived within ten blocks of a florist's window; she had not been more than a five-cent car ride away from the public parks; but she had

never dreamed of faring forth for herself, and no one had taken her. Her conception of America had been the untidy street in which she lived and had made her long struggle to adapt herself to American ways.

Jane Addams' work became famous. All sorts of unexpected projects started at Hull-House. The Little Theater movement, of amateur actors putting on plays to entertain themselves and their friends, developed and spread all over the country. She started a book bindery and a music school.

Settlement houses on the Hull-House model appeared in big cities everywhere. Future playwrights, actors, composers, and musicians who had happened to be born into poor slum families now found their chance.

For the first time many thousands of immigrants discovered that somebody else cared about them. Jane Addams—without the aid of governments or politicians—had helped make America the promised land.

America had always been a land of help-yourself. Before long some of the most energetic Reformers came from the immigrants. But it was not easy for Newcomers to become leaders. So many respectable institutions remained in the hands of the Oldcomers—whose families had been here for a century or more. For example, Harvard College—the oldest college in the country, where young bluebloods had learned their ideas of Anglo-Saxon superiority—was run by Oldcomers. It was hard even to become a student there if you were not one of them.

New institutions offered the best chance for Newcomers. Among the most remarkable—and most American—of the new institutions were the scores of new colleges and universities.

At the outbreak of the Civil War there were only seventeen State universities. Then, in 1862 an energetic Congressman, Justin S. Morrill from rural Vermont, secured the passage of the Morrill Act. This act granted government lands from the Public Domain to States—30,000 acres for each of the State's Senators and for each of its Representatives in Congress—to support new State colleges. There students would be taught to be better farmers. These were called "Land Grant" Colleges.

After the Civil War, hundreds of other colleges and universities were founded. In the later years of the nineteenth century, some of the wealthiest Go-Getters gave millions of dollars to found and endow still more institutions of higher learning. In 1876 Johns Hopkins University was founded by a fortune left by a Baltimore merchant. In 1885 a railroad builder, Leland Stanford, in memory of his son, founded Leland Stanford Jr. University. In 1891 John D. Rockefeller, the Go-Getting oil millionaire, founded the University of Chicago. And there were scores of others.

Many of these college-founders were men who themselves had never gone to college. But they shared the American faith in education. Even before the end of the century, the United States had more colleges and universities than there were in all western Europe. And a larger proportion of the citizens could afford to go to college here than in any other country. The children of poor immigrants, along with millions of other Americans, now had a better chance to rise in the world.

The new labor unions also became centers of new leadership and of self-

Mayor Fiorello La Guardia, during a newspaper strike, reading the comics aloud over the radio.

help. Samuel Gompers, who had been born in London, came to New York as a boy. He worked at starvation wages as a cigarmaker before becoming president of his Cigarmakers Union and then the first president of the American Federation of Labor (1886). Sidney Hillman, who came from Lithuania when he was twenty, led the Amalgamated Clothing Workers, the union that did most to help the new immigrants in big-city sweatshops.

In politics the support of your fellow immigrants counted for something. Crowded together in the cities, the immigrants of any one nationality found it easy to stick together to support one of themselves. Soon new political leaders from among the Newcomers themselves were livening up City Hall and even the halls of Congress, which began to sound like a United Nations. The representatives of Italian-Americans and German-Americans, and of the new arrivals from everywhere, gave a new spice to American politics.

One of the most colorful of these was Fiorello La Guardia. His mother and father had come from Italy, and Fiorello was born in New York City only three years after they arrived. His father, a musician, joined the army and soon became the leader of an infantry band. On an army post in Arizona in the 1880's Fiorello saw the pioneer West. He found it "a paradise for a little boy. We could ride burros. Our playground was not measured in acres, or city blocks, but in miles and miles. We could do just about anything a little boy dreams of. We talked with miners and Indians. We associated with soldiers, and we learned to shoot even when we were so small the gun had to be held for us by an elder."

Out there La Guardia had his first glimpse of corruption. And it was something he would never forget. The men who had been paid to supply wholesome beef to feed the army were supplying diseased beef instead, and then pocketing the money themselves. La Guardia's father became so ill from eating this diseased beef that he had to be discharged from the army and a few years later he died. No wonder Fiorello spent his life fighting corruption.

For several years he worked at United States consulates in eastern Europe. He learned about the problems of the immigrants in their homelands. When La Guardia returned to New York in 1906 he joined the Immigration Service on Ellis Island. There the Newcomers were examined before being admitted to this country. La Guardia knew Croatian as well as German and Italian. While he worked as an interpreter, he learned the immigrants' troubles and the immigrants' hopes.

In 1917 La Guardia went to Congress, where he began his long fearless career of defending the poor and of fighting corruption. He carried on his fight when he became mayor of New York City in 1934. Now the city was his family and all the city's problems were his. With the broad-brimmed cowboy hat he had learned to wear out in Arizona, his familiar figure bounced all over the city. He especially liked to be on hand at trouble spots. Whenever there was a big fire La Guardia somehow arrived with the fire chief. In twelve years as mayor he did more than any New Yorker before him to remove the blot of the slum and to brighten big-city life.

PART THREE

BRINGING PEOPLE TOGETHER

BRINGING PEOPLE TOGETHER

After the Civil War the United States was as large and varied as all western Europe. From the alpine heights of the Rockies and Sierras to the tropical everglades around the Gulf of Mexico there stretched nearly every kind of landscape.

And this variety made the nation more attractive to immigrants from all over. Just as the English could feel at home on the rolling landscape of "New" England, the Swedes felt less strange on the snowy stretches of Minnesota and the Dakotas, and Italians found familiar sunny seacoasts in southern California. The imported people spread across the land.

From Chicago to New York was as far as from London to Rome. And if you traveled all the way from London to Constantinople and back to London you had still not gone quite as far as if you went from New York to San Francisco. How could these spread-out people ever become a nation?

People in the United States wanted and needed new ways to feel closer together. This challenged American know-how. And American know-how—using telegraph wires, rails, and new-style bridges—organized new ways to bind a nation.

The nation of many cities remained a nation of many centers. Chicago and St. Louis and Denver, even before the end of the nineteenth century, were rivaling Boston, Philadelphia, and New York—the capitals of the eastern seaboard. And by mid-twentieth century Los Angeles on the Pacific was one of the nation's fastest-growing big cities.

Even before the continent began to seem overcrowded, American know-how, with materials and techniques borrowed from everywhere, sent skyscrapers high in the air, collecting thousands to live and work in a single towering building. In American cities—in the once-wilderness of open spaces and fresh air—people were close-packed together as never before.

The telegraph instrument patented by S. F. B. Morse.

CHAPTER 13

Everybody Shares the News

Newspapers were not very newsy until nearly the time of the Civil War. They used up much of their space to print stories and poems and essays and the strong opinions of their owners. And they copied much of their "news" from other newspapers which arrived by slow mail. The best-known papers were owned or controlled by political parties. They praised their own side and slandered the other. If you wanted to know what was happening far outside your neighborhood you had to wait for a traveler to come by.

Businessmen and generals organized their own systems to send urgent messages over great distances. One of the oldest was the "semaphore" (from the Greek words meaning "signal-bearer"), sometimes called the "visual telegraph." People arranged in advance what their signals would mean. Then they built fires, sent up smoke, or arranged a pattern of boards on a high tower. All these could be seen at a far greater distance than the voice would carry. The Greeks and Romans and the American Indians had used rows of these semaphore stations to relay messages for many miles. By the mid-nineteenth century a French semaphore system used 556 separate stations to stretch three thousand miles.

In the 1840's a young New England Go-Getter, Daniel Craig, decided to try sending news by carrier pigeons. He ordered pigeons from Europe and trained them for his Pigeon Express. Soon newspapers subscribed to his service. In his boat he would go out into the Atlantic for many miles to meet a ship arriving from Europe. The captain would throw him a watertight canister containing the latest London newspapers. Then Craig would quickly summarize the news on thin pieces of paper. These he would attach to the legs of his pigeons, who swiftly flew to the newspapers.

His pigeons went all the way from Halifax, Nova Scotia, to a newspaper in Washington, D.C. The New York *Sun* even built a dovecote for its own carrier pigeons on the roof of its new building. But the pigeon service, too, was unreliable. And there was a limit to how much news a pigeon could carry.

It was hard to imagine a system that did not depend on seeing signals, or on sending written messages. Samuel F. B. Morse found a way to make an electric current do the job. Morse was a man of many talents. At Yale he painted portraits of his fellow students for five dollars apiece. Then he went to London where he studied at the Royal Academy,

In the days before the telegraph or radio, sending news "by air" meant using carrier pigeons.

the honor society of English artists. When Morse came back in 1815 he was a famous artist but he nearly starved because people would not buy his large paintings. Once again he made a living by painting portraits. At the age of thirty he went to Italy and France, the headquarters for painting at the time.

Among Morse's fellow passengers on the sailing ship *Sully* coming back from Europe in 1832 was a talkative young physician from Boston, Charles T. Jackson. In Paris, Dr. Jackson had learned a great deal about electricity. To while away the six-week ocean trip, Morse asked him lots of questions. Morse was an educated man, but he still knew very little about the new science. Would electricity flow through a long wire?

How fast did it travel? Why, Morse asked, couldn't electricity be used to send messages? Others before him had asked the same question—and got nowhere with their answers. But Morse did not know enough about the subject to be discouraged. He suddenly decided to make an electric "telegraph" (from the Greek words for "far writer").

As an artist Morse had a bold imagination about new shapes of things. Then and there he began to invent his telegraph. In our National Museum of American History in Washington, D.C., we still have the shipboard notebook in which Morse every day wrote his new ideas. Before he reached New York he had drawn a picture of a telegraph instrument very much like that used today. He had even begun to use dots and dashes for his new Morse code.

"Well," Morse told the captain of the ship as they arrived in New York on November 16, 1832, "should you hear of the telegraph one of these days, as the wonder of the world, remember the discovery was made on board the good ship *Sully*."

It took Morse five years to make a telegraph instrument that would work. During that time he supported himself by giving painting lessons.

To build a telegraph line would require a small fortune. Most people thought the telegraph was nothing but a toy—"a thunder and lightning 'jim crack.'" Morse decided to change their minds by a public demonstration. He took his machine with him to Washington, where the Committee on Commerce of the House of Representatives allowed him to demonstrate his telegraph in the Capitol. It was a sensation. "The world is coming to an end," one witness declared. "Time and space are now annihilated." President Martin Van Buren and members of his Cabinet came to see the new electric marvel.

The chairman of the House Committee, Congressman "Fog" Smith of New Hampshire, saw his own chance to make a fortune. When he asked Morse to make him a partner in a firm developing the telegraph, Morse could hardly refuse. For Congressman Smith had the power to persuade the House of Representatives to give Morse the money to build a telegraph line.

The Congressional debate was hilarious. Opponents jokingly proposed that the money be split among Morse's telegraph and the supporters of hypnotism and the crackpots who believed the world was about to end. Finally, in 1843, eleven years after Morse had his first inspiration, Congress appropriated $30,000. With this money Morse was supposed to stretch a telegraph line from Baltimore to Washington.

At first Morse and his partners tried burying the wire. They spent $23,000 before they discovered that, because the wire was defective, the buried line would not work. They then started all over again by stringing a wire on poles. They were in a hurry to get the job done before the whole Congress began to believe the telegraph was a hoax. Mile after mile, they placed 24-foot-high chestnut poles two hundred feet apart. In holes they bored in the poles, they stuck the necks of old bottles which served very well as insulators.

Luckily, at that very moment in May 1844 both the main political parties were holding their national conventions

As the railroads pushed westward across the continent, telegraph lines kept pace.

in Baltimore. This gave Morse his chance to impress all the people in Washington who were especially anxious to learn the names of the candidates. But when the candidates were actually selected, Morse's wire still reached only twenty-two miles—from Washington to Annapolis Junction.

To demonstrate his telegraph, Morse had the news brought by train from Baltimore to Annapolis Junction. Then —to beat those who had to carry the news all the way by train—he flashed it over the wire to his telegraph receiving machine in the Capitol. The politicians there were amazed when Morse told them (before anyone else in Washington knew) the names of the Whig Party candidates—Henry Clay for President and Theodore Frelinghuysen for Vice-President. This was the first news ever flashed by electric telegraph.

The telegraph soon impressed people

by other sensational uses. When a thief escaped from Washington by train, his description was telegraphed ahead to the station in Baltimore. There he was arrested as he stepped off the train. Newspaper editors predicted that before long there would be no more crime, since criminals would be too afraid to be "struck" by this telegraphic "lightning."

Morse joined two newspapermen to form the Magnetic Telegraph Company. They built new lines—from Philadelphia to New York, from Philadelphia to Baltimore, and around to all the larger cities. By 1848 the telegraphic network reached northward to Portland, Maine, southward to Charleston, and westward to St. Louis, Chicago, and Milwaukee. Regular newspaper columns offered the latest bulletins under the heading "BY MAGNETIC TELEGRAPH." Newspapermen boasted of the "mystic band" that now held the nation together.

The Mexican War of 1846–48, the Gold Rush beginning in 1848, and the national troubles that foreshadowed a Civil War—all these whetted the Americans' appetite for news. And the more news people had the more they wanted.

Because it was expensive to gather news by telegraph, the newspapers came together in groups. Since they all shared the latest dispatches, each of them had to pay only part of the cost of telegraphing the news. In 1848 six New York daily newspapers formed the first Associated Press. Their man in Boston took the news brought by ships from Europe and put it in one telegram to the New York office. Then the Associated Press sold its speedy and reliable dispatches to newspapers in Boston, Philadelphia, and elsewhere.

Gathering and selling news became a big business. With the news-gathering experience of the Civil War behind them, Go-Getting newsmen extended the Associated Press throughout the nation. Then every member newspaper supplied its own local news to all the hundreds of other members. Since there were so many members, they could also afford to open offices with full-time reporters all over the world. This increased the quantity and improved the quality of news. The Associated Press stories tried not to be prejudiced or one-sided, for their readers were members of all political parties. Papers would not buy the "A.P." news unless it gave the straight facts. By the early twentieth century there was also a United Press and an International News Service.

At the same time many other new inventions were helping to turn out papers fast and by the millions. In the early nineteenth century an ingenious Englishman improved the presses used by big-city newspapers. Instead of using a frame that went up and down he used a cylinder. The blank paper was attached to the cylinder and rolled evenly against the type. This was much faster because the cylinder could be kept going continuously and a new piece of paper put in every time it went around.

Then Richard Hoe, a young New Yorker, had a still better idea. Why not put the *type* itself on a cylinder and roll the type smoothly and rapidly against the paper? By 1855, his Hoe Rotary Press was printing 10,000 newspapers in an hour.

The next step was to manufacture paper in long rolls instead of sheets. In 1865, a Philadelphian, William Bullock, made the first machine that printed on a continuous roll of paper—and it printed both sides of the paper at once. The finishing touch came with a gadget that actually folded the papers as they came off the presses.

Some metropolitan papers soon put out six different editions each day. Newspapers became larger and larger. Sunday newspapers—including advertisements, comics, magazine sections, book reviews, and everything else—became big enough to fill the whole day for Americans who did not go to church.

Richard Hoe's speedy web printing machine was among the new wonders shown in Machinery Hall at the Centennial Exposition in Philadelphia. This new-style press, instead of printing on separate sheets, used a continuous roll of paper, which could be more than four miles long.

CHAPTER 14

Letters in Every Mailbox

A workable national mail system was slow in coming to the nation. The framers of the Federal Constitution in 1787 had given Congress the power "to establish Post Offices and Post Roads." A Post Road was a main road with special stations to provide fresh horses for the riders who carried the mail. For some years, almost all postal service was on one Main Post Road along the Atlantic coast. People used the mail very little. When George Washington was President the letters in the mail averaged less than *one* for every *twelve* Americans each *year!*

In those early years the postage on a letter was usually paid by the person who received it. If he did not want to pay the postage he never got your letter.

Of course there was no home delivery. To get your mail you had to go to the post office. Even after Philadelphia had a population of 150,000 everybody in the city who wanted his mail had to wait in line at the post office.

Then in 1825 came the dim beginnings of modern mail delivery. The postmaster in each town was allowed to give letters to mail carriers to deliver to people's homes. The carriers still got no government salary. They lived by collecting a small fee from anybody to whom they delivered a letter. If you were not at home to pay they would not leave your letters in your mailbox.

By the 1840's the growing country desperately needed a cheap and efficient postal system. The government service was still so haphazard and expensive that there was widespread demand to abolish the Post Office. People called it an "odious monopoly" and said that private businesses could do much better.

As a result in 1845 Congress passed a law establishing cheap postage and tried to reform the whole system. At first each postmaster printed his own stamps and there was chaos. Then, in 1847, the reformed Post Office Department issued the first national postage stamps—a five-cent stamp showing the head of Benjamin Franklin and a ten-cent stamp with the head of George Washington.

Now the postage would be paid by the person who mailed the letter. Some people objected. They said that if a person really wanted to receive a letter, the least he could do was pay the postage. Before postage stamps, people would simply fold their letters and write the address on the outside. But now letters became more private because everybody began to use envelopes which could be sealed.

With the growth of the railroads just before the Civil War it was possible to carry the mail much faster than on horseback or by stage coach. But when a train arrived at a railroad station and dropped several large bags of mail they had to be sorted all at once. That caused annoying delays. Then in 1865 the Railway Mail Service began using specially designed railway cars to sort the mail while it was in transit.

There were still problems of how to pick up mail from small towns along the track where the trains did not even stop for passengers. With a clever new gadget—the mail-bag catcher—the speeding train, as it passed, could snatch a bag of mail hanging beside the track.

Postage stamps, too, became a way of bringing Americans together. The pictures on stamps reminded the nation of its heroes (like Franklin and Washington) and told of great events, past and present. The first "commemorative" series of American postage stamps appeared in 1893 at the time of the World's Columbian Exposition in Chicago. Sixteen large stamps in different denominations showed scenes of Columbus and the discovery of America. In 1938 the Post Office issued a complete series of Presidents. From the very beginning the Post Office had a rule against using the images of persons still alive.

Even after postage stamps were introduced, at first they paid for delivery only as far as the post office. They did not include delivery to anybody's home. About the time of the Civil War, when private letter-carrying businesses were actually delivering mail to the home address on the envelope, they were often speedier than Post Office mail. To compete with them the Post Office began to provide the same service.

Finally in 1863 Congress provided a regular salary for letter carriers. They took the mail from the post office and delivered it to home addresses. This serv-

Paying the postman for a letter received.

ice was offered only in the cities. By 1887 a city had to have at least 10,000 people to be eligible for free home delivery. But most Americans still lived on farms or in small towns. As late as 1890 nearly three-quarters of the people in the United States never received a letter unless they went to the post office to collect it.

The old-fashioned system had its points. People did not receive "junk" mail they didn't want. The general storekeeper was commonly the village postmaster. When the post office was in a corner of the general store—between the drygoods and the farm tools—the system brought customers to the general store. There, too, farmers would enjoy meeting friends from the whole countryside who had come for their mail.

But it was also a nuisance. The farmer never received mail unless he came to town. He was out of touch with the news. No wonder the farmer had a reputation for being out-of-date.

In 1889 a Go-Getting department-store pioneer from Philadelphia, John Wanamaker, became Postmaster General. He saw that it was time for a change. The whole nation would profit if *everybody*—not just the city dweller—had mail delivered to his mailbox. Wanamaker's plan would finally bring the mail to the farmer. It would be called "Rural Free Delivery"—RFD for short.

"RFD!" became the farmers' battlecry. And there really was a battle. On one side were the farmers who wanted mail-order catalogs and mail-order packages and newspapers delivered to their doors. They wanted to be in touch with the world every day. On the other side were the village storekeepers. They wanted to keep the farmers coming into their stores to get their mail—and incidentally to do some shopping. If it became too easy to shop by mail, the farmers

might buy all their goods from Sears and Ward's and the country stores would lose their customers.

At the same time, in the 1890's, many American farmers in the West were suffering from drought and hard times. Farmers were organizing in their Grange Clubs (which had supported Ward's) and in their Populist political party. And many city people, too, wanted to help the farmer—especially if it could be done in some way that would help make the cities prosper.

In 1896 Congress adopted RFD. Incidentally, Congressmen were glad to create lots of new jobs—and perhaps win new votes. In one of the great American organizing achievements of the nineteenth century, the Post Office laid out nine thousand new routes in one year. The Postmaster General approved the design for a standard rural mailbox, which ever since has been the trademark of country life.

RFD helped open the world to the farmer. Now when he ordered from Sears and Ward's, his goods came promptly by RFD. Soon farmers insisted on—and were getting—the latest styles and the newest improvements. The farmer was no longer a "back number" as he used to be called.

Now, at last, he shared with other Americans all the news of the world. When his only way of receiving mail had been his weekly trip to the village, no sensible farmer would subscribe to a daily newspaper. Who wanted an armful of stale newspapers once a week? But now the newspaper came to the farmer's mailbox every day. In 1911 over a billion newspapers and magazines were delivered over RFD.

A Railway Mail Service employee aboard a moving train, using the improved "catcher" to snatch a mailbag from a post beside the track.

In the days before the automobile, mail wagons like this brought letters and packages by Rural Free Delivery to the farmer's own mailbox.

CHAPTER 15

The Sun Is No Longer Boss

In the days before the railroad, people did not worry much about being on time. George Washington or Thomas Jefferson did not consider a person late simply because he arrived fifteen or twenty minutes after the time they had agreed on. When Benjamin Franklin listed in his *Autobiography* the thirteen virtues he would practice till he became perfect in them, he included "sincerity" and "cleanliness"—but he did not include punctuality.

In colonial days it was hard to be on time anyway, because watches were expensive and not many people carried them. Most people depended on the clock they saw—or heard—on the town hall or the church steeple. "Grandfather clocks" struck the hour and the half-hour to tell time to people who had no watches. If you took a trip, there was no regular timetable. Stagecoaches left whenever they had arrived from some other place or whenever the driver and

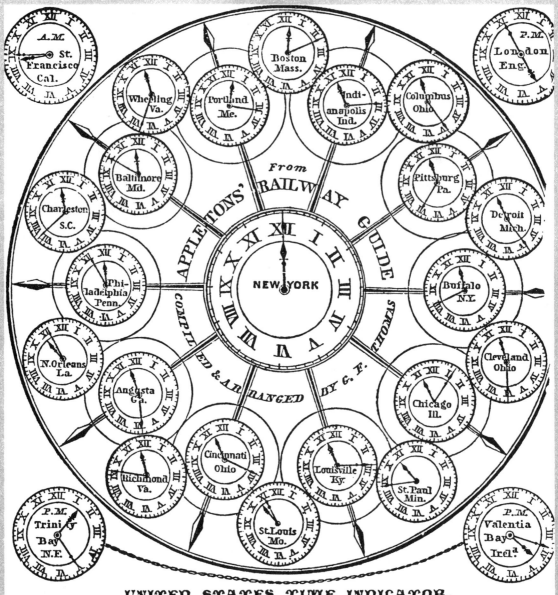

UNITED STATES TIME INDICATOR,

*Showing the Difference of Time between the various Cities of the United States : including
San Francisco, California ; Trinity Bay, Newfoundland ; Valentia Bay, Ireland ; and
London, England.*

It will be perceived. by glancing at the "Indicator," that when it is noon at New York, it is 12 minutes past 12 00 at Boston, 25 minutes past 1 00 at Trinity Bay, 24 minutes past 4 00 p. m. at Valentia Bay ; when it wants 15 minutes of 9 00 a. m. at St. Francisco, Cal., it wants 5 minutes of 5 00 p. m. at London, England. Thus, by a little calculation, the reader will readily perceive the difference of time between the several points, and obviate the necessity of moving the hands of his watch to be in time.

There is no standard railway time in the Union, each Railway Co. adopting the time where its principal office may be located ; we would, therefore, suggest to the traveller the necessity of consulting t "Indicator," and, if possible, to be at the depot som few minutes previous to the departure of the trains

To Travellers.—As our object is to publish *reliable Guide*, regardless of expense, we woul thank the travelling community if they will notif us of the incorrectness of a Time Table, and we wil not only exclude it from the "Guide," but notif the public of the same.

*Before Standard Time. This cover of Appletons' Railway Guide shows the time in different
cities when it was noon in New York.*

the horses were ready.

In a stagecoach on a good road you might average five miles an hour. After the railroads were built you could average forty. And you could travel on schedule. When a single track was used for trains in both directions, the engineer had to know exactly what time the train was due from the other direction so he could be on the siding to let it pass. Trains ran by the minute.

And now, with trains speeding from city to city, there were strange new problems that nobody had ever noticed before. The trouble was that every town had its own clocks set to its own particular time. The astronomers said that it was "noon" when you saw the sun reach its zenith—the highest point in the heavens. Since the earth was constantly in motion, and since the sun rose sooner when you were more to the east, then when it was noon obviously depended on *where* you were. Since you saw the sun rise earlier if you were in New York than if you were in Chicago, and still earlier in Chicago than in San Francisco, the time was different in those places.

There actually was a difference in the "astronomical" time, between any two places if one was to the west of the other —that is, if the places were on different longitudes. When it was precisely noon (that is when the sun had reached its zenith) in Boston, it was still only 11:56 in the morning in Worcester (slightly to the west). And when it was precisely noon in Chicago it was already 12:06 in Indianapolis (slightly to the east).

Cities became as patriotic about their own time as about the splendor of their city hall or the grandeur of their hotel. In every city the people said God had given them their "own" time, when He fixed the sun in the heavens.

Imagine what this meant for a railroad! The Pennsylvania Railroad tried to use Philadelphia time on its eastern lines. But that was 5 minutes earlier than New York time and 5 minutes later than Baltimore time. In Indiana there were 23 different local times, in Illinois 27, and in Wisconsin there were 38.

Even in any one town people disagreed about what the time really was. Each jeweler might have his own special time, which his customers were loyal to. To keep business running smoothly, and so that people would know when the stores would open and close, and when to meet their appointments, each city somehow had to announce its own time. Some used chimes on a town clock. Others blew a whistle or used a ball, called a "time ball" (held up on a pole in a conspicuous place) which was dropped at the precise moment of noon.

Generally the railroads used the local time for their arrival in each station. In between cities there was the greatest confusion. Yet for speeding express trains a few minutes could make the difference between a clear track and a fatal collision.

It is not surprising, then, that railroad men were among the first to try to bring order out of this confusion. But it was not easy. If you began tampering with their time, citizens were as outraged as if you tried to change the name of their city. And, of course, the astronomers really had a point. If you measured time by the sun in the heavens, then it was not man but nature that had made the confusion. And then perhaps nothing could be done about it.

But maybe, others said, this way of handling time was only a matter of habit. Suppose people simply stopped using sun time or astronomical time. And suppose that instead they used a new kind of "Railroad Time"—which could be the "Standard Time."

Suppose you managed to persuade the different cities along the railroad line to set their clocks to the same time. Take, for example, the train which ran west from Boston to Worcester. Although Worcester's astronomical time was 4 minutes earlier than Boston's, the people of Worcester might be persuaded to set their clocks to the same time as those in Boston.

For the United States as a whole, you could mark off on the map a few conspicuous time belts—up and down the whole country. You would need only four—Eastern Time, Central Time, Mountain Time, and Pacific Time— each several hundred miles wide. Standard Time would be exactly the same for all the places within each belt. At the edge of each belt, the time would change by a whole hour. These time belts would be marked on all maps, and then everybody could know exactly what time it was everywhere.

This was a sensible plan. But it took many years to persuade Americans. The leader of the campaign was William Frederick Allen, an energetic man who was not afraid to make enemies. He had seen the confusion when he had been an engineer on the Camden and Amboy Railroad before he joined the staff of the *Official Guide of the Railways*. And he made time reform the main purpose of his life. Allen aimed to provide a railroad timetable that everybody could understand and could rely on. This would help make railroad travel safer and speedier. His plan for Standard Time finally was adopted by the railroads to go into effect at noon, November 18, 1883.

Everywhere people prepared for the dramatic moment. At 11:45 in the morning according to the old Chicago time, conductors and engineers gathered in the lobby of the railroad station in Chicago. With their old-fashioned stem-winding pocket watches in their hands they looked at the clock on the wall. When the official Chicago railroad clock reached noon, it was stopped. The switch instantly connected it by telegraph wire to the new official clock for the whole Central time belt. At what would have been 9 minutes and 32 seconds past noon by the old Chicago time, the clock was started again. The railroad men all set their watches. Now everybody was on Standard Time!

Some people still objected. They thought the railroads were trying to take the place of God. "It is unconstitutional," warned Mayor Dogberry of Bangor, Maine, "being an attempt to change the immutable laws of God Almighty and hard on the workingman by changing day into night." He told churches not to ring their bells according to the new Standard Time. The editor of the Indianapolis *Sentinel* was outraged:

The sun is no longer boss of the job. People—55,000,000 of them—must eat, sleep and work as well as travel by railroad time. It is a revolt, a rebellion. The sun will be requested to rise and set by railroad time. . . . People will have to marry by railroad time, and die by railroad time. Ministers will be required to preach by railroad time.

One minister in Tennessee was so disgusted at this effort to take the place of God's own sun time that he took a hammer into his pulpit and smashed his watch to pieces just to shock his congregation.

But others found reason to be pleased. "The man who goes to church in New York on November 18th," applauded the New York *Herald*, "will hug himself with delight to find that the noon service has been curtailed to the extent of nearly four minutes, while every old maid on Beacon Hill in Boston will rejoice to discover that she is younger by almost 16 minutes."

Gradually people forgot their outrage. They discovered that it was wonderfully convenient to have Standard Time. One city after another changed its clocks to agree with the clock on the railroad station. In 1918 Congress finally gave the Interstate Commerce Commission the legal power to mark off time belts. The government simply followed the time belts that William Frederick Allen had persuaded the railroads to adopt thirty-five years earlier.

Standard Time helped to draw all the nation's railroad lines together. But other steps were needed too. In 1860 there were about 350 different railroad companies and about 30,000 miles of railroad tracks in the United States. Yet there was not really a national railroad network.

The main reason was that the many railroad lines were not on the same "gauge." The gauge is the distance between the two rails, measured from

the inside of one rail to the inside of the other. There were many different gauges. Some railroad builders put their tracks six feet apart but some put them closer together, and there were at least eleven different gauges in general use. A railroad car that would just fit the six-foot gauge would not run on the narrower gauges.

If you wanted to send a package any distance by railroad it had to be taken out of the car that fitted one gauge and moved into a car to fit the gauge of the next railroad. In 1861 a package sent by railroad from Charleston, South Carolina, to Philadelphia, had to change railroad cars eight times.

Moving a package from one railroad to another made work for porters and teamsters. At the same time the passengers, who had to wait in the town while they changed trains, made business for hotels, restaurants, and storekeepers. Naturally enough, then, town boosters were not anxious to have all railroads on the same gauge.

From the beginning, quite a few lines happened to have the same gauge. George Stephenson, the English railroad inventor, had designed his locomotive to measure 4 feet 8½ inches between the wheels—the usual distance between wheels on a wagon. When Stephenson locomotives were imported to the United States, they had this "Standard Gauge." And many early railroad lines naturally built their tracks to fit the imported trains.

By 1861 about half the railroad tracks in the United States were on Standard Gauge. These were mainly in New England and the Middle Atlantic States, where most of the early railroads had

THE LAST SPIKE
OF OUR
COMMERCIAL UNION

SOUTH

NORTH

OUR STANDARD (GAUGE) ADOPTED ALL OVER THE UNION.

Thomas Nast, who drew this cartoon, came to New York from Germany as a child. He supported the Radical Republicans, attacked corrupt politicians, and invented the Republican Elephant and the Democratic Donkey.

been built. But the other half of American railroad tracks were on every sort of gauge—from about three feet to about six feet.

The Civil War brought an urgent need to ship arms and men quickly across the country. In the Confederacy, lines which ran into Richmond on Standard Gauge were hastily connected to one another. Now passengers and freight could go straight through. In the North, too, the war hurried progress. For the first time through service connected New York City with Washington, D.C.

At the end of the war Americans, North and South, saw the overwhelming advantages of a uniform gauge. And when the transcontinental railroad was completed with Standard Gauge in 1869, that settled the question. Now if a railroad builder wanted to join the traffic across the continent, he had to set his rails 4 feet 8½ inches apart.

By 1880 about four-fifths of the tracks in the United States had been converted to Standard Gauge. Most of the other gauges were in the Old Confederate South. Finally, in 1886, representatives of Southern railroads decided to change the gauge of all their 13,000 miles of track to the national standard.

A month in advance, crews went along loosening the old track. They measured the distance for the new Standard Gauge and put spikes along the wooden ties. On May 31 and June 1, 1886, the men worked frantically. One record-breaking crew on the Louisville and Nashville Railroad changed eleven miles of track in 4½ hours. June 1, 1886, was a holiday along the Southern tracks. By 4:00 P.M. the Southern railroads had joined the Union.

CHAPTER 16
Company Towns and Garden Cities ᏇᏉᏋ

The American West was known for its "instant cities." Even before the Civil War, these grew quickly if they happened to be located at way stations where the westward travelers passed—at the joinings of riverways, on lake ports, at railroad terminals, or near new mines. As these cities grew, their boosters competed with one another to attract new settlers who, of course, would also be new customers. Each city hoped to become "bigger and better" than all the others. Some of them—Cincinnati, Chicago, Denver, Omaha, Kansas City, and others—became the great cities of the new Middle West.

But after the Civil War, as the whole country became more citified, there grew up new kinds of instant cities. These had not been way stations on the road west. They were found all over the country. At first their aim was not to grow big, but to stay small—and so escape the troubles of the crowded metropolis. They were actually planned— by businessmen, real-estate developers, and others—and they had common patterns.

Businessmen were looking for new places to put their factories. Workers were anxious to escape the dumbbell tenements and the darkened, crowded cities. Prosperous merchants and lawyers and doctors were eager to raise their families out in the open air.

With the new railroad network there was less reason than ever for factories to stay in big cities. Almost everywhere along a railroad line would do. For raw materials could be brought in from anywhere and finished products could be transported to anyplace.

Then why not build a "Company Town"? If an industrialist built his factory away from a big city, the workers would not have to live in slums. Where land was so much less expensive, each worker could have an attractive little house with his own garden. The employer could provide parks and playgrounds, and workers might be more content. After the Civil War many energetic businessmen had this idea.

In 1881 Andrew Carnegie, a Go-Getting steel industrialist, built a steel plant and a whole new town called Homestead seven miles up the Monongahela River from Pittsburgh. Besides small houses for the workers and their families, Carnegie provided a library and even bowling alleys. Homestead was not beautiful, but at least it lacked the crowds and the filth of the city slums.

George M. Pullman, inventor of the Pullman sleeping car for railroads, also decided to build a new town ten miles outside Chicago. In 1884 he bought a tract of land on the shores of Lake Calumet. He named it after himself and hoped it would be a model for other Company Towns. Pullman's architect designed the whole town, including a central square with town hall, churches, a library, and parks. All the buildings, including the small houses for the workers, were of dark-red brick.

Then in 1893 Granite City was founded outside St. Louis, to manufacture "graniteware" pottery. The Diamond Match Company and the Pittsburgh Plate Glass Company built Company Towns near Akron, Ohio. The United States Steel Company in 1905 built Gary in Indiana (not far from Chicago), named after Elbert Henry Gary, the head of the company.

Company Towns sprang up all over the country. There workers escaped the worst horrors of the big city. But they found some new horrors. Living in a Company Town was something like being a feudal serf in the Middle Ages. The company not only controlled your job, but it also decided where you would live, where (and at what price) you could buy your food. The company controlled your schools, and even hired your police.

Some of the most violent strikes were in these Company Towns. When the Carnegie Steel Company cut wages at its Homestead plant in 1892, the angry workers went on strike. In the resulting violence a dozen men were killed. When the Pullman Company cut wages but kept up its rents during the business depression of 1893, their whole town went on strike against the company and for months the nation's railroads were paralyzed. For Americans who wanted to run their own lives the Company

*Homestead, Pennsylvania, the company town built by Andrew Carnegie, where workers es-
caped the city slum but lived in a pall of smoke from the blast furnaces.*

Town was a spiritual failure.

But the Company Town was not the only new-style instant city which appeared at the end of the nineteenth century. On the "suburban frontier" there appeared the Garden City. An English reformer, Ebenezer Howard, who had come to America as a young man and had spent five years around crowded Chicago, tried to design a suburban utopia. Howard's *Garden Cities of Tomorrow* (1898) was his blueprint for a better life. He wished to combine the best features of the city and the country. He urged people to group together to build Garden Cities—new small towns out in the country. These towns, he said, should be planned with a garden belt all around. Then, if the Garden City was connected to the big city by a railroad, it gave its residents the best of both worlds.

Some rich men who owned summer houses in the country near cities began living out in the suburbs year-round. For example, some businessmen who worked in New York City preferred living in Old Greenwich, Connecticut, three-quarters of an hour away on the railroad. Since there was not enough traffic to persuade the railroad to stop there, they would hop on or off the train outside Old Greenwich as it slowed down for a bridge. By the 1880's when enough New York businessmen were living there, they built their own railroad station, and the train stopped for them. These rich suburban pioneers built their own country clubs, and tried to keep their communities "exclusive"—for Oldcomers.

Soon other Americans, following Ebenezer Howard's advice, were building Garden Cities. These were no longer only for the very rich, but they were not yet for people of modest means. Lake Forest outside Chicago and Shaker Heights outside Cleveland showed a special effort to make the Garden City more romantic than the big city. Instead of the monotonous parallel streets of checkerboard city blocks, the Garden City streets wound up and down the hills and by the trees of the countryside. Wide lawns separated the houses from the roads and from one another. Before long, Garden Cities like Radburn, New Jersey, were being specially planned for people of modest income. In 1910 a New York architect made a new design for space-saving "garden apartments" with "kitchenettes" (a new American word for a compact kitchen and pantry). Now you no longer needed to be rich to live out in a garden suburb.

Ebenezer Howard's diagram (1898) of the ideal arrangement of lands in a Garden City. Houses were to be built in a circle around a park. Outside the Circle Railway there were to be farms and forests.

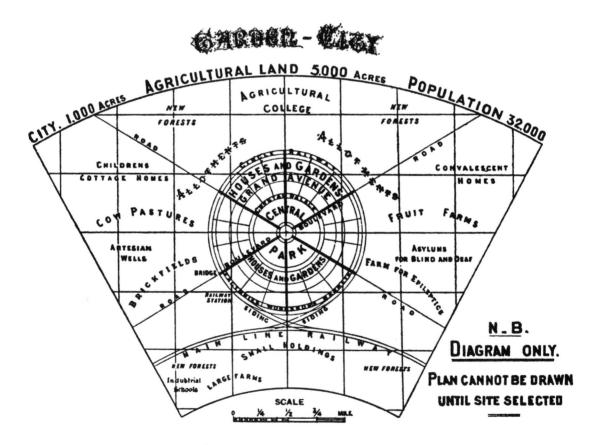

CHAPTER 17

Bridge-Building Heroes

Many fast-growing American cities had started on the banks of wide rivers. To expand, they had to find ways of carrying the railroad—and thousands of daily passengers—out beyond the old city limits. The growth of these American cities, and their ability to hold their citizens together, depended on their ability to span the neighboring waterway. Go-Getting American engineers transformed the ancient art of bridge building to help the cities to reach out to their new frontiers.

Something about bridge building specially attracted the American inventive genius. James Buchanan Eads, the man who built the bridge for St. Louis, had first shown his inventive talents during the Civil War as an adviser to the Union navy. In 1861 he proposed a fleet of ironclad gunboats to control the Mississippi River. When the government took up his suggestion he manufactured the needed ships in sixty-five days. After the war the people of St. Louis, which was on the west bank of the Mississippi, saw that they had to bring the railroad across the wide river and into their city if St. Louis was to grow.

Many different schemes were offered. But all were rejected until Eads appeared. As a boy he had worked on a river steamboat. When only twenty-two years old, he had invented a diving bell to salvage ships that had sunk in the river. And then he had done a lot of walking underwater on the very bottom of the Mississippi. He knew that river bottom almost as well as other men knew the city streets.

What Eads had learned was important. Building a bridge across the Mississippi depended first on finding solid support under the sandy river bottom. As Eads had moved along 65 feet below the surface of the water, he saw the swift currents churning up the sands. He knew that the supports for his bridge would have to go far below those river sands—all the way down to bedrock.

In 1867, when Eads began construction, his first problem was to lay the foundations of the two stone towers which would hold up the arches of the bridge in midstream. The towers would rise 50 feet above water level. The foundation of one would have to go down 86 feet below water level, and the other, where bedrock was deeper, had to go down 123 feet. But was this possible?

Eads's plan was to use his own diving bell together with some new caissons—watertight working chambers—that had recently been perfected in England. The 75-foot-wide caissons would keep out the water while the men dug, and the men would keep digging beneath the river sands until they reached solid rock.

Stages in the building of Eads's bridge to span the Mississippi River at St. Louis. From the two stone towers in midstream, steel arches thrust out to meet arches thrusting from other towers on the shore.

When his men finally reached bedrock, they were working ten stories below the surface of the water! Because of the great pressures at that depth, the men could stay down only 45 minutes at a time. They had to come up slowly. Between shifts they rested long periods. Despite all precautions thirteen men died of "caisson disease" (sometimes called "the bends") from too rapid change in air pressure.

The Mississippi River boatmen and ferrymen feared competition from the new railroad that would cross the bridge. They tried to persuade the Secretary of War to dismantle the towers when they were half built. President U. S. Grant knew St. Louis and he had faith in Eads. He knew the bridge would be important to the future of the city and to the growth of the Middle West. And he saw that it would help bind the nation together. He ordered the engineers in the War Department to keep the project going.

For the three vast arches of the bridge Eads decided to use steel, though it had never been used in such a large struc-

ture. When the usual carbon steel did not meet his tests, he ordered large quantities of the new chromium steel, and then supervised its production. While chromium steel was more costly, it was rustproof and needed no covering.

It took Eads seven years to bridge the Mississippi. Finally in 1874 in a grand ceremony the former Union general, William T. Sherman, pounded the last spike of the double-track railroad crossing the bridge. Then fourteen locomotives, two by two, chugged triumphantly across the river. President Grant came to St. Louis to proclaim Eads an American hero.

And there were other heroic bridge builders who helped open ways to the suburban frontiers. Few other cities were quite so hemmed in by water as New York. Manhattan Island, heart of the city, was surrounded by the East River, the Hudson River, and the Atlantic Ocean. For a half-century there had been proposals for a bridge across the East River, connecting lower Manhattan Island to Brooklyn. When the fierce winter of 1866–67 stopped all ferry

service and isolated Brooklyn from Manhattan for days, it was plain that something had to be done.

John Roebling was ready with a plan. When he came to the United States from Germany as a young man he opened the first factory for making wire rope out of many strands of wire twisted together. This new material was wonderfully suited for reaching over wide rivers where it was difficult or impossible to build masonry towers in midstream. From high towers on both ends you could suspend the strong wire rope to hold up the bridge.

If the Niagara River, for example, was to be spanned near the Falls, it would have to be by such a "suspension" bridge. In 1855 Roebling completed a wire-supported bridge over the Niagara —strong enough to carry fully loaded trains. This feat made John Roebling famous. In 1860 he completed another suspension bridge, just outside Pittsburgh, reaching a thousand feet across the Allegheny River. And by 1867 he had completed still another outside Cincinnati, across the Ohio River.

A suspension bridge, Roebling style, could solve New York's problem. For the bridge from Manhattan to Brooklyn had to stay high above water level in order to allow the sails and smokestacks of large ocean-going vessels to pass underneath. Roebling's ambitious plan in 1867 proposed towers 271 feet above water level, holding up a main suspension span of 1,595 feet.

During the very beginning of construction in 1869, a ferry crushed John Roebling's foot against the dock and he died from tetanus infection in two weeks. John Roebling's son, Washington Roebling, was ready to carry on. He too was a man of courage. He had enlisted in the Union army as a private on the day after President Lincoln's first appeal for volunteers. By the time of the Battle of Gettysburg, young Washington Roebling's services had earned him the rank of colonel. On the second day of the battle, with his own hands he helped drag a cannon up to a strategic hilltop, and so helped to prevent the defeat of the Union Army.

On his father's death, Washington Roebling at once took over the building of the bridge. In 1872, when fire in the Brooklyn caisson threatened the whole project, Roebling stayed below in the

THE EAST RIVER BRIDGE.

ON this page we give several views of the Brooklyn caisson of the East River Bridge, which a few days since narrowly escaped destruction by fire. The interior of the caisson is divided into chambers by temporary partitions of planking calked with oakum. It was in one of these partitions that the fire occurred. It originated from the blaze of a candle held too near the partition by a workman. Once kindled, the fire was driven by the immense force of the compressed air within the caisson with such rapidity as to defy all ordinary methods of extinguishment; and it was not until the interior was flooded with water that the engineers of the work felt satisfied that they had effectually subdued the mischievous element. It is thought that the injury to the caisson can be fully repaired at a very slight expense.

The caisson, as our readers will see from the sectional view, is an immense wooden box, without bottom, covering a space of 102 by 168 feet, or about three-eighths of an acre of ground—nearly seven city lots. Its present height is 24 feet 6 inches. The roof is of solid timber 15 feet thick (except that the upper ten courses have narrow spaces filled with concrete, to increase the weight). The sides of the air chamber are V shaped, and are of solid timbers bolted very firmly together. The lower edge is heavily shod with iron. This V is 9 feet 6 inches high, 8 inches thick at the bottom, and 9 feet thick at the top. The timber joints, from the edge to the top of the fifth roof course, are thoroughly calked and pitched. Between the fourth and fifth roof courses is a sheet of tin, which is continued down the sides underneath the outside sheathing; this is intended to prevent all escape of air from the inside.

The air or working chamber is divided by massive timber trusses or frames into six rooms, in each of which fifteen to twenty men are employed. Some are drilling the immense boulders preparatory to blasting, others pulling stone from the trenches by means of tackle; gangs of men are wheeling material that has been excavated and dumping it into the pools under the water-shafts, and here others are constantly shoving the material under the shafts, from whence it is taken by the dredging buckets. The interior is lighted by fourteen calcium lights: the gas being let into the caisson through pipes connected with receivers placed outside.

The caisson is supported mainly by blocks placed 12 feet apart in the trenches, and wedged tightly up to the frames; and the lowering is effected by clearing material from under the V, and in taking out the blocking and replacing it at a little lower level. The movement downward is imperceptible, but it goes on steadily at an average rate of three inches per day.

The water or excavating shafts are essentially barometers, which measure accurately the pressure of air in the caisson. The shaft is the barometer tube, but is filled with water instead of mercury, and the pool at the bottom is the cistern. Every pound above the atmospheric pressure (which is, of course, bearing on top of the column) forces the water a little more than two feet higher in this tube. At the present time the pressure inside is 12 to 15 pounds in excess, and the water column is therefore 27 to 34 feet high.

The two smallest shafts shown in the sectional view, called supply shafts, are for the purpose of passing cement, sand, and gravel into the caisson, after the excavation is completed. The whole interior space will then be filled with concrete, made from these materials, forming one massive stone.

The two remaining shafts are the air shafts, through which the laborers descend by ladders to the chamber below. The enlarged cylinders at the top are the air locks, and it is in these that the change of pressure is experienced in either ascending or descending. In changing the gangs about twenty men enter each lock at one time, and the time occupied in shifting the entire force is less than half an hour. One of the air pipes from the compressors enters one of these shafts, and the other one of the supply shafts.

The spaces left around the shafts are inclosed by coffer-dams, to prevent water entering from without through the masonry. There are now 18 feet of masonry completed. It is of massive blocks of limestone and granite, weighing from one and a half to six tons each. The arrangement of derricks and railway track is so complete that it is not an uncommon thing to unload and set twenty of these blocks in an hour.

There were used in the construction of the caisson over 3,000,000 feet, board measure, of yellow pine timber, and about 35 miles of bolts.

THE BROOKLYN PIER—GENERAL VIEW OF FOUNDATION.

WORKING BENEATH SHOE OR EDGE OF CAISSON.

AIR CHAMBERS FOR THE INGRESS AND EGRESS OF WORKMEN.

SENDING UP DÉBRIS THROUGH THE WATER SHAFT.

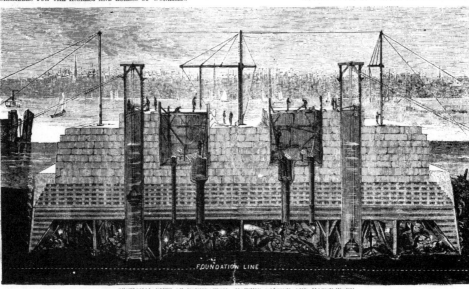

FOUNDATION LINE

SECTIONAL VIEW OF FOUNDATION, SHOWING CAISSON AND MASON-WORK.

Building Brooklyn Bridge was one of the wonders of the age. The problems of working far underwater were just as challenging as the later problems (brought by the skyscraper) of working far into the air.

compressed-air chamber for seven hours. As a result he acquired "caisson disease."

Washington Roebling never fully recovered. Too weak to supervise the bridge on the spot, he would sit in a wheelchair in his apartment and watch the work through field glasses. Then he would give instructions to his wife, who carried them down to the bridge. All his communications with the world were through her. Efforts were made to remove him from the job, but his mind remained active and he would not give up the command.

At 1:30 on the afternoon of May 24, 1883, fourteen years after John Roebling had begun the job, President Chester A. Arthur and his Cabinet joined with Governor Grover Cleveland of New York for the formal opening of the Brooklyn Bridge. Six warships anchored below the bridge fired a resounding salute, and from the center of the bridge came a dazzling display of fireworks. The orator of the occasion declared that this, the world's greatest bridge, was a triumph of "the faith of the saint and the courage of the hero."

The "saint," Mrs. Roebling, herself attended the celebrations. But Washington Roebling, the heroic bridge-building son of a heroic father, was too ill to leave the room from which he had overseen the work. The President of the United States went to Roebling's simple apartment at No. 110 Columbia Heights to give his congratulations.

CHAPTER 18

Going Up!

Oddly enough, although the growing United States had lots of land to spare, the most distinctive American way for a city to grow was not to stretch *out*. After the Civil War, Americans began using their own know-how—together with materials and know-how from all over the world—to stretch their cities *up*. Although some Americans were moving to the suburbs, more people than ever before wanted to live and work right in the center. Businessmen wanted to be where the action was. And many people who could afford to live in the suburbs, still preferred to live downtown.

With old kinds of construction the tallest buildings had seldom been over five or six stories high. There were two problems which had to be solved before buildings could go higher.

The first problem—how to get the people up and down—was beginning to be solved even before the Civil War. In a few luxury hotels, elevators already carried guests up to the fifth and sixth floors. And in some early department stores the elevator was an attractive curiosity.

But elevators were thought to be dangerous. People feared that if the rope holding up the elevator cage should

On opening day at Lord & Taylor's, a new department store in New York City, the elevator was one of the chief attractions.

break, the passengers would drop to their death. Elisha Graves Otis found a way to dispel the public fears. He invented a simple automatic safety brake. If the rope broke, instead of the cage plummeting to the bottom, the brake would automatically clamp the cage safely to the sides. Otis staged a demonstration in New York in 1854. He rode the elevator to the top. Then an attendant cut the rope while breathless

spectators watched. As the cage was clamped in place, Otis bowed nonchalantly to the crowd.

Otis' early steam-driven elevators moved only 50 feet a minute, which amounted to about half a mile an hour. To Americans, who now could speed along on railroads at forty miles an hour, this steam-driven "vertical railway" seemed to climb like a snail. But before 1880 the improved "hydraulic" elevators (pushed up by water pressure in a long vertical cylinder) were climbing at 600 feet a minute. By 1892 an electric motor was carrying passengers up so fast that it "stopped" their ears.

The second problem—how to hold up the building—began to be solved when James Bogardus and others had used cast iron for their Buyers' Palaces. No longer was it necessary to build a tall building like a pyramid, with thick supporting walls on the lower floors. Cast-iron construction helped the department stores keep the lower floors wide open, with broad vistas and narrow pillars, allowing attractive show windows in between. But iron construction also made it possible to build higher and higher. Soon an eight-story building like Stewart's Cast Iron Palace would seem small.

The time was ripe for the "skyscraper." Of course Bogardus was only dreaming when he forecast buildings "ten miles high." But he was not far wrong when he told American builders that only the sky would be the limit.

Bogardus himself constructed one of the first buildings of true skyscraper design. Its frame was a tall iron cage. If the cage was strong and rigid, and solidly anchored at the bottom, then the building could go up high without needing thick walls at the bottom. This was "skeleton" construction. The building was held up, not by wide foundations at the bottom, but by its own rigid skeleton.

The first time Bogardus actually tried this, his structure did not have any rooms at all. It was a skeleton-framed tower for an ammunition factory. In those days lead shot was made by pouring molten lead through a sieve inside a high tower. The little liquid balls of lead dripped through, a few at a time. As these plummeted down through the air they became naturally rounded. And as they fell into the tank of water at the bottom they hardened into their rounded shape—ready for use in a rifle or a cannon.

In 1855, when the McCullough Shot and Lead Company needed a new shot tower in New York City, Bogardus gave them his radical new design. He built them an octagonal iron tower eight stories high. A tall iron cage, it needed no filled-in, weight-bearing walls to hold it up. Yet it was strong. When the openings in the iron frame were covered with brick, it served just as well as any heavy column of stone.

It was one thing to build a shot tower but quite another to trust the lives of hundreds to such a newfangled way of building. The first real try was in Chicago where the pioneer was William LeBaron Jenney. An adventurous man of wide experience, he had helped build a railroad across Panama before there was any canal. In the Civil War he served on General Sherman's staff as an engineer.

In 1884 when the Home Insurance Company decided to construct a new office building in Chicago, they gave him the job. Jenney, who had probably heard of Bogardus' shot towers built twenty years before, decided himself to use an iron skeleton. In the next year his building was completed.

Even before Jenney's first skyscraper was completed, a better new material had been perfected. This new material was steel. The first six floors of the Home Insurance Building had been

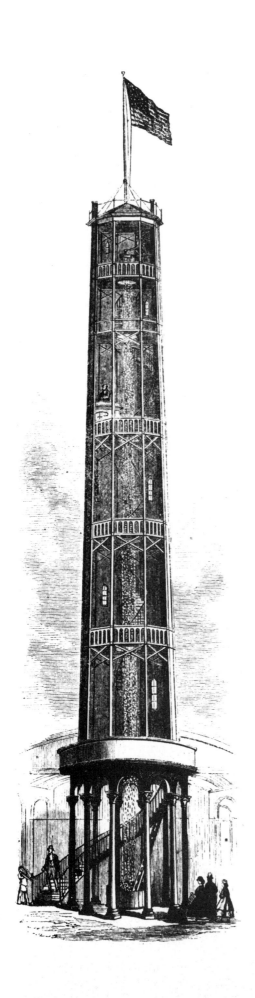

LEFT: *In the Bogardus tower, pieces of lead became rounded as they fell through the hollow center down into a well of water below.* ABOVE: *A New York City fire tower, also designed by Bogardus. The drawing is by Winslow Homer, who first became famous from his Civil War drawings for* Harper's Weekly. *Later he settled on the coast of Maine and had a second career as a painter of fishermen and the sea.*

framed with wrought iron. The top three stories were framed in steel. Steel, like wrought iron, was made almost entirely from iron ore, but steel was far superior. While wrought iron was easily shaped into beams and connecting plates, it bent readily. It was not ideal for a skyscraper frame. Steel was the answer. And it was the material that made higher and higher American skyscrapers possible.

Though men had known how to make steel for centuries, the process had been difficult and time-consuming. Therefore steel was so expensive that it was used only for small objects. The swords used by knights in the Middle Ages were made by endlessly hammering and re-heating and then again hammering the blades. Until the mid-nineteenth century this was the usual way to harden iron to make it into steel.

Then an Englishman, Henry Bessemer, invented his new mass-production steel furnace. By blowing air through the molten iron mass, the carbon in it was burnt out much more quickly. Now it was possible to produce a hundred tons of steel from a single furnace in twelve hours. Before the end of the nineteenth century, the United States—borrowing English methods, improved by American know-how—was producing about twice as much steel as Great

Steel skeleton for a pioneer skyscraper, Chicago's Reliance Building, 1894.

Britain, and now led the world. Better, cheaper steel meant more tall buildings.

Jenney's example in Chicago was followed in New York. The skeleton system was especially useful for building high structures on the tiny lots of crowded Manhattan Island. In 1888 an architect, Bradford Gilbert, was asked to design an 11-story building on Broadway, on a lot that was only 25 feet wide and 103 feet deep. With the old-fashioned heavy masonry the walls would have had to be so thick on the ground floor that there would have been no space for any rooms there. Gilbert designed a true iron-skeleton building—the first in New York City.

At first the building inspectors refused a building permit for Gilbert's Tower Building because they believed that no iron-skeleton building could stay up. Even after the building was completed, Gilbert had to show his confidence by taking the offices at the very top for himself. The age of the skyscraper had arrived.

Twenty-five years later, on the night of April 24, 1913, President Woodrow Wilson pressed a button in Washington to light the tallest habitable building in the world—the Woolworth Building in downtown Manhattan. The Woolworth Building, with its 55 stories rising 760 feet to the base of a towering flagpole, was a monument to the American Go-Getter.

The Woolworth Building was the biggest advertisement in the world. It advertised the success of Frank W. Woolworth, who had begun thirty years before as a poor farm boy in upstate New York. His empire of Five-and-Ten-Cent Stores with their brilliant red-and-gold storefronts now covered the nation. The biggest building in the world had been built from the selling of millions of little things. In that very year the 611 Woolworth stores sold 27,576,000 pairs of hosiery, 12,000 gross (1 gross = 12 dozen) of mousetraps, 300,000 gross of clothespins, 10,000 gross of tin toys, 3,000 gross of baby pacifiers, 368,000 gross of pearl buttons, and 186 tons of hairpins!

The Woolworth Building was a city in itself. With its thirty high-speed elevators it held 15,000 office workers and service employees. Its own power plant generated enough electricity to light fifty thousand homes.

Frank Woolworth wanted an office grand enough to go with the building. On a European tour in 1913 he selected the design of the Empire Room of Napoleon's palace in Paris for "the handsomest office in the country and possibly the world." For the Napoleon of American merchants, why not an office that was truly imperial? And beside his desk he placed a bust of Napoleon.

Skyscrapers still went up and up. Above the Woolworth Building rose the Chrysler Building in 1930. Then in 1931 came the Empire State Building. With its 105 stories reaching up 1,250 feet (almost twice as high as the Woolworth Building), it long remained the highest structure in the world.

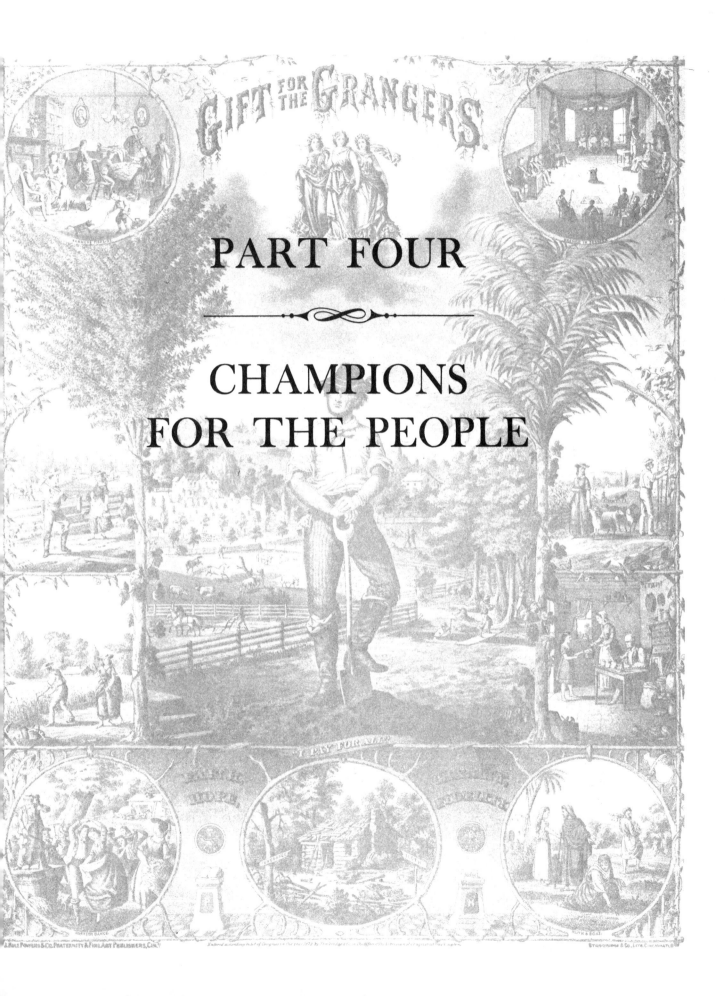

PART FOUR

CHAMPIONS
FOR THE PEOPLE

CHAMPIONS FOR THE PEOPLE

The Old World had long been ruled by aristocracies. In France and England and Germany, men who had inherited their titles and their lands held power over the life of the whole nation. For centuries government was by a privileged few looking after the silent many. Even after the European revolutions of the late eighteenth and early nineteenth centuries the old aristocrats still controlled the government in most countries.

In the United States, while some people were richer than others, there was no old-style aristocracy. If the people did not look after themselves, who would look after them?

In these years after the Civil War, there came a great new test for self-government. Could a nation so vast and varied find national leaders to speak for all its citizens?

The nation was growing strong and rich. It was becoming more and more citified, with bigger and bigger businesses. Could it find loud clear voices to speak for the farmer, for the small businessman, for the individual factory worker—and for all those others who had little wealth or power and who were in danger of being left out?

Grangers' meeting in Illinois. One sign says: "President $50,000 a year. Farmers 75 cents a week."

CHAPTER 19

The Farmers Find a Voice

During the Civil War many farmers—in both North and South—prospered. There was a great demand for food to supply the armies, there were fewer people working on farms, and the prices for farm products went up.

But within a few years after Appomattox the farmers' troubles began. A bushel of wheat, which in 1873 still sold for $1.21, twelve years later had gone down to 49 cents. A pound of cotton, in 1873 priced at 21 cents, in twenty years sank to 5 cents. At the same time the farmer's expenses went up.

Millions of farmers—like many homeowners today—were painfully buying their farms on mortgage loans. In good times and bad, the farmer had to make regular payments. The heartless sheriff with a long moustache who threatened to "foreclose" the mortgage was no joke to the poor farmer between about 1870 and 1900.

"In God we trusted," the farmers' saying went, "and in Kansas we busted." In the Depression of 1893 when factories closed, many unemployed workers went back to the farm and added to the farmers' burdens. Banks foreclosed their mortgages. Farm families walked the country roads in desperation.

But they did not take their troubles lying down. As early as 1867 they had begun to organize. Within ten years the Patrons of Husbandry had members all over the country in the 20,000 local lodges they called "Granges." On the Fourth of July, 1873, groups of farmers had met to hear a "Farmers' Declaration of Independence."

Farmers who believed they needed their own political party formed a "Farmers Alliance" and then organized the Populist Party in Omaha, Nebraska, in July 1892. Crusaders like the rabble-rousing Tom Watson of Georgia spoke for them in Congress, and spoke loud and clear. "Before I will give up this fight," Watson warned, "I will stay here till the ants tote me out of the keyhole."

One of the farmers' loudest demands was for "cheap money." That meant a high price for wheat and corn and cotton. For the farmers, who were always in debt, were most worried about how to keep up the yearly payments on their mortgages, so they could hold onto their farms.

Suppose for example, that a farmer owed $500 on his mortgage every year. Then if the price of wheat was $1 a bushel, he would have to raise 500 bushels of wheat to pay the $500. But if there was "cheap money"—say, if the price of wheat went up to $2 a bushel—

then the farmer could pay off his yearly debt by selling only 250 bushels of wheat. Of course the banker, to whom the farmer owed the $500 each year, would rather have seen all prices kept down, so the money he received would buy more things.

"Cheap money" meant finding ways for the government to mint as much money as possible. The more money there was around, the more likely people would pay higher prices for farm produce. On the other hand the bankers were against "cheap money" and wanted "hard money." They wanted the "Gold Standard." This meant keeping gold as the *only* basis for money. Since the amount of gold was extremely limited, and was not likely to increase much, the Gold Standard was one way of keeping prices down.

In the 1860's large new deposits of silver had been found in Nevada, Colorado, and elsewhere in the West. The farmers saw that if the government would be required to mint all this silver into money, then the quantity of money would be much increased. The price of wheat and corn and cotton would go up, and the farmers' problems might be solved. This program for minting silver was called "Free Silver" because it meant the "free," that is the unlimited, coining of silver into dollars.

Free silver, then, had a sure-fire appeal. It appealed to debt-burdened city laborers as well as debt-burdened farmers all over the country. And it appealed also to miners and prospectors in the Western States who wanted a guaranteed market for their silver. When the farmers put together their Populist Party to run their own candidates in the Presi-

dential election of 1892, they demanded Free Silver.

The farmers' colorful leaders were not afraid to shock the comfortable people. The handsome, unladylike Mary Elizabeth Lease of Kansas was the mother of four. "What you farmers need to do," she urged, "is to raise less corn and more *Hell!*" She also said:

> Wall Street owns the country. It is no longer a government of the people, by the people and for the people, but a government of Wall Street, by Wall Street and for Wall Street. The great common people of this country are slaves, and monopoly is the master.

Then, also from Kansas, there was "Sockless Jerry" Simpson. Once when he ran for Congress he accused his well-dressed opponent of wearing silk stockings. A reporter then sneered that Simpson was so crude that he wore no socks at all. Simpson made this into a boast. Always after he was known as "Sockless Jerry."

The famous farmer-orator, Ignatius Donnelly, came to be known as "the Sage of Nininger," after the town he had tried to build. Before the Civil War he had bought some Minnesota land, and hoped to get rich by making it into a boom town. When the town died, he plowed up what were supposed to be city lots and downtown streets, planted them with wheat, and so became a farmer.

Donnelly wrote many books and he loved outlandish ideas. His *Great Cryptogram* (1888) offered a secret code that was supposed to prove that the plays of Shakespeare had really been written by Sir Francis Bacon. Donnelly could attract a crowd anywhere. Some people were afraid to go hear him because they feared he would make them believe things against their will.

When the regular Democratic and Republican politicians saw the appeal of these farm crusaders, they naturally wanted to steal the Populist thunder. The Populist Platform of 1892 demanded many different reforms. But what would appeal most to the farmers was some one cure-all—a single reform that would solve all their problems at once.

It was not hard to believe that the cure-all might be Free Silver. There was something magical and mysterious about money. The amounts of money somehow seemed to change the value of everything else. Money seemed a medicine for everybody's ills.

Many Democrats and Republicans were especially afraid to see the country get into control of a third party. They called Populists the "lunatic fringe."

Inside the regular parties the most successful of the farm crusaders was William Jennings Bryan. Some called him "The Great Commoner" (because he championed the common people). Others called him "The Prairie Avenger," or "The Boy Orator of the Platte" —after the Nebraska river near his home. Born in Salem, Illinois, he studied law in Chicago and then practiced law in small towns. He distrusted rich people and people of "good family."

Bryan had a holier-than-thou way of speaking. He liked to preach against sin. Proud that he did not drink or smoke or gamble, he was always telling others how to behave. He also had a great appetite. One of his Sunday School class-

Mary Elizabeth Lease, a founder of the Populist Party, and one of the most colorful political leaders of the day.

mates recalled that Bryan was too good a boy to help steal the watermelons— "but he would enjoy eating them when the other boys had secured the booty." As a boy he would carry around bread in his pockets "for an emergency." His enormous appetite became famous. On his political campaigns it was not uncommon for him to eat six full meals a day.

A tall man of great energy, Bryan loved a political battle. And he had a talent for making every issue seem very simple. After he had explained it, every political battle seemed to be between Bryan and God on one side, and his opponents and Satan on the other. His enemies said Bryan did not really understand how complicated the problems

During the Presidential campaign of 1896, Democratic candidate Bryan traveled strenuously about the country carrying his rousing message to anyone who would listen.

were. Even his friends had to admit that what made him famous was not a sharp mind but his loud musical voice.

The "silver-tongued" William Jennings Bryan had decided that "Free Silver" would cure the ills of all mankind. When Bryan arrived at the Democratic Convention in Chicago on July 7, 1896, he was thirty-six years old—one year over the minimum age for a President. He had served only four years in Congress and was barely known outside of Nebraska. Unlike the other leading candidates, he did not have rich supporters.

As the Convention met, it was still not decided whether the Democratic Party would stay with the Gold Standard or whether they would join the farmers for

Free Silver. President Grover Cleveland, the Democrat in the White House, was strong for the Gold Standard. But he had lost the support of many laborers and farmers by using federal troops against the railroad workers in the big strike at Pullman. He had a reputation as spokesman for big business.

Until Bryan came to the platform, the speakers at the Chicago convention had been dull and long-winded. Since there was no public-address system most of the speakers could hardly be heard. Bryan was the final speaker for Free Silver.

This was young Bryan's great chance. The first sound of his ringing voice awakened the perspiring audience. They responded to his words with laughter and applause, "like a trained choir" (as he said), down to his last syllable. He spoke without hesitating, for he had given substantially the same speech many times before—to farm audiences all over Nebraska. "We will answer their demand for a Gold Standard," he ended, "by saying to them: You shall not press down upon the brow of labor this crown of thorns. You shall not crucify mankind upon a cross of gold."

The crowd went wild. Their yelling and cheering lasted for an hour. The delegates from Alabama led a "grand march of glory" around the hall. Others reached for Bryan, proud even to touch his coat. They lifted him and marched him in triumph. After they put him back in his seat, admirers sat in his lap, "hugged him until his collar wilted, shook his hand, shouted into his ears, danced all over his feet, and hemmed him in until he could scarcely get his breath." This one speech had transformed a Nebraska small-town lawyer into a front runner for President!

On the next day, the Democratic Convention voted him to lead their ticket.

Bryan was a rousing candidate. From millions of admirers he received all kinds of gifts—ostrich eggs, a stuffed alligator, four live eagles, a cane supposed to have belonged to Andrew Jackson, and lots of rabbits' feet for good luck. "If all the people who have given me rabbits' feet in this campaign will vote for me," Bryan declared, "there is no possible doubt of my election."

The campaign offered one of the most spectacular contrasts in American history. "The Boy Orator of the Platte" went careering about the country by

Meanwhile Republican candidate McKinley sat calmly on his own front porch.

train, making speeches far into the night at every little town, and often in between. On some days he made thirty-six speeches. Meanwhile, his conservative Republican opponent, William B. McKinley, remained calmly seated on his front porch in Canton, Ohio. McKinley made almost no speeches. When he did, he was careful to say nothing in particular—except that he was in favor of "sound money" (the Gold Standard) and "restoring confidence."

Mark Hanna, a clever Cleveland businessman and political boss who had secured the Republican nomination for McKinley, managed McKinley's campaign. Hanna counted on letting Bryan talk himself to defeat. And he used every trick to convince voters that Bryan was a dangerous radical. For example, he persuaded some factory owners, as a stunt, to pay their workers in Mexican dollars (worth only 50 United States cents). This was supposed to show the workers what their wages would really be worth if Bryan won.

Hanna's tactics succeeded. The election went to McKinley by a narrow margin. But Bryan had attracted so many votes that the Democratic leaders could not ignore him. Twice again—in 1900 and 1908—he was named the Democratic candidate for President. Bryan never won.

The Age of Reform had arrived. Free Silver, the simple-minded cure-all, was never adopted. But other Populist reforms—the regulation of railroad rates, control of monopolies, limits on the hours of labor, and a federal income tax —all these finally became law. The Populists had done more than anybody else to advertise the farmers' troubles. And the big, old parties—the Democrats, and then the Republicans—got the message. They adopted the main Populist reforms as their own. The Populists, who had lost many noisy battles, finally won a silent victory.

CHAPTER 20

From Umpire to Guardian

Everything seemed to be growing. While at the outbreak of the Civil War, the country had numbered thirty million people, by 1900 there were over seventy-five million. From thirty-four States, the number had grown to forty-five. Before the war the nation's population was mostly between the Mississippi River and the Atlantic Ocean, plus a few sparsely settled States on the Pacific Coast. By 1900 four transcontinental railroads poured people into the great heart of the continent, filling lands between the Mississippi River and the Sierra Nevada Mountains.

There were more cities, more big cities, and the big cities were bigger than ever. In 1860 there were only nine places that contained 100,000 people or more. But by 1900 there were nearly forty. And there were three giant metropolises each with over a million people.

Businesses were growing bigger. Now you bought your clothes and furniture not from a friendly storekeeper, but from a huge mail-order house or a vast department store. In the old days, you dealt with men you knew personally. Now more and more of everybody's needs were supplied by big companies.

Your goods were manufactured in large factories thousands of miles away. Whom would you complain to? Whom could you count on? Many families who had braved the wilderness and had known loneliness, who had faced the horrors of Civil War, were now frightened by the new menace of Bigness.

What had happened to the old neighborly spirit?

The dangers of Bigness were not only imaginary. As the companies that made the things you needed became larger and larger, the number of different companies supplying your needs became

THE ROAD TO DIVIDENDS.

Newspapermen and cartoonists joined in the popular campaign against Big Business. "Muck-rakers" awakened the nation's conscience by accusations, real and imaginary, against all men of wealth.

fewer and fewer. For example, by 1880 the Standard Oil Company controlled over 90 percent of the lamp-oil refining in the United States. In those days before electric light, if you wanted oil to light your house at night you had to pay whatever price that company asked.

Bigness meant monopoly. And monopoly meant that a few men had the power to dictate to everybody.

Everywhere, it seemed, some company was squeezing out its competitors. In the 1890's, if you wanted sugar for your table, you had to buy it from the company that controlled 98 percent of the sugar refining in the whole country. For tobacco, you were in the clutches of the American Tobacco Company. Almost every machine—along with the many new ships and bridges and sky-scrapers—now had to use steel. In 1901

the United States Steel Company became the country's first billion-dollar corporation.

The Go-Getters (with the help of their lawyers) invented new ways to combine small businesses into big. And they found ways to keep their control secret. One new kind of company, whose only business was to own other companies, was called a "trust." The men who owned a trust really (but sometimes secretly) controlled smaller companies that still carried on under their own name.

In these ways ambitious Go-Getters built their businesses into empires. Soon there were Banking Empires and Mining Empires, Steel Empires and Railroad Empires. The men who built them were full of imagination and energy, but some of them were as arrogant and as ruthless as the despots of the Middle Ages. Some believed that the only law they had to obey was the law they made for themselves. Once when J. P. Morgan, the giant of American banking, heard that his company was being prosecuted for violating the laws, he went to see the President. "If we have done anything wrong," he explained, "send your man [the Attorney General of the United States] to my man [Morgan's lawyer] and they can fix it up."

Congress passed a law in 1890 making it a crime for businessmen to combine in order to prevent competition. This Sherman Antitrust Act was supposed to punish "restraint of trade or commerce." But like other laws, the law against trusts would work only if the government enforced it.

Presidents did not want to offend the powerful businessmen who had helped them get elected and who might help again at the next election. They pretended that the law did not exist. In the rare case when a President dared to use the law, the Supreme Court saved the trusts by thinking up technicalities. For example, in 1895 the Attorney General prosecuted the one company that controlled 98 percent of the sugar refining in the whole country. But the Supreme Court said that the company really was *not* guilty of preventing competition under the Sherman Antitrust Act—because it was in "manufacturing" and not in "commerce."

The President who actually started using the power of the national government to protect ordinary Americans was Theodore Roosevelt. He had been elected Vice-President on the Republican ticket with William B. McKinley in 1900. When President McKinley joined the festivities at the Pan-American Exposition in Buffalo on September 6, 1901, a man he had never seen before walked up and fired two shots at him. Within a week McKinley was dead.

The man who shot President McKinley called himself an anarchist, which meant that he was against all government. But by making Theodore Roosevelt President, he actually helped to give the national government strong powers.

No one who had visited Theodore Roosevelt as a child would have guessed that he would become a champion of the ordinary American. His father was a well-to-do New York banker who owned country houses and used to take his family to Europe for vacations. Among Teddy Roosevelt's early memories were seeing the Pope during a walk in Rome, and visiting the tomb of Napoleon in Paris.

Young Teddy had no worries about money. But he had other worries. He suffered from asthma, which made it hard for him to exercise, and his eyesight was poor. He became seriously interested in nature and began collecting specimens of plants and animals. When he was twelve, his mother told a maid to throw away some dead mice that the boy had stored in a dresser drawer. "The Loss to Science," Teddy lamented. "The Loss to Science!"

His father built a gymnasium at home. There Teddy worked with a punching bag and did pull-ups on the horizontal bars. He also took boxing lessons. By the time he was seventeen he was expert in track events including running, pole vaulting, and high jumping. On his grandfather's country estate at Oyster

Bay on Long Island he became an enthusiastic horseman and a crack shot. All his life Teddy Roosevelt felt that he had to make up for the childhood weakness of his body.

Roosevelt never lost his boyish excitement. He continued his boxing. After he was hit in the eye while boxing with a young army officer, his left eye became completely blind. He managed to keep this secret, and he devised ways to prevent people knowing that he could see in only one eye. He even became world-famous as an explorer and big-game hunter in Africa and South America.

From the White House he preached "The Strenuous Life." Some genteel European diplomats dreaded being assigned to Washington when "TR" was in the White House. They could not do their diplomatic duty by sipping tea and making polite conversation. TR expected them—along with panting Cabinet members and generals—to join his exhausting tramps through the countryside. "You must always remember," a British ambassador once explained, "that the President is about six years old."

TR liked a good fight—not only in the boxing arena, but also in politics. He had been shocked that earlier Presidents had not enforced the laws against monopolies, and he was disgusted by the Supreme Court's technicalities. The growing power of corporations worried him. "Of all forms of tyranny," he complained, "the least attractive and the most vulgar is the tyranny of mere wealth, the tyranny of a plutocracy."

No sooner had TR moved into the White House than he had his chance. The owners of the anthracite coal mines had become reckless about the safety

Teddy Roosevelt as a boxer at Harvard.

of their men. Workers were dying needlessly each year. In 1901 alone, 441 men were killed in mining accidents in the anthracite coal fields of Illinois, Ohio, Pennsylvania, and West Virginia.

The men had received no raise in wages in twenty years. They were paid by the weight of the coal they dug, but the companies were not weighing honestly. Sometimes they made a man dig four thousand pounds before giving him credit for a ton. Miners were forced to spend their wages in "company stores" which charged high prices.

By 1902 the miners could endure no more. The union leaders decided to take action. John Mitchell, then the energetic young president of the United Mine Workers of America, was the son of a miner who had lost his life in the mines. Mitchell himself had begun mining at the age of twelve. His union—

Membership certificate of the United Mine Workers. Labor unions in their beginnings were often organized like social clubs or lodges, and followed elaborate rituals.

150,000 strong—included thousands of Newcomers who spoke over a dozen different languages.

The coal miners went on strike in May 1902. By October, with winter coming, people feared that the railroads would have to stop running and that the nation would freeze.

President Roosevelt came to the miners' rescue. Regardless of who owned the mines, Roosevelt insisted, nobody owned the miners. He shamed the mine owners into granting most of the workers' demands. When the strike ended TR had shown how, in the new age of big business, it was possible for the federal government to help. He had proven himself a champion of the ordinary American.

This was only a beginning. President Roosevelt enforced the law against trusts—even when it offended the richest men in the country. He added to the Cabinet a Secretary of Commerce and Labor, one of whose jobs was to keep an eye out for monopolies. He sponsored a law making it a crime for the railroads to show favoritism (for example, by giving secret refunds or "rebates") to anybody.

It was just as important, Roosevelt saw, to protect future Americans against the greed of living Americans as it was to protect mine workers against greedy mine owners. This was what he meant by "Conservation." As a young man out West he had enjoyed the open spaces. From his Dakota ranch he himself had ridden the range and explored the wilderness. He loved everything about the West—the cowboys, the life of the trail, fishing and hunting. And he was shocked to see lumber companies wast-

ing forests which had taken centuries to grow. He knew that the wilderness could never be put back.

He saw some parts of the country troubled by floods while others lacked water. Saving rivers and streams was just as important as protecting the land or the forests. To the White House he called scientists, Governors, Supreme Court Justices, and others, to plan an inventory of the natural wealth. Soon "Conservation" was a popular word.

During most of American history, the money to run the federal government had been raised by selling lands from the Public Domain in the West, by customs duties on imports, and by "excise" taxes on certain kinds of goods (for example, liquor and tobacco). These taxes were not democratic enough for Roosevelt. Shocked by the "swollen and monstrous fortunes," he wanted the rich to pay a bigger share.

But the Constitution said that the only "direct" taxes Congress could pass were those apportioned according to the *population* of the States. Income was a very different thing from population. During the Civil War the government somehow had got around these technicalities and had actually passed a tax on income. But after the war the income tax was dropped.

Later, when Populists and others demanded an income tax, the Supreme Court stood in the way. The Supreme Court said that an income tax was exactly the kind of tax that the Constitution had prohibited. President Roosevelt then demanded an amendment to the Constitution. Within a few years, the required number of States had passed this income-tax amendment.

Now Congress had the power to tax the rich Americans more heavily than the poor.

Now taxes themselves would protect most Americans by making it harder for any Americans to become monstrously rich. The income tax was a "progressive" tax. The higher you progressed up the ladder of wealth the larger the *proportion* of your income you had to pay. This was a sign that Americans were beginning to think in a new way.

After Theodore Roosevelt, fewer Americans believed it was good enough for the government to be only an umpire. Even in a prosperous democracy, the powers of different citizens and corporations were not equal. In the twentieth century more and more Americans expected their government to be a guardian. They expected it actually to help protect the weak from the strong.

CHAPTER 21

Who Killed Prosperity?

During the twenty years after President Theodore Roosevelt left the White House in 1909, the United States seemed a land of miracles. Never before in history were factories making so many new things. Never before had the daily life of a nation been so quickly transformed.

At the opening of the twentieth century the automobile was still such an oddity that in Vermont the law required the driver to send someone an eighth of a mile ahead with a red flag. But before Herbert Hoover took his oath as President in 1929 the American automobiles made each year came to five million.

Back in 1900 the closest thing to a movie was the crude "nickelodeon." In return for your nickel you looked into a box to see pictures move for a few minutes. But in 1929 one hundred million tickets were being sold to the movies every week, and the movies could actually talk!

Until World War I most Americans had not even heard of the radio. But by 1929 the annual turnout of radio sets numbered over four million. Television was still in the future—but it seemed amazing enough that voices could be sent without wires.

Americans were making the highest wages in history—and working shorter hours.

The American diet was more varied. Most homes had refrigerators, and even city people could have their fill of milk and of fresh fruit and vegetables at all seasons. With advancing medical knowledge, now at last the diseases which most threatened children—typhoid, diphtheria, and measles—were coming under control. Americans were healthier and were living longer than ever before.

Education in the United States was better and reached a larger proportion of the people than in any other country. By 1928 the money that Americans

Unemployed New Yorkers in 1932 (at the Hudson River and 75th Street), using old boxes and discarded mattresses for shelter. They entertained themselves with a wind-up phonograph.

spent each year for education was more than that spent by all the rest of the world put together. In most European countries only a grade-school education was free. But in the United States a free high-school education was normal, and millions could hope to go to college.

Progress seemed endless. Then suddenly, in late October 1929, came terrifying signs that the success story might have an unhappy ending.

The first hint was the Great Stock Market Crash. The New York Stock Market was where people bought and sold stocks—"shares" in the largest American corporations. The owner of a share in a company really owned part of the company. If the company grew and made a large profit, then the owner of the share would be paid a dividend as his part of the profit. Then, too, the value of that share went up. Naturally, everybody wanted to own shares in the most profitable companies.

But by 1929 many people who bought shares hoped to make their profits, not from the earnings of the company, but from the higher price that other Stock Market gamblers would pay them for their shares. More and more people began risking their money in the Stock Market. They expected to get rich when the price of their shares would suddenly go up. And with the money they made they would buy other shares, which they hoped would also go up.

Stock Market gambling became a national mania, a contagious disease. Americans who never would have thought of borrowing money to bet on the horse races now were actually borrowing to bet on stocks. The more the stock mania grew, the less connection there was between the real value of a company and the price people were paying for that company's shares on the Stock Market. People came to expect every stock to go *up*.

The "impossible" began to happen on October 24, 1929. All prices seemed to be falling. On that day thirteen million shares were sold. Then, it seemed, *everybody* wanted to sell his stocks—and as fast as possible, before they went further down.

In the months that followed the prices of stocks sank faster than ever. A share in United States Steel which had sold for $262 soon brought only $22, while a share of Montgomery Ward sank from $138 to $4, and a share of General Motors went from $73 to $8.

In the panic, people forgot an important fact. Even though the market price of a share of General Motors went down to nearly zero (simply because Stock Market gamblers no longer bet on it) the automobile factories and the men with know-how were all still there, just as good as ever. The wealth of the land and the energy of the people were still there.

But were they? People who never really understood why American progress had seemed so endless, now, of course, had no better understanding of why prosperity had vanished. In unreasoning fear, Americans who heard of this "impossible" drop in the price of stocks began to wonder. Perhaps this was only the first signal of the collapse of all America. If stocks could so quickly lose their value (they sank by forty billion dollars before the end of 1929), maybe nothing else was worth as much as people thought.

They lost faith in their banks. Of course, one way banks make money is to lend out at interest much of the money that people deposit with them. Usually only a few people at any one time want to draw out their money, and banks keep enough on hand to take care of them.

But during the Crash nearly every-body seemed to want to draw his money out at the same time. By the hundreds, then, banks, which could not suddenly produce all that cash, failed. Many people lost their life savings. Over six hundred and fifty banks failed in 1929, thirteen hundred failed in 1930, twenty-three hundred failed in 1931. Eventually the federal government itself would provide a new kind of insurance guaranteeing the depositors their money in an emergency. But there was nothing like that at the time of the Great Crash.

After the Great Stock Market Crash came the Great Depression. Manufacturers, finding fewer customers for anything they could make, began slowing down their factories, making fewer automobiles, fewer refrigerators, and fewer radios. They laid off their workers. And workers out of a job could not afford to buy things. Then still more factories closed down. Storekeepers went bankrupt. Soon, it seemed, collapse of the prices of stocks on the Stock Market had signaled the collapse of American business and American industry.

By the end of 1932 about thirteen million able-bodied Americans—about one in every four—were out of work. They could not afford to pay their own rent and had to squeeze in with friends or relatives. Young people with no money, no job, and no prospects did not dare marry. Within three years, the number of marriages was down by one-quarter. College enrollments sank.

Millions did not have enough to eat. Children cried for the food their parents could not give them. Hungry, sad Americans were actually wandering down alleys, routing through garbage pails for scraps to keep their families alive.

Unemployed war veterans, who had joined the "Bonus March," waiting outside the Capitol as the Senate in a special night session in July 1932 debated the bonus. The Senate voted it down.

Desperate unemployed went on hunger marches. In Henryetta, Oklahoma, three hundred men broke into food stores. In Iowa and Nebraska, farmers, who could no longer pay the money due on their mortgages, used pitchforks to drive off the sheriffs who came to seize their land. In the spring of 1932 thousands of unemployed veterans formed a "Bonus Army." Demanding that the government pay them a bonus for their service fourteen years earlier in World War I, they marched on Washington. President Herbert Hoover called out the army to drive them from government buildings and parklands that they had occupied.

Where would it end?

But before Americans could cure what ailed the country, they had to know what really was the disease. Who —or what—had killed prosperity? In the panic many Americans lost their heads. Everybody wanted to have somebody to blame it on. Crackpot leaders quickly appeared with fantastic explanations and imaginary cure-alls. Abolish banks! Print more money!

The unlucky man in the White House, the Republican Herbert Hoover, had been elected President in November 1928 by the second largest popular majority until then in all American history. But he had the misfortune to be inaug-

The young Herbert Hoover as a mining engineer.

urated in March 1929, just in time to get the blame for the Great Stock Market Crash.

Never was there a more honest or a more hard-working President. Hoover, a poor boy raised in a small Iowa town, went to Stanford University where he studied engineering. Then he made a fortune working as a mining engineer—in Australia, Africa, China, Latin America, and Russia. He became world-famous during World War I, when he headed the Relief Commission that fed starving Europeans. He was also in charge of conserving food in the United States so Americans could share it with their European allies. He had proven himself a great humanitarian and a remarkable organizer.

But Hoover was no politician. He did not like to try to persuade people. He did not enjoy the arts of compromise. As an engineer, he felt he saw problems clearly. After he had carefully prepared his solution he expected people to follow his instructions without arguing. Wearing a high stiff collar, he was a stiff man who inspired respect but not love. He had none of William Jennings Bryan's eloquence, nor any of Theodore Roosevelt's pep. In ordinary times he might have been a good President to keep America on the familiar road to success.

These were not ordinary times.

President Hoover was the handiest person to blame, even though the Depression had actually begun to happen almost before he had moved into the White House. The shacks made of cardboard and flattened tin cans, where some unemployed lived, were soon called "Hoovervilles." One folk song of the unemployed declared, "Hoover made a souphound out of me." A man's empty pocket, turned inside out, was called a "Hoover flag."

But when the collapse came so unexpectedly, President Hoover did not sit still. He used all the familiar ways to relieve suffering. He called upon cities, States, and all private charities to help feed the hungry. He brought business leaders and labor leaders to the White House, where they promised to try to keep up wages and keep the factories going. At the same time he started an ambitious new plan to use government money to hold up the price of tobacco, cotton, corn, and wheat in order to help the suffering farmers. He actually cut his own Presidential salary by one-fifth.

What Hoover did helped some, but it was not enough. The disaster was more unfamiliar than President Hoover realized. And it required remedies even more unfamiliar than he could imagine.

CHAPTER 22
Nothing to Fear but Fear Itself

When the election of 1932 came around and Herbert Hoover ran for President again, almost anybody could have beaten him. Who wanted to vote *for* the Depression? But the Democrats happened to pick one of the most winning men in American history. He was a distant cousin of Theodore Roosevelt, and his name was Franklin Delano Roosevelt.

Although only a few people in the country realized it at the time, Franklin Delano Roosevelt was a man of heroic character. From his youth he had enjoyed athletics. He had always loved politics and had been the Democratic candidate for Vice-President in 1920. One August day in 1921 he was stricken with polio and left paralyzed. This single, sudden thunderclap of bad luck reduced him from a bouncy, athletic, runabout politician to a bedridden invalid. A man of weaker character might have given up.

Instead, after his misfortune, he became more determined than ever to be an active politician. An old friend who came on a sympathy visit to the hospital was surprised when FDR unexpectedly gave him a strong, good-natured wallop. "You thought you were coming to see an invalid," FDR laughed from his bed. "But I can knock you out in any bout."

People who went to cheer him up found that FDR gave them a lift instead.

Franklin Delano Roosevelt and his wife Eleanor (right), eight years before his paralysis. Eleanor, who was a niece of the Republican President Theodore Roosevelt, later became world-famous for her humanitarian activities.

Sometimes he joked about his affliction. FDR wrote a friend that he had "renewed his youth" by "what was fortunately a rather mild case of *infantile paralysis.*"

But his case really was far from mild. He was never able to walk again. Only after long and painful exercises and by wearing heavy braces did he learn to use his hips so he could get around on crutches. He told his friends that he had an advantage, because while they were running around he could sit still and think. He used his long period of recovery in bed to write hundreds of letters to politicians all over the country—not about his personal problems, but about politics and how to build a stronger Democratic party. All over the country Democratic politicians valued his advice.

FDR made a fantastic comeback. When the Democratic Convention in Chicago in 1932 nominated Franklin Delano Roosevelt to be their candidate for President, it was really not because of his heroic personal qualities. For he had already proven himself a spectacularly successful politician in New York. In 1928, only a few years after he had been stricken with infantile paralysis, he managed to be elected Governor of his State. After a successful term as Governor he ran again in 1930, and he won by the biggest majority ever.

With his broad, contagious smile, he was a wonderful persuader. He loved people, and could make them love him. People cheered up when they saw his jaunty long cigarette holder and felt his warm firm handshake. He had all the human qualities that Herbert Hoover lacked. And these were what the nation wanted in that dangerous year of 1932.

FDR was no radical. In fact, during his campaign he was careful not to offend anybody. When he made speeches, he sounded more like William McKinley than like William Jennings Bryan. Some people, who thought the nation needed strong medicine, criticized FDR.

They said he was too eager to please everybody. They were afraid that he was simply "a pleasant man who would very much like to be President."

Those critics were wrong. For FDR had courage in politics just as much as in his private life. And as soon as he took office on March 4, 1933, he showed it.

"A New Deal for the American people!" This was what FDR had announced in Chicago when he accepted the nomination. He promised to *experiment*. The nation and all its wealth were still there, he reminded people in his inaugural address. "We are stricken by no plague of locusts. Compared with the perils which our forefathers conquered because they believed and were not afraid, we have still much to be thankful for. Nature still offers her bounty and human efforts have multiplied it. Plenty is at our doorstep." He had faith that there really were lots of new ways that could be tried.

"The only thing we have to fear," he said, "is fear itself." His courage and his optimism, like his smile, were contagious. Americans were encouraged most of all because they believed that their new President really would experiment. He would try one thing, and then another—until ways would be found to put the country back on the track, and to put people back to work.

FDR began trying things from his first day in the White House. In order to preserve people's life savings, he ordered all banks closed for four days while ways were found to restore confidence in them. He called Congress into special session to pass laws for the emergency.

Congress, on his urging, arranged special loans to help people pay their mortgages so they could keep their farms and homes till the crisis was over. A fund of over two billion dollars helped citizens start new construction—of homes, offices, shops, and factories—and thus create new jobs. Over three billion dollars was appropriated for new government buildings, and a half-billion dollars for outright relief. New laws guaranteed workers their right to organize into unions. New laws prohibited child labor, set minimum wages and maximum hours. A new program was passed for the farmer, to keep up the price of his crops.

Some experiments were not so successful. For example, one of FDR's pet projects was a law—the National Recovery Act or NRA—enforcing new "codes" to be made by representatives of business and labor in each industry. These codes aimed to keep up prices and wages. They said what should be manufactured, how many of everything, and at what price. They made many of the kinds of arrangements which big businesses had been punished for making when they fixed prices by monopoly. But the new law said that the antitrust rules did not apply. Small businessmen objected. They said the big businessmen were simply using the law to protect their own monopoly profits.

The Supreme Court declared the NRA codes unconstitutional. Congress, the Court said, was trying to give away the power to make laws. But the Constitution had assigned the lawmaking power only to Congress.

Still, on the whole, FDR seemed to be making headway. By the end of his first term in office, there were fewer people without jobs. The country was looking up. When FDR ran again in 1936, he was reelected by an even bigger majority.

All over the rest of the world, desperate people were handing over their liberty to dictators who promised them food and jobs in return. In Italy, only ten years before FDR was inaugurated, Benito Mussolini and his gang of fascists marched on Rome. They seized the government, abolished democracy, destroyed the liberties of the Italian people —all on the promise that they would provide more and better jobs.

In Germany, too, in the very month when FDR took his oath of office, Adolf

---

President Franklin D. Roosevelt (seen here by cartoonist Gluyas Williams) reached the American people through the new and democratic devices of the press conference and the radio fireside chat.

Copr. © 1942, The *New Yorker* Magazine, Inc.

Adolf Hitler addressing the 160,000 Storm Troopers who, by spreading terror, helped "persuade" the German people to become Nazis.

Hitler, with his gang of Nazis, was made dictator. Screaming slogans of race hate and fear, the Nazis destroyed the universities. They used secret police and concentration camps. They murdered, robbed, and tortured. They abolished liberty and decency. And the civilized German people somehow tolerated it all because many of them needed jobs, their children were hungry, and they believed Hitler's promise of prosperity.

FDR had faith that it did not need to happen here. He tried all sorts of experiments—democratic experiments—to restore hope and prosperity, while strengthening American liberties. He consulted with business leaders, labor organizers, university professors, social workers, judges, scientists, lawyers, and doctors. Anybody who had an idea

knew that somebody in the New Deal would listen. Of course some people accused FDR of wanting to be a dictator. But he never lost his faith in democracy and in the ability of Americans to handle the unexpected.

"Happy Days Are Here Again!" had been FDR's campaign song. Many Americans wanted to believe that FDR was a kind of magician who could suddenly bring back prosperity. Of course, FDR did not believe government had a magic formula.

He did believe, though, that there were many helpful things the government could always do, and had to do. And he believed that the government did not need to wait till the next emergency. It ought to promise people help in advance. Then, if Americans felt sure they would get the emergency help they needed, they would be more cheerful and less worried about their future. This itself might help bring back prosperity and keep prosperity alive.

FDR therefore proposed a scheme of insurance. While a person had a job, he paid a small amount every month out of his wages, and his employer paid the same amount. This went into the federal treasury. Then when the worker was out of a job or when he became too old to work, he received back a payment every month. He could be sure that he would never starve.

The people who received their insurance payments did not feel they were charity cases. Since they had been putting in their own money when they were prosperous, they felt they were only getting what they were entitled to when times were bad. This system was called Social Security. It aimed to make everybody in the whole society feel more secure.

Following the lead of the Republican Roosevelt, FDR set up a grand new plan for conservation, to prevent the soil from being used up or washed away, and so to help farmers make a better living. And he found other ways to preserve resources for the future.

FDR enlarged Teddy Roosevelt's idea to include "People Conservation." The government spent millions of dollars encouraging artists by employing them to decorate post offices and other government buildings. Government programs also provided useful work for young people who could not afford to go to college.

One of the most ingenious plans was to "conserve" the people of a whole re-

gion. In the mountains of western Kentucky, Tennessee, and Alabama, around the valley of the Tennessee River, there lived about 3,500,000 people. Most of them lived poorly. Their land was exhausted. Electricity was too expensive, yet without electricity they could not modernize their farms or bring in the factories to provide jobs.

FDR's idea was to build a great dam on the Tennessee River. This would protect against floods. At the same time the water flowing through the dam would turn generators to make cheap electricity. And two old munitions plants left over from World War I could be made into factories for fertilizer to improve the farms. These were FDR's plans for the Tennessee Valley Authority (TVA).

The lives of thousands of people in the Tennessee Valley were brightened. Public Health doctors used this chance to rid the countryside of malaria. Librarians sent "bookmobiles" into the farms. Better houses and better schools were built. Again, some people objected that FDR was trying to be a dictator. They accused the government of competing unfairly with private electric and fertilizer companies.

Yet the experiment was a success. Of course, it did not solve all the problems of the poor farmers in the Tennessee Valley. But it showed how much *could* be done if a democratic government was willing to help.

Hope came back to America. FDR had found ways to cure the symptoms of the Great Depression. But had he cured the disease? Many Americans were not sure. Prosperity did not fully return until World War II put the fac-

These energetic young men were among the three million members of the Civilian Conservation Corps, one of many New Deal programs to put people to work. The CCC planted more than seventeen million acres of forests, stocked over a billion fish in hatcheries, built trails in the National Parks, fought forest fires, and worked on countless other useful outdoor projects.

tories back to working full steam. Some people said the real end of the Depression did not come till then. But Americans had learned a lot about how to deal with the dangers of unemployment and how to keep the factories working in peacetime.

Americans too had lost many of their old fears of economic Ups and Downs. That itself was a gain. The Great Depression proved that, the more people were frightened, the worse things became.

Americans had discovered a new strength. Through the crisis the federal Constitution proved adaptable, and came out stronger than ever. Americans had proved that they could survive their worst peacetime disaster—without spreading hate, without taking away liberties, without installing a dictator.

This was a great and reassuring discovery. It was as important as anything Americans had ever learned about their land or about themselves.

CHAPTER 23

Who Was Left Out?

When prosperity returned, Americans boasted that this was a land where *every*body had a fair chance. But that still was not quite correct. When you surveyed the whole country and all the people in it you had to wonder. Many Americans were not getting their full fair chance. Some were almost entirely left out.

The United States was, of course, a nation of minorities. Had there ever before been a nation built of so many different groups?

There were many kinds of minorities. Of the religious minorities, for example, in some parts of the country Catholics were commonly discriminated against. It was taken for granted that no Catholic could ever be elected President—until the 1960 election of John F. Kennedy. Although the Jews had a long tradition of learning, even before they arrived in this country, strict quotas in colleges and medical schools kept out all but a few, even if they were the best qualified. The Mormons, who were a distinctive American religion, actually had laws passed against them.

We have seen how the Oldcomers— in New England, for example—had looked down their noses at Newcomers. And it was especially easy to be snobbish when the Newcomers looked different. Mexican immigrants, who came across the border for seasonal farm work, were not allowed to buy land, or to get an education, or to find a better job. The Chinese and Japanese, who had been imported to help build the Western railroads, afterwards in some places were not permitted to live equally among other Americans, or to own land, or to become voting citizens.

The American Indians, of course, were the oldest of the Oldcomers. But they were deprived of their best land and forced onto barren "reservations" of desert wastes and rocky mountain slopes. They were not allowed to become full-fledged Americans. And there were many others.

The largest single group of left-out Americans were the Negroes. This was especially disappointing because the whole nation had fought its most terrible war and had even split families apart so that all Americans would be treated like men. While the Civil War was, of course, a war for Union, it was also emphatically a war to help the Negro. For that cause a quarter-million Union soldiers had given their lives.

Never before in history had so many people fought for the freedom of others. In relation to the Negro, the United States had shown its best and its worst. Some Americans had kept him a slave. But other Americans fought and died to make him free.

After the Civil War, as we have seen,

Some American Indians have carried on their traditional crafts. But these Americans, the oldest of the Oldcomers, were sometimes treated as if they were not Americans at all. An Act of Congress in 1924 finally admitted all Indians born in the United States to full citizenship.

the United States had as hard a job as faced any nation. The millions of Americans who had been treated as *things* were suddenly to be given their rights as *people*. They had owned no property and had not even been allowed to go to school. Now they were suddenly to become citizens with the duty to govern themselves and to help govern others. All this had to be done in the shadow of the hateful "peculiar institution," slavery, which had bred fears and hates on all sides. And all this had to be done in the aftermath of a bloody war which had bred still more fears and hates.

The mark of slavery could not be erased by magic. The South—and Southerners—might take generations to recover. The full tragedy of slavery was only now appearing.

Yet by the early twentieth century there had been progress. When the Freedmen's Bureau ended in 1872, money to educate former slaves and their children then came from churches and missionary associations.

Wealthy men and women, mostly from the North, gave millions of dollars to help educate the Negro. By 1900 there were already about thirty thousand Negro teachers. John D. Rockefeller, for example, had contributed over $50 million of the money he had made from oil, most of it to train more teachers for

Negro schools. Every year more Negroes owned their own farms. And in the long run, better education, better wages, and more property would help the Negro to equality.

But a small number of Americans still actually *wanted* a Two-Nation America. These people were afraid that if Negroes had their share of education and owned their share of property, they really would become equal. And they were especially afraid to let the Negroes vote. Most of these fearful Americans were in the South. Less money was spent there than in other parts of the country for all kinds of education. In the South Negroes had to attend separate, and inferior, schools. There, especially, Negroes found it hard to borrow money in order to buy houses or farms.

The whole South suffered. By 1938 President Franklin Delano Roosevelt called the South "the nation's No. 1 economic problem." Almost any way you measured—by the health of the people, the quality of schools or houses, the number of automobiles, the amount of farm machinery, or the income of the families—the South was the worst-off section of the whole United States. And in the South, the Negroes were generally even worse off than others.

In 1930, 80 percent of American Negroes were still living within the boundaries of the old Confederacy. Yet new forces were working on all America. One of the most important of these was the Negro himself. Emancipation gave him a new power to be heard.

Even before the Civil War, a few eloquent Negroes like Frederick Douglass had managed to speak up loud and clear against slavery. Douglass, the slave son of an unknown white father, had been working on the Baltimore wharves. One day in 1838, at the age of twenty-one, he stowed away on a ship sailing for New York. After that he became one of the best propagandists against slavery. His books described the sufferings of slaves, and urged everybody to help them escape. Beginning in 1847, Douglass' newspaper, *The North Star,* worked for many reforms, including women's right to vote.

As more Negroes were educated and acquired property, more were able to help themselves. But how could they do it best? Negro leaders could not agree.

One way was proposed by Booker T. Washington. Born a slave, Washington was a self-made man. He worked as a janitor and at all sorts of jobs to support

Frederick Douglass helped recruit Negroes for the Union army. After the Civil War he became U.S. Minister to Haiti.

himself in school. Before his death he was famous throughout the world. For his own story of his life, *Up From Slavery* (1901), was read by millions.

"No man," he said, "... black or white, from North or South, shall drag me down so low as to make me hate him."

He preached a gospel of love and common sense. He told the Negro to make the most of himself and of his opportunities. He told white Southerners to show new respect for the Negro, to realize that only by bettering the Negro's life could they make a better South for everybody. Self-respect, self-education, and self-help, he said, would bring Negroes the opportunities they deserved. Some people thought he sounded old-fashioned. This might have been Benjamin Franklin speaking!

But Booker T. Washington did not merely talk. In 1881 he founded Tuskegee Institute in Alabama, which became one of the most powerful forces in American education. There he trained thousands of Negroes to be better farmers and mechanics, to make a good living, and to help build their communities.

He believed in a step-by-step way "up from slavery." First, he said, Negroes should get education and get property. But he believed in a special kind of education. Most important for Negroes right away was not a "liberal" education of the kind American college students were getting all over the country. He did not want Negroes to spend their efforts learning history and literature and foreign languages and science and mathematics. Instead, he said, they should train quickly for jobs—and mostly for jobs they could do with their hands. The vote, he said, could wait.

The Negro first should become a free man with a job before he became a free man with a vote.

Many who admired Booker T. Washington still did not agree with his program for the Negro. One-step-at-a-time was not good enough. Americans were quick with their know-how, quick in covering the continent and building cities. Why should they be slow to give *all* Americans *all* their rights?

Twenty-five years after Booker T. Washington started his Tuskegee Institute in Alabama, a group met at Niagara Falls. They demanded for Negroes all the rights of Americans. *Now!*

Their Negro leader was W. E. B. Du Bois. His life had been very different from that of Booker T. Washington. Born in Massachusetts after the Civil War, he studied at the University of Berlin in Germany and then received a Ph.D. degree from Harvard in 1895. While Booker T. Washington's roots were in the South, Du Bois's roots were in abolitionist Massachusetts, and in the whole world. Du Bois was a poet, and a man of brilliant mind and vast learning. Why should anyone try to tell Du Bois and others like him to be satisfied to work with their hands?

In 1905 the Declaration by Du Bois's Niagara Movement expressed outrage. It demanded for Negroes *all* their human rights, all their rights as Americans, and *at once*. It opposed all laws and all customs that treated Negroes as if they were different from other people. And, of course, it demanded the right to vote.

After the Civil War, white Southerners who believed in a Two-Nation South (run by the whites) had used all sorts of tricks to deprive Negroes of their rights

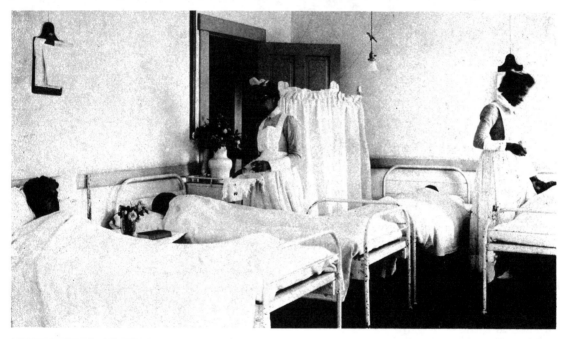

Booker T. Washington's Tuskegee Institute aimed to train its students for skilled and useful jobs. ABOVE: *Young men learn upholstering.* BELOW: *Young women learn nursing.*

as citizens. The Fifteenth Amendment, adopted during Reconstruction, plainly declared that the right of citizens to vote should not be denied "by the United States or by any State on account of race, color, or previous condition of servitude." This set a real puzzle for the Two-Nation Southerners.

They tried using the "grandfather clause." They simply passed a law in the State Legislature giving the right to vote to those persons who *did* have the right to vote on January 1, 1867 (before the Fifteenth Amendment had been passed) and to those persons' descendants. Anybody else who wanted to vote had to pass all sorts of impossible tests. Of course that included Negroes. *They* would not be allowed to vote simply because their *grandfathers* did not have the right to vote! Beginning in 1895, seven Southern States passed "grandfather" laws. Not until 1915 did the United States Supreme Court declare

Booker T. Washington (left) believed that permanent progress must come slowly. W. E. B. Du Bois, himself a scholar, feared that Booker T. Washington's "gradualist" program would keep Negroes in lowly jobs.

that these laws violated the Constitution.

Another trick was the so-called Literacy Test. It was as dishonest as the Literacy Test which Oldcomers had tried to use to keep out immigrants from certain countries. It pretended to limit the vote to people who could read. But prejudiced election judges gave ridiculously complicated tests (which they themselves probably could not have passed) whenever Negroes came to vote. They would ask a Negro to explain the most difficult part of the Constitution. But a white person only had to read out a simple sentence.

Some Southern States also used the Poll Tax. That was a tax that everybody was required to pay before he could vote (or go to the "poll"). Most Negroes in the South were so poor they really could not afford the few dollars for the tax. And even if a Negro paid his tax, the election judge could always find some technical mistake in his tax receipt, and

so keep him from voting.

The craftiness of Two-Nation Southerners seemed endless. They even went so far as to pretend that the great political parties in the South were not political parties at all, but only private clubs. Therefore, they said, nobody except the white "members" had a right to vote in the primary election when their "club" picked its candidates.

Since the Democratic Party was in complete control in most of the South, whoever won in the Democratic primary automatically won the office. By keeping a person from voting in the primary, then, you would actually be taking away his vote. Finally, in three separate decisions—in 1944, 1947, and 1953—the United States Supreme Court declared that these laws violated the Fourteenth Amendment to the Constitution. But it took a special Twenty-fourth Amendment to the Constitution, adopted in 1964, to outlaw the Poll Tax.

CHAPTER 24

"A Triumph for Freedom"

Intelligent citizens all over the country were beginning to be ashamed and disgusted that the nation had been so slow to give all Americans their simple rights. The Niagara Movement, sparked by Du Bois and aided by white Americans who gloried in the anti-slavery tradition, became stronger. To help prevent shameful race riots like the one in Springfield, Illinois (Lincoln's birthplace) in 1908, a new organization, the National Association for the Advancement of Colored People (NAACP), was founded in 1909 on Lincoln's birthday.

Americans of all races and religions, from all parts of the country, joined hands. People like Jane Addams, who already were working for the poor of all races in the northern city slums, gave money to pay for lawyers to help Negroes secure their rights in the South. The president of the NAACP, a famous Boston lawyer, argued the case before the Supreme Court in 1915 when the "grandfather" laws were declared unconstitutional. The NAACP also won other important cases. One of these declared that no trial of a Negro could be a fair trial (as the Constitution required) if Negroes were kept off the jury. During the next years the NAACP was the most important group trying to awaken all Americans to the rights of Negroes.

Things were getting better for the Negro. But the progress was painfully slow—even considering the long distance the Negro needed to rise from slavery.

For millions of Negro Americans—especially in the South and in the big city slums in the North—there still seemed almost no change. Negro workers were the last hired and the first fired. Negro children still had less money spent on their education. Negroes were not allowed to live wherever they could afford, but had to live in special neighborhoods. Even under the New Deal, Negroes were not always given their share. For example, they were not allowed to live in the model towns built with government money in the Tennessee Valley. Most of the Negroes whom Du Bois called the "Talented Tenth" still had to take lowly jobs.

Some, in fact, gave up. Du Bois, for example, joined the Communist Party and then renounced his United States citizenship. In 1961 at the age of 93 he moved to the new African country of Ghana, which before 1957 had been a British colony. Others kept their faith in America and struggled for new ways to keep the nation true.

During two World Wars, Negro Americans fought for their country. In World War I, Negro soldiers numbered over a third of a million. In World War II they numbered a million. In both wars they proved their bravery and their loyalty. The wars gave them other chances, too—to move outside the South, away from their farms and villages, into the larger world.

They discovered that the prejudices which some white Southerners had inherited from the days of slavery were not found everywhere. They mixed with other Americans from all over the country, and they went abroad. They had new experiences and new adventures.

Yet, even in the army and navy and air force, Negro Americans still were not given equal rights. In World War I, Negroes found it difficult to become officers. They were not allowed at all in the Marines, and in the navy they had no hope for promotion. Even in uniform, they were often insulted. It took great faith and patriotism, then, for a Negro American to risk his life for a country that was not yet giving him his full rights as a citizen.

President Woodrow Wilson was leading the country in a war "to make the world safe for democracy." Yet President Wilson himself, born in Virginia before the Civil War, had never outgrown the feelings of the Two-Nation South. Though elected on the slogan of the "New Freedom," after he came to Washington he actually segregated Negroes working in the government. And he took government jobs away from Negroes in the South.

In World War II things were better for the Negro soldier. The Marines no longer kept him out, and before the war was over there were 17,000 Negro "Leathernecks." It became easier for qualified Negroes to become officers. Even the navy, which before had taken in Negroes only for kitchen work and as waiters, began to open up. The air force trained Negro officers and pilots, and more than eighty won the Distinguished Flying Cross.

But the long shadow of the Two-Nation South remained. Negroes, once more fighting for democracy, were usually still segregated.

Finally, though, the stain of slavery was washed away in the armed services. President Harry S Truman in 1946 appointed a national committee to recommend action. By 1949 the army, navy, and air force had all abolished racial quotas. They made it their policy to give all Americans an equal chance. By the time of the Korean War in 1950–1953 *all* Americans were fighting for democracy side by side.

During these later wars, even more than during the Civil War, Americans moved all around the country. Many went to new war jobs. Returning soldiers settled in new places. Before World War I only about 10 percent of Negro Americans lived outside the South. After that war the number rose to 20 percent. And after World War II about one-third of all Negro Americans were living outside the Old Confederacy.

Negro Americans, like other Americans, were becoming more and more citified. Outside the South nearly all of them were living in cities. Even in the South they too were moving off the countryside. Many Americans—including, of course, more Negroes—were churning quickly and easily around the whole country. It was harder than ever for the South to keep its old ways.

In Africa, new republics were declaring their independence from the old colonial powers. First came Ghana in 1957, and by 1965 there were over thirty new African members of the United Nations. When they sent their ambassadors to the United States, the discrimination against Negroes here was more embarrassing than ever.

Then, too, the United States Supreme Court began to wake up. In a series of decisions it began to outlaw those Southern practices and laws which had taken from the Negro his full rights as an American. Back in 1896 the Court actually had declared that laws which required Negroes to stay separate—to use separate washrooms, separate schools, and separate railroad cars—did *not* violate the Fourteenth Amendment. It was all right, the Court said, for any services to be separate so long as they were "equal." But this was a trick argument. Anyone who knew the South could

have known that the white Southerners who ran the government would *say* they were providing "equal" schools. But who had the power to complain if the schools were not really equal? Negroes, who still were not allowed to vote, had no way of forcing government officials to listen. The Supreme Court had okayed the Two-Nation South.

In the South, Negroes continued to have the worst of everything. Their schools and hospitals, and even their washrooms and water fountains, were inferior.

Anyway, the whole idea of "separate but equal"—even if it could have been enforced—was wrong. It was not only wrong, it was nonsense. Because, in a democracy, people who are forced to be separate, forced to use washrooms and water fountains and schools not used by other Americans, are not being allowed

Segregated water fountain.

"Freedom Riders" in a Montgomery, Alabama, bus station (May 1961) integrating a lunch counter with a nonviolent "sit-in."

to be equal. The special separate schools for Negroes could not possibly be equal —simply because they were separate.

Finally in 1954, in one of the most important decisions it had ever made, the Supreme Court ordered that, under the Constitution, public schools could not be separate. Americans had a right to go to school with all other Americans of their age and grade. This was a part of their education. No American should be deprived of that right. The opposite of separation was "integration"—bringing together into one. And the Supreme Court ordered that all public schools in the United States had to be "integrated."

These changes in American life, in American thought and feeling all over the country, made the time ripe for the work of Martin Luther King, Jr. His work began in a small way and in one place. Within only a few years his message had carried to the world.

Born in Atlanta in 1929, son of a minister, he attended Morehouse College and received a doctor's degree from Boston University. He was a natural leader, American to the core. He combined the common sense of a Booker T. Washington with the impatient visions of a Du Bois.

On December 1, 1955, a tired Negro seamstress returning from work boarded a crowded bus in Montgomery, Alabama. She took a seat. But the seat she took was in the part of the bus reserved for white passengers. When she was asked to give up her seat to a white person, she refused. The police arrested her for violating the law.

Martin Luther King, who was then a Baptist minister in Montgomery, decided it was time for action. It was time to stop any Americans from being degraded.

Although King was indignant and saddened, he was not angry. He was a thoughtful man, and a Christian, and he decided to try a new way. He called it the only true Christian way. It was the way of nonviolence.

He did not tell people to burn the buses or to fight the police. No, he said. All people need to be educated in the ways of peace and decency. If you fight your enemies with violence, you are using their weapons and brutalizing yourself. But if you are peaceful and simply do not go along with them, you will eventually prevail. And if you win this way, your victory will not merely be the truce in a running battle. It will actually be peace. Your enemies then

will understand, and they will begin to be decent, too.

So he preached to the Negroes in Montgomery. He told them to stop using the buses until the buses gave them their place as Americans. Of course many Negroes were angry. But Martin Luther King begged and pleaded with them to keep their heads, and to keep love in their hearts, even while they joined the bus boycott.

For 381 days the Negroes of Montgomery refused to ride the buses. It was inconvenient. Some formed car pools. Many were given rides by friendly white neighbors. Many walked miles to work. Others simply did not get to their jobs and had to lose their wages.

And the bus company was about to go bankrupt.

In the end the Negroes and all the decent people of Montgomery won. When the buses ran again, every passenger was treated like all the others. Martin Luther King called this a "Stride Toward Freedom." And he was right.

It was not only a stride toward freedom. It was a step along a new path. Many Americans were encouraged to walk along that path in the years that followed. By 1960 many Negroes in the South were using this new way to fight segregation. They sat down at lunch counters where they had not been allowed to sit. They swam in public swimming pools that had been denied to Negroes. And they worshiped in churches that had kept out Negroes. They did not fight the police or strike out at anyone. Quietly and peacefully, they simply acted like decent Americans who knew their rights.

The movement spread. In 1963—a

full century after the Emancipation Proclamation—there came a climax. In February, the season of Lincoln's birthday, President John F. Kennedy sent a Civil Rights Bill to Congress. The bill would guarantee the vote to all Americans, outlaw segregation in all public places, and protect the right of all Americans to use motels and hotels and barber shops and restaurants. But Congress did not act. The Two-Nation Southerners and a few of their Northern supporters blocked the law. They acted as if the Civil War had never been fought—or as if it had been won by the South.

Americans of all races became impatient. Members of all religious groups—Catholics, Protestants, and Jews—leaders of labor unions and many others decided to show Congress how strongly Americans felt. They planned a "March on Washington." The purpose of their march was peaceful, entirely in line with Martin Luther King's ideas. They did not want to fight the police or take over the government. They simply wanted to use their democratic right to show their representatives in Congress how many Americans were demanding equality for everybody.

On August 28, 1963, nearly a quarter-million Americans gathered at the Lincoln Memorial in Washington, D.C., within sight of the White House and the Capitol where Congress met. The meeting was orderly and eloquent. It was the largest number of Americans until

The March on Washington, August 1963. Americans of all faiths and races and several labor unions joined hands in demanding equal rights for all. In the center of the front row was Dr. Martin Luther King.

President Lyndon B. Johnson speaking with Dr. Martin Luther King during the televised ceremony at the signing of the Civil Rights Act of 1964.

that time ever gathered in one place for any purpose in peacetime.

Some were afraid there might be trouble. But trouble did not come. Americans could ever after be proud that so many of their countrymen cared enough for the rights of all Americans to make that meeting possible, and to keep it peaceful.

Congress still delayed. They did not want to act when it might seem they were acting under threat. Then, on November 22, 1963, the nation was shaken by tragedy. While riding in an open car in Dallas, Texas, President Kennedy was shot. He died within minutes. But the spirit of all who believed in America, and in the promise of equality, lived on.

The new President was Lyndon B. Johnson. His first act was to address

Congress demanding immediate passage of the Civil Rights Bill. He also offered a new Voting Rights Act, with effective new ways of protecting the right of everybody to vote—even in the South.

These acts meant business. The day of legal trickery had passed. "Today is a triumph for freedom," President Johnson declared when these acts became law, "as huge as any victory that's ever been won on any battlefield. . . . Today the Negro story and the American story fuse and blend." He could have called this peaceful victory even bigger than the victories in war.

Still, the forces of hate and fear—of a Two-Nation America—were not yet dead. Martin Luther King himself was shot while he stood on the balcony of a Memphis motel on April 4, 1968. No American who knew history could be surprised that the spirit of hate still walked the land—and it found new preachers of hate in all races.

The twentieth-century battle for rights left new wounds, stirred new fears and hates. The future of the nation would depend on the ability of all Americans to remember the long struggle which *all* Americans shared. And also on their ability to forget harsh words and old insults. The nation needed a renewal of the generous, forgiving spirit of Lincoln.

The next years showed that the spirit of Lincoln was alive and well. There was a long way to go to make up for the years of slavery. Even after the Civil War, Negroes were only half-free, for in many parts of the country and for many kinds of jobs, they had no chance.

Now the nation's conscience was awake. Some of the most important new opportunities were in education. The old segregated classrooms were changed by school busing. Now white and Negro children sat happily together. Colleges that had never seen a Negro in the lecture hall opened their minds and their doors. The best colleges, law schools, and medical schools in the land, instead of finding reasons to keep them out, went in search of qualified Negroes. Special scholarships were offered to Negro students. Negro professors who once could find jobs only in Negro colleges could take their rightful place in any university. These great changes were going on behind the scenes.

Out front, too, there were great changes that no one could miss. Thurgood Marshall, a Negro appointed by President Lyndon Johnson, now sat on the Supreme Court. And when you turned on your TV set, you saw Negroes not only as maids or chauffeurs, but as police captains, businessmen, news reporters, priests, doctors, and lawyers.

The civil rights movement was contagious. If Negroes should have a new chance, why not others? What about women? It had taken a long time for women to get the right to vote, to be admitted to universities with men, and to have their fair chance to study law, medicine, and business administration. Now a woman, Sandra Day O'Connor of Arizona, had been appointed by President Ronald Reagan to sit on the Supreme Court. And by the 1980's there were six women governors of States of the Union. On TV, too, women were seen not only as wives and mothers but as people who could handle any kind of job—from truck driver to airplane pilot. Once the nation's eyes were opened, they would never be closed again.

PART FIVE

❦

TO THIS
WHOLE WORLD
—AND BEYOND

TO THIS WHOLE WORLD—AND BEYOND

Until the Civil War the United States had seemed a world of its own. It had been easy for Americans to imagine that they really did not need the rest of the world. The continent was so large. It offered so many different climates. Almost every needed crop or animal, almost every mineral, was found somewhere within the nation and its territories. When the first settlers had called this a New World they were speaking the sober truth.

Then after the Civil War, more and more Americans discovered that America needed the world. The nation still wanted to import people by the millions. And it needed the outside world for many new reasons.

The prosperity of American farmers and factory workers and businessmen now depended on faraway customers and on the ability of Americans to deliver their goods overseas. American consumers were coming to rely on silk from Italy and China, on rubber from the Congo and Sumatra, on coffee from Brazil, on tin from Malaya, on gold from Rhodesia—and on a thousand other items from across the oceans.

The United States became the world's know-how center—for trying new ways of making and doing.

And people everywhere expected to learn from America. Americans began to feel it their duty to help make the whole earth into a New World.

But could the United States preach democracy and help other nations become democratic without trying to choose other peoples' governments for them?

Could Americans take their place in the world competition for customers and for raw materials without making remote peoples into a new kind of colonies?

Could the most powerful nation on earth resist the temptation to run the affairs of mankind?

Could the nation do its duty in the battles of the Old World and yet stay free of the Old World curse of endless wars?

Could the nation become the most modern, most intricately organized people on earth, and yet preserve self-government and the spirit of adventure?

CHAPTER 25

Ocean Paths to World Power

After the Civil War, Americans realized that the United States had become a two-ocean nation. The Atlantic seaboard looked eastward toward Europe and Africa. The Far Western States looked across the Pacific toward Australia and Asia.

Some Americans were beginning to think differently about their place in the world. An Annapolis graduate, Admiral Alfred T. Mahan, wrote a powerful book called *The Influence of Sea Power Upon History* (1890). What *Uncle Tom's Cabin* was to the Civil War, Mahan's *Sea Power* would be to the Spanish-American War.

Sea Power, Mahan said, was the key to all history. A nation became great and kept its greatness only if it ruled the waves. Americans, he said, had long shown "the instinct for commerce, bold enterprise in the pursuit of gain, and a keen sense for the trails that lead to it." Yet these were not enough. The nation also needed to be rich in all kinds of ships. Then, of course, she would need colonies in faraway places where her ships could refuel and find protection.

A few years after Mahan began preaching Sea Power he found one of his strongest allies in Theodore Roosevelt, whom President McKinley appointed Assistant Secretary of the Navy in 1897. Even before he had finished at Harvard,

Teddy had begun writing *The Naval War of 1812*, which was published in 1882, only two years after he graduated. He remained fascinated by ships. And he was especially intrigued by the puzzle of power. What really made a nation strong? He was delighted by Mahan's writings.

At that time trouble was brewing only a few miles off the coast of Florida. The island of Cuba had been a colony of Spain ever since it was first sighted by Columbus. In the nineteenth century Spain was tyrannizing over the inhabitants. And the Cuban rebels declared their independence in February 1895.

The Spanish government sent out troops and put the island under a ruthless general, Valeriano "Butcher" Weyler. On February 10, 1896, General Weyler ordered that "all the inhabitants of the country" who were still outside the towns should "concentrate themselves in the towns." Anybody found outside a town would be shot. This made Cuban towns into "concentration camps." The whole island became a prison. Men, women, and children were herded together. Some were tortured, others died of disease and starvation— including some United States citizens.

American newspapers splashed the stories of "Butcher" Weyler's atrocities on the front pages of papers which went out in six editions a day to the cities and at least once a day (by RFD) even to remote farms. Joseph Pulitzer, an energetic Hungarian immigrant who had bought the New York *World,* was anxious to make his paper popular. The more copies he sold, the more he could charge for advertising—and advertising supported the paper.

Pulitzer was brilliant at finding new ways to attract readers. For example, he hired a clever cartoonist, Richard F. Outcault, to make the first color comic strip. It showed the adventures of a bad boy called the "Yellow Kid" who ap-

in whether they were true. Because they featured the Yellow Kid these newspapers—and others like them—were soon called the "Yellow Press."

The United States had a long-standing interest in Cuba. Back in the early nineteenth century Thomas Jefferson himself had said he hoped to see Cuba become part of the United States. Now American businessmen had invested over fifty million dollars in Cuban sugar. In 1895 the rebels destroyed sugar plantations and mills, hoping to prod the United States to intervene. Then, in 1896, William McKinley was

Sensational headlines in Hearst newspaper.

peared regularly in the Sunday edition. Outcault's cartoons were so successful that Pulitzer's leading competitor, the Go-Getting William Randolph Hearst, hired the same cartoonist to do another Yellow Kid series for the Sunday edition of *his* paper, the New York *Journal.*

While on Sundays both papers used the Yellow Kid to attract readers, every day they competed by printing shocking stories. They were more interested in whether the stories were shocking than

elected President with a promise to help Cuba become independent.

When Spain began to negotiate with the United States about freedom for the Cubans, it seemed there would be no need to fight. But on February 9, 1898, the New York *Journal* printed a stolen letter in which the Spanish ambassador called President McKinley a coward and other nasty names.

To protect American lives and property, the United States battleship *Maine* had been sent to Havana harbor. At 9:40 P.M. on the night of February 15, 1898, the *Maine* was shattered by an explosion, and 260 officers and men were killed. The navy's court of inquiry reported that the cause was an underwater mine, but they could not say for sure whether the Spanish were to blame. Anyway the Yellow Press called for war against Spain, and headlined the slogan, "REMEMBER THE MAINE!"

When the excitable Assistant Secretary of the Navy, Theodore Roosevelt, heard that McKinley was hesitating, he said the President "had no more backbone than a chocolate éclair." On February 25 the Secretary of the Navy made the mistake of taking the afternoon off. That left impatient Teddy as Acting Secretary—in charge of the whole United States navy. Without consulting anyone, he instantly cabled his friend Admiral George Dewey, who commanded the United States fleet in Asiatic waters. Make sure, he ordered, that Spanish ships do not leave the coast of Asia. Begin "defensive operations" against the Spanish colony out there— the Philippines!

When the Secretary of the Navy returned to his office next day, he was astonished. "Roosevelt," he wrote in his diary, "has come very near causing more of an explosion than happened to the *Maine*." But it was too late to change the order. And even *before* war had begun in nearby Cuba, Teddy had arrayed the United States fleet for war on the other side of the world.

If President McKinley had been a stronger man he would not have been afraid to keep the peace. The government of Spain now actually told him

Joseph Pulitzer, a painting by John Singer Sargent, who was famous for his portraits of notable Americans.

they would give Cuba her independence. But the Yellow Press was still demanding Spanish blood. The "jingoes" —the people who loved to see a fight— wanted war. On April 11, the day *after* President McKinley learned that Spain would agree to do everything Americans said they wanted, he asked Congress to declare war.

The war lasted only a few months— but that was long enough to create the greatest confusion. At the training camp in Tampa, Florida, commanding officers could not find uniforms, while for weeks fifteen railroad cars full of uniforms remained on a siding twenty-five miles away. The commander of United States troops in Cuba, Major General W. R. Shafter, weighed three hundred pounds and was therefore "too unwieldy to get to the front." Unprepared for combat,

"Charge of the Rough Riders at San Juan Hill," a painting by Frederic Remington, who went to Cuba as an artist-correspondent. The "Rough Riders" had to run up the hill on foot. Teddy Roosevelt, leading them on horseback, made himself the most conspicuous target.

the army committed every foolishness known to man.

The navy was in better shape. On May 1, when Admiral Dewey, following Roosevelt's impulsive orders, attacked the Spanish warships in the Philippines, he finished off the Spaniards in seven hours. The remnant of the Spanish fleet, which was in North American waters, then sneaked into Santiago harbor on the southeastern tip of Cuba.

Meanwhile Teddy Roosevelt had himself appointed lieutenant colonel of a new regiment of cavalry. At a training camp in San Antonio, Texas, he gathered cowboys, sheriffs, and desperadoes from the West, and a sprinkling of playboy polo players and steeplechase riders from the East. They came to be known as Roosevelt's Rough Riders.

Roosevelt himself was preparing for serious combat. What worried him most was his bad eyesight. If he broke or lost his glasses he could not see where he was going, much less find the Spaniards

to shoot. He ordered a dozen extra pairs of steel-rimmed eyeglasses. He then stowed them separately all over his uniform and even put several extra pairs inside the lining of his campaign hat.

On June 22, Roosevelt's Rough Riders arrived in Cuba. They were given the job of storming San Juan Hill, which overlooked Santiago bay. To capture the steep hill his "Rough Riding" cavalry (who had been selected for their horsemanship) actually had to dismount. "I waved my hat and went up the hill with a rush," Roosevelt recalled. After a bloody fight, they reached the top.

Theodore Roosevelt never suffered from modesty. When Roosevelt published his book *The Rough Riders*, the humorist "Mr. Dooley" said Teddy should have called it "Alone in Cuba."

The decisive naval battle occurred even before the Americans could place their big guns on San Juan Hill to bombard the enemy navy below. When the Spanish fleet tried to run for the open sea the United States navy exterminated every last warship of Spain. All over the United States, enthusiastic Americans celebrated their victory.

By the standards of American history, this had not been a full-size war. There were 385 battle deaths—less than one-tenth the deaths in the American Revolution, and only one-twentieth the deaths at the Battle of Gettysburg alone. While the American Revolution had lasted nearly eight years and the Civil War had lasted four years, the Spanish-American War lasted only four *months.* Even this "little" war cost a quarter-billion dollars and several thousand deaths from disease.

And the little war marked a big change in the relationship of the United States to the world. The tides of history were turned. Cuba, given her independence, became an American protectorate.

The defeated Spain forfeited to the United States an empire of islands. This nation, born in a colonial revolution, would now have her own colonies. All were outside the continent, some were thousands of miles away. The United States acquired Puerto Rico at the gateway of the Caribbean, along with Guam, important as a refuelling station in mid-Pacific. The Philippine Islands (there were seven thousand of them, of which over one thousand were inhabitable) off the coast of China were sold to the United States for the bargain price of twenty million dollars.

These new American colonies added up to one hundred thousand square miles, holding nearly ten million people. That was not much, compared to the vast empires of England, France, or Germany. But for the United States it was something quite new.

The meaning of this Spanish-American War in American history, then, was actually less in what it accomplished than in what it proclaimed. The American Revolution had been our War of Independence. Now the Spanish-American War at the threshold of the twentieth century, was our first War of Intervention. We had joined the old-fashioned race for empire—on all the oceans of the world.

Many Americans were worried. Some were saddened, and even angry. They called themselves "Anti-Imperialists," for they hated to see the United States become an empire. To be an empire, they said, meant lording it over people in faraway places. Anti-Imperialists included Democrats and Republicans, of all sections and classes—labor leader Samuel Gompers, industrialist Andrew Carnegie, President Charles W. Eliot of Harvard and President David Starr Jordan of Stanford, the philosopher William James, the social worker Jane Addams, and the popular writer Mark Twain.

Theodore Roosevelt, however, believed that the United States could accomplish her mission only if she was a great world power. We must be willing to have colonies, he said, while we help the people learn to be democratic.

He built a great navy. In the Spanish-American War we had only five battleships and two armored cruisers. But before Roosevelt left the White House in 1909, we had twenty-five battleships and ten heavy cruisers. We had become, next to the British, the strongest naval power in the world.

President Roosevelt foresaw some grand accomplishments which would never have been done by stay-at-homes. For years Americans going westward had tried to find ways to shorten the voyage to California. Now, as a world power, the United States had to be able to move its navy speedily from one ocean to another. This was an urgent new reason to cut a waterway through Central America.

When TR came to the White House, a French company had already been working on a canal for twenty years. But they were stymied by tropical disease. Their progress was slow and international complications seemed to make the whole enterprise hopeless.

TR would let nothing stop him. First he tried to make a treaty with the little Republic of Colombia, which then included the part of the Isthmus of Panama where the canal had to be built. When the government of Colombia blocked Roosevelt's treaty in 1903, a revolution suddenly occurred in Panama. A lucky coincidence for the United States! But there was evidence that American money had helped the "coincidence" to happen. Immediately, the new "independent" Republic of Panama made a treaty granting the Canal Zone to the United States.

Within only ten years after construction began, ships were actually passing through the canal. The canal cost over a half-billion dollars.

Building the canal had produced some world-wide benefits that even TR had never dreamed of. In order to build the canal through the fever-infested swamps, the Americans had to conquer tropical diseases. When Americans occupied Havana after the Spanish-American War, Dr. Walter Reed had discovered the mosquito that carried the deadly yellow fever. Then Dr. William Gorgas, who had worked with Reed in Cuba, applied this discovery in Panama. His work finally made the canal possible —and incidentally helped conquer that tropical disease all around the world.

CHAPTER 26

How Submarines Killed the Freedom of the Seas

With world power and an island empire came a greater need to use the ocean highways. Ever since the eighteenth century, the civilized nations had agreed on certain rules. Since wars were always going on somewhere in the world, the purpose of these rules was to allow the neutral countries to carry on their commerce in peace.

The countries that were not fighting had certain Neutral Rights. The most important was their right to send their ships anywhere, and to have their citizens be safe wherever they traveled.

Warring nations were allowed to seize certain war materials ("contraband"— explosives, guns, and ammunition) even from a neutral ship. But they were not supposed to seize the other goods carried by neutrals. Before sinking any

ABOVE: *The luxury liner Lusitania at the dock in New York. When launched in 1907 it was the largest steamship in the world.* BELOW: *A German submarine in World War I. Posing a new threat to warships and passenger vessels, it was too small and crowded to rescue its victims.*

passenger ship, the attacker was required to give warning, to take the passengers on board, and do everything else reasonable to save civilian lives. Since warships were large vessels, they could normally be seen at a great distance, which automatically gave some warning. And anyway it was not too inconvenient for large warships to carry some extra passengers.

Such rules as these were what people meant by International Law. There was no court or police force to make nations obey. But the rules were still called "Law" because so many people believed they ought to be obeyed. The special rights of neutrals were also called Freedom of the Seas.

In 1914, when World War I broke out in Europe, these rules were still substantially the same as they had been for about two centuries. But the navies had changed. Most important was a new kind of ship—the submarine. The submarine's great strength was its new power to surprise. At the same time, however, the submarine was a crowded, tight-packed little vessel. With barely enough room for its own crew and food and ammunition, it had nowhere to put passengers from the ships it sank.

To say that all warring nations still had to follow the old rules would automatically outlaw the submarine. This would not have bothered Great Britain, for she had the greatest navy in the world. She commanded the seas anyway. But for Germany, with her relatively small navy, submarines would make all the difference. To forbid the submarine, then, was only another way of saying that Britain must forever rule the waves.

Great Britain made it plain that she had no intention of giving up her control of the oceans. She declared a blockade of Germany and enlarged the list of contraband to include all sorts of goods that neutrals had always been allowed to carry. Britain declared that she would even stop ships from carrying goods to neutral countries if any of those goods would eventually get to Germany. None of this was according to International Law.

Germany could hardly be expected to sit still and let herself be strangled. Her submarines could do their deadly work only if they, too, disobeyed International Law. Germany therefore decided to use the submarine for all it was worth, and to let others worry about the old rules. The Germans advertised in American newspapers urging Americans not to travel on British ships.

Then, on the night of May 7, 1915, the British luxury liner *Lusitania* was sunk without warning off the coast of Ireland by the German submarine U-20. Of nearly two thousand persons on board, 1,198 died, including 128 Americans. The ship sank within eighteen minutes of the time she was torpedoed. She was carrying 4,200 cases of small-arms ammunition and 1,250 shrapnel cases (which under International Law made the whole ship contraband and liable to be sunk).

President Woodrow Wilson sent a strong protest to Germany. He insisted on Neutral Rights. And he said this meant the right of Americans to travel wherever they pleased—even on the ships of the fighting nations, and right into the war zone. Wilson said this was a matter of national honor.

Woodrow Wilson's family background had not aroused his interest in naval or military affairs. His father, a Presbyterian minister who taught in a seminary, wanted young Woodrow to train for the ministry. Although Woodrow Wilson decided against becoming a minister, in some ways he always thought and talked like an old-fashioned minister.

Like Theodore Roosevelt, Wilson was a literary President, the author of many books. But in almost every other way he was TR's opposite. While TR's first book was on sea power, young Wilson wrote about moral questions for the North Carolina *Presbyterian*. While TR adored "The Strenuous Life," Wilson lived in the world of ideas, "longing to do immortal work." At the age when TR was learning to ride broncos and was bunking with cowboys, Wilson was sitting in post-graduate seminars on political science at Johns Hopkins University.

Wilson was an indoor sort of man. After a bright career as a professor he was elected president of Princeton University, where his educational reforms made him nationally famous. Then in 1910 he was elected Governor of New Jersey, and in 1912 he received the Democratic nomination for President. He could inspire people in large groups or from the printed page. But face to face he was stiff and stand-offish.

While Wilson had some of William Jennings Bryan's religious appeal, his tone was very different. Bryan sounded like the preacher at a country tent meeting, but Wilson could have been the minister of the best church in town. Both could persuade voters that they were joining the Army of the Lord. Wilson, like Bryan, championed the

Woodrow Wilson as president of Princeton University.

struggling farmers and underprivileged workers. As a more moderate kind of Bryan, Wilson had a wider appeal.

In 1916, two years after the outbreak of war in Europe, Wilson was reelected on the slogan, "He Kept Us Out of War!" But one thing after another was taking Americans further down the road. The German foreign minister, Arthur Zimmermann, sent a foolish message to the German ambassador in Mexico. Zimmermann asked Mexico to join the German side, and in return Germany promised to help the Mexicans recapture from the United States all of Texas, Arizona, and New Mexico. The message was intercepted and decoded by the British, who then eagerly relayed it to the United States.

Meanwhile, powerful unseen forces were drawing Americans naturally like a magnet toward the British. After all, we spoke the English language, our laws were built on English foundations, and we had fought our American Revolution to preserve our rights as Englishmen. Early in the war, the British succeeded in cutting the transatlantic cable that brought news to America direct from Germany. After that, all news from Europe was channeled through England. This gave the British a great advantage that very few people noticed.

Even before we declared war the United States was already supporting the British side. Because of the British blockade against Germany and her allies, the value of American goods sent to Germany and Austria plummeted from nearly $170,000,000 in 1914 to about $1,000,000 in 1916. During the same two years, American trade with Britain and her allies rocketed from $800,000,-000 to over $3,214,000,000. While the United States was still technically neutral, American bankers had actually loaned the British allies $2,300,000,000 to buy war supplies.

On April 2, 1917, within a month after the Zimmermann Note was published, President Wilson went to Congress to demand a declaration of war against Germany. He no longer spoke only about Neutral Rights. He would not ask Americans to die for a technicality. "The world," Wilson said, "must be made safe for democracy." Americans must fight "for the rights and liberties of small nations," to "bring peace and safety to all nations and make the world itself at last free."

There was, in fact, a good reason why the United States did not want to see the British lose. While European nations had spent their treasure on armies and navies, Americans had put their own wealth into schools and factories and railroads, into a better life for all citizens. Why had Americans been allowed to go about their business in peace? One reason was that the United States had the good luck to be protected by British Sea Power.

While the friendly British ruled the waves, they let us carry our cargoes and our people all over the world. The British, like the Americans, did not want to see other European nations build new empires in North or South America. The Monroe Doctrine—that European countries should not make new colonies in America and should not interfere in American affairs—had actually been enforced by the British navy. It had been very economical and extremely convenient, then, for Americans to have the British control the seas. But no one could predict what might come from a victorious Germany, with its new imperial ambitions.

In January 1918, President Wilson went before Congress again—to explain the American program for the future of the world. He listed Fourteen Points. They were a noble list. And if they could have been lived up to, there would never have been any more wars. All secret diplomacy was to be abolished— to make statesmen ashamed to barter away other people's lives and liberties. Freedom of the Seas would be restored. National boundaries would be adjusted so that all peoples could govern themselves. And, finally, there would be a League of Nations to preserve peace and insure justice.

The Fourteen Points impressed the world. They meant more to people outside the United States than any American statement since the Declaration of Independence or the Emancipation Proclamation.

President Wilson had proved himself one of the greatest preachers in modern history. He had lifted the spirits of the battle-worn, and he expressed the hopes of millions everywhere. But to make even half his dreams come true required a master politician. Could Wilson do the job?

CHAPTER 27

Winning a War, Losing a Peace

When the United States entered the war in April 1917, our Allies had almost lost.

In Europe the land war was in a new style. The trench warfare was like nothing ever seen before. When the war broke out in 1914, both German generals and French generals had their own plans for a knockout blow to end the war in a hurry. But the new automatic weapons were deadly and accurate against attack. The advantages of the defensive had so increased that *both* armies immediately went on the defensive.

This was Stationary Warfare. Both armies dug their trenches, lived underground, and fired at each other from fixed positions. For three and a half years, the trenches stretched from the Swiss border to the North Sea. The battle lines had hardly moved.

On both sides the trenches became elaborate systems. There was usually a line of front trenches, held as outposts. Behind were networks of supply and command trenches, sometimes stretching back as far as five miles. These were connected by complicated tunnels, and sometimes even by specially designed railways. Soldiers became human moles,

hiding by day and digging by night. As soon as darkness fell, they went to work, digging new trenches, stringing barbed wire, and connecting telephone lines.

Instead of the higher officers leading their men into battle, these officers often stayed far back in command posts located in comfortable chateaus. Men in the front trenches had a terrible feeling of isolation. They were threatened not only by enemy gunfire, but by darkness, cold, and mud. Out of the filth and fatigue arose new ailments, which came to be called "trench fever," "trench foot," and "trench mouth."

In this kind of warfare, a "battle" was when large numbers of men from one set of trenches rushed out and tried to break through the enemy's trenches. The hope was always to force a big gap so your troops could pour through and then attack the whole enemy line from the rear. But advancing soldiers were tangled in barbed wire and mowed down by deadly machine-gun fire.

In the opening battles in 1914, even before the trenches were dug, each side lost a half-million men, which was more men than had been in the entire German army fifty years before. Then, during the whole year of 1915, the British and French did not advance more than three miles at any point. Still the French lost nearly a million and a half men in 1915, and a million in 1916. At the Battle of the Somme alone, the Germans lost more men than had been killed during the whole four years of the American Civil War.

Never before had so many men been slaughtered so rapidly or so senselessly. Before the war was over, the soldiers killed on both sides would number ten million, and another ten million civilians would die from disease, starvation, and the revolutions that grew out of the war.

When the United States finally plunged in, both sides were weary and sick of the bloodshed. In May 1918, the Germans had pushed their trenches to within fifty miles of Paris. They aimed at all costs to reach Paris and so force the surrender of the Allies before American troops could make a difference.

But the Americans came just in time. In July, 85,000 Americans arrived to help save Paris and to join a new counter-offensive. By August an American army of a half-million under General John J. Pershing advanced against the Germans on the southern front. Before the end of September a million and a quarter Americans were fighting in France.

After a bloody battle in October, the Americans advanced to Sedan, fifty miles behind the trenches which the Germans had held for three years. The Americans then cut the railroad line that

"Battle of the Marne," an eyewitness drawing by an artist-reporter. In the days of Stationary Warfare armies advanced on foot with fixed bayonets, hoping to break through the enemy's entrenchments.

had supplied the German army, and the whole German defense disintegrated. With this American encouragement, the French and the British were advancing too.

The German generals and the German Emperor had badly miscalculated. They had thought they would win the war before the United States came in. They could not imagine that American help at the last moment could possibly turn the tide. Though the Americans arrived late in the battle, they actually made the difference that decided the war. The United States lost 50,280 men in action.

That bloodiest war yet in history ended with the Armistice on November 11, 1918. In New York and San Francisco and Dallas and Chicago and Atlanta, Americans danced in the streets.

The Germans, in agreeing to an Armistice in November, believed that the peace would be based on Wilson's generous Fourteen Points.

When President Wilson himself decided to go to a Peace Conference in Paris, he gave ammunition to his critics. They said he was more anxious to be the Preacher to the World than to be the Protector of the United States. No President while in office had ever before gone to Europe.

In Paris, the three Allied leaders whom Wilson had to bargain with—the Prime Ministers of Great Britain, France, and Italy—were clever and tough. Each of them remembered the enormous cost of the war to his country during the four bloody years. Each wanted to get as much as possible in lands and wealth

"Blitzkrieg," Hitler's new technique of warfare in World War II, sent motorcycles and tanks speeding over highways to get behind the enemy's lines before he knew what was happening. Support by airplanes (not shown here) was crucial. This scene: Poland, 1939.

and power for his own country, and hoped to punish the enemies so they would never rise again.

The victorious European statesmen were irritated by the self-righteous American President who always said he was worrying about "all mankind." They compared the Points that Wilson had announced from Washington with the Commandments given to Moses on Mount Sinai. "Mr. Wilson bores me with his *Fourteen* Points," the French Prime Minister, Georges Clemenceau, sneered. "Why, God Almighty has only *ten!*"

The treaty that came out of the Paris conference rooms was not as selfish or as vengeful as the European leaders would have wished. Nor was it nearly as just and noble as President Wilson might have hoped. Each victorious power got territories it had been promised in secret treaties. The German colonies were parceled out among the Allies. At the same time, some new smaller republics—like Czechoslovakia and Poland—were created so that at last these people could govern themselves.

The provisions most poisonous for the future of Europe had to do with "reparations." These were payments the Allies demanded from Germany to "repair" all the war damage. When the Germans signed the Armistice they did understand they might have to pay for the damage to civilians.

But the British and the French raised the damages to include the *total* cost of the whole war to all the Allies. This meant not only the homes and farms and factories destroyed, but also the cost of guns and ammunition, the uniforms and pay for soldiers, and even the pensions to wounded Allied soldiers and to their

relatives. This sum was so vast and so hard to estimate that the Allies refused to name a figure—or even to name a time in the future when the Germans would be allowed to stop paying.

President Wilson did manage to put his own scheme for permanent peace—the League of Nations—in the very same package with all those things the other Allied powers really wanted. He believed that, even if the whole treaty was not perfect, his new League of Nations could correct the mistakes later.

When President Wilson returned to the United States, he was greeted like a returning hero. An escort of festive warships accompanied him into New York harbor. Ten thousand people welcomed him at the Union Station in Washington.

His triumph was short. Now his political mistakes came home to roost. When Wilson had appointed the American Peace Commissioners to go to Paris, he snubbed both the Republican Party and the Senate. Yet the Republicans held the majority in the Senate. And before any treaty became law, the Senate would have to approve it by a two-thirds majority.

President Wilson simply could not believe that there were reasons why sensible Americans might not want to approve his treaty. What frightened Americans most was the plan for a League of Nations—but especially Article 10. Wilson, with typical obstinacy, said that Article 10 was the heart of the whole League, and that the League was the heart of the treaty.

In Article 10 each League member promised to respect and preserve all the other members of the League against "external aggression." At first sight that looked harmless enough. But the real purpose of the Article was to make each member of the League regard an attack on any other member as an attack on itself. And in that case, each League member would be expected to prepare for war.

To agree to this would overturn one of the oldest American traditions. Should the United States let herself be *required* to plunge into some future European war?

Two able, contrasting Republican statesmen led a relentless battle against allowing the United States to join Wilson's League. One was William E. Borah, Senator from the Far Western State of Idaho. Borah, like President Wilson himself, was the son of a Presbyterian minister, who wanted him also to go into the ministry. A graduate of the University of Kansas, he was as eloquent as Wilson, but had more experience in politics. Although technically a Republican, he supported many Democratic measures when he happened to agree with them. He had worked for the income tax and had fought against trusts and monopolies.

Just as Senator Borah's own personal rule in politics had been to stay independent, and then support whatever measures were best, so he believed the United States should always stay independent in her relation to other countries. He bitterly opposed our joining the League of Nations, for fear it would take away our independence.

The other leader of the anti-League forces was the learned Senator Henry Cabot Lodge of Massachusetts. He, too, had had a long career as a politician.

But he came from a wealthy and aristocratic New England Oldcomer family. After attending Harvard, he wrote many books on American history. At the time of the World War he was chairman of the Senate Committee on Foreign Relations, which had the power to recommend to the Senate whether or not they should adopt the treaty. Unlike Senator Borah, he was a man of strong personal hates. He distrusted Woodrow Wilson and so he feared Wilson's League.

Then President Wilson made his fatal decision to appeal direct to the American people. In early September 1919, though already in ill health, he traveled eight thousand miles, visited twenty-nine cities, and gave forty speeches in twenty-two days. At Pueblo, Colorado, he collapsed and had to be taken back to the White House. For nearly eight months President Wilson could not even meet his Cabinet. His wife carried messages back and forth from everybody else to the President—and it was never quite clear which messages actually reached him.

Before the election of 1920 Wilson made another grave political blunder. If he had been willing to work with Senator Lodge, he might still have found some compromise and so might have passed the Treaty and the League through the Senate. Instead Wilson once again became the preacher. "Shall we," he asked "or shall we not, redeem the great moral obligation of the United States?" He declared that the Presidential election of 1920 would be a "solemn national referendum" on the League of Nations.

The Democratic candidate for President, Governor James M. Cox of Ohio, stood up for the League. The weak but likeable Republican candidate, Senator Warren G. Harding of Ohio, opposed the League and said vaguely that he favored some sort of "association of nations." Americans chose the Republican Harding by a resounding majority of seven million votes.

The United States never joined Wilson's League of Nations. Wilson was saddened that the American people chose a "barren independence." But he did not give up hope that what a union of States had accomplished in North America, a union of nations might someday accomplish for the whole world.

CHAPTER 28
The Battlefield Is Everywhere

When Franklin Delano Roosevelt moved into the White House in March 1933, the world prospects once again were grim. Italy, Russia, and Japan—three former American allies in the war "to make the world safe for democracy"— had become threats both to democracy and to peace. Germany, the leading enemy in that war, had risen from defeat, was building an enormous new army, was manufacturing weapons at frightening speed, and soon proclaimed her intention to rule the world. Any one of the new military powers had a bigger army and was beginning to have stronger armaments than the old democracies. Each proclaimed its intention to fight.

In the United States the national slogan had become, "Never Again!" Many Americans were becoming pacifists, saying they would never go to war for *any* reason. Others were becoming Isolationists, looking for ways to fence off the New World. And others refused to give up the old-fashioned hope that the country could always stay neutral. But by

1935 the idea that neutrals had rights which everybody would respect was more unrealistic than ever.

Each of the new warlike powers wanted not just a bigger empire for itself. It wanted its own kind of world —Communist, Fascist, or Nazi. All were battling for the minds of men. The winner aimed to take all.

This meant that, whether Americans liked it or not, the battlefront was everywhere. Now the airplane had made nearly all traditional thinking about war out-of-date. What the submarine had done to Freedom of the Seas, the airplane was doing to almost all the other rules of warfare.

Just as Admiral Mahan had once argued for the decisive influence of Sea Power on history, so during World War I the brilliant and energetic Billy Mitchell began to advertise Air Power.

Air Power was still so new that few took it seriously. In the Spanish-American War one light observation balloon had actually been used in Cuba. But "military ballooning" (as it was

Billy Mitchell, commander of United States aviators in France during World War I, was a bold and enthusiastic pioneer of Air Power.

called) was considered mostly a sport or a hobby. In 1913 when Mitchell was a young officer in the Signal Corps he began to be intrigued by the airplane's military possibilities. Then, during World War I, as General Pershing's Chief of Air Service he was impressed by the effectiveness of British and French warplanes.

At the end of the war, American generals and admirals still considered the airplane at most merely another new weapon. Like a new machine gun, it was to be used by either the army or the navy in their own regular operations.

Billy Mitchell had other ideas. His experience as a flyer and his other wartime observations persuaded him that airplanes really ought to be organized into an entirely new military unit, under a command all their own. So long as Americans thought of airplanes as only helpers in traditional army and navy maneuvers, he argued, Americans were sure to be left behind. They would lose the next war to nations who recognized that Air Power was something new and world-shaking.

Air Power, Mitchell said, had actually shifted the main targets. No longer were they the enemy *armies*. Now the most important targets were the "vital centers"—the centers of industry, the centers of supply, and the centers of the enemy's will to resist. "Armies themselves can be disregarded by air power," he explained, "if a rapid strike is made against the opposing centers."

Americans could not bear the thought of a new warfare that was so horrible. They hated to believe that whole cities might have to be destroyed.

Mitchell was an expert at getting publicity. He wrote magazine articles and books, and made speeches to alert all citizens to the importance of Air Power. Many of his fellow officers disliked him for it. Some called him "General of the 'Hot Air' Force."

But Mitchell was not discouraged. To prove that airplanes were an effective and economical force against battleships, he planned a spectacular demonstration. He arranged to have the German battleship *Ostfriesland*, which had been surrendered at the end of World War I, hauled to a position sixty miles off the Virginia coast. The battleship had a reputation for being "unsinkable." Now it was a ghost ship, with not a soul on board.

Just before noon on July 21, 1921, a flight of Mitchell's army bombers left Langley Field eighty-five miles away. As they arrived over the battleship, they dropped six 2,000-pound bombs. Within twenty minutes the "unsinkable" battleship was at the bottom of the ocean. It was the first time a battleship had ever been sunk by planes.

When admirals and generals still refused to grasp the full meaning of Air Power, Mitchell tried other tactics. He publicly denounced "the incompetency, criminal negligence, and almost treasonable administration of the National Defense by the Navy and War Departments." This was the sure road to court-martial—and that seemed to be his purpose. On December 17, 1925, a panel of generals found Brigadier General Billy Mitchell guilty of "conduct which brought discredit upon the military service." They sentenced him to a five-year suspension from active duty.

But his publicity campaign had already forced President Calvin Coolidge to take some action. The committee he appointed did not support all of Mitchell's demands, but they did urge the buildup of an American air force.

Then, on May 21, 1927, a young air-mail pilot named Charles A. Lindbergh surprised and delighted the world by flying his light monoplane, *The Spirit of St. Louis*, nonstop from New York to Paris. Americans were proud of his courage and his modesty. He called his book *We* (meaning his plane and himself).

Charles Lindbergh at Curtiss Field, New York, before beginning his solo flight across the Atlantic. When he arrived at Le Bourget Airport outside Paris, to his astonishment he was greeted by 100,000 people.

As the military meaning of Lindbergh's feat sank in, Americans began to realize that Billy Mitchell's "wild" ideas no longer were so wild. Now it seemed quite possible that some day the United States might be attacked by airplanes which came nonstop across the ocean. The nation began to take Mitchell, and Air Power, seriously.

In 1935 the new American long-range B-17 bomber (soon called the "Flying Fortress" and equipped with the super-accurate Norden bombsight) first went into the air. Now it was hard for Americans to doubt that Air Power would change the meaning of war. Air war against "vital centers" would be as different as possible from the old stationary trench warfare.

Adolf Hitler's shocking new strategy depended on Air Power. The German name for it was *Blitzkrieg*, which means "lightning war." The idea was to strike with lightning speed. Using the fastest new vehicles (airplanes, tanks, trucks, and even motorcycles) the Nazis would rush quick and deep into enemy territory. The sluggish, unprepared enemies would be overwhelmed.

Blitzkrieg also meant war that struck like lightning—from the sky. Air Power made it possible. Leaping over "standing" armies, over water barriers and coastal fortifications, the Nazi air force would strike abruptly at the heart of the defenseless nations.

On September 1, 1939, Hitler invaded Poland, which fell before the end of the month. Then, on April 9, 1940, he horrified the world by invading Denmark and Norway. One month later he rushed into the Netherlands, Belgium, and Luxembourg, and then lunged deep into France around the "impregnable" Maginot Line. On June 14 his Nazis marched into Paris. Thousands of weeping Frenchmen lined the streets, helpless against this lightning barbarian invasion.

Luckily, President Franklin Delano Roosevelt recognized the Nazi menace. Even before the Nazis had overrun France he had sent a special message to Congress warning the nation to rearm. He announced his plan to turn out fifty thousand planes in the next year and every year until the Nazis were beaten. In one of his most effective "fireside chats" over the radio, he alerted the nation:

> The Nazi masters of Germany have made it clear that they intend not only to dominate all life and thought in their own country, but also to enslave the whole of Europe, and then to use the resources of Europe to dominate the rest of the world. . . . We cannot escape danger, or the fear of danger, by crawling into a bed and pulling the covers over our heads. . . . No nation can appease the Nazis. No man can tame a tiger into a kitten by stroking it. . . . Let not the defeatists tell us that it is too late. It will never be earlier.

But still there were those who believed they could ward off the Nazi menace by the old-fashioned magic word, "Neutrality!"

The Isolationists had passed a Neutrality Law requiring that all military supplies sent abroad had to be "cash-and-carry." This law required all the warring countries to pay for the goods they bought here before the goods left our shores and then also required them to carry the goods in their own ships. The Isolationists hoped this would keep the United States out of the war.

The British had run out of cash and were running out of ships. If this law was not quickly changed the United States might not be able to get help to the British before they were defeated by the Nazis.

President Franklin Delano Roosevelt showed his usual genius for compromise and for persuasion. He offered a clever plan called "Lend-Lease." We would "lend" or "lease" to the British—or any other country whose defense the President considered vital to the defense of the United States—whatever war supplies we could make. In that way the British would not need cash, and the hesitating Congressmen might be per-

suaded that we were getting value in return.

At the same time, in January 1941, in his annual message to Congress, President Roosevelt proclaimed the Four Freedoms. After the war he hoped for "a world founded upon four essential human freedoms"—freedom of speech, freedom of religion, freedom from want, and freedom from fear. Later that year, after a secret meeting with British Prime Minister Winston Churchill on a warship off the coast of Newfoundland, the two men issued the Atlantic Charter. This was an up-to-date version of Woodrow Wilson's Fourteen Points.

Meanwhile Hitler made his fatal blunder. In his maniac belief that all battlefields were alike and that *Blitzkrieg* could conquer all, on June 22, 1941, only

The bombing of Pearl Harbor by Japanese war planes helped convince all Americans that the age of Air Power had arrived.

a year after mastering France, he suddenly invaded Russia. But Russia was bigger—and colder—than Hitler had imagined. When the Russian winter arrived, the fingers of Nazi soldiers became numb. Frozen oil paralyzed the motors of his tanks. The Russians counterattacked and Hitler's *Blitzkrieg* was buried in the snow.

At the same time, halfway around the world, the Japanese suddenly forced even the most Isolationist of Americans to realize that Air Power had already put them on the battlefield. On the morning of December 7, 1941, while Japanese diplomats were pretending to discuss peace at the White House, a fleet of 189 Japanese warplanes attacked American airfields at Pearl Harbor in Hawaii. Then they attacked the ships of the United States navy anchored in the harbor. An hour later came a second fleet of 171 Japanese warplanes.

The surprise had been perfect. 150 American warplanes—the bulk of our air force in the Pacific—were destroyed on the ground. It was a better demonstration than Billy Mitchell could have imagined, and the fulfillment of his direst prophecies. There were eighty-six American ships in Pearl Harbor at the time. The most powerful of these, the eight battleships, were put out of action, together with three cruisers and three destroyers, and one battleship was actually sunk. 2,323 men were killed. This was the worst naval catastrophe in American history.

The very next day Congress announced that we were at war.

CHAPTER 29

The Exploding World of the Atom

As soon as Americans had been plunged into battle by this lightning stroke of Air Power, it was plain that the new kind of war was even newer than anyone had imagined. Now the battlefield was everywhere—but especially in the hearts of civilians. Warplanes sometimes flew so high they could not be seen and could barely be heard, to strike at homes and factories.

At first the bombing of Germany followed an American plan of "pinpoint" daylight attacks. Since daylight bombers could actually see their targets they could focus their bombs on the crucial factories. But at the same time the Germans could see the approaching planes, and they downed a disastrous number. The damage to the whole German war machine was slight.

By contrast with the American scheme of "precision" bombing, the British bombers went over at night and bombed whole areas. Incendiary bombs set fire to entire cities. Since these attacking bombers could not be seen, the British losses were much lower. And the damage to the "vital centers"—to the enemy's production, communication, and transportation and the enemy's will to

Massed United States bombers attacking a target in Germany in World War II.

resist—was far greater.

Now the war came home to the people on both sides. Never before in the history of warfare was there so much suffering by civilians. The Germans sent their bombers over London and other British cities, killing thousands. The Americans and British sent their bombers back over Germany. Finally it was the destruction of factories and cities behind the lines that broke the Nazi will to war. Allied planes had killed nearly a third of a million Germans and had destroyed over five million homes.

When the defeat of the Nazis appeared to be in sight, in February 1945, President Roosevelt met with the Allied leaders, British Prime Minister Churchill and Russian Dictator Josef Stalin. They met at Yalta, a Russian summer resort on the Black Sea. There they agreed on their plans for the Nazi surrender. Germany was to be taken apart. The Germans once again would have to

pay enormous "reparations," with Russia receiving half.

At first Stalin demanded that Poland, on the Russian border, be put under a Communist puppet government. Then when Roosevelt and Churchill objected, Stalin promised to let the Polish people choose their own government by free elections.

The Russians agreed to declare war against Japan soon after the defeat of Germany, and they agreed that they would join the United Nations. In return the Russians gained certain Japanese islands and would be allowed to conquer Outer Mongolia—a vast area twice the size of Texas—on the Russian border in central Asia. At the same time, Stalin solemnly promised not to interfere in the countries along the Russian border in eastern Europe. He promised to let those countries choose their own governments.

Of course Churchill and Roosevelt

knew that for years the communist leaders had called democracy a fraud. But since the Russian armies still had unrivaled power in eastern Europe, the British and American leaders did not have much choice. From their Russian ally all they could expect was promises. They considered themselves lucky to get those. Soon enough they would discover what Stalin's promises were really worth.

Within one short month the Nazi armies crumbled—caught between the Russian communist armies speeding westward and the Anglo-Americans speeding eastward.

General Dwight D. Eisenhower was Supreme Commander of Allied forces. Now his decision could change the history of Europe. If he wanted, he could quickly move his forces into Berlin, the capital of Germany, and also into Prague, the capital of Czechoslovakia.

In Anglo-American hands, Berlin and Prague would be strongholds to help the democracies enforce the Russian agreement to let eastern Europe decide its own fate.

On the other hand General Eisenhower could wait to mop up the German troops behind his own lines—meanwhile letting the Russians overrun more of eastern Europe and consolidate their positions in the capitals. In communist hands, those capitals would help the Russians to foist their dictatorship on all the surrounding peoples. The Russians could make Poland, Czechoslovakia, Hungary, Rumania, and Bulgaria into "satellites" revolving around Moscow.

The far-sighted Winston Churchill saw the threat. "I deem it highly important," he warned General Eisenhower, "that we should shake hands with the Russians as far to the east as

General Eisenhower talking to American paratroopers in June 1944 just before "Operation Overlord"—the successful landing on D-Day of Allied troops on the German-held coast of France. The paratroopers were assigned to drop behind enemy lines before the Allied landing.

possible." But General Eisenhower was anxious to avoid the loss of more American soldiers. Instead of rushing his democratic forces eastward, he decided to halt fifty miles west of Berlin at the River Elbe. Stalin applauded this decision, for now both Berlin and Prague were left to the Russians.

Until the last minute, Churchill was still trying to warn President Roosevelt. The new "mortal danger to the free world," he said, was our "ally," Russia. It would be tragic, after the long struggle against the Nazi tyranny, to hand over half of Europe to a communist tyranny.

Before Churchill's wisdom could prevail in Washington, President Roosevelt was dead. Worn down by wartime burdens, he had gone for a rest to Warm Springs, Georgia, where he often went for treatment of his paralyzed limbs. On April 12, 1945, he complained of a bad headache, and within a few hours a blood vessel had burst in his brain. The cheerful leader, who had helped raise his fellow Americans from the depth of their Great Depression and who had organized their battle against Nazi barbarism, finally did not have the satisfaction of receiving the Nazi surrender.

The nation grieved as it had grieved for few Americans since Lincoln. Men and women wept in their offices, at home, and in the streets. They felt they had lost not only a national leader, but a personal friend.

To the White House in his place came the courageous, peppery Vice-President, Harry S Truman. He was destined to make some of the most fateful decisions in the history of modern warfare. But when he solemnly took his oath of office

and asked the nation to pray for him, he could not have imagined what was in store. He still had not even heard of the super-secret project that was already nearing completion—to build an atomic bomb.

Those who made the American bomb possible (in addition to many American scientists) were a "Who's Who" of world science. From Germany came the greatest physicist of the age, Albert Einstein. Because he was a Jew, the Nazis had taken away his German citizenship and seized his property. From Italy, as a refugee from Mussolini, came the brilliant Enrico Fermi, who was one of the first to propose an atomic bomb as a practical possibility. Scientists, engineers, and mathematicians came also from Hungary, Austria, Denmark, and Czechoslovakia—refugees from all the enslaved parts of Europe.

To build the atomic bomb certain theoretical questions first had to be answered. Was it really possible to achieve "the controlled release of atomic energy"?

The answer came at 3:25 on the afternoon of December 2, 1942, in a squash court on the campus of the University of Chicago. Professor Enrico Fermi supervised the experiment. When everything was prepared, he gave the signal to pull out the control rod. Suddenly the Geiger counters resounded with telltale clicks from the radiation made by the successful breaking up of uranium atoms. The dignified scientists let out a cheer. They had produced a chain reaction that transformed matter into energy! The Atomic Age had begun.

One of the physicists hurried to the long-distance telephone and gave the code message to be relayed to the President of the United States.

"You'll be interested to know," he reported with mock casualness, "that the Italian navigator has just landed in the New World. The Earth was not as large as he had estimated, and he arrived in the New World sooner than he had expected."

"Is that so?" he was asked. "Were the natives friendly?"

"Everyone landed safe and happy." This meant that Professor Fermi (the "Italian navigator") had succeeded even ahead of schedule. The "New World" was, of course, the uncharted world of Atomic Power.

In May 1942, seven months before the Fermi experiment succeeded, President Roosevelt had set up the super-secret "Manhattan Project" to be prepared to build a bomb. Within less than three years and at a cost of two billion dollars, "Manhattan Project" did its job.

At 5:30 on the morning of July 16, 1945, in the remote desert near Alamogordo, New Mexico, the moment came to prove that the bold thinking of the scientists could be matched by the practical know-how of engineers. The answer required no delicate Geiger counter to detect it. The world's first atomic bomb exploded—with a blinding flash and a mushroom cloud such as had never been seen before.

By the time the bomb was perfected, the Germans and Italians had already surrendered. Of the enemies now only Japan remained. On July 26, the Allied leaders gave the Japanese a solemn warning that "the alternative to surrender is prompt and utter destruction."

Still they did not surrender.

Should the United States use the atomic bomb? President Truman alone had to decide. No one knew how long Japan would hold out. Despite the terrifying fire raids of March 1945, when much of Tokyo was destroyed, the Japanese militarists showed no signs of giving up. If the war dragged on and Americans had to invade Japan, it might cost a million lives. The atomic bomb, President Truman knew, might kill hundreds of thousands of innocent Japanese. But life for life, the odds were that it would cost less.

Devastation at Nagasaki, Japan, after the dropping of the second United States atomic bomb on August 9, 1945.

On August 6, 1945, three weeks after that first blinding blast on the New Mexico desert, a single American plane dropped an atomic bomb on Hiroshima. About eighty thousand people were killed. The Japanese still held on. A few days later another plane dropped an atomic bomb on Nagasaki. The Japanese caved in. They announced their surrender on August 14, 1945.

CHAPTER 30

"Little" Wars and Big Risks

World War II was over. The menace of Nazi barbarism and of Japanese militarism was destroyed. But the world was haunted by new fears. Could democracy survive in a world where the Russian communists were more powerful than ever before—and more determined than ever to conquer the world?

By now the United States had joined a modernized version of Wilson's League of Nations. The United Nations had been organized in San Francisco in 1945 even before the German surrender. President Truman hoped the United Nations would help keep the world at peace. But he had fought in France in World War I and he remembered the letdown after that war. Therefore he scaled down his hopes and made plans to fit. He did not promise perpetual peace or freedom for all men on earth.

Instead President Truman offered a simple two-pronged plan. People weakened by the war would receive American machinery and food and money. This would make them stronger to resist tyranny. He would also use American force, wherever it was needed, to help any particular country fight off a takeover by the communists from the outside. This was called "Containment" because it aimed to "contain" the communists and prevent them from taking over the world.

The Truman Doctrine was not as inspiring as Wilson's dream of an entirely democratic world. It was a country-by-country approach. It aimed to help free people stay strong and to help weak people stay free.

And, on the whole, it worked. The exhausted countries of western Europe —Great Britain, France, West Germany, and Italy—which might have been easy pickings for the Russian communists, became stronger in these postwar years. On the shaky borderlands of Greece and Turkey, the communist threat was held back.

The first armed test of the Truman Doctrine came in far-off Korea. The communists set up a puppet government in North Korea—like the puppets they had already set up in eastern Europe— and they claimed the right to rule the whole country. The United Nations (supported by the United States) proposed free elections so all the Koreans could choose their own government. But the Russians objected. And on June

American troops like these, fighting in Korea under the United Nations command, struggled over a hilly country, often barren and frigid.

25, 1950, an army of 100,000 men, who had been armed and trained by the Russian communists, swooped down to take possession of South Korea.

President Truman instantly sent in American troops. The United Nations condemned North Korea as an aggressor. And a United Nations army was organized with troops drawn from fifty-three member nations, commanded by the American General Douglas MacArthur. At first the United Nations forces drove back the invading North Korean communists.

Then suddenly the whole picture changed. Communist China, aided by the Russians, poured in masses of its own troops against the United Nations. They came down from north of the Yalu River. Now the Chinese communists threatened a third World War—if the United Nations forces stepped over the Yalu River into Chinese territory.

On March 24, 1951, General MacArthur, supreme commander of American forces in Korea, publicly warned that he would attack communist China if her forces did not withdraw from South Korea. Unlike President Truman, General MacArthur was willing to risk World War III.

But President Truman had not forgotten the powers of the President. The Constitution said that the President was Commander in Chief of all the United States armed forces. And the general had disobeyed the President's orders by refusing to keep the war inside Korea. President Truman called a surprise press conference at one o'clock in the morning on April 11, 1951, to announce that General MacArthur had been removed.

When the picturesque General MacArthur returned to the United States, admiring crowds greeted him in San Francisco, Chicago, and New York. In

Washington on April 19, he gave an oration to Congress. "In war," he urged in his deep baritone voice, "there can be no substitute for victory."

But even as the sound of the general's voice died away, more and more Americans saw that President Truman was talking common sense. You could no longer talk about "victory" in the general's simple phrase. Communist Russia now had its own atomic bomb. If there was another World War both "winners" and "losers" would go up in atomic blasts. The only hope for mankind, said President Truman, was to keep the fighting limited. Now even "little" wars carried big risks.

When General Eisenhower cam-paigned for President in 1952, he promised that if he was elected he would go to Korea to find a way to end the war. And the Korean War ended in a compromise, arranged by President Eisenhower, on July 27, 1953. The American dead numbered thirty-five thousand. The Korean peace was no "victory" for the United States. But since it removed the most immediate threat of an atomic war, it was a kind of victory for mankind.

The expanding forces of communism had been warned that any attempt to conquer their neighbors would be extremely costly. They had not been defeated, but they had been held back. It was not all that Americans really wished

An American military adviser in Viet Nam (third from right) with South Vietnamese Marines at the edge of a rice paddy. At far left are two enemy (Viet Cong) prisoners.

but it was probably the best that could be expected for some time to come.

Within a few years after the Korean truce, again on a peninsula which bordered on communist China, came another test of Containment. In April 1954 the United States met at Geneva with communist Russia, communist China, and countries that once had colonies in Southeast Asia. They agreed that Indochina, the old French colony, should be divided into new independent nations. The people in the area called "Viet Nam" were already split between the communists in the north (on the border of communist China) and the anti-communists in the south. It was therefore agreed to set up *two* Viet Nams.

But then, as in Korea a few years before, communist forces from the North began invading the South.

Would the United States again try to hold back the expanding forces of communism?

In October 1961, President John F. Kennedy made the decision to intervene. Then, after the assassination of President Kennedy in November 1963, Congress on President Lyndon B. Johnson's request voted to use American forces. By 1967 there were nearly a half-million American soldiers in Viet Nam.

This new War of Containment was in many ways similar to the war in Korea. But there were some important differences. Now it was not the whole United Nations but the United States forces with only a few allies who were fighting.

This was the most unpopular war in American history. College students and others objected to being drafted to fight in a strange far-off country. Why, they asked, should the United States be trying to settle Viet Nam's problems? They were told that the countries in Asia were like dominoes standing in a row. If one fell over to communism, the others could not help falling.

On television Americans saw our young soldiers dying and our bombs killing thousands of Vietnamese villagers. Hard-fighting American forces could not win, but they did not quite lose. This undeclared war was unlike any other war in American history. It was not fought on the battlefield but in steamy jungles against communist guerrillas who knew every inch of their own territory.

It was clear after years of fighting that the war in Viet Nam could not be won. Never before had Americans lost a war. After his election in 1968, President Nixon promised to bring our troops home. This was easier said than done. While he began bringing the Americans back, he kept up the bombing attacks to force the communists to come to the conference table. Not until January 1973, after long and tiresome negotiations, was a cease-fire declared.

The war was a great tragedy for the people of Viet Nam, and for Americans, too. At least two million Vietnamese had died. More than 46,000 Americans lost their lives, 1,200 were missing, and 300,000 were wounded. The war had shown the patriotism of young Americans. But it had also shown that the American people would not support a war whose purpose they did not understand.

CHAPTER 31

Windows to the World ᨕᨏᨕᨏᨕᨏᨕᨏᨕᨏᨕ

By 1960 there were many more automobiles in the United States than in all the rest of the world put together. Two-thirds of American households had at least one automobile.

Perhaps more than anything else that Americans had made by the millions, the automobile expressed their new civilization. All American wealth and ingenuity and organizing ability had been required to give Americans their cars.

The automobile was democratic. Just as ready-made clothing had made it harder in the United States than anywhere else to tell a man's occupation or social class by what he wore, so it was harder than anywhere else to guess an American's bank account by the car he drove.

The automobile was a symbol of freedom. A man who owned a car was free to live at a considerable distance from where he worked. He could take his family to the country on weekends, and to far parts of the continent on vacations.

The automobile was a symbol of speed. With it a man could go as fast as the fastest locomotive, and he could make his own timetable. Americans had always valued their ability to go where and when they wanted. In the twentieth century it was the automobile that helped make this possible.

While automobiles took Americans all around their own country, they no longer had to be rich to vacation abroad. In 1930 less than a half-million Americans traveled overseas, but in 1970 the number reached three million. Jet airplanes took them on three-week holidays to all the continents. And the enormous jumbo jet began to carry four hundred passengers from New York City to London in less time than a farmer used to spend on his weekly drive to the village post office.

Each American felt closer to others, too, when messages came to him more quickly and more easily. But it was almost the time of the Civil War before the U.S. mail had begun to be speedy and reliable. Before Lincoln came to the White House, Morse's telegraph had made it possible for Americans to share the news, which reached newspaper readers throughout the whole nation within a day after it happened. In 1866 the transatlantic cable, which had taken twelve years to complete, brought messages instantly from the Old World.

Then came the telephone. Alexander Graham Bell was twenty-three when he immigrated from Scotland with his family in 1870. Young Bell, following his father's interests in helping the deaf, studied acoustics (the science of sound) and electricity.

Bell determined to find a way to use

American automobiles, about 1913, on a group excursion to the Great Oregon Caves. Some critics feared that Americans would stop going to church and instead would spend Sundays in their automobiles.

electricity to carry the human voice. For Morse's telegraph would carry nothing but dots and dashes.

By 1876 Bell's new electromagnetic telephone was being displayed at the Centennial Exposition in Philadelphia as a great curiosity. Bell, like Edison, was a skillful organizer, and in the early twentieth century his telephone company had overtaken U. S. Steel to become the largest corporation in the United States.

On remote farms and ranches, medical-care-by-telephone saved the life of many a child—and incidentally saved the doctor a long ride. New businesses were started by new-style Go-Getters who sold their goods exclusively by telephone. The telephone (like the typewriter, which was perfected about the same time) provided new jobs for women.

Within a century after Bell made his invention, it was unusual for any American family to be out of reach of a telephone. The nation's hundred million telephones were more than half of all those in the world. By 1970 three hundred million separate phone conversations were carried on in the United States each day.

Back in the 1880's it was hard enough for people to imagine that a voice could be sent on a wire. But how much harder to imagine that messages could be sent even *without* a wire!

Before 1890 a German physicist, Heinrich Hertz, had discovered the existence of radio waves. At first people called them "Hertzian waves." These had the amazing quality of being able to pass through solid objects—even through wooden and brick walls.

In 1894 a young Italian named Guglielmo Marconi, still in his teens, happened to see a magazine article on "Hertzian waves." The idea fascinated him. He retreated to his room on the third floor of the family home near Bologna, locked the door, and experimented with "Hertzian waves" for hours

A boy learning to draw by listening to lessons broadcast over the newfangled invention, the radio (about 1924). The term "broadcast" (used on page 32) now had a new meaning.

on end. His first success was to use these waves to ring a bell across a room or downstairs. The very next year, when he was still only twenty-one, he succeeded in sending these waves outdoors (the distance of a twenty-minute walk) and even across the neighboring hill.

In 1896 Marconi and his mother went to England with a "little black box" containing his invention. Encouraged by the chief of telegraph in the British Post Office, he pursued his experiments and soon was sending messages nine miles. In 1897 Marconi received a British patent for his "wireless telegraph" and founded Marconi's Wireless Telegraph Company in London. His company was a great success.

His wireless equipment was installed in three British battleships in 1899. And in that year Marconi came to the United States.

Americans, with their new colonial empire, had special reasons to want news quickly from everywhere. During the Spanish-American War, when Admiral Dewey reported his victory at Manila Bay, he first had to send dispatch boats to Hong Kong. There the news was telegraphed westward (on British-controlled cables) by way of the Indian Ocean, the Red Sea, the Mediterranean, and then across the Atlantic, before it finally reached the President in Washington. Now wireless might make it possible (without depending on cables owned by the British or by anyone else) to get messages to Washington instantly from anywhere. The American Marconi Company prospered.

But Marconi's wireless still sent only dots and dashes. It would not send voices or music. The next step was taken by Reginald Aubrey Fessenden, a Canadian who had worked with Edison in his "invention factory" in the 1880's.

Fessenden had a simple but revolutionary idea. Marconi, using wireless waves, had sent out dots and dashes by stopping and starting electrical signals. Suppose, said Fessenden, the wireless message was sent out in a *continuing* wave of radio rays. Then, by making the waves correspond to the vibrations made by sounds, you could actually transmit speech and music. Fessenden experimented with this idea at the laboratory of the General Electric Company, which had grown out of Edison's invention factory.

The startling result occurred on Christmas Eve, 1906. That night, wireless operators on ships at sea, wearing their earphones, were listening for the usual stream of dots and dashes. To their amazement, they suddenly heard a human voice. A woman sang a Christmas carol, someone played a violin, then someone read a passage from the Bible, and finally Fessenden's own voice wished them Merry Christmas.

The very word broadcast took on a new meaning. In the 1901 dictionary it usually meant "the act or process of scattering seeds." But by 1927 *broadcast* usually meant "to scatter or disseminate, specifically, radio messages, speeches, etc."

Within the twenty years after Fessenden's first Christmas broadcast in 1906, events moved with a peculiarly American speed. Many other Go-Getters, inventors, and adventurous businessmen joined in.

One of the most remarkable of these Go-Getters was Lee De Forest, born in Council Bluff, Iowa, in 1873. His father went to Alabama, to be president of Talledega College, which had been founded by missionaries just after the Civil War to help educate the Negro freedmen.

Like Marconi, young De Forest began to read about the new "Hertzian waves." His summer job pushing a chair for sightseers at the World's Columbian Exposition in Chicago in 1893 gave him the opportunity to study the electrical exhibits. He worked his way through Yale College, sometimes rising at 4:00 A.M. to mow lawns. And he studied hard. But he was not popular with his classmates, who voted him both the "nerviest" and the "homeliest" of their year.

After graduation—and for the rest of his life—De Forest gave his enormous energies to inventing ways to improve radio. His new radio tube which he patented in 1906 was called the Audion. It was based on a tube that Edison had made in his laboratory when working on the incandescent lamp. With the Audion tube it was easier to tune in, all reception became louder and clearer, and the broadcast of voice and music was much improved. Before his death De Forest had received over three hundred patents.

The man who did more than anyone else to bring radio and then television into American homes was David Sarnoff. He showed that the Go-Getting spirit was as alive in the mid-twentieth century as it had been in the days of the trailblazer John Iliff or the merchandising giants, Montgomery Ward and Richard Sears.

David Sarnoff's life was an American saga. He was born in southern Russia in 1891, to a poor family who intended him to become a rabbi. Even before he was nine he was reading the sacred texts in Hebrew. Then his father, who had gone to America a few years before, sent back money for the family's transatlantic passage.

When the Sarnoffs settled in a crowded immigrant section of New York City, David still did not know a word of English. But he went to public school and soon spoke like an American. When his father became too sick to earn a living, David at the age of ten began supporting the whole family with the profits from his newsstand on Tenth Avenue.

David was ambitious. Deciding to become a wireless operator, he taught himself the Morse code and was hired by the American Marconi Company.

Then, by luck, Sarnoff happened to be the only operator at a New York wire-

David Sarnoff as a teen-age telegraph operator working for Marconi.

less receiver when word came dimly through on the afternoon of April 15, 1912, that the luxury liner *Titanic* had struck an iceberg and was sinking in mid-Atlantic. He gave the news to the press, and stayed at his instrument (while all other stations were ordered off the air) to alert other ships to send help. The name of David Sarnoff reached everyone who read the newspapers.

When the American Marconi Company was taken over by the Radio Corporation of America (RCA), Sarnoff joined the new firm. By 1921 Sarnoff was running the large company, making plans to sell the new "radio music boxes" by the millions.

During World War I the soldiers hidden in trenches had needed the radio to keep in touch with their units. And radio sets improved in wartime, when the different manufacturers had been required to pool their know-how. After the war, radio entered American homes. With the new sets listeners no longer had to wear earphones. Now they could receive the program over a loudspeaker.

In 1920 the Department of Commerce issued the first license for a regular commercial broadcasting station to KDKA in Pittsburgh. Within two years there were over five hundred licensed commercial broadcasting stations, and over a half-million radio sets were being produced annually. Before World War II, the annual production of radio sets numbered ten million.

Sarnoff was just as bold in forecasting the success of television. He invested large sums in the RCA television research laboratory where another Russian immigrant, Vladimir Zworykin, was making remarkable progress.

While Zworykin was collaborating

with a large staff in the costly RCA laboratory, another inventor was working quietly by himself. Philo Taylor Farnsworth, born to a large Mormon family on a farm near Beaver, Utah, in 1906, began studying electronics on his own when he was still in high school. Encouraged by his science teacher, he tried to make a television set. Then a businessman furnished a small laboratory for him in California. Philo worked alone and in secret, with the blinds drawn. Once the police (suspecting he was building a still to make illegal whiskey) raided his laboratory. At the age of only twenty-four, Farnsworth had patented his own new system for television.

World War II delayed the manufacture of television for the home. But out of wartime needs came "radar"—a word made up from *ra*(dio) *d*(etecting) *a*(nd) *r*(anging). Radar used radio waves to locate enemy planes and ships. The many returning servicemen with radar experience were well prepared to work on television.

By 1948 television was booming. Sarnoff's foresight had paid off. In that year alone nearly one million television sets were produced. In the very next year production reached three million, and in the year following 7,500,000. By the mid-1960's it was hard to find an American household without a television set.

When people could see a movie at home for free, why should they go to the movie theater? Thousands of movie theaters closed. Fewer new movies were made for the theater each year, yet old movie spectaculars (like *Gone With the Wind*) were still successful.

Old movies, especially Westerns, found a new life on television. There was a new interest in experimental movies. Though shown in small theaters, they aroused widespread interest. And now it was possible to rent or buy cassettes of new movies, too, and play them through your television set at home.

Television gave everybody a window to the world. Now everyone—whether he lived on a farm or in the city, whether his neighborhood was rich or poor, whether in Oregon, New Mexico, Maine, or Florida, whether young or old, sick or well—could look through the television window at the very same world. Now, as never before, Americans shared their experience.

Even in the days before television, when President Franklin Delano Roosevelt broadcasted his first inaugural address on radio he received in response a half-million pieces of mail. During the Great Depression and World War II he skillfully used his radio "fireside chats" to bring all Americans together.

Now with television all Americans could not only hear their candidates. They could actually see them in action. They could watch the expression on a candidate's face and could follow his gestures. In this new way, American voters could feel personally acquainted with their leaders.

In 1948, for the first time, the National Party Conventions were telecast. While sitting in the White House, President Truman saw the nomination of his Republican rival, Governor Thomas E. Dewey, in Philadelphia. During the campaign President Truman seemed relaxed and homey on television while

One of television's "Great Debates" in 1960. LEFT: John F. Kennedy. RIGHT: Richard M. Nixon. Presiding: Howard K. Smith of ABC. William Jennings Bryan's strenuous campaigning had brought his voice to a few million Americans; each of the Great Debates reached about seventy million.

Governor Dewey (his opponents said he looked like the bridegroom on a wedding cake) appeared stiff and formal. This new opportunity for American voters to size up the personalities of the candidates on television helped explain why President Truman won reelection.

In the Presidential campaign of 1960 the two candidates appeared together on television. In the "Great Debates"—a series of four one-hour programs—John F. Kennedy, the Democratic candidate, and Richard M. Nixon, the Republican candidate, discussed the issues. These were not really "debates" like the old-fashioned Lincoln-Douglas Debates a century earlier. For now newspaper reporters put the questions. Each Presidential candidate had 2½ minutes in which to give his answer. Then he had 1½ minutes for reply after the other candidate had made his brief statement.

These "Great Debates" probably reached the largest audience in history up to that time. Seventy million people were watching each program. Television's new window to the world had made American life more democratic. Television showed more Americans more about everything and everybody in their country. American technology—drawing on the know-how of Americans and of the whole world—had come to the service of American democracy.

But there were dangers. The man who showed up best on television was bound to be the man who was the best "performer." He was the man who could give the cleverest response in 2½ minutes to questions he had just heard. But was that the best test of a President?

"Telstar," an American satellite, made it possible to exchange television programs between continents. With television Americans could even reach out beyond this world. And by looking through the window in his living room every American would join the nation's adventures to the New Worlds of outer space.

CHAPTER 32

Footprints on the Moon

When the first Europeans came to America, they came in their familiar ships "over the vast and furious ocean." They feared the ocean, but they knew its perils. When the first Americans pushed off into outer space, they had to invent new kinds of ships. And they had to brave the unknown perils of a new kind of ocean.

By the time of World War II, of course, a great deal was known about airplanes. But airplanes would not work in outer space. For every airplane engine then known—whether an internal-combustion engine like an automobile's that used gasoline to turn a propeller, or a jet engine that pushed ahead by burning gases—depended on the air. From the air came oxygen to explode the gasoline or to burn the gases. But in outer space there is no air. Out there you would need a very special kind of engine.

The pioneer American space scientist, Robert H. Goddard, proposed propelling spacecraft by rocket. A rocket carries its own fuel, and also carries its own "air"—usually in the form of liquid oxygen—which it uses to burn the fuel. The shooting of the rocket behind pushes the spacecraft forward.

In 1914 Goddard received a patent for his liquid-fuel rocket engine. In 1920 he wrote a technical report for the Smithsonian Institution in Washington explaining how his rocket engine worked. He said it might even be possible someday to reach the moon by rocket. The New York *Times* and other respectable newspapers wrote editorials ridiculing his idea. For the rest of his life Goddard distrusted newspapers. Unlike Billy Mitchell he kept his work secret and hated publicity. And he went ahead perfecting his rocket engine. He finally secured 214 patents on rocket improvements.

When he died in 1945, few Americans yet believed that man would ever travel through interplanetary space.

The people of London, however, already had sad reason to know that rock-

Robert Goddard with his first successful rocket. His imaginative experiments with small rockets laid the groundwork for later American achievements in space.

ets provided a fantastic new source of Air Power. Raining down from the skies in 1944 came thousands of German V-2 rockets. Aimed from distant launching pads in Germany they did not carry pilots but still reached their English targets with terrifying accuracy. They traveled at a speed of 3,500 miles an hour and each dropped a ton of explosives.

The V-2 rockets were the work of a group of German scientists who had been experimenting since 1932. When the Nazis came to power and plunged the world into war, the Nazis had provided these scientists with a secret new laboratory in Peenemuende, a little fishing village on the Baltic Sea in northeastern Germany.

By 1944, about twelve thousand Germans were engaged in making the V-2 rockets which were pouring down on England every day. The name "V-2" came from a German term meaning "Vengeance Weapon, No. 2." It was the most terrifying weapon of the war because no defense against it had been found. If the Nazis had only perfected this weapon earlier, they might have won the war. But by mid-1944 Germany was near collapse.

When the Russians speeded westward across Europe in their final triumphal march, they hastened to Peenemuende to capture the German rocket factory—for their own future use. When they arrived they were dismayed to find that the most valuable resource, the rocket scientists themselves, had already fled westward.

"This is absolutely intolerable," Dictator Stalin complained in a rage. "We defeated the Nazi armies; we occupied Berlin and Peenemuende; but the Americans got the rocket engineers!" Stalin was especially irritated because the Russian communists were not strong in big bombing planes. Their only weapon, then, for a possible long-distance attack on the United States was transatlantic rockets.

Some far-sighted American generals organized a new project under the code name "Operation Paperclip." They collected 118 of the best German rocket scientists (including Wernher von Braun), and signed them up to work on rockets and space travel for the United States. Wernher von Braun became head of the U.S. Army rocket research.

The United States and communist Russia began a competition in rockets. By 1956 the chief of the Russian Communist Party boasted that soon Russian military rockets would be able to hit any target on the earth. The Russians had improved the old V-2 into a new weapon called the T-1.

Then, on October 4, 1957, the Russians sent up the first man-made earth satellite. It was a package of instruments weighing 184 pounds. They called it "Sputnik" which in Russian meant "fellow traveler" (of the earth). One month later they launched a much heavier satellite, Sputnik II. It weighed 1,120 pounds and for experimental purposes carried a dog named Laika.

The Space Race was on!

Early American efforts were not always successful. The White House announced that on December 6, 1957, the United States would launch its own satellite with a Vanguard rocket. While the whole nation watched on television this much-advertised rocket collapsed on the wet sand around the launching pad.

The next try did succeed. Two months later Explorer I, the first American satellite, went into orbit. And it made some important scientific discoveries.

But Americans still worried about the "Space Gap." Within the next few years, both Russia and the United States performed spectacular feats in space.

On April 12, 1961, the Russians sent up Yuri Gagarin, the first man in space. He went whirling around the earth in a satellite, and made nearly a full orbit —in 89 minutes. A year later the United States sent John H. Glenn, Jr., into orbit in the American spaceship called Friendship 7. Probably Russia and the United States each would have lagged if it had not been for the competition of the other.

President John F. Kennedy at first had doubts about space exploration. He doubted whether man could survive outside the earth's atmosphere. He feared another Vanguard fiasco. And he thought that the enormous sums of money might be better spent on earth. But his persuasive Vice-President Lyndon B. Johnson was a great space enthusiast. After the Russians had sent Yuri Gagarin into orbit, President Kennedy announced that the United States would aim to land a man on the moon before 1970. When President Johnson came to office, he gave space exploration his strong support.

The moon-landing project did need all the support it could find. For there were great risks and vast expenses. When a fire exploded in 1967 during tests of a spaceship, three of the most experienced astronauts were killed. The costs of preparing for the moon shot came to over $25,000,000,000. But this meant new industries, new products, and employment in new jobs for a third of a million people all over the country.

"We work in a place," boasted someone at the Manned Spacecraft Center in Houston, Texas, "where 13,000 men can feel like Columbus."

Finally, after nine years of preparation and two voyages around the moon and back, on July 16, 1969, Americans set out to land on the moon. Neil Armstrong commanded the mission, Michael Collins piloted the command ship Apollo 11, and Edwin E. Aldrin, Jr., was to work with Armstrong when they landed on the moon.

None of them was a great scientist. None came from a family that was rich or famous. They all had a passion for

American on the moon, July 20, 1969.

flying. Armstrong had made a reputation as a daring yet reliable test pilot. Aldrin's father, an army colonel, had studied with the space pioneer Goddard. Aldrin himself, after graduating from West Point in 1951, piloted a Sabrejet in the Korean War, and then earned a doctor's degree in aeronautics at Massachusetts Institute of Technology. Collins had been born in Rome while his father, a professional army officer, was stationed there. He graduated from West Point, joined the Air Force, and became a test pilot. As an astronaut, he had taken a 5½-hour space walk, the longest ever. All three men were athletes, in top physical condition. They were all modest men, who had practiced working together.

The moon trip was unlike earlier explorations of unknown lands. For this voyage was watched on television by the whole world—including the explorers' own families. Hundreds of millions of people could share the adventure and the suspense.

The three astronauts shot up in the command ship Apollo 11, which took them orbiting around the earth. Then, after 2½ orbits, they steered Apollo 11 off toward the moon, over two hundred thousand miles away. After a three-day journey through interplanetary space, they arrived in their moon orbit. Armstrong and Aldrin climbed into a small "lunar module" attached at the nose of Apollo 11. They called this little ship "Eagle."

They separated Eagle from the mother ship. After orbiting the moon to the agreed position, they landed Eagle on the moon at 4:17 P.M. Eastern Daylight Time on July 20, 1969.

There were risks till the last instant of the landing. As the computer guided them down, Armstrong noticed they were about to settle in a deep crater about the size of a football field, filled with large boulders. He seized the controls and guided Eagle to a safe, smoother site.

By the original plan, Armstrong and Aldrin were supposed to take a long nap within their Lunar Module before risking the strain of the moon walk. But they were impatient and in no mood for napping. After receiving permission from the Mission Control Center in Houston and putting on their complicated space suits, they opened their hatch, six and a half hours after landing.

The first man, an American, stepped out on a heavenly body. For that moment the whole world, except those whose dictators forbade them to know, watched proudly together.

Surrounded by the footprints of the first earthlings on the moon is the launching stand from which Armstrong and Aldrin took off from the moon, in their Lunar Module. And on it is a plaque that may remain forever. For on the moon there is no oxygen to rust and no water to erode. The message on the plaque boasts an American achievement and proclaims the hope of the world. "Here men from the planet earth first set foot upon the moon, July 1969, A.D. We came in peace for all mankind."

But already—long before American dreams to make the world safe for democracy could come true, long before world-wide peace was in sight—Americans back on earth were asking the familiar American question, "Where next?"

Chapter 33

No More Secrets: The World Is Watching

Because travel on the sea was so much easier than travel on land, the Puritans had managed to cross the three-thousand-mile ocean to this mysterious New World in only seven weeks. That was how they escaped the government that was persecuting them. Back home in England people could not really know what the Puritans were doing and even whether they were still alive.

Our world of airways is a whole new world. There are no more secrets. The three American astronauts in the *Apollo 11* were jammed into a spacecraft. But the whole watching world heard their voices. Their success depended on the Mission Control Center in Houston, Texas, where thirteen thousand people were joining the adventure. The whole nation in front of their television sets on July 16, 1969 felt *they* were somehow going along in the tiny *Apollo 11*. All across the country the people who had supplied materials, and with their taxes provided the billions of dollars for the voyage, watched anxiously.

Space voyages and the new triumphs of air travel would depend on inventions never imagined by the astronauts' grandfathers. When a vehicle sped through outer space to the moon—more than 238,000 miles in only three days—it had to be steered precisely and kept on its lightning-fast course. The slightest delay or tilt in the wrong direction might send the *Apollo 11* and its three passengers into the nowhere of outer space.

What made this speedy control possible was the computer. It was based on the ideas of a brilliant refugee from Hungary, John von Neumann, who had helped design the atomic bomb and then turned to making computers to work with fantastic speed. These miraculous machines could in the wink of an eye make computations that before had taken days. New ways were found to make computers smaller and smaller. Some were on the *Apollo 11*, and there were many at the space center. It was von Neumann's idea that made possible the computers we now use in homes, factories, businesses, and classrooms.

Travelers through the ocean of outer space could not have the privacy of *Mayflower* passengers. They could not sneeze without the controllers at home base knowing it and without making the nation's television watchers worry. Houston had to guide them, and without Houston's help they would be lost.

The trip to the moon was only a beginning. The astronauts had been picked up by navy vessels 940 miles southwest of Hawaii in the Pacific Ocean, where the *Apollo 11* splashed down. But the *Apollo 11* could not be used again for another space flight.

The next step was a space shuttle. This was an old word but a new idea. *Shuttle* is a word for the reel used in weaving to carry the thread to the woof back and forth between the threads of the warp. It has come to mean anything that goes back and forth—for example, the bus between a suburban parking lot and downtown. The new idea was a space shuttle unlike the *Apollo 11*: one that could come back and land at an airport like any other airplane. It could be used again and again and save millions of dollars.

The first space shuttle took off from Kennedy Space Center in Florida on April 12, 1981, and landed at Edwards Air Force Base in California two days later. Then shuttle trips became routine. They served many purposes. Some had military uses. One tested the effect of outer space on human blood. Another carried cages with two monkeys and twenty-four rats to learn more about life processes during space travel. All took spectacular photographs of earth.

For the twenty-fifth shuttle it was decided to include a teacher in the crew. After a nationwide search Christa McAuliffe, a social studies teacher from Concord, New Hampshire, was chosen. And she took off with the six other crew members from Kennedy Space Center on January 28, 1986. That morning was bitter cold, unusually cold for Florida. But the *Challenger* took off anyway. To the horror of the nation, 73 seconds after takeoff the *Challenger* exploded in full sight of the world watching on television. There had been failures in the American space efforts before, but none so terrible. All seven astronauts were killed on that day of tragedy. President Reagan ordered a prompt public study of the causes. And on television he led the nation's memorial service for these soldiers on our newest frontier. Before the *Challenger* the nation had begun to take for granted the courage of the astronauts. Now the nation saw with its own eyes the mortal risks of space heroes.

Before the year 1986 was out, the saddened nation would have its spirits lifted—not by another voyage into outer space but by a more familiar kind of adventure.

For nearly five hundred years seafarers had planned voyages circling our planet earth. The bold Portuguese Ferdinand Magellan started from Spain with five ships in 1519. After a horrendous voyage through the Strait of Magellan (later named after him) at the tip of South America, he sailed his ships into the Pacific. That ocean proved much vaster than he had imagined. The starving crew desperately chewed the pieces of leather that held the sails in place, and even ate the rats they found on board. Magellan himself was killed by natives in the Philippines, but one of his ships did manage to reach home. This first round-the-world trip had taken three years and had cost four of the five ships and the lives of all but eighteen of the more than two hundred fifty men who had begun the voyage.

Other adventurers have kept trying to find a speedier, safer way to circle our globe. The French writer Jules Verne's fantastic tale *Around the World in Eighty Days*, published in 1873, followed the breathless hero on ships, trains, and balloons to complete his journey to win a bet. Astronauts in outer space orbited beyond the atmosphere, but that was not the same as circling through the earth's air and weather.

Americans had always been in a hurry to set records. The story of the *Voyager* is another chapter in this wonderfully American quest. One day in March 1981 test pilot Dick Rutan and his friend and fellow pilot Jeana Yeager were having lunch with Dick's brother Burt Rutan, an airplane designer, near Burt's airplane factory in Mojave, California. Dick and Jeana were looking for adventure. Burt described a new carbon-fiber featherweight material for making a light aircraft which could carry more fuel; thus it could go farther without needing to refuel.

Jeana urged that they build a plane of this new material. Then and there on a restaurant napkin Burt sketched a plane to fly around the world nonstop without refueling. Instantly they agreed to "do this thing or die trying." Burt would design the plane and they would all help build it. Dick and Jeana, good persuaders, would raise the two million dollars needed and secure donations of costly equipment from manufacturing companies. They spent three years along with a few volunteers building the plane with their own hands.

The plane they finally put together was like none ever seen before. With propellers front and back it resembled sketchy plans for a kite. It really was a flying fuel tank, designed to carry four times its own weight in fuel. The two pilots were squeezed into a cockpit three and a half feet wide by seven and a half feet long. They were so close to the engine that earphones for them had to be specially designed to cancel out the engine sounds to avoid permanent

damage to their hearing.

With Dick and Jeana wedged inside, the *Voyager* took off from Edwards Air Force Base on the edge of the Mojave Desert in California on December 14, 1986. The plane's seventeen fuel tanks would keep the plane perfectly balanced by allowing fuel to flow from one tank to another as it was consumed. But the fuel load was so heavy on takeoff that the sagging wing tips were damaged by scraping the runway. The *Voyager* went westward across the Pacific, South Africa, and the Atlantic, then across the southern United States and back to Edwards. As the trip advanced, the plane used fuel and became lighter. But the less the *Voyager* weighed, the slower it flew. At the end it was going only 75 miles an hour. For the whole trip the speed would be about what Charles Lindbergh averaged on his way to Paris, 107 miles per hour.

Brother Burt Rutan was at mission control, nervously watching this proof of his design while the whole world, with television glimpses of the plane tumbling through African storms, followed the trip moment by moment. This trip that Dick and Jeana could not wait to make was no picnic. They carried only twenty-two pounds of food and ten and a half gallons of water. Each day they ate one hot meal specially packaged like the food for astronauts. In between they chewed peanut butter crunch or other dry food. The weather was especially rough, because they traveled at eight thousand to twelve thousand feet above the earth—much lower than the forty thousand feet where passenger liners fly. They did not want to waste fuel to pressurize the plane for the higher altitude. And they did not have enough oxygen to fly high. Juggled by turbulence, Jeana suffered severe bruises. Once the front engine scared them by quitting. Another time the rear engine stopped for a terrifying five minutes. Luckily, Dick was able to get fuel to that engine, and the outside flow of air turned the propeller and started the engine again.

An autopilot, working automatically by computer, operated the controls. This saved the energy of the two live pilots, who had many tasks and had to work frantically to see that the fuel flowed from one tank to another to keep balance. Each pilot took a turn at the controls while the other slept. It was a rocky trip. Dick, who had been shot down in combat in Viet Nam, finally said, "Compared to this flight, I felt a lot safer in combat."

Just nine days, three minutes, and forty-four seconds after takeoff, Jeana Yeager and Dick Rutan had covered the

25,012 miles around the earth—without ever stopping to take fuel. They landed back at Edwards Air Force Base before cheering thousands while the world shared their joy and relief on the television screen.

When before had a sketch on a napkin made so much history? Both Dick and Jeana had risked their life's savings and their lives on what aviators called "the last plum" to be picked. "What kind of world would there be," Dick asked, "if there were no daring?"

How many of the thousands in 1927 in New York City who had welcomed Lindbergh from his sensational nonstop flight to Paris could have imagined that just sixty years later Americans on the other side of the continent would be celebrating a two-person nonstop voyage around the world? American technology and daring were no longer merely links between New York and Paris, ties to the Old World from which Americans had come. Now Americans were circling the whole world with the whole world watching!

* * *

The land that began as the best-kept secret had become the best-known land in the world. Everybody shared the adventures of astronauts and round-the-world pilots. Television, added to movies and radio and newspapers and books, now made it possible for Americans to know more about the world and themselves. The world had become one big television screen. Now all could share the suspense. American history had been a story of surprises. Like the past, the future was sure to be full of the unexpected. And these surprises were just another name for America.

Voyager on its first test flight in 1984.

INDEX

DANIEL J. BOORSTIN, the Librarian of Congress Emeritus, is one of our nation's most eminent and widely read historians. He is the author of the best-selling book *The Discoverers*, now translated into thirteen languages. And his celebrated earlier trilogy, *The Americans*, was awarded the Bancroft, Parkman, and Pulitzer prizes.

Prior to his twelve-year tenure at the Library of Congress, Dr. Boorstin served as director of the National Museum of American History of the Smithsonian Institution. Earlier he had been the Morton Distinguished Service Professor at the University of Chicago, where he taught for twenty-five years.

Born in Georgia and raised in Oklahoma, he received his B.A. from Harvard University and his doctorate from Yale. He has spent a good deal of his life viewing America from the outside, first in England as a Rhodes scholar at Balliol College, Oxford, and more recently as a professor in Rome, Paris, Kyoto, Cambridge, and Geneva.

His wife and collaborator, Ruth Frankel Boorstin, is a graduate of Wellesley College and holds a master's degree in social science from the University of Chicago. She has contributed as an editor to all of her husband's books.

The Boorstins live in Washington, D.C. They have three grown sons and four grandchildren.

Photo by Bern Schwartz